T0396244

Texts & Translations of Transcendence & Transformation
Series Editors: Adam Bremer-McCollum & Charles M. Stang

THE

PEARLSONG

Adam Bremer-McCollum

The Center for the Study of World Religions
Harvard University Press
2025

Adam Bremer-McCollum. 2025. The Pearlsong. Texts & Translations of Transcendence & Transformation 1. Cambridge, Mass.: Center for the Study of World Religions.

This title can be downloaded at: `https://cswr.hds.harvard.edu/publications/4t`

ISBN: 978-0-67430-146-7

Signature Printing
5 Almeida Ave, East Providence, RI 02914
E-mail: ken@signatureprinters.com

EU GPSR Authorised Representative
LOGOS EUROPE, 9 rue Nicolas Poussin, 17000, La Rochelle, France
E-mail: Contact@logoseurope.eu

Cover: Martha Doyle Lindman
Design: RDW Group, Providence, Rhode Island
Typesetting: Adam Bremer-McCollum

Contents

Dedicated to the memory of my mother,
Kathy Lynne Carter Mathis (1957–2018)

Foreword

Among the various collections of apocryphal acts of the early Christian apostles is one conventionally known as the *Acts of Thomas*, which narrates the apostle Judas Thomas "the Twin"'s evangelism in the East, especially in India. It is generally thought to have been composed in Syriac, and then translated into Greek, in the early third century CE. The *Acts of Thomas* is well attested, with something on the order of six Syriac and seventy-five Greek manuscripts. In only one of the Syriac manuscripts, and in only one of the Greek manuscripts, we find a text that has come to be called the "Hymn of the Pearl" or "of the Soul" – or, as Adam Bremer-McCollum has dubbed it, *The Pearlsong*. Whatever else *The Pearlsong* is, it is a poem, spoken in the first person by a young prince from the East who journeys westward to Egypt to recover a pearl from a slumbering serpent, is then called home to his royal family and accompanied by various guides, human and otherwise. The poem, like the *Acts*, survives in Syriac and in a Greek translation, although oddities in the Syriac suggest that it might too be a translation from a lost original in a different dialect of Aramaic. In both manuscripts of the *Acts* that include *The Pearlsong*, the poem is recited in the first person by Thomas while he is imprisoned, so the prince's voice, and arguably his quest, becomes the apostle's own.

The very fact that *The Pearlsong* appears in only two manuscripts suggests that it was not original to the *Acts* but inserted later: by whom, when, and exactly why remain matters of dispute. It was almost certainly an independent composition. Unlike the *Acts*, *The Pearlsong* contains no obviously Christian content. It might have originated in a different religious milieu and was then repurposed for Christian readers. But there is little or no agreement on what its religious milieu, if any, was; or where it was composed, or exactly when, between the first and fourth centuries.

I included my own interpretation of *The Pearlsong* in my 2016 book, *Our Divine Double*, which interpretation I will briefly rehearse here.[1] As I mentioned, the poem is spoken in the first person: a young prince tells of his royal family in the East – a father, mother, and brother – and how he is stripped of his royal garment and sent to Egypt to retrieve a pearl guarded by a slumbering serpent. On his journey westward, he is at first accompanied by guardians and then alone and finds in Egypt the serpent he is seeking. He meets a countryman from the East, but adopts the dress of the Egyptians to blend in. They see through his disguise, however, and make him eat of their food, and he forgets his parentage and his quest. His parents learn of his predicament and send a flying magical letter to awaken him: it reaches and awakens him, and he in turn enchants the serpent and recovers the pearl. He is led home by the magical letter, and then greeted along the way by his parents' stewards bearing his royal garment. In the end, he returns to his father's kingdom, with pearl in hand and clothed in his cloak, and is welcomed into the royal court.

In *Our Divine Double*, I confidently asserted that *The Pearlsong*, or "hymn" as I called it, is quite obviously an allegory. I was leaning on the good work of, among others, Bentley Layton.[2] If *The Pearlsong* is an allegory, then we must ask who or what this prince is supposed to signify. There are two common interpretations. The first interprets the prince as the savior or redeemer figure who is sent into the world to rescue the human soul (the pearl) but becomes ensnared in that world and so is himself in need of saving. This was often alleged to be a fundamental Gnostic myth of the "redeemed redeemer" or *salvator salvandus*. There is, in my view, very little to recommend this interpretation of *The Pearlsong*. Much more compelling, I argued, is a second interpretation, according to which the prince stands not for the savior but for the human soul itself that departs its heavenly origin (the East) and descends into embodiment (Egypt). The drama is therefore of the soul's exile and return.

[1]Stang, *Our Divine Double*, 135–143.

[2]Layton, *The Gnostic Scriptures*, (Garden City, NY, 1987), 366; I also acknowledged the dissent of Gerard P. Luttikhizen, "The Hymn of Jude Thomas," 112–113.

One problem with this second interpretation, however, is that it does not furnish an obvious meaning for the pearl. I argued that the pearl and the serpent serve principally to explain how the prince (soul) finds himself in Egypt (embodied exile). The real interest of the allegory, then, is how the embodied soul comes to realize its divine parentage and to return home. This interpretation suggests that "the letter and the garment ... are much more important to the development of the story" and that "the pearl plays only a supporting part in the story, just as the serpent does."[3] I argued that the scholarly convention of labeling this interpolated hymn the "Hymn of the *Pearl*," therefore, is somewhat unfortunate insofar as it leads the reader to think that the drama centers on the prince's recovery of the prized pearl from the serpent. Whereas the prince's recovery of the pearl is narrated in a few short verses, *The Pearlsong* devotes almost twenty verses to his parents' letter to him, and nearly thirty-five to his return home, including detailed descriptions of how the letter guides him and especially how his royal garment meets him on his way home. In short, I argued, this is a hymn, not of the pearl, but of the letter and the garment. I would revise that and say: if *The Pearlsong* is a song, it is a song of the soul, and of soul's many divine doubles.

That should come as no surprise, since that was the topic of my book. Perhaps I was seeing doubles everywhere. The truth is, however, that *The Pearlsong* furnishes plenty of them. There is the brother the prince leaves behind in the East, called his "second" or "double." There is the countryman he meets in Egypt, whom he makes his "intimate friend" and "companion." Or, as Bremer-McCollum translates this scene,

> I saw someone there from my people, freeborn from the East:
> A lovely, charming boy
> My age had come and joined me.
> I made him my expedition partner and brought him in as an associate.[4]

[3]Gerard P. Luttikhuizen, "Hymn," 104-105.

[4]Bremer-McCollum, *The Pearlsong*, ll. 24-27.

There is the letter his parents and brother send, which flies to him in the form of an eagle, which lands by him and "becomes speech." Its voice and the sound of its flight awakens him from his slumber; the prince reads the letter, only to learn that its words were already written on his heart (*lebbå*). The letter is his textual double, as it were: it mirrors back to him his inner inscription, which had been obscured by exile. The prince is something of a palimpsest, and his textual double renders his inner inscription once again legible.

Having recovered the pearl, he turns east and begins the journey home, led by the letter, "my awakener, in front of me on the road ... leading me with its light."[5] The letter had reminded him of his "shining clothes," his "luxurious cloak," and of his brother, with whom he expects to inherit his parents' kingdom. On the journey home, his parents' treasurers meet him along the way, bearing his "shining garment," which likeness he had forgotten:

> Suddenly, when I'd faced it, the garment seemed like my mirror:
> I saw all of it in all of me, and in it likewise I faced all of me,
> Because we're distinctly two, but still one, with one form.[6]

Like the letter, the garment speaks to him, and he rushes to put it on. Now resplendent, the prince returns to the royal court, reunited with his brother in their parents' court.

It was, and remains still, hard for me not to interpret this litany of characters (human and otherwise) "allegorically," namely that the brother, countryman, letter, and shining garment are the prince's various alter-egos, other "I"s, divine counterparts calling him home to the light of the East, where he can be, as he always was, two and yet one. This allegory, I argued, was inserted into the *Acts of Thomas* precisely because it resonated with – or *echoed* – the *Acts* narrative of the apostle Judas Thomas as "the Twin" of Christ. While *The Pearlsong* didn't originate in this apocryphal collection, I argued that as an allegory it

[5]Bremer-McCollum, *The Pearlsong*, ll. 64-65.
[6]Bremer-McCollum, *The Pearlsong*, ll. 76-78.

harmonizes well with the theology of the *Acts*. Just as the letter serves as the textual double to the prince in *The Pearlsong*, so *The Pearlsong* serves as an interpolated textual double of the *Acts* – facilitated by the apostle Thomas speaking the part of the prince, reciting his verses as his own. Just as the shining garment appears as the mirror image of the prince, so the divine double is our mirror image, or rather we are its mirror image. I argued that *The Pearlsong* and the *Acts* mirror each other, and we, the readers poised between the two as if in a *mise en abyme*, begin to see, to know, our own divine double(s).

In his Introduction, Bremer-McCollum signals his skepticism of an allegorical reading of *The Pearlsong*. He insists that it "is first and foremost a story," with elements both "pedestrian" and "weird," "and it's mainly as a story" that he reads and interprets it, "while still open to symbolic readings."[7] He is not alone: contrary to Bentley Layton (and me), Jürgen Tubach comes to the "unavoidable conclusion that the poet of *The Pearlsong* didn't intend the text to be understood as an allegory."[8] While Bremer-McCollum keeps his distance from Tubach's confident claims about the intentions of the poem's original author and remains open to "allegories waiting to be activated by new readers and hearers at the right time and place," he is sympathetic with Tubach's note of caution: "An allegorical reading that assigns specific philosophical or religious meanings to the text and demands a specific kind of understanding is unnecessarily limiting, and fails to let the story do its work." Such one-to-one correspondences (e.g. the prince's journey to Egypt represents the soul's descent into embodiment) can easily descend into "heavy-handed" and "bland equations."[9] Bremer-McCollum wants to invite "multiple and shifting readings" and cites as support the summary statement of the great historian of religions Ioan

[7]Bremer-McCollum, *The Pearlsong*, 2.

[8]Tubach, "Zur Interpretation," 245; cited by Bremer-McCollum, *The Pearlsong*, 10n24.

[9]Bremer-McCollum, *The Pearlsong*, 10-12.

Culianu, "It can only be said with certainty that *The Pearlsong* means many things."[10]

Bremer-McCollum also finds support from another, perhaps surprising corner: the contemporary writer, scholar, and journalist Erik Davis. Although Davis is an old friend, colleague, and collaborator, until working with Bremer-McCollum on this edition of *The Pearlsong* I did not know that he had written about this poem, or rather about one recent and passionate reader of it, namely the twentieth-century science fiction writer Philip K. Dick. Bremer-McCollum pointed me to Davis' book, *High Weirdness: Drugs, Esoterica, and Visionary Experience in the Seventies*, and especially Chapter Four on Dick, or "PKD" as he is often known. Dick was fascinated with *The Pearlsong*, a text he knew, as so many others did, as the "Hymn of the Soul."

Davis also thinks that treating the poem as an allegory runs certain risks: "in treating the Hymn as a philosophical allegory, we flatten something Dick recognized even in the clipped *Britannica* paraphrase he first encountered: the Hymn's peculiar power *as a story*."[11] How did Dick understand its peculiar power as a story? In order to answer that question, we have to rehearse a story from Dick's own life. Dick was himself an avid storyteller, and his life reads as one hell of a story – nothing "flattened" about it. One can divide his writerly life in two, separated by a chasm, a series of disquieting and transformative experiences he would constellate and call "2-3-74." On February 20, 1974 – so the story goes – he came home after having a wisdom tooth extracted. His wife arranged for the pharmacy to deliver his pain medication, and when the doorbell rang, he was met by a messenger, a young delivery woman with "black, black hair and large eyes very lovely and intense."[12] He later admits to being mesmerized by her, although that was common for Dick: he was a serial monogamist of ever-younger women. In particular, he was mesmerized by her gold necklace and the fish symbol that hung from it. He asked after it, and she explained that it was a "sign" used by early Christians. After all, Jesus found his first disciples

[10] Culianu, "Erzählung und Mythos im 'Lied von der Perle,'" 71; cited in Bremer-McCollum, *The Pearlsong*, 16.

[11] Davis, *High Weirdness*, 348; cited below by Bremer-McCollum, 12n30.

[12] Davis, *High Weirdness*, 299.

among the fishermen of Lake Galilee, and promised they would become "fishers of men" (Matthew 4:19). The sign or symbol of the fish, in Greek ἰχθύς, also came to serve as a coded acrostic for the phrase Ἰησοῦς Χριστός θεοῦ Υἱός Σωτήρ, "Jesus Christ, Son of God, Savior." The fish was a very simple and common early Christian symbol, eventually replaced by another simple symbol in the fourth century: the cross. Both fish and cross were drawn by two simple, intersecting strokes: arcs for the fish, and straight lines for the cross.

In the months and years after 2-3-74, Dick returned to this experience, almost obsessively, turning it over and over in his mind, clothing it in different words and interpreting it with different frameworks. There is no "standard account" of it, but rather a jumble of letters and journal entries, some of which found their way into his sprawling text, the *Exegesis*. But a curious detail recurs: a shimmer of sunlight on the golden fish first catches his eye and leaves him dazed and confused: time and space collapse and he remembers "who I was and where I was." The young woman and he were simultaneously living in two worlds: in California in the 1970s *and* in ancient Rome, where both of them were "secret Christians" hiding from detection and persecution. Several years after the experience, he says that he came to apply to this experience the Greek word *anamnesis*, which he translates literally as "loss of forgetfulness."[13] In one sense this sign stabilized his identity – he understood himself as a Christian – but it also cracked his world *wide* open. In the wake of 2-3-74, other messages and messengers – voices, dreams, encounters with entities, transmissions, and transcriptions – started streaming in. If you're interested in learning more about this impossible influx, you should read Davis' compelling chapter.

I wish only to highlight that Dick came to interpret 2-3-74 through the prism of *The Pearlsong*. In February of 1975, a year after the experience, he writes a letter to a friend in which he speaks of the "Hymn of the Soul," his knowledge of the text drawn from the *Encyclopædia Britannica*. By the late 70s, however, we know that he had read Hans Jonas' influential book, *The Gnostic Religion*, and that his attention is laser focused on the hymn's flying letter. Jonas regarded the flying let-

[13] Davis, *High Weirdness*, 301.

ter that spoke as a symbol of the "call from without," and an example of how "the transmundane penetrates the enclosure of the world and makes itself heard therein as a call." Jonas goes on to say that "the call as such is its own content, since it simply states what its being sounded will effect: the awakening from sleep."[14] In *The Pearlsong*, the call awakens the prince to his person and his pursuit, his identity and quest. In Dick's life, the call of 2-3-74 became in Davis's words a "conundrum": "a clarion blast ruptured Dick's reality field, but, with the exception of some remarkable epiphanies, the message itself was terminally postponed."[15] If *The Pearlsong* is best understood as a story, it is a simple one, with resolution; but while this simple story gave Dick an ancient or perhaps a timeless template for thinking through his own call, he was never able quite to find his way home to his own East and royal family. Davis brilliantly brings contemporary theory to bear on Dick's predicament, including Peter Sloterdijk's notion of "message ontologies" and Giorgio Agamben's analysis of the apostle Paul's call (*klēsis*) as that which "calls for nothing and to no place."

In his endless exegesis of 2-3-74, Dick began to suspect, and to hide, his own hand. In *The Pearlsong* the hymn's letter reads out the prince's inner inscription: he already knew, but had forgotten, what was written on his heart. But Dick began to wonder whether the young prince sent the letter to himself – after all, his brother the "second" or "double" remained at home. Dick could never find any corroborating evidence for the young woman who appeared at his door: the pharmacy denied using anyone of her description for deliveries. Did he imagine her and her fish sign? Had he made it all up? Had he sent himself "a very convoluted letter"? If so, what was the self, the "I," who was both sender and receiver, who had forgotten and remembered? In *Cannibal Metaphysics*, Eduardo Viveiros de Castro insists, that "When everything is human, the human becomes a wholly other thing."[16] If the self is both sender and receiver, at home and in exile, in contemporary California

[14]Jonas, *The Gnostic Religion*, 74, 80; cited in Davis, *High Weirdness*, 348, 350.

[15]Davis, *High Weirdness*, 349.

[16]Eduardo Viveiros de Castro, *Cannibal Metaphysics*, translated by Peter Skafish (Minneapolis, 2017), 63.

and ancient Rome, with feet on both banks of the river Lethe, then indeed such a self is a wholly other thing.

Dick's dance with *The Pearlsong* was new to me, and I'm grateful to Davis for his brilliant and balanced exploration of it. Just as Dick was ramping up his fascination with *The Pearlsong* in the 1970s, a contemporary of his by the name of Henry Corbin (1903-1978) was winding his down. Temperamentally Dick and Corbin could not be further apart, although they both wrote furiously, and were committed to the tradition of commentary. I am also struck by some curious correspondences in their understanding of *The Pearlsong*. Henry Corbin was a French philosopher of religion, a scholar of Islam and pre-Islamic Iran, and professor of Islamic Studies at l'École pratique des hautes études. He is often remembered today, along with Mircea Eliade and Gershom Scholem, as one of the three principal intellectuals active in the postwar Eranos seminars, held every summer on the shores of Lake Maggiore in Ascona, Switzerland.[17]

Corbin was long fascinated with the "Hymn of the Soul," as he knew it. I don't know when he first crossed paths with it, but he mentions it several times in his first book, *Avicenna and the Visionary Recital*, published in 1954.[18] Corbin regards *The Pearlsong* as a kind of archetype for what he calls a "visionary recital." Both the famed rationalist philosopher Avicenna (c. 980-1037) and the infamous *ishraqi* ("illuminationist") philosopher Sohravardi (1154-1191) each wrote a small number of

[17] See H. T. Hakl, *Eranos: An Alternative Intellectual History of the Twentieth Century* (Montréal, 2013), 154-168. See also, W. Hanegraaff, *Esotericism and the Academy: Rejected Knowledge in Western Culture* (Cambridge, 2012), 295-314; for a critical appraisal of these three, see S. M. Wasserstrom, *Religion After Religion: Gerschom Scholem, Mircea Eliade, and Henry Corbin at Eranos*, (Princeton, 1999). For a more sympathetic and sophisticated engagement with Corbin, see the forthcoming volume, edited by Hadi Fakhoury, *New Perspectives on Henry Corbin*, Palgrave Studies in New Religions and Alternative Spiritualities (forthcoming).

[18] Henry Corbin, *Avicenne et le récit visionnarie* (Teheran, 1954). English translation by Willard R. Trask, *Avicenna and the Visionary Recital* (Princeton, 1960). My comments on Corbin's views of *The Pearlsong* are drawn from this book, although he mentions it in other works of his, including, as Bremer-McCollum notes, *En Islam Iranien*, vol. 2, 258-334.

strange fables, full of symbols, and Corbin's book is an interpretive study of Avicenna's trilogy of such. They have generally been regarded as peripheral texts in these giants' respective bodies of work, but Corbin insists that these recitals are the key to their philosophy and spirituality. A visionary recital is a "dramaturgy," the staging of one's own drama, "a personally lived adventure." It has several consistent features. First, a visionary recital is spoken in the first person, because it inalienably belongs to an individual person (which begs the question of what significance *others'* visionary recitals have for *me*). Second, a visionary recital is a description of a journey: you go somewhere. The "where" you go is also the "how": you use the faculty of the imagination, nearly atrophied in the modern period, to enter the "imaginal" realm – a place that is not at all "imaginary," but very much real, and populated with images that are appropriate to your vision. You *see things* there, and you are in part the painter of what you see. But there is also some consistency across imaginal worlds, correspondences between different reports of this realm. Third, in a visionary recital you "repeat from memory" this journey, most often a quest, which includes allies and adversaries.

The fact that *The Pearlsong* was set in Parthia, the ancient Iranian empire, was no coincidence for Corbin. He was convinced, certain even, that Iran had a "special vocation": its philosophers knew how to enter and navigate the imaginal realm, the world of soul, which lies between our customary world of sense perception and the intelligible world from which both others are derived. According to Corbin, the West, and especially the modern West, has largely lost its way: we no longer know *that* there is a soul, nor *how* to get to know it. And because soul lies between body and mind, and mediates between the two, to lose sight of soul is to be reduced to a flatland of sense perception, a bleak "empiricism" that aches for transcendent dimensions whose existence it denies. The embers have not gone completely cold in the West, however. Certain figures and traditions have preserved imaginal knowledge: Platonism, Hermeticism and alchemy, certain esoteric strands of Christianity, in the East and West, including decidedly *Protestant* visionaries and mystics. Corbin was a French Protestant, and chose to highlight the esoteric, visionary, and mystical aspects of Protestantism, which he felt were alive in, for example, Emmanuel Swedenborg and Joseph Smith. According to Corbin, soul binds the universe together because it is only in the world of soul that I encounter my guide, my counterpart or *alter-ego*, the angel out in front of me. Everyone, every *being* in fact, has an angel: like you I have the capacity to meet and unite with my higher self, on an ever-ascending scale of angelic ecstasies, until I finally face the faceless source. We are each our own individual chain of being, and the "I" I know is but a link it, and in the realm of soul I meet my angel, the next highest link in my chain, in which I experience a hole at the center of myself, filled with someone else who is also none other than me.

This vision of Corbin's, especially as it is found in *The Man of Light*, was an inspiration for *Our Divine Double*.[19] But reading Bremer-McCollum's introduction to *The Pearlsong*, I suspect I fell short of that vision in one important respect. This brings me to the fourth feature of a visionary recital: it narrates the encounter with one's angelic avatar *in symbols*. It seems easier for Corbin to explain what symbols are *not*: they're not signs, metaphors, or allegories. He regards signs and metaphors as arbitrary and "artificially constructed." This in contrast to symbol and symbolized, between which there is a "strict connection": the symbol *participates in* – I am tempted to say "ontologically" although Corbin does not – the symbolized. In other words, the symbolized is *present* in the symbol, if one knows the hermeneutics of "making present." If you don't, you will string together a series of signs and metaphors into an "allegory," a one-to-one correspondence or code: this means that, this that, etc.[20] I fear this is what I and others have done with *The Pearlsong*, collapsing the range of symbolic senses into a fixed allegorical meaning. In my defense, I often feel that Corbin does much the same when he is interpreting Avicenna's own recitals: his commentary seems to slip into allegory, suggesting that allegory is something of a temptation, or perhaps better, that symbol is easier to anticipate than to enact, to talk than to walk. Like the angel, the symbol is out ahead of us.

[19] Henry Corbin, *L'homme de lumière dans le soufisme iranien* (Paris, 1971); English translation by Nancy Pearson, *The Man of Light in Iranian Sufism* (New Lebanon, NY, 1994).
[20] Corbin, *Avicenna and the Visionary Recital*, 30-31.

A symbol is the experienced image of the imaginal realm. It is given to us, in some sense by us, and when we bring it back to this world, its power resides in its ability to "make present" whatever reality we experienced there. In this sense, you can't assign a meaning to a symbol (e.g. prince = soul; Egypt = embodiment); once it is recited, a symbol is something that has to be activated in the present, by an interpreter or a reader. A symbol is more of an event than a sign, something that has *to happen*, to be continually re-earned, re-activated, made present *again*, now rather than then. The name for this kind of interpretation, Corbin tells us, is *ta'wil*, which means to bring a symbol back to its source, its origin, the first thing (*al-awwal*). To perform *ta'wil* on a symbol, however, is simultaneously to perform *ta'wil* on oneself. As you let the symbolized shine through the symbol, you meet your angel and ascend the chain of being. For Corbin, all exegesis, whether the "text of a book or cosmic text," is exegesis of the soul. You come to know yourself only through interpreting symbols.[21]

The fifth and final feature of a visionary recital is its curiously consistent orientation. Visionary recitals move across a landscape defined by East and West, by the sun's rising and setting, orient and occident. These cardinal directions point not only to geographic regions, the "East" and the "West," but more fundamentally they name existential stances: existential Easterners, what Corbin calls "orientals," are those who are properly oriented, that is, who face the rising sun and look for the angel out ahead; existential Westerners, or "occidentals," turn away from that "man of light." He often played on this ambiguity: he, a geographical "occidental," was in fact an existential "oriental," and he understood himself as gathering such "orientals" from East and West, from Iran and Europe, in a shared quest to preserve and protect the knowledge of soul.

I hope you can see why, with these five features of a visionary recital, Corbin might think that *The Pearlsong* was an archetype of those recitals that would come after, which he spent his time editing, translating, and interpreting. *The Pearlsong* has all five of these features: it is spoken in the first person, about a soul's journey and its quest; a recitation of that

[21] Corbin, *Avicenna and the Visionary Recital*, 31-32, among many other places.

quest from memory, including friends and foes; friends who are also guides, counterparts, intimates, and mirror images – divine doubles, if you will – recited and rendered as symbols, whose meaning cannot, or should not, be assigned; and a drama played out between East and West, themselves symbols of deeper orientations and identities.

I am persuaded by Bremer-McCollum that we, that I, should ease up a bit on the allegorical interpretation of *The Pearlsong*. But I do not think that the simple shift from allegory to story is sufficient to our task, to whatever call a visionary recital issues us. More deeply, I am persuaded by Corbin that these stories, these fables that are not fantasies, should be treated as symbols, that the task is to make present for each of us whatever needs to shine through. It is my great privilege and pleasure to introduce you to *The Pearlsong*, if you are new to it, or even if, like Dick, you suspect that it is an inscription you have read before, a letter you may have sent to yourself. To whatever degree this edition, translation, and commentary, and my foreword, help further orient us and deepen our *ta'wil*, I will be grateful and proud.

Charles M. Stang
Epiphanytide
Cambridge, Massachusetts

Acknowledgments

As *The Pearlsong*'s protagonist had the advantage of helpers and guides along the journey, I've had support from several directions while writing this book. First, I would like to thank Charles Stang, with whom I co-edit the series, Texts & Translations of Transcendence & Transformation (4T). The idea for our series became clear in conversations between Charles and me about typography, the breadth of Late Ancient literature, and parallel text-and-translation editions.

Gosia Sklodowska's planning for the series and careful editing of the text in its final stages have been a major help. Heather Dubnick saved the book from scores of inconsistencies and typos. Janet Timbie read my English translations of the Coptic texts and offered several translation alternatives, which made my renderings read more smoothly. Byron MacDougall looked over an early draft of my English translations of the Greek *Pearlsong* texts, and Brayden Hirsch read these and my other translations from Greek. Thanks especially to Brayden's detailed remarks, these translations now both sound better and more closely reflect their Greek sources. I have Nathan Tilley to thank for a host of helpful comments in each of the book's parts, but his remarks on my translations of the Syriac texts and his suggestions for moving parts of the book around have especially improved the result.

Michael Penn at various times gave enthusiastic support for the project. His hope to see it published and in the hands of students has been an encouragement. I read *The Pearlsong* with students of Syriac various times and learned anew each time. In particular, I would like to mention Chia-Wei Lin, who has been an almost weekly interlocutor on Syriac, Iranian languages, Georgian, and more, and Erfan Dianat, with whom I had the good fortune to discuss both *The Pearlsong* and Sohravardi, and who also read parts of the draft of the book.

I warmly thank my colleagues at the CSWR for their interest and support. Nick Low patiently read through early – and long! – drafts of the introduction and helped me trim it and rearrange it. Gio DiRusso, generously offered pointed ideas for improving the book in a few places. Fabien Muller has been a frequent conversation partner for the 4T series; in addition to always being ready to discuss Hunter and Barlow lyrics, he has constantly offered a voice in support of my work on the book and the series.

Lydia Bremer-McCollum not only read the book in various incarnations, she also endured hearing me talk about it incessantly at times. Her advice on both the arrangement and the details have made it a much better book. More than this, she made and makes every day brighter by being in it. Two of my children, Isaac and Stephen, read my translations of *The Pearlsong* texts and the story is now part of our own shared story together.

Although it's been many years since I sat in their classrooms and read with them, my teachers Isaac Jerusalmi (ע״ה) and Stephen A. Kaufman are always with me when I read and think about not only the languages and texts I studied with them, but also the languages and new things I have studied since then.

Translations of all texts into English are my own, with just one exception, Emily Wilson's *Odyssey*. These sources, both ancient and modern, are always also given in the source language (in footnotes) to accompany my English translations. Languages, writing systems, and translation are not only major components of philological scholarship, they're a joy to explore, and I hope that different kinds of readers will find different things to appreciate in the linguistically and visually diverse textual richness presented here. In any case, scrutinizing and critical readers can readily compare my renditions with the source texts.

Typesetting the book, while also being its author and the series co-editor, has included the responsibility for making all sorts of decisions, minute and global. I am very grateful for the askers and answerers of questions on LaTeX forums, where I often found very specific help on typesetting issues.

It has been a pleasure to work with the team at RDW Group (Providence, Rhode Island). I am especially grateful to Stephanie Nademlynsky, and to Martha Doyle Lindman, who created a beautiful, fittingly enchanting cover for *The Pearlsong*'s story.

I'm grateful for the opportunity to have written this book, to think with these texts, to see and say these words in other languages. I'm grateful for the lifetimes of labor devoted to old texts and languages by previous editors, type compositors, translators, commenters, and lexicographers.

I'm grateful for the peaceful environment I could write in. I'm grateful for the music I listened to while writing and while thinking about *The Pearlsong*. Among several songs cited in the book, the Shangri-Las' "Remember (Walkin' in the Sand)" from 1964 was a favorite of my mother, Kathy Lynne Carter Mathis (1957-2018). I dedicate the book to her memory. I miss our conversations and our shared smiles and laughs. These and other memories keep her close every day.

Adam Bremer-McCollum
February 2, 2025

Abbreviations and Transliterations

Abbreviations

See the bibliography for fuller details.

AIOA	Kaufman, *Akkadian Influences*
Akk	Akkadian
AMS	Bedjan, *Acta Martyrum et Sanctorum*
BB	Bar Bahlul's lexicon: see Duval, *Lexicon Syriacum*
CAD	Reiner and Roth, eds., *Chicago Assyrian Dictionary*
CPA	Christian Palestinian Aramaic
DJBA	Sokoloff, *Dictionary of Jewish Babylonian Aramaic*
DJPA	Sokoloff, *Dictionary of Jewish Palestinian Aramaic*
DMMPP	Durkin-Meisterernst, *Dictionary of Manichaean Middle Persian and Parthian*
ILS	Ciancaglini, *Iranian Loanwords in Syriac*
JBA	Jewish Babylonian Aramaic
JPA	Jewish Palestinian Aramaic
KAI	Donner and Röllig, *Kanaanäische und aramäische Inschriften*
KMK	*Mani Codex* from Cologne: see Koenen and Römer, *Mani-Kodex*
Kph	*Kephalaia of the Teacher*: see Polotsky and Böhlig, *Kephalaia*; Böhlig, *Kephalaia*; and Tardieu, "Diffusion"
MHm	Manichaean *Homilies*: see Polotsky, *Homilien* and Pedersen, *Homilies*
MS	manuscript

MP	Middle Persian
MPb	Manichaean *Psalmbook*: see Allberry, *Psalm-book* and Richter, *Psalmengruppe*, *Bema*, and *Herakleides*
Pa	Parthian

For the Syriac *binyanim*, or stems, the following letters are used:

G	*pʕal*	tG	*ʔetp̄ʕel*
D	*paʕʕel*	tD	*ʔetp̄aʕʕal*
A	*ʔap̄ʕel*	tA	*ʔettap̄ʕal*
Q	[quadrilit.]	tQ	[*t*-quadrilit.]

Transliterations and transcriptions

Texts in several different languages and scripts are quoted (and translated) below. They are generally quoted in their own conventional script, where this is possible (i.e. the script is in Unicode).

Syriac

The consonants of Syriac (and other Aramaic languages) are transliterated and transcribed as follows:

ʔ b g d h w z ḥ ṭ y k l m n s ʕ p ṣ q r š t

The six consonants having alternating "hard/soft" allophones – the *bgdkpt* letters – are transcribed *b/ḇ g/ḡ d/ḏ k/ḵ p/p̄ t/ṯ*.

The Syriac transcriptions reflect a plausible early (≈ 3rd-5th centuries) form of Syriac reading and pronunciation, much of which also lines up with (early) East Syriac reading tradition. The vowels are *a, å, e, ē, i, o, u*. (Alongside the characteristic *å* > *o*, West Syriac reading tradition merges *ē, i* > *i*, *ē, e* > *e*, and *o, u* > *u*, resulting in a shorter list of vowels.) The vowel I transliterate as *å* is commonly transcribed as *ā*. Given that it is a *long a* [aː]/[ɑ], tending toward [ɔ], and that it's pronounced *o* in West Syriac, the transcription *å* is fitting. The generally predictable ultrashort vowel [ə], unwritten in Syriac script, is also unmarked in the transcriptions.

Greek

Other than in Greek script, Greek is sometimes given in italics in transliteration, that is, a letter-for-letter conversion from Greek script into Latin script. It is *not* a transcription indicating a particular pronunciation.[22]

Other

Inscriptions in Aramaic languages, in this case Old Aramaic, Palmyrene, and Nabatean are given in Phoenician and Palmyrene script, respectively, and in transliteration in angled brackets < >. Mandaic is in Mandaic script and in transcription.[23] Middle Persian and Parthian texts, whether Zoroastrian or Manichaean, are given in transcription in italics following usual conventions, as in DMMPP (Manichaean) and MacKenzie, rather than just in transcription. Other languages – Coptic, Akkadian, Jewish Babylonian Aramaic, Arabic, Armenian, etc. – are given in their usual scripts or transliterated following norms that will be clear to readers and students of those languages.

[22] For example, in a pronunciation appropriate to these texts – Byzantine or "modern" pronunciation – the vowel *η/ē* and the original diphthong *ει/ei* are both [i], δ/*d* is [ð], etc. So, for example, *τρυφή* is transliterated *trup^{h}ē*, but in Byzantine pronunciation this is something like [tri'fi].

[23] Rather than Macuch's transliteration system, I use a transcription based on Mandaic reading tradition and (less so) comparative Aramaic dialectology. Here are a few forms in each system for comparison, with Macuch's version in boldface: **abuia** for *aḇūy* "his father," **bnia/ʿbnia/abnia** for *ebnī* "children," **b(i)riata** for *beryāṯā* "streets," and **libai** for *lebbay* "my heart."

1 Introduction

1.1 A Late Parthian-era Aramaic Poem

Tucked away inside a single Syriac manuscript of a long hagiography devoted to Thomas, the saint, is a poem of just over 100 lines. While widely accepted as a parable or allegory, the poem itself is a first-person narrative with a trip, a giant snake keeping a pearl by the sea, a magic sleeping-spell, literal telepathy, a flying letter that talks, and more. With these and other endearing charms, *The Pearlsong*, as I'll call it, has so captivated readers that it's often considered on its own, apart from its position in the *Acts of Thomas*.[1] However much it's a part of the saint's life, it is and has been treated as a separate text all on its own, as it is here.

This Syriac text, along with two Greek versions, is the subject of this book. The Syriac text of *The Pearlsong* is known from a single manuscript, among other Thomas manuscripts lacking it. Similarly, most Greek manuscripts of the *Acts of Thomas* have no *Pearlsong*, with just one including it. In addition to these late ancient texts in Syriac and Greek, there's a paraphrase in a Byzantine homily by Niketas of Thessaloniki (perh. eleventh century). All three texts are given below with English translations.

At its most basic, *The Pearlsong* is a first-person narrative in verse, told by a prince sent as a child to Egypt by his parents to retrieve a pearl from a giant snake in the sea. Once in Egypt, abandoned by his guardian-guides, he tries to disguise himself as an Egyptian, and he gets tricked into joining them in serving their king and eating their food. He forgets why he's there and where he came from. But his

[1]For a synopsis of the *Acts of Thomas*, see Saint-Laurent, *Missionary Stories* 17-35. For recent research see Gallarta and Lanzillotta, *New Trends*.

parents are somehow aware and they write a rousing letter that triggers his memory. The letter flies from sender to receiver, whom it wakes from slumber by making sounds and by actually speaking. The traveler-prince, now reawakened and reminded, recites a sleeping spell over the giant snake using the names of his royal family. The snake is now unconscious, so the prince makes off with the pearl. At this point our protagonist makes his way home, finding the letter in front of him as a guiding light. His parents also sent the prince a shining or sparkling garment belonging to him, but unlike the letter, the garment doesn't fly: two members of the royal staff deliver it to him on the road, and it becomes a revelatory mirror. Like the letter, the shining garment speaks, too. Now the traveler-prince is ready to return home and rejoin his family, on the best terms with king and court.

While specific allegorical or symbolic interpretations are possible, *The Pearlsong* is first and foremost a story, with all the possibilities of meaning, appropriation, and remixing. A reader or hearer may identify, for example, with one or more actors in the narrative, at different times, and take some "meaning" – encouragement, sympathy, inspiration, direction, a reason to laugh – from the story that's not directly philosophical or religious, domains where allegory and symbolism tend to reside. Like Shakespeare's *Tempest*, the world of *The Pearlsong* is

> a created world which is neither allegory nor psychology, but rather a world in the true sense; an alien place at the other side of the mirror, or at that world from which we snatch glimpses when we dream. Like learning of a new continent, we can see the similarities and also the dissimilarities to our own world; there's people there, some of which may look like us, others which may look or behave in a way that appears to us quite surreal; they move about in a landscape where some of our natural laws seem to hold, while others don't. We may spot creatures, strange as things from another planet, whom we soon come to learn.[2]

[2]Lundborg, *Psychedelia*, 65.

The Pearlsong has characters that are strange, uncanny, or supernatural, like a letter that can fly like an eagle, and parents telepathically aware of their child's dire straits. Altogether the pedestrian elements and the weird and unexpected combine to make up the story, and it's mainly as a story that I will read and discuss it, while still open to symbolic readings.

1.1.1 Is it really a hymn?

In the Syriac manuscript of the *Acts of Thomas*, the text is titled a *madrâšâ*, and in Greek *psalmos*.[3] Either of these terms can reasonably be translated as "hymn," and the text is typically referred to in English as "the hymn of the pearl (or soul)," but does "hymn" really fit this text?

First, in the Thomas story itself, Thomas "says" the poem: he's not singing. The verb used for Thomas's performance of *The Pearlsong* is the normal, everyday verb of speaking in Syriac, the verb *ʔemar*. By contrast, the other piece of verse in the *Acts of Thomas* that the title character shares is something at a wedding, but in this case, Thomas unambiguously sings it, with the verb *zmar* used: "Thomas started singing this song."[4] By contrast, *The Pearlsong* is introduced in the *Acts of Thomas* this way: "Thomas started reciting this *madrâšâ*."[5]

Second, in English "hymn" brings to mind a piece of verse sung in praise of someone or something, maybe in a liturgical setting or style, whether a selection from *The Southern Harmony and Musical Companion* or an Egyptian hymn to Amun-Ra, for example. *The Pearlsong* is not mainly in praise of anyone or anything: neither the prince, the pearl, nor even the royal family and realm the prince leaves and returns to.

Third, regarding the Syriac term *madrâšâ*: this word refers to a major type of Syriac religious poetry associated especially with the famous Syriac writer Ephrem, and it is regularly translated "hymn" in that context. As discussed in Appendix I, a *madrâšâ* normally means a

[3]When the Greek translator calls the *madrâšâ* a *psalmos*, this already indicates at least a small semantic shift Christianward (Tubach, "Zur Interpretation," 241).

[4]AMS 3 8: ܘܫܪܝ ܗܘܐ ܬܐܘܡܐ ܕܢܙܡܪ ܙܡܝܪܬܐ ܗܕܐ

[5]AMS 3 110: ܫܪܝ ܗܘܐ ܬܐܘܡܐ ܕܢܐܡܪ ܡܕܪܫܐ ܗܢܐ

kind of Syriac poem following a set of stanzaic patterns. *The Pearlsong*, though, clearly follows a distinctly different metrical arrangement and thus cannot be a Syriac "hymn" in this technical sense.

So why is the text called a *madrāšā*? The Syriac term is cognate with Hebrew *midrāš*. Midrash is a well-known, if not easily defined, genre of late ancient (and later) Jewish literature. At the most generic level in this context, it means a theory-oriented (as opposed to practice) interpretive instruction based on an authoritative text, generally part of the Bible.[6] It's nearly impossible to fit *The Pearlsong* even into this loose definition. In short, it's not a *madrāšā* as *midrāš*.[7]

So, if it's not really a hymn, or a *midrāš*, and we want to call it something else, what might work? Niketas refers to it as τραγῳδίαν τινά "a tragedy." Is it enough simply to call it a "poem"? Maybe "lore" or "lore-song"? I prefer "Pearlsong" because, first, unlike "hymn," "song" can include rhythmical recitation without music; and second, it conveys both whimsy and uniqueness – like the article in "*the* hymn of the pearl." "Pearlsong" is no more invented than "hymn of the pearl" and it's a better match.

Beyond the title, it's important to keep in mind the text's more concrete features: a first-person narrative focused on the speaker's movements and changes, recorded in Syriac with a baseline rhythm of six-

[6] Strack and Stemberger, *Introduction*, 234-235.

[7] While it's better known within Rabbinic literature, the term *midrāš* occurs in the Hebrew Bible, too: the ways and words of so-and-so "are written in the *midrāš* of prophet ʕiddō," and similarly, "written on the *midrāš* of the kings' scroll" (2 Chronicles 13:22: כתובים במדרש הנביא עדו, and 24:27: כתובים על־מדרש ספר המלכים). Both times it's singular and in a bound ("construct") relationship with another noun, and most importantly, it explicitly refers to some kind of written document with a known title. In the Syriac translation of these verses 2 Chronicles 13:22 has *madrāšē* and 24:27 has *madrāšē da-spar malkē*, both plural, and in a place that doesn't seem to have anything to do with "hymns." (In the Old Greek of the first verse, it's βιβλίον "letter, document, scroll, volume, book," and 24:27 has γραφή "inscription, document, list, book, writing.")

A cognate to Syriac *madrāšā* shows up not only in Hebrew, but also in other Aramaic languages beyond Syriac, even if relatively rarely. In Jewish Babylonian (JBA) and Jewish Palestinian Aramaic (JPA), it mostly shows up in the phrase *be(t) madrāšā* "school, place to study" (DJPA 94, 292; DJBA 214). A related compound expression, in JBA, the person in charge of a *be madrāšā* can be called *rēš madrāšā* "school-leader," but *rēš mtibtā* "session-head" is more common with this meaning (DJBA 1081).

syllable couplets. It's not in praise of anyone or anything. It's not obviously written for music, and at least the way it's presented in the *Acts of Thomas*, it wasn't experienced as a melodic song. That said, there's nothing to bar the text or narrative from a musical setting, and the name *Pearlsong* remains open and inviting for that prospect.

1.1.2 What does it mean?

Within the *Acts of Thomas*, *The Pearlsong* plays a limited role. First, it's notable that it's completely absent from all but one manuscript each in Syriac and Greek of the *Acts of Thomas*. In these manuscripts lacking *The Pearlsong*, the narrative flows without a hitch. Even in the two manuscript instances where the *Acts of Thomas* includes *The Pearlsong*, no effort is made to interpret it in light of the *Acts*. Nevertheless, upon closer comparison, resonances and contrasts emerge, as outlined by Saint-Laurent:

> This story inverts a version of the missionary story itself, warning of the dangers that befall a traveler who forgets the intent of his mission. The type/antitype patterning of the hymn's images relates to themes from the dominant narrative. The values of the hymn compare to the ideals of the *Acts of Thomas*. Unlike Thomas, who maintains his course to Christ through prayer, even in imprisonment, the prince of the hymn begins with purpose but loses his way. The hymn reunites a family broken apart; the *Acts of Thomas* breaks up earthly families and discourages marriage. The hymn celebrates royalty; the *Acts of Thomas* promotes simplicity and anonymity. The prince of the "Hymn on the Pearl" must hold fast to his material possessions, whereas the *Acts of Thomas* promises freedom through poverty. Thomas, though a pauper and magician in the temporal world, emerges as a superior double of the royal son. Both the prince and Thomas move from freeborn social statuses into slavery. Both complete missions in service to a lord. Both fall into a decadent society

> but Thomas resists its temptations. He, unlike the prince, never forgets his royal lineage.[8]

So the prince of *The Pearlsong* can be interpreted as a foil for Thomas.[9]

These narrative mirror-images from the hagiography aside, just as *The Pearlsong* was inserted into the *Acts of Thomas* and thereby enriched it, so too it can be extracted from Thomas's presentation and given its own stage. As such, with an immediately appealing narrative, whether read superficially or symbolically, and with several themes that resonate widely, it has found devotees not just among readers of early Christian literature. Discussions of the work of Fyodor Dostoyevsky, Philip K. Dick, and Cormac McCarthy refer to *The Pearlsong*'s narrative and its allegedly "saved savior" main character.[10]

It bears highlighting that nothing about the narrative or the actors, human and non-human, necessarily assumes a specifically Christian narrator or audience. There is no deity, no trinity, no congregation, no faith, etc. This, despite the fact that *The Pearlsong* is known, in terms of manuscripts and textual ancestry, through channels of Christian hagiography.[11]

Birger Pearson claims, "The religiosity reflected in the hymn matches that of the *Acts of Thomas*,"[12] but what is it in *The Pearlsong* that might be reflecting this religiosity? The story has no god or other divinity, no worship or prayer or sacrifice, and no teaching or preaching, social or doctrinal. With Pearson's assumption that *The Pearlsong* is a plain

[8] *Missionary Stories*, 25.

[9] For other possibilities of reading *The Pearlsong* with the *Acts of Thomas* as a whole, cf. Stang, *Our Divine Double*, 142.

[10] See respectively Moskvina, "Гностический миф;" Davis, *High Weirdness*, 347-358; and Hillier, Rev. Mundik. Dick's connection to *The Pearlsong* is the most robust. His encounter with a "vast active living intelligence system"–VALIS, an encounter he called 2-3-74, was triggered on 2 Feb 1974: "Like the winged letter that appears in the Gnostic 'Hymn of the Pearl,' the delivery woman's necklace served as a trigger for mystical memory" (Davis, *Techgnosis*, 331).

[11] "The fact that it contains no obviously Christian content, moreover, raises the question of whether it originated in a different religious milieu and was subsequently repurposed for a Christian audience in these apocryphal *Acts*" (Stang, *Our Divine Double*, 135).

[12] Pearson, *Ancient Gnosticism*, 261.

Christian text, it's a small step to assuming further that its supposed Christianity fits in with the *Acts of Thomas*, but it's still just an assumption, if not a forced reading. Not only is *The Pearlsong* not obviously Christian, it's not even particularly "religious." We wouldn't be wrong to call it "doctrinally neutral."[13]

Given this apparent doctrinal neutrality, interpreters have been quick to fill the void with suggested religious or philosophical contexts. In the year William Wright first published *The Pearlsong*, 1871, Wright's friend and frequent correspondent, Theodor Nöldeke, reviewed the book, spending a disproportionate amount of attention on the few pages (out of 333) that have *The Pearlsong*.[14] Nöldeke's characterization of *The Pearlsong* as "Gnostic," that wide-ranging tag of heresiologists, proves enduring.

> This is without a doubt *an unadulterated Gnostic song, and a Syriac original at that*. We have here the old Gnostic hymn of the soul, where the soul is sent to earth from its heavenly origin and there forgets its origin and mission, until it's awakened by a higher revelation, fulfills its mission, and then returns home on high, where it rediscovers its heavenly garment, its ideal likeness, and reaches the highest powers of heaven.[15]

---

[13]The phrase is Poirier's: "a piece as doctrinally neutral, at least at first glance, as the *Hymn of the Pearl*" / "un morceau aussi doctrinalement neutre, du moins à première vue, que l'*L'Hymne de la Perle*" (Poirier, "Codex Manichaicus," 242).

[14]For letters between the two scholars, see Maier, *Gründerzeit* and *Semitic Studies*.

[15]Nöldeke Rev. Wright, 677:

> Dies ist unzweifelhaft *ein unverfälschter gnostischer Gesang, und zwar ein syrisches Original*. Wir haben hier das alte gnostische Lied von der Seele, die, vom himmlischen Ursprung, auf die Erde gesandt wird und hier ihren Ursprung und ihre Aufgabe vergisst, bis sie durch höhere Offenbarung erweckt wird, ihren Auftrag vollzieht und nun nach oben zurückkehrt, wo sie das himmlische Kleid, ihr ideales Ebenbild, wiederfindet und in die Nähe der höchsten Himmelsmächte gelangt.

However slippery the term "Gnostic" is, Nöldeke specifies his meaning.[16] If a Gnostic labeling means what Nöldeke describes, then *The Pearlsong* resonates with a wide range of texts, in both language and story, such as texts from the Nag Hammadi codices,[17] and Mandaean literature.[18]

A more general reading might take cues from and find resonant language in a broader Platonic framework, like this famous snippet from Plotinus:

> So what's the way? What's the means of access? How can anyone see "inaccessible beauty" of the sort that stays inside holy sanctuaries and does not go outside for someone uninitiated even to see? ...

[16]On the use and abuse of "Gnostic" labeling, see King, *What is Gnosticism?*, and Williams, *Rethinking "Gnosticism"*.

[17]The Nag Hammadi codices (named for where in Egypt they were found) are a group of fourth-century manuscript books in Coptic of varied contents, but often broadly and generically characterized as "Gnostic." In general, see Markschies, *Gnosis*, 48-58, and chapters 6 and 7 of King, *What is Gnosticism?*. As a representative of the move to read the Nag Hammadi texts as from a Christian context, rather than some Gnostic environment, see Lundhaug and Jenott, *Monastic Origins*. I cite *The Gospel of Thomas*, *The Apocryphon of John*, *The Gospel of Philip*, *The Sentences of Sextus*, *The Apocalypse of Adam*, and *The Sophia of Jesus Christ/Eugnostos*, all from the Coptic editions in Robinson, ed., *The Coptic Gnostic Library*, where they are also accompanied by English translations.

[18]Mandeans are adherents of a "Gnostic" belief system – the name "Mandean" comes from *manda* "knowledge," like *gnōsis* – with particular focus on John the Baptist as a prophet, and a consequent practice of baptism. In general, see Buckley, *Mandaeans* and *Great Stem of Souls*, and Van Bladel, *From Sasanian Mandaeans*. See Adam, *Psalmen*, 68-70, for some possible connections between *The Pearlsong* and Mandean literature, at least as then known. Two Mandaic texts, in particular, show up in the discussion below: *The Baptism of Hibil-Ziwa* and a parallel text from the *Qolasta* and *Left Ginza*. E.S. Drower wrote a short article ("Hibil-Ziwa") noting some similarities between *The Pearlsong* and the *The Baptism of Hibil-Ziwa*, as well as a facsimile text and an (archaizing) English translation. I cite according to the text at the Comprehensive Aramaic Lexicon (CAL) site and in Al-Mubaraki, *Hibil-Ziwa*. The *Qolasta* text was edited by Lidzbarski, with a German translation of its parallel text in the *Left Ginza* (*Qolasta* prayer 73 in Lidzbarski, *Mandäische Liturgien*, 111-114 [text and German translation] ≈ *Left Ginza*, 3.27 [p. 108], *Ginza der Schatz*, 552-554). I cite the text by page in Lidzbarski's edition of the *Qolasta*. See also Drower, *Canonical Prayerbook*.

> Indeed, "let's take flight to our dear homeland,"[19] someone might more truly advise. So what is this flight, and how is it taken? Let us set sail in the way that, Homer says, Odysseus did from the witch Circe or Calypso – telling enigmatically, I think, that he was not happy to remain, even though he had pleasures for his eyes and was living with a great sensory beauty. Indeed our "homeland" is where we came from, and our father is there.
>
> So what is the journey and the flight? One cannot finish it on foot, since feet just take us everywhere on earth, from one place to another. Nor do you need to prepare a vehicle with horses or one for the sea. Rather, forget all this, and stop looking: with your eyes closed, switch to and awaken another kind of sight, one which everyone has, but few use.[20]

The focus here on a homecoming to the "father" particularly resonates with *The Pearlsong*.

While it may share language and imagery with texts called Gnostic or Neoplatonic, *The Pearlsong* doesn't definitely and straightforwardly

---

[19]See *Iliad* 9.27, and elsewhere.

[20]*Enneads* 1.6.8 (text in Armstrong, *Enneads*):

> Τίς οὖν ὁ τρόπος; Τίς μηχανή; Πῶς τις θεάσηται κάλλος ἀμήχανον οἷον ἔνδον ἐν ἁγίοις ἱεροῖς μένον οὐδὲ προιὸν εἰς τὸ ἔξω, ἵνα τις καὶ βέβηλος ἴδηι; ...
>
> Φεύγωμεν δὴ φίλην ἐς πατρίδα, ἀληθέστερον ἄν τις παρακελεύοιτο. Τίς οὖν ἡ φυγὴ καὶ πῶς; Ἀναξόμεθα οἷον ἀπὸ μάγου Κίρκης φησὶν ἢ Καλυψοῦς Ὀδυσσεὺς αἰνιττόμενος, δοκεῖ μοι, μεῖναι οὐκ ἀρεσθείς, καίτοι ἔχων ἡδονὰς δι᾽ ὀμμάτων καὶ κάλλει πολλῶι αἰσθητῶι συνών. Πατρὶς δὴ ἡμῖν, ὅθεν παρήλθομεν, καὶ πατὴρ ἐκεῖ.
>
> Τίς οὖν ὁ στόλος καὶ ἡ φυγή; Οὐ ποσὶ δεῖ διανύσαι· πανταχοῦ γὰρ φέρουσι πόδες ἐπὶ γῆν ἄλλην ἀπ᾽ ἄλλης· οὐδέ σε δεῖ ἵππων ὄχημα ἤ τι θαλάττιον παρασκευάσαι, ἀλλὰ ταῦτα πάντα ἀφεῖναι δεῖ καὶ μὴ βλέπειν, ἀλλ᾽ οἷον μύσαντα ὄψιν ἄλλην ἀλλάξασθαι καὶ ἀνεγεῖραι, ἣν ἔχει μὲν πᾶς, χρῶνται δὲ ὀλίγοι.

warrant a philosophical or religious label. Beyer speaks of the background "religion" for the text as "a syncretic religion in the wake of Plato, easily joined with Christian ethics. Its imagery is shared with Gnosticism and the other ancient redemptive religions, with no one able to say for sure where they've been adopted from."[21] This categorization is perhaps almost too loose to be useful, but it underlies an important point: *The Pearlsong* is furtive in its religious or philosophical allegiances (if it has any), and it appeals to a range or readers, not just the adherents of one particular school or belief. This characteristic is reflected in the history of the text's interpretation.[22]

In Tubach's view, had the poem been intended as an allegory from the beginning, its exact meaning would have been made clearer.[23] While I agree that *The Pearlsong* isn't just an allegory, this implies an insight into "the poet," or even the poem, that I don't find possible. There may be allegorical possibilities in the poem that were and are unknown to the poet, allegories waiting to be activated by new readers and hearers at the right time and place. This allegorical potentiality is supported by a reading that takes the story seriously as an actual story, with all the possible visions, scapes, and sounds that that might evoke.

An allegorical reading that assigns *specific* philosophical or religious meanings to the text and demands a specific kind of understanding is unnecessarily limiting, and fails to let the story do its work. In a note to a line in Ephrem's poetry, Brock and Kiraz flatly describe *The Pearl-*

[21] Beyer, "Perlenlied," 241: "Das ist eine synkretische Religion in der Nachfolge Platons, die sich auch leicht mit der christlichen Ethik verbinden läßt. Ihre Bilder teilt sie mit der Gnosis und den anderen antiken Erlösungsreligionen, ohne daß man sicher sagen kann, wer sie von wem übernommen hat."

[22] As Poirier puts it (120), "people are happy to explain the hymn by using a source offering a more or less exact parallel with the general outline of the hymn" ("on se contente d'expliquer l'hymne en utilisant une source qui présente un parallèle plus ou moins précis avec le schéma général de l'hymne").

[23] "If the poet had conceived of the song as an allegory, the meaning of the symbolism would have to have been more straightforwardly framed than it actually is. This leads to the unavoidable conclusion that the poet of *The Pearlsong* didn't intend the text to be understood as an allegory." "Hätte der Dichter das Lied als Allegorie konzipiert, müsste sich die Auflösung der Symbolik einfacher gestalten als das tatsächlich der Fall ist. Das führt zu dem unausweichlichen Schluss, dass der Dichter des Perlenliedes den Text nicht als Allegorie verstanden wissen wollte" (Tubach, "Zur Interpretation," 245).

song as "where the Royal Son goes down to Egypt to rescue the pearl (i.e., soul) from the dragon."[24] Similarly, Stang declares, "The text is quite obviously an allegory."[25] Over a century ago, Burkitt remarked, "Although the narrative is never once interrupted by preaching or philosophy, the general scope of the Allegory is clear."[26] Maybe we should take that "Although" more seriously? Birger Pearson, who treats *The Pearlsong* as undoubtedly Christian, similarly sums up the poem with bland equations:

> This hymn is an allegory of the human soul, a prince whose home is in heaven. Sent down to the earth, he is bereft of the divine image (the robe). His mission is to deprive Satan (the serpent) of his power and obtain the pearl, his true self. But, as an alien in a world of demons (Egypt), he forgets his commission and falls asleep, until he is awakened by the gospel of Jesus (the letter). He then realizes what his task is, and overpowers the serpent in the name of the Father, the Son, and the Holy Spirit. (The Holy Spirit is feminine in Syrian Christianity, and is depicted in the hymn as the queen mother.) With the pearl in hand, he returns as a king's son to his heavenly homeland, is reunited with Christ, his brother, and receives again the divine image that he had lost.[27]

This kind of automatic recourse to specific allegorical or symbolical correspondences strikes me as heavy-handed. It too readily relies on "counterfeit promises of meaning," to use an expression by Emily Witt.[28] *The Pearlsong* does not have to be an allegory, and even if it *is* an allegory, it doesn't have to be mainly about the soul. As in the Middle English *Perle* poem, both symbolic and straightforwardly narrative readings can co-exist and even enrich each other.[29] Stressing the

[24] Brock and Kiraz, *Ephrem*, 255n5.

[25] *Our Divine Double*, 136.

[26] Burkitt, *Hymn*, 7.

[27] *Ancient Gnosticism*, 260.

[28] *Health and Safety*, 224.

[29] As Jane Beal says, "While there is clearly a literal, elegiac sense to the poem, there are also allegorical meanings," and further, "For once the possibilities of allegorical inter-

symbolism, potential or otherwise, even runs the risk of taking something away from the poem, rather than enriching it. As Erik Davis notes, "But in treating the *Hymn* as a philosophical allegory, we flatten something [Philip K.] Dick recognized even in the clipped *Brittanica* paraphrase he first encountered: the *Hymn*'s peculiar power *as a story*."[30]

The interpretive history of the poem has focused especially on author, geographic origin, religious label and genre. As a possible author of *The Pearlsong*, Bardaisan has often been suggested, Burkitt going so far as to name his 1899 translation of it *The Hymn of Bardaisan*. Bardaisan (154-222) is known in antiquity to both Syriac and Greek writers as an important philosopher or theologian.[31] With Marcion and Mani, Bardaisan makes up the triumvirate target of Ephrem's polemical prose, and he's also a favorite enemy in his *Hymns against Heresies*.[32] In addition to both the prose and poetry he penned, mentioned and discussed by ancient authors but now lost except in some quotations, Bardaisan is the main speaker in the famous early Syriac dialog, *The Book of Laws of Countries*, which *is* extant.[33] Although what he wrote can be known only obscurely and impartially, Bardaisan is considered an important figure in late ancient philosophy in Syrophone and Iranophone environments. That he is the author of *The Pearlsong* is much less likely. The main reason for this is, again, *The Pearlsong*'s lack of an obvious interpretive key. As an early piece of Syriac verse with a speculative air to it, it could be by Bardaisan, but there's not necessarily anything in the text or its trail of transmission that overwhelmingly moves the needle in Bardaisan's direction.

---

pretation are re-captured, readers gain a richer sense not only of the elegiac meaning of the poem but also of the greater signifying power of *Pearl*" ("Signifying Power," 53, 54).

[30] *High Weirdness*, 348.

[31] Generally see Drijvers, *Bardaiṣan of Edessa*; Skjærvø, "Bardesanes;" and Camplani, "Rivisitando Bardesane." For more focused studies, note Ehlers, "Bardesanes von Edessa;" Aland, "Mani und Bardesanes;" and Possekel, "Bardaisan of Edessa."

[32] E. Beck, "Bardaisan und seine Schule."

[33] It's known from a single manuscript, BL Add. 14658, which also includes other philosophical texts (logic, cosmology, ontology, and more), several translated from Greek. The Syriac text of *The Book of Laws of Countries* was published in 1907 by F. Nau, with a Latin translation, in *Patrologia Syriaca* 1.2, cols. 490-697 (1907). For an English translation (and Syriac text in Estrangela), see Drijvers, *Book of the Laws of Countries*.

The question of a possible author is of course related to its possible geographic origin. We discuss the strangeness of the text from a Syriac perspective below in Appendix II, with some features pointing, if anywhere, toward a kind of Aramaic that is western, rather than eastern. As mentioned there, this is surprising, given the stated home of the prince, and given the few toponyms mentioned on the way to Egypt. The attention given to Mesene, in particular, has led some scholars to name southern Mesopotamia as the poet's home.[34] Again, if this is true, it conflicts with the linguistic evidence.

Thanks to *The Pearlsong*'s polyvalent potential, it can be and has been read as Christian, Manichaean, Gnostic, although it is none of these in terms of its explicit language and narrative.[35] *The Pearlsong* resonates particularly with Manichaean texts.[36] Among the named disciples of Mani, one named Thomas makes the list in anti-Manichaean Christian sources: in particular the *Acta Archelaei* (written in Greek but surviving in full only in Latin), a polemical text by Alexander of Lycopolis. In addition, in a line from a fragmentary text in Coptic by Severus of Antioch someone named "Thomas" is specifically called Mani's disciple.[37]

[34] As Beyer says, "The surprising detour for Mesene (where Mani also grew up, 216-240 CE) – which means an n-shaped route – and the particular emphasis on this border area between the shining east and the tarnished west, makes one consider Mesene as the author's homeland." ("Der auffällige Umweg über Mesene (wo auch Mani 216-240 n. Chr. aufwuchs), der zu einer N-förmigen Reiseroute führt, und die besondere Hervorhebung dieses Landes (18.70f.73b) an der Grenze zwischen dem lichten Osten und dem befleckten Westen lassen an Mesene als Heimat des Verfassers denken," Beyer, 238.) And similarly, Tubach: "The poet's surprising interest in southern Babylon is best explained, if we assume either that he grew up there or lived there for a long time. His accurate placement of Charax Spasinou allows his homeland to be narrowed down further." ("Das auffällige Interesse des Dichters am südlichen Babylon erklärt sich am besten, wenn man annimmt, daß er dort entweder aufgewachsen ist oder längere Zeit gelebt hat. Seine richtige Lokalisierung von Charax Spasinou erlaubt es ferner seine Heimat noch näher einzugrenzen," Tubach, "Weg," 101.)

[35] Cf. Poirier, "Codex Manichaicus," 243.

[36] Generally on Manichaeism see Tardieu, *Manichaeism* and Lieu, *Manichaeism*. For more concise introductions, see also Lieu and Gardner, *Manichaean Texts*, 1-45; Klimkeit, *Gnosis* (which, despite the name, just covers Manichaean texts), 1-26; and Boyce, *Reader*, 1-14. Two recent studies of the Kellis Manichaean community in Egypt, see Brand, *Religion*, and Teigen, *Manichaean Church*.

[37] Crum ("Coptic Anecdota," 181n9) equates the "Thomas" of the Manichaean "Thomas Psalms" with Jesus's disciple, Thomas. (Adam devoted a monograph to linking both

Some have even suggested that *The Pearlsong* is a hymn *to* Mani,[38] others that it was Manichaeans who were most likely to have found *The Pearlsong*'s story especially appealing, and that they not only added it to the *Acts of Thomas*, but used it as an inspiration for Mani's story in the Cologne *Mani Codex*.[39] If only for their similarity in language and settings, I cite numerous Manichaean texts (in Parthian, Coptic, and Greek) below in the commentary.[40]

Interpreters have variously characterized *The Pearlsong* as a didactic poem, a narrative poem, a mini-epic, or an epic.[41] It has been called a parable itself, or a *midrash* to the parable of the pearl from the Gospel of Matthew.[42] If it's an allegory, is it about the soul's relationship to the material world? A Christian's time on earth among contrary forces? Tubach calls *The Pearlsong* "a story in verse, framed in the style of a

these Psalms of Thomas and *The Pearlsong* to a pre-Christian Gnostic tradition.) Here's the relevant part of the text (180): "Having abandoned the books of God-inspired scripture, he read what the myth-speakers of his polluted heresy have said, i.e. Mani and Thomas, his disciple, together with what all the heretics have said" (ⲉⲁϥⲕⲱ ⲛⲥⲱϥ ⲛⲛϫⲱⲱⲙⲉ ⲛⲧⲉⲅⲣⲁⲫⲏ ⲛⲛⲓⲃ[ⲉ] ⲛⲧⲉ ⲡⲛⲟⲩⲧⲉ ⲁϥⲱϣ ϩⲛⲛⲉⲛⲧⲁⲛⲣⲉϥϫⲉ ϣⲃⲱ ϫⲟⲟⲩ ⲉⲧⲉⲛⲁⲧⲉϥϩⲁⲓⲣⲉⲥⲓⲥ ⲉⲧⲥⲟⲟϥ ⲛⲉ ⲉⲓϣⲁϫⲉ ⲉⲙⲁⲛⲏ ⲙⲛⲑⲱⲙⲁⲥ ⲡⲉϥⲙⲁⲑⲏⲧⲏⲥ ⲙⲛⲛⲉⲛⲧⲁⲩϫⲟⲟⲩ ⲛϭⲓ ⲛϩⲁⲓⲣⲉⲧⲓⲕⲟⲥ ⲧⲏⲣⲟⲩ). (Given the fragmentary nature of the text, the referent for the "he" isn't absolutely clear.)

38 Bousset's view, for example. See Adam, *Psalmen*, 61-62.

39 Poirier, "Codex Manichaicus," esp. 242-244. For the Mani-Codex (in Greek), see Koenen and Römer, *Mani-Kodex*.

40 For the Greek *Mani Codex*, see Koenen and Römer, *Mani-Kodex*. The Coptic texts are, first, the *Psalmbook* (Allberry, *Psalm-book*, with English translation; re-edited, with the first part, and German translation in Richter, *Psalmengruppe*, *Bema*, and *Herakleides*), the *Kephalaia of the Teacher* (Polotsky and Böhlig, *Kephalaia*; Böhlig, *Kephalaia*; Tardieu, "Diffusion"), the *Homilies* (Polotsky, *Homilien*, with German translation; re-edited with additional fragments and an English translation in Pedersen, *Homilies*), and *Mani's Epistles* (Gardner, *Epistles*, with English translation). Finally, Parthian sources include some lines from hymns (Boyce, *Reader*, 160-162 [text cv]; cf. Poirier, *L'Hymne*, 89n218; Klimkeit, *Gnosis*, 146-148, and more generally, Durkin-Meisterernst and Morano, *Mani's Psalms*) and the "Zarathustra-fragment" (Boyce, *Reader*, 108 [text ay]; cf. Poirier, *L'Hymne*, 98n247, and Klimkeit, *Gnosis*, 47-48).

41 See especially Russell, "Epic," 53-56, who discusses epic-with-dragon-combat as a language-crossing genre of Late Antiquity.

42 Matthew 13:45-46, cf. *Gospel of Thomas* 76.

New Testament parable, except with first-person narration."[43] Calling on parables from the Gospels as the main comparanda, though, is unnecessary, even if the gravitational pull of the Christian context is strong. As mentioned above, Pearson sees *The Pearlsong* as nothing if not a straightforwardly Christian text: "The prince in this hymn can be construed as Adam, whose fall from Paradise and restoration are paradigmatic of the human soul that is awakened to eternal life by the Christian message," even going so far as to baldly declare, "The *Hymn of the Pearl* exemplifies the theology of Syrian Christianity as it was lived in Mesopotamia in the second century."[44] How is this characterization based on, or supported by, the actual text? *The Pearlsong* itself does not "exemplify" *any* theology.

Detailed coverage of the history of interpretation of *The Pearlsong* up to 1980 is available in Poirier's study.[45] It's beyond our scope to retrace that history here, but a common thread running through interpretations of the text is that they change and vary, even in the thought of individual interpreters.[46] Reitzenstein, for example, first saw the poem as especially related to Mandaic texts, but alchemical texts made him change his views.[47] There is nothing amiss with fluid readings and un-

[43] "... eine Geschichte in Versform, die im Stil eines neutestamentlichen Gleichnisses gehalten ist, aber abweichend davon in Ich-Form erzählt wird" ("Zur Interpretation," 242).

[44] Pearson, *Ancient Gnosticism*, 260.

[45] *L'Hymne*, 31-167. Poirier marks three stages in this history: 1871-1904 (from Wright to Preuschen), 1905-1933 (Reitzenstein to just before Bornkamm), and 1933-1980.

[46] Poirier, *L'Hymne*, 113.

[47] Poirier, *L'Hymne*, 100, and Reizenstein, "Heilswanderung und Drachenkampf," esp. 44-48. Cf. Poirier (103-104):

> This shift in thinking, in our opinion, is not the fruit of research carried out directly on the Hymn of the Pearl, but just the reflection of the general evolution of Reitzenstein's thought: he uses the hymn as an example or illustration, more than as proof, of the myth of the *salvator salvatus*, gradually transferring it from Egypt to Iran as he pushes the cradle of the myth eastward.
>
> Ce changement d'opinion n'est pas, à notre avis, le fruit d'une recherche qui aurait porté directement sur l'HP, mais simplement le reflet de l'évolution générale de Reitzenstein: il s'est servi de l'hymne comme exemple ou illustration, beaucoup plus que comme preuve, du mythe du

understandings of a text, but this tendency among *The Pearlsong*'s interpreters points perhaps to something ill-fitting in these approaches and assumptions. *The Pearlsong* doesn't readily match up with text patterns well-known from Late Antiquity, such as homily, hagiography, epic, or philosophical treatise, nor does it fit the hagiographic manuscript context it's found in either, something reflected in its absence from most manuscripts of the *Acts of Thomas*. Further, *The Pearlsong*'s Syriac isn't quite normal Syriac. It's an ambiguous text, and it invites multiple and shifting readings, even more so than a more regularly situated text from this period. As Ioan Culianu says, "It can only be said with certainty that *The Pearlsong* means many things."[48]

1.2 Date and Original Language

The Pearlsong seems firmly set in the time and places of the late Parthian Empire (to 224 CE), and it was written in an Aramaic language, even if not necessarily Syriac. Especially given the idiosyncrasies of language in the text, it may be that the poem was composed in a non-Syriac Aramaic language first and then adapted, more or less, to Syriac before or when it was incorporated into the *Acts of Thomas*. The Syriac form of *The Pearlsong* is in verse, but it's difficult to say what the metrical layout of a pre-Syriac version of the poem might have been. Given that Syriac hardly has a monopoly on Aramaic poetics, a verse-to-verse adaptation is reasonable.[49]

If the text is known in Syriac by the early third century, that makes it an early piece of Syriac literature. This early dating rests especially on its Parthian setting. As Nöldeke said early on, "In any case, the song is very old. The fact that the Parthians are named speaks decisively, I believe, in favor of its being older than the foundation of the Sasanian

Saveur sauvé, le faisant passer progressivement d'Égypte en Iran au fur et à mesure qu'il repoussait ver l'Est le berceau de ce mythe.

[48]"Mit Sicherheit läßt sich nur sagen, daß das L.P. vieldeutig ist," ("Erzählung," 71).

[49]For non-Syriac Aramaic poetry, see Greenfield, "Early Aramaic Poetry;" Tal, "Samaritan Literature;" Lieber, *Jewish Aramaic Poetry*; and Pereira, *Studies in Aramaic Poetry*.

Empire."[50] Similarly Burkitt almost three decades later: "in its imagery the Parthians are still the ruling power of the East ... No Poet would place his ideal heaven in the home of a newly fallen empire."[51]

There is a translation of *The Pearlsong* in one manuscript of the Greek version of the *Acts of Thomas*, and there's also a later Greek paraphrase from a Byzantine sermon. The Greek version of the *Acts of Thomas* is considered to have been translated as a whole from Syriac, including *The Pearlsong*.[52] A major feature that points toward an Aramaic or Syriac origin is that the text is metrical, while in the Greek version it's just simple prose. (The Byzantine retelling is also prose, but of a higher register.) This, together with its "thoroughly Aramaic coloring," led Nöldeke to assume a Syriac original.[53] This remains the predominant view, although, as discussed in Appendix II, the language in its present form is unusual Syriac, and it may have its origins in another kind of Aramaic. Given the setting – the prince's homeland and places named along his route – some kind of eastern late Imperial Aramaic would be reasonable.

1.3 The Parts of the Book

The **Syriac and Greek texts with facing English translations** are the centerpiece of the book. First, you'll find a new edition of the Syriac text of *The Pearlsong*, based, first, on my own reading of the sole known manuscript (details in the Syriac chapter), and then on the scholarly discussions of the text that have arisen since its publication in 1871. I

---

[50] Rev., 677: "Jedenfalls ist das Lied seht alt. Ich glaube, der Name der Parther spricht schon entschieden dafür, dass es älter ist als die Stiftung des Sasanidenreiches."

[51] *Hymn*, 5. See also Adam, *Psalmen*, 58, and Poirier, *L'Hymne*, 38.

[52] See also Poirier, *L'Hymne*, 40–42. For a recent contrary voice, see Lanzillotta, "Syriac Original," who argues for a Greek, not Syriac origin of the *Acts of Thomas*, from the second century even, and that *The Pearlsong* is not an insertion, but original to the hagiography.

[53] "That the song is a Syriac original is clear not only from the thoroughly Aramaic coloring of the language, but also from the fact that it's metrical;" "Dass das Lied ein syrisches Original ist, geht nicht bloss aus der durch und durch aramäischen Farbe der Sprache, sondern auch daraus hervor, dass es *metrisch* ist" (Nöldeke 677).

have made or followed a number of conjectures and emendations, all changes clearly indicated in the apparatus to the Syriac text.

The Syriac text was copied in Estrangela in the manuscript, unvocalized as is typical. Both for more immediate readability and for a clear indication of how I am reading it, I have fully vocalized the text, yielding an edition in West Syriac script with western vocalization for the most part.[54] The critical apparatus indicates the text of the manuscript in unvocalized Estrangela where there's an emendation in the edited text.

I have also included a complete Syriac transcription into Latin script. For one reason or another, the text in this form may be more accessible or clear to some readers, whether they know Syriac script or not.

The texts of the Greek translation and of Niketas's retelling are based on earlier editions, but I have included a small critical apparatus to indicate some alternate readings.

The English translations of both the Syriac and the Greek texts, and indeed throughout the book, are not intended as a crib, reliant on part-of-speech equivalences and consistent lexical correspondences. I have aimed intentionally for language that feels present, current, and lively, and at times colloquial, trying to avoid staid or archaizing language. Nevertheless, I have not intentionally smoothed over places that seem especially awkward or unclear in Syriac or Greek, and this is reflected in the translations.

There are **glossaries** (Syriac-English and Greek-English) for the texts. Thorough, but not comprehensive, these are for students, language-learners, and other readers as an immediate lexical resource for reading any of the three texts included here. The glossaries include transliterations, and others may also find having a general wordlist of the Syriac and Greek texts handy for some other reason. The Syriac glossary also serves as a concordance.

The **commentary** follows the English translation of the Syriac, with discussions of the narrative and content, the Syriac text, interpretive

[54]The vowels are predominantly those of the West Syriac system, but East Syriac vowel-signs are occasionally used, as where they reflect a more specific vowel than the western sign.

cruces, Syriac-to-Greek translation, textual conjectures and emendations, and more. There's no pretense about its non-comprehensiveness, however comprehensive a commentary can be. I have been keen to include and compare textual resonances from various sources, with the hope that these quotations will enrich both the reading of *The Pearlsong* and these other texts, too. As Russell puts it, "The Mandaean gnosis of Mesopotamia, and the Persian writings of Sohravardi, then, speak the same language as that of the Hymn, in the places the Prince traversed on his way down into Egypt ... "[55] Textual connections that have resonated with *The Pearlsong*'s language range from Akkadian poetry[56] to inscriptions from various periods in Aramaic languages,[57] to Manichaean texts, the Nag Hammadi codices, Mandaean liturgical texts,

---

[55]"Epic," 67.

[56]Namely, the *Enūma eliš*, the Babylonian creation story, and the *Epic of Anzu*, where the god Ninurta must confront the fearsome bird Anzu to retrieve the tablet of destinies. The reason these come up is that they're memorable and picturesque literary examples of human-monster fight scenes, and stealing something and bringing it home. I cite both texts from the *electronic Babylonian Library* (eBL) based at Ludwig-Maximilians-Universität München. Available at `https://www.ebl.lmu.de`. See also Talin, *Enūma Eliš*; Kämmerer and Metzler, *Enūma eliš*; and Annus, *Epic of Anzu*. See also Parpola, "Mesopotamian Precursors," here esp., 184, for these and other Mesopotamian resonances with, or "precursors" to, *The Pearlsong*. For the *Enūma eliš* and *The Pearlsong*, see also Wikander "Job," 268, and *Unburning Fame*, 141–142; Wikander follows a common interpretation, calling *The Pearlsong* "gnosticizing," with the dragon = chaos.

[57]Including Old Aramaic (eighth century BCE), as well as much later Palmyrene inscriptions, which are from a time more contemporaneous with *The Pearlsong*. Palmyrene inscriptions are cited from Hillers, Nabatean from the *Corpus inscriptionum semiticarum* (CIS), and the Old Aramaic inscriptions (Bar-Rakib I and II, Sefire I and III) from Donner and Röllig, *Kananäische und Aramäische Inschriften* (KAI). The Aramaic languages have a long documented history, from the ninth century BCE to the present, and connections between these inscriptions and *The Pearlsong* highlight a continuity of vocabulary and phrasing across time and place.

Sohravardi,[58] Old and Middle English poetry,[59] and the occasional modern musical lyric.

Underlying these connections is an open attitude of fun and play across these texts, in opposition to a strict and stodgy hermeneutic narrowly focused on single, fixed interpretations with assumed certainty. This openness to hermeneutical possibility reaches to *The Pearlsong*'s language and phrases as well as its meaning content-wise. Of encounters with non-human entities, Erik Davis mentions "the risky move of trying to take them seriously without taking them literally."[60] We can likewise take *The Pearlsong* seriously as a mirror of human experience and a reminder of human connections, in a multitude of possible ways, without taking it either literally or according to a conventional allegorical reading. While it's true that we may be dealing with "an es-

---

[58]Šehāb ad-Din Sohravardi was a twelfth-century philosopher and mystic, writing in Persian and Arabic. Thanks especially to Henry Corbin, Sohravardi's *Story of Western Exile* (*qiṣṣat al-ġurba al-ġarbīya / qiṣṣéy-e ġorbat ġarbiye*) has been linked to *The Pearlsong* (Corbin, *En Islam Iranien*, vol. 2, 258-334.) Of the two texts, Corbin remarks, "They should both be included in the corpus that may one day reunite all the scattered pieces of the extensive family of gnosis." ("Ils auraient à figurer l'un et l'autre dans le *corpus* qui, un jour peut-être, réunira tous les *disjecta membra* de l'immense famille de la gnose," 266). Sohravardi's story is written in Arabic, but there's also an early Persian translation, together with a commentary (Corbin, *En Islam Iranien*, 270n380). Both texts and an English translation of the Persian are in Thackston, *Suhrawardi*, 106-124. Where it's quoted below, I generally give both the Arabic and the Persian, with my English translation being more directly based on the Arabic.

[59]These are the two well-known Old English poems known as *The Wanderer* and *The Seafarer*, meaningful here for their poignant verbal capture of what it feels to be alone, away from home, and in potential peril. The text of both poems is available in Robinson and Mitchell, *Old English*.

In Middle English, the fourteenth-century poem known as *Perle*, made up of 101 heavily alliterated stanzas in 1212 lines, recounts the narrator's experience coming to terms with the loss of his "pearl," that is, after his infant daughter has died. Simply because both the Syriac poem and the Middle English poem are ostensibly about a pearl in some way, they invite comparison and co-reading, and they turn out both to bear reflections on separation from someone or something treasured, on wandering alone, and even on sleep. For the text see Gollancz, *Pearl*, and Osgood, *Pearl*. (There's a "modern" translation in Gollancz, but it's sometimes more opaque than the Middle English.) See also the essays in Conley, *Pearl*, and Beal's more recent article, "Signifying Power."

[60]*High Weirdness*, 6.

oteric tradition that is arguably so esoteric and potentially multivalent that anything can come to signify anything else,"[61] this possibility of finding meaning in the echo of other texts invites continued reflection on a long human conversation in different languages and places.

Four **appendices** include additional material of varied type. The focus of Appendix I is a discussion of Syriac poetic meter generally and in terms of *The Pearlsong*. Appendix II covers some linguistic features of the Syriac text that make it unique, namely: the particle *yåṯ-*, the use of the absolute state, the high frequency of bound constructions, and the vocabulary (especially loanwords).

Appendix III contains English translations of three excerpts from the Syriac *Acts of Thomas*. The point here is to supply a broader context for the hagiographic setting *The Pearlsong* is found in, as well as simply to give a longer sample of the *Acts of Thomas* irrespective of *The Pearlsong*. The first text is the start of the saint's life, including another poetic text, the wedding-song that Thomas sings. Next I give Thomas's interaction with a giant, talking snake; it's unrelated directly to the snake in *The Pearlsong*, but an immediate reminder that daunting confrontations with monstrous snakes, while not everyday occurrences, are just part of being a hero or saint. Third, there is a translation of part ten of the *Acts of Thomas*, which is where *The Pearlsong* is recited. So this excerpt provides the entire immediate hagiographic context in which *The Pearlsong* is transmitted.

Finally, in addition to those mentioned in the commentary, in Appendix IV I give a few excerpts from various sources that mention pearls.

[61] Hillier, Rev. Mundik, 99.

2 *The Pearlsong* in Syriac

2.1 Introduction

2.1.1 The manuscript

The Syriac text of *The Pearlsong* is known from a single manuscript: British Library, Additional manuscript (= Add.) 14645, ff. 30v-32r.[1] As already mentioned, the manuscript context of *The Pearlsong* is hagiographic. Not only is it embedded in a saint's life, but that hagiographic text itself inaugurates a series of forty-one stories about monks and martyrs. In the manuscript, within the *Acts of Thomas*, *The Pearlsong* itself is marked off by a rubricated title:

ܡܕܪܫܐ ܕܝܗܘܕܐ ܬܐܘܡܐ ܫܠܝܚܐ ܕܒܐܬܪܐ
ܕܗܢܕܘܝܐ

THE POEM OF THE APOSTLE JUDAS THOMAS WHEN HE WAS IN INDIA

The poem's end is likewise signaled by a rubricated finish:

ܫܠܡ ܡܕܪܫܐ ܕܝܗܘܕܐ ܬܐܘܡܐ ܫܠܝܚܐ ܕܐܡܪܗ ܒܝܬ
ܐܣܝܪܐ ܀

THE END OF THE POEM OF THE APOSTLE JUDAS THOMAS, WHICH HE RECITED IN PRISON

Other than these markers for the beginning and end of *The Pearlsong*, nothing distinguishes it paleographically or codicologically: it's just like

[1] See Wright, *Catalogue*, vol. 3, 1111-1116. Nöldeke signals how especially meaningful another manuscript of this text would be: "There is no other text you feel the absence of a second manuscript with like this one;" "Bei keinem Stück vermisst man so schmerzlich eine zweite Handschrift wie bei diesem" (Nöldeke, Rev., 678).

the rest of the *Acts of Thomas*, which is just like like the other saints' lives in the codex.

The text is copied in two long columns per page, of about 34–38 lines each. The scribe's handwriting is a bit unusual and does not fit well into the conventional neat division of Syriac scripts into Estrangela, Serto, and East Syriac.[2] This manuscript's scribe uses an almost even mixture of Estrangela and West Syriac script forms, rather than distinctly one of these two. The scribe's versions of <ʔ, d, h, w, r, t> are of the Serto form, while the letters <b, g, ṭ, k, l, ʕ, ṣ, q, š> are of the Estrangela form. Final <m> is Estrangela, while in other positions it's Serto. (Other letters are relatively the same in each script.) It's not unusual to see some Estrangela forms in an otherwise Serto manuscript, or vice versa, but the easy mixture of so many forms, as we see in this manuscript, is noteworthy. In addition to this Estrangela-Serto medley, the ductus itself is peculiar, meriting descriptors such as sharp and spindly. Some letters at word-end have a slight flourish (<l, b, y, š>), and words and letter-shapes tend to stretch horizontally across the line.

As for the date, as Wright points out, there is a note on p. 430 of the manuscript with the Seleucid era date 1247 (corresponding to 935/6 CE). This date is given with reference to a specific text – not the *Acts of Thomas*, nor less the entire manuscript – namely, the story of a monk from Scetis, John the "lesser." This story was *translated* (ܐܬܦܫܩܬ *ʔeṯpaššqaṯ*) in that year.[3] This is not the date of the manuscript's copying, just the date of the translation of this individual text. Unfortunately, Wright doesn't translate the note itself and misleadingly says, "there is a note stating that the manuscript was written in the convent of the Syrians in the desert of Scete ...." Again, this note just gives the date and place of the translation of the last text in the manuscript, not "the manuscript." This note echoes the details of the final text's beginning rubric on 396v. Here are both together:

> Our holy father, Mar Zakarya, bishop of the city of Sakha, carefully rendered and translated it. After some educated and virtuous people had congregated to him and asked

[2] Cf. Penn, Crouser, and Philip Abbott, "Serto."

[3] Wright, *Catalogue*, vol. 3, 1116.

> him for the favor, he consented and dictated it. This he did on the day they were gathered together in memory of our holy father John, twenty people, Egyptians and Syrians, on the 17th of the month Tešri I.
>
> [end] ... it was translated from Arabic into Syriac. ... It was translated in the Monastery of the Syrians in the Scetis desert in the year 1247 of Alexander, son of Philip the Macedonian.[4]

This date corresponds to approximately 17 October, 935. So, based on this note, the manuscript cannot be earlier than 935, but it might be from some subsequent year. Based on the scribe's Syriac handwriting, it may be more likely that the manuscript itself was copied in the next century, the eleventh.

Finally, and incidentally, the scribe thought it important enough to leave a note mentioning that a saint Ḥananya is also sometimes called Ḥannina:[5] "In another copy we found it as *Ḥannina*, instead of *Ḥananya*: say whichever one you like." Does the fact that the scribe made this onomastic observation, but said nothing at all about *The Pearlsong*, mean that *The Pearlsong* wasn't especially unusual or unique to them? It's an argument from silence, but it is possible that, to this scribe, at least, *The Pearlsong* wasn't the textual anomaly it's now known as, however few copies of it there are in Syriac or Greek.

---

[4] F. 396v:
ܐܬܛܦܝܣ ܕܝܢ ܘܦܩܕܗ ܘܬܪܓܡܗ ܐܝܟ ܡܢܝܢܐ ܡܢ ܕܢܚܐ ܐܦܝܣܩܘܦܘܬܐ
ܕܗܕܐ ܡܕܝܢܬܐ. ܐܡܪܗ ܕܝܢ ܒܗ ܐܬܟܢܫܘ ܟܐܕܘܗܝ ܐܢܫܐ ܠܥܣܪܝܢ ܘܡܨܪܝܐ.
ܘܬܒܥܘ ܡܢܗ ܕܢܟܬܒ ܘܢܗܒ. ܗܘ ܕܝܢ ܐܫܬܡܥ ܠܗܘܢ. ܘܐܡܪܗ ܒܝܘܡܐ ܕܒܗ
ܡܬܟܢܫܝܢ ܠܕܘܟܪܢܗ ܕܐܒܐ ܩܕܝܫܐ ܝܘܚܢܢ. ܡܬܟܢܫܝܢ ܕܝܢ ܥܣܪܝܢ ܐܢܫ
ܡܨܪܝܐ ܘܣܘܪ̈ܝܐ. ܘܕܬܫܪܝܢ ܩܕܡ ܒܫܒܥܬܥܣܪ ܒܗ [430v] ... ... ܐܬܦܫܩܬ ܡܢ
ܥܪܒܝܐ ܠܫܢܐ ܠܣܘܪܝܝܐ ... ܐܬܦܫܩܬ ܕܝܢ ܒܕܝܪܐ ܕܣܘܪܝܝܐ ܕܒܡܕܒܪܐ ܕܐܣܩܝܛܝܣ
ܒܫܢܬ ܐܠܦ ܘܡܐܬܝܢ ܘܐܪܒܥܝܢ ܘܫܒܥ ܕܐܠܟܣܢܕܪܘܣ ܒܪ ܦܝܠܝܦܘܣ ܡܩܕܘܢܝܐ

[5] F. 178r; Wright, *Catalogue*, vol. 3, 1113b: ܒܢܘܣܚܐ ܐܚܪܢܐ ܚܠܦ ܚܢܢܝܐ ܚܢܝܢܐ
ܐܫܟܚܢ. ܘܗܘ̇ ܕܨܒܐ ܠܟ ܗ̇ܘ ܐܡܪ

2.1.2 *The Pearlsong* within the *Acts of Thomas*

The *Acts of Thomas*, which probably originates in Syriac in the third century CE, is well attested, known in at least six Syriac manuscripts and seventy-five Greek manuscripts. Wright's edition of the *Acts of Thomas* is based solely on BL Add. 14645, while Bedjan's includes (some) variants from another manuscript, Sachau no. 222 (= Berlin syr. 75), a late copy prepared for Eduard Sachau on a trip to "Syria and Mesopotamia" in 1881.[6] As can be seen from Bedjan's noted variants, and even from the translations included below in Appendix III, these two manuscripts, the BL and Berlin, clearly have the same text, broadly considered, but there are many places where the language differs slightly, and some places where the BL text is much longer and includes more, such as *The Pearlsong*.

In the context of the *Acts of Thomas*, the titular character recites the poem in prison. Just before this episode, the text reads:

> While he was praying, all those imprisoned were watching him do so and they asking him to pray for them, too. When he had prayed and sat down, he began to recite this poem.

The Pearlsong follows immediately in the BL MS, but the much younger Berlin MS lacks *The Pearlsong*, and instead of referring to a *madrāšā* here, it has *tešbohtā*, "praise-song." At this point this manuscript indeed has a short praise-song in place of *The Pearlsong*. Folio 37r is where *The Pearlsong* would be in the Berlin manuscript. It has *tešbohtā*, rather than *madrāšā*, and moves immediately – no rubric, division, or marginal note – into the *tešbohtā*. There's no hint of a missing text. The BL MS, which has *The Pearlsong*, also has the Berlin copy's praise-song, but it's actually much longer in this older manuscript. An English translation of this part of the *Acts of Thomas*, with the praise-song and more, is included in Appendix III below.

[6]Bedjan, AMSS III: vi. Sachau, *Verzeichnis*, vol. 1, 289-291. *The Acts of Thomas* occupies ff. 2r-54r. For his travel at this time, see Sachau, *Reise*.

2.1.3 Principles of the edition

The Syriac text given here is a new edition based on the single known manuscript described above. The Syriac text edition of *The Pearlsong* is printed in West Syriac script and is fully vocalized.[7] The vowels, to be clear, are not from the manuscript: they are my additions based on Syriac grammar and lexicon, both for grammatical clarity as to my interpretations and for the practical benefit of Syriac-language readers.[8] For the same reasons, a complete transcription follows the text edition. So as not to overly clutter the Syriac text, *rukkåḵå* and *quššåyå* – marking the soft : hard opposition in the pronunciation of <bgdkpt> consonants – are not comprehensively marked, but only sometimes. In the transcription, however, these differences are clearly visible in every case. Like the text edition, the glossary's Syriac is given in both vocalized West Syriac script and in transcription.

Where I have adopted an emendation, the reading of the manuscript is given (in unvocalized Estrangela) in the critical apparatus, along with the name of the critic who suggested the change.[9] Many of the emendations I have followed more easily fit the poem's six-syllable meter (for which see Appendix I). Others are discussed in the commentary.

---

[7]The vowels are given in a mixed, but predominantly West Syriac system.

[8]Syriac script, like Arabic script and Hebrew script, includes, but does not require extra vowel marks. There are exceptions, especially among East Syriac manuscripts, but Syriac manuscripts are typically only sparsely vocalized, if at all, except, sometimes, for copies of the biblical books.

[9]See especially the editions and studies of Wright, *Apocryphal Acts*, 294-299; Hoffman, "Zwei Hymnen;" and Beyer, "Perlenlied." Cf. Poirier, *L'Hymne*, 329-342, for another Syriac edition and a fuller apparatus.

2.2 Syriac Text and English Translation

ܟܕ ܐܢܐ ܫܒܪ ܝܠܘܕ ܘܥܡܪ ܒܡܠܟܘܬܐ ܕܒܝܬ ܐܒܝ.
ܘܒܥܘܬܪܐ ܘܒܦܘܢܩܐ. ܕܡܪ̈ܒܝܢܝ ܡܢܝܚ ܗܘܝܬ.
ܡܢ ܡܕܢܚܐ ܒܝܬܢ. ܙܘܕܘ ܐܒܗ̈ܝ ܫܕܪܘܢܝ.
ܘܡܢ ܥܘܬܪܐ ܕܒܝܬ ܓܙܢ. ܐܒܪ ܙܘܕܘ ܠܝ ܡܘܒܠܐ.
ܪܒܐ ܗܘܐ ܘܩܠܝܠܐ. ܕܐܢܐ ܠܚܘܕܝ ܐܫܩܠܝܘܗܝ.
ܕܗܒܐ ܗܘ ܕܒܝܬ ܓܝܠܢ̈ܝܐ. ܘܣܐܡܐ ܕܓܙܟ ܪܒܐ.
ܘܟܪ̈ܟܕܢܝ ܗܢܕܘ. ܘܦܛܕܐܢܐ ܕܡܢ ܒܝܬ ܩܘܫܢ.
ܘܚܙܩܘܢܝ ܒܐܕܡܘܣ. ܕܒܦܪܙܠܐ ܗܘ ܚܫܝܠ.
ܘܐܫܠܚܘܢܝ ܠܙܗܝܬܐ. ܕܒܚܘܒܗܘܢ ܥܒܕܘܗ ܠܝ.
ܘܠܬܘܒܢܝ ܕܙܚܘܪܝܬܐ ܕܥܠ ܩܘܡܬܝ ܡܡܫܚ ܗܘܐ.
ܘܥܒܕܘ ܥܡܝ ܫܘܘܕܝܐ. ܘܟܬܒܘܗܝ ܒܠܒܝ ܕܠܐ ܐܬܛܥܝܐ
ܕܐܢ ܬܚܘܬ ܠܡܨܪܝܢ: ܘܬܝܬܝܗ ܠܡܪܓܢܝܬܐ:
ܗܝ ܕܐܝܬܝܗ ܒܓܘ ܝܡܐ: ܒܚܕܪܘܗܝ ܕܚܘܝܐ ܫܪܘܩܐ.
ܬܠܒܫܝܗ ܠܙܗܝܬܟ. ܘܠܬܘܒܢܟ ܕܥܠܝܗ ܡܢܝܚ.
30vb ܘܥܡ ܐܚܘܟ ܬܪܝܢܢ. ܝܪܬܐ ܒܡܠܟܘܬܢ ܬܗܘܐ.
ܢܦܩܬ ܡܕܢܚܐ ܢܚܬܬ. ܟܕ ܥܡܝ ܬܪܝܢ ܦܪ̈ܘܘܢܝܢ.

---

6 ܕܒܝܬ ܓܝܠܢ̈ܝܐ] conj : MS ܕܒܝܬ ܓܠܝܐ
8 ܘܚܙܩܘܢܝ] corr Wright Hoffmann Bevan : MS ܘܚܙܩܘܢ
9 ܠܙܗܝܬܐ] corr Bevan Hoffmann : MS ܠܙܘܗܝܬܐ
12 ܠܡܪܓܢܝܬܐ] del Hoffmann : MS ܠܡܪܓܢܝܬܐ ܚܕܐ
16 ܢܦܩܬ] ܢܦܩܬ

2.2 Syriac Text and English Translation

When I was just a little child, living in my kingdom in my father's palace
And enjoying the riches and luxuries of my caretakers,
My parents outfitted me and sent me off from the East, our country.
They had loaded my luggage from our treasury's riches.
It was a lot, but light enough that I could carry it on my own –
The gold of Elam, the silver of great Ganzak,
The chalcedonies of India, and brocade from Kushan –
And they packed iron-grinding diamonds for my trip,
But they stripped me of the shining garment they had lovingly made me,
And my scarlet cloak, measured and woven to my size.
They made a pact with me and inscribed it in my heart, lest it be forgotten:
"If you go down into Egypt and you bring down the pearl,
The one that's in the sea near the breathy snake,
Then you should put on your shining garment and the cloak resting on it,
And with your brother, our second, become my heir in our kingdom."
I left the East and went down, with two guardians accompanying me,

ܘܐܘܪܚܐ ܕܚܝܠܐ ܘܥܛܠܐ. ܘܐܢܐ ܥܒܪ ܐܢܐ ܠܡܪܕܝܗ.
ܥܒܪܬ ܠܬܚܘܡܝ ܡܝܫܢ ܪܘܟܐ ܕܬܓܪ̈ܐ ܡܕܢܚܐ.
ܘܡܛܝܬ ܠܐܪܥ ܒܒܠ. ܘܥܠܬ ܠܫܘܪܝܗ ܕܣܪܒܘܓ.
ܢܚܬܬ ܠܝ ܠܡܨܪܝܢ. ܘܫܒܩܘܢܝ ܡܢܝ ܦܪܫܘ.
ܐܙܠܬ ܠܘܬ ܚܘܝܐ ܚܕܪܘܗܝ ܘܐܫܪܝܬ ܫܪܝܬ.
ܥܕ ܢܢܘܡ ܘܢܕܡܟ. ܘܡܢܗ ܠܡܪܓܢܝܬܝ ܐܫܩܘܠܝܗ.
ܘܝܚܝܕ ܗܘܝܬ ܘܡܫܬܢܐ ܗܘܝܬ. ܠܒܢ̈ܝ ܐܬܪܝ ܢܘܟܪܝ ܗܘܝܬ.
ܬܡܢ ܚܙܝܬ ܒܪ ܚܐܪ̈ܐ: ܡܢ ܡܕܢܚ̈ܝܐ ܐܝܟ ܕܝܠܝ.
ܛܠܝܐ ܫܦܝܪܐ ܚܣܝܕܐ.
ܒܪ ܡܫܘܚܢܝ. ܘܠܝ ܐܬܐ ܢܩܦ.
ܘܥܒܕܬܗ ܒܪ ܚܒܪܝ. ܚܒܪܐ ܕܐܫܬܘܬܦܬ ܠܗ ܬܘܓܪܬܝ.
ܐܙܗܪܬܗ ܡܢ ܡܨܪ̈ܝܐ. ܘܡܢ ܢܩܦܘܬܗܘܢ ܕܛܢܦ̈ܐ.
ܘܐܦ ܒܐܣܟܡܗܘܢ ܐܬܟܣܝܬ. ܕܠܐ ܢܚܫܕܘܢܝ ܕܡܢ ܠܒܪ ܐܬܝܬ.
ܕܐܫܩܠܝܗ ܠܡܪܓܢܝܬܐ. ܘܢܥܝܪܘܢܝ ܚܘܝܐ ܥܠܝ.
ܘܒܐܢܫܐ ܡܢ ܬܘܠܠܬܐ. ܘܝܕܥܘ ܠܝ ܕܠܐ ܗܘܝܬ ܒܪ ܐܬܪܗܘܢ.
ܘܚܠܛܘ ܠܝ ܒܢܟܠܝܗܘܢ. ܐܦ ܐܛܥܡܘܢܝ ܡܐܟܘܠܬܗܘܢ.
ܘܛܥܝܬ ܕܒܪ ܡܠܟܐ ܐܢܐ. ܘܦܠܚܬ ܠܡܠܟܐ ܕܝܠܗܘܢ.
31ra ܛܥܝܬܗ ܠܡܪܓܢܝܬܐ ܕܥܠܝܗ ܐܒܗ̈ܝ ܫܕܪܘܢܝ.
ܘܒܝܘܩܪܐ ܕܬܘܪ̈ܣܝܗܘܢ ܢܚܬܬ ܒܫܢܬܐ ܥܡܝܩܬܐ.

---

26 ܒܪ ܡܫܘܚܢܝ] MS : conj (cf. Beyer) ܒܪ ܡܫܘܚܐ
26 ܢܩܦ] MS : corr Hoffmann ܘܢܩܦ
29 ܢܚܫܕܘܢܝ] MS : corr Beyer ܢܚܫܕܘܢܢܝ
33 ܘܛܥܝܬ] MS : corr Hoffmann ܛܥܝܬ
34 ܛܥܝܬܗ] MS : corr Hoffmann ܘܛܥܝܬܗ
35 ܕܬܘܪ̈ܣܝܗܘܢ] MS : corr Hoffmann (cf. Nöldeke) ܕܛܘܪܣܝܗܘܢ

Since the road was scary and hard, and I was too young to travel it.
I crossed the borders of Mesene, the meeting-spot for eastern traders.
I made it to Babylon and entered Sarbug's walls.
I went down into Egypt and my attendants left me.
I headed for the snake, and I camped around its lair,
Waiting until it dozed and slept, and I could take my pearl from it.
Because I was one person, left alone, I was a stranger to my fellow lodgers.
I saw someone there from my people, freeborn from the East:
A lovely, charming boy
My age had come and joined me.
I made him my expedition partner and brought him in as associate.
I warned him about the Egyptians and from joining these polluted people.
I dressed like them so they wouldn't suspect that I'd come from abroad
To take the pearl, and then rouse the snake against me.
But some way or other they figured out I wasn't one of them.
They tricked me into joining them and they accustomed me to their fare.
I forgot I was a son of kings, and I served their king.
I forgot the pearl my parents had sent me for,
And weighed down with their food I fell into a deep sleep.

ܘܗܠܝܢ ܟܠܗܝܢ ܕܓܕܫܢ. ܐܒ̈ܗܝ ܪܓܫܘ ܘܚܫܘ ܥܠܝ.
ܘܐܬܟܪܙ ܒܡܠܟܘܬܢ. ܕܟܠܢܫ ܠܬܪܥܢ ܢܬܗܠܟ.
ܡܠܟ̈ܐ ܘܪ̈ܫܐ ܦܪܬܘ. ܘܟܠ ܪܘܪ̈ܒܢܝ ܡܕܢܚܐ.
ܘܬܪܥܘ ܥܠܝ ܐܬܪܥܝܬܐ. ܕܐܢܐ ܒܡܨܪܝܢ ܠܐ ܐܫܬܒܩ.
ܘܟܬܒܘ ܠܝ ܐܓܪܬܐ. ܘܟܠ ܪܒ ܚܬܡܗ ܠܗ ܐܪܡܝ.
ܡܢ ܐܒܘܟ ܡܠܟ ܡܠܟ̈ܐ. ܘܐܡܟ ܐܚܝܕܬ ܡܕܢܚܐ.
ܘܡܢ ܐܚܘܟ ܬܪܝܢܢ. ܠܟ ܒܪܢ ܕܒܡܨܪܝܢ ܫܠܡ.
ܩܘܡ ܘܣܩ ܡܢ ܫܢܬܟ. ܘܫܡܥ ܡ̈ܠܝ ܐܓܪܬܢ.
ܐܬܕܟܪ ܕܒܪ ܡܠܟ̈ܐ ܐܢܬ. ܚܙܝ ܥܒܕܘܬܐ ܠܡܢ ܦܠܚܬ.
ܥܗܕܝܗ ܠܡܪܓܢܝܬܐ. ܕܥܠܝܗ ܠܡܨܪܝܢ ܐܫܬܕܪܬ.
ܐܬܕܟܪܝܗ ܠܬܘܠܒܟ. ܘܠܐܣܛܠܟ ܝܩܝܪܬܐ ܥܗܕ.
ܕܬܠܒܫ ܘܬܬܥܛܦ. ܘܒܣܦܪ ܓܢܒܪ̈ܐ ܫܡܟ ܢܬܩܪܐ.
31rb ܘܥܡ ܐܚܘܟ ܦܩܝܕܢܢ. ܥܡܗ ܒܡܠܟܘܬܢ ܬܗܘܐ.
ܘܐܓܪܬܝ ܐܓܪܬܐ ܗ̱ܝ. ܕܡܠܟܐ ܒܝܡܝܢܗ ܚܬܡܗ.
ܡܢ ܒ̈ܢܝܐ ܒܝ̈ܫܐ ܒܒܠܝ̈ܐ. ܘܕ̈ܝܘܐ ܡܪ̈ܝܕܐ ܕܠܒܘܪܝܢܬܘܣ.
ܦܪܚܬ ܒܕܡܘܬ ܢܫܪܐ. ܡܠܟܐ ܕܟܠܗ ܦܪܚܬܐ.
ܦܪܚܬ ܘܢܚܬܬ ܠܘܬܝ. ܘܟܠܗ ܗܘܬ ܠܗ ܡܠܬܐ.
ܒܩܠܗ ܘܒܩܠ ܪܓܫܗ. ܐܬܥܝܪܬ ܘܩܡܬ ܡܢ ܫܢܬܝ.

---

40 ܪܒ] conj Nöldeke : ܪܘܪܒܢܐ MS
48 ܦܩܝܕܢܢ] corr : ܦܩܝܕܢܢ MS
50 ܡܪ̈ܝܕܐ] corr Hoffmann : ܡܪ̈ܕܝܐ MS

My parents sensed everything happening to me and they hurt for me.
It was announced in our kingdom that everyone should come to our court:
Kings and leaders of Parthia and all the magnates of the East.
They devised me a plot, so I wouldn't be left in Egypt.
They wrote me a letter, and each of the leaders signed it with their name.
"From your father, the king of kings, and your mother, ruler of the East,
And from your brother, our second: greetings to you in Egypt, son!
Wake up! Get up from your sleep, and listen to the words of our letter!
Remember that you're a son of kings: look whom you've served!
Remember the pearl you were sent to Egypt for!
Recall your shining clothes, and remember your luxurious cloak,
To wear them, decked out, since you are named in *The Book of Heroes*,
So that with your brother, you'll be our successor in our kingdom."
And my letter was a letter that the king had sealed with his right hand,
Because of the perverse Babylonians and the riotous devils of Sarbug.
It flew like an eagle, king of all the birds:
It flew and landed by me, and the whole thing became speech.
Waking at its voice and the noise of its movement, I rose from my sleep.

ܫܩܠܬܗ ܘܢܫܩܬܗ. ܘܩܪܝܬ ܐܢܐ ܟܬܒܗ ܩܪܝܬ.

ܘܥܠ ܗܘ ܕܒܠܒܝ ܪܫܝܡ. ܩܠܝܗ ܕܐܓܪܬܝ ܐܬܟܬܒ.

ܥܗܕܬ ܕܒܪ ܡܠܟܐ ܐܢܐ. ܘܚܐܪܘܬܝ ܒܥܝܐ ܓܢܣܗ.

ܥܗܕܬ ܠܡܪܓܢܝܬܐ. ܕܥܠܝܗ ܠܡܨܪܝܢ ܐܫܬܕܪܬ.

ܘܫܪܝܬ ܡܡܓܕܦ ܐܢܐ ܠܗ ܒܚܫܘܡܐ ܕܚܝܠܐ ܘܗܡܣܐ.

ܐܢܝܡܬܗ ܘܐܕܡܟܬܗ. ܕܫܡ ܐܒܝ ܥܠܘܗܝ ܐܬܕܟܪܬ.

ܘܫܡܗ ܕܬܪܝܢܢ. ܘܕܐܡܝ ܡܠܟܬ ܡܕܢܚܐ.

ܘܚܛܦܬܗ ܠܡܪܓܢܝܬܐ. ܘܗܦܟܬ ܕܐܬܐ ܠܒܝܬ ܐܒܝ.

ܘܠܒܘܫܗܘܢ ܨܐܐ ܘܛܢܦܐ. ܫܠܚܬ ܘܫܒܩܬܗ ܒܐܪܥܗܘܢ.

31va ܬܪܨܬܗ ܠܡܪܕܝܬܝ ܕܐܬܐ. ܠܢܘܗܪܐ ܕܒܝܬܝ ܡܕܢܚܐ.

ܘܠܐܓܪܬܝ ܡܥܝܪܢܝܬܝ ܡܨܝܬ ܒܐܘܪܚܐ ܐܫܟܚܬ.

ܘܐܝܟ ܕܒܩܠܗ ܐܥܝܪܬܢܝ. ܐܦ ܒܢܘܗܪܗ ܗܘ ܡܕܒܪܐ.

ܕܫܪܝܐ ܒܫܘܫܝܦܐ. ܡܢ ܩܕܡ ܒܢܘܗܪܗ ܡܢܗܪܐ.

ܘܒܩܠܗ ܗܘܢܘܬܗ. ܬܘܒ ܕܪܗܛܬܝ ܡܬܚܦܛܐ.

ܘܒܚܘܒܗ ܢܓܕܐ ܠܝ.

ܢܦܩܬ ܥܒܪܬܗ ܠܣܪܒܘܓ. ܫܒܩܬ ܠܒܒܠ ܠܣܡܠܝ.

ܘܡܛܝܬ ܠܡܝܫܢ ܪܒܬܐ. ܠܠܡܐܢܗܘܢ ܕܬܓܪܐ.

ܕܝܬܒܐ ܥܠ ܣܦܪ ܝܡܐ.

ܘܠܒܘܫܝ ܕܫܒܩܬ ܗܘܝܬ. ܘܠܛܘܒܣܝ ܕܥܡܗ ܡܟܪܟܐ ܗܘܐ.

---

59 ܥܠܘܗܝ] ܐܢܐ ܥܠܘܗܝ transp MS : del Hoffmann (< ܥܠܘܗܝ ܐܢܐ)

63 ܬܪܨܬܗ] ܘܬܪܨܬܗ MS : corr Hoffmann

65 ܐܥܝܪܬܢܝ] ܐܥܝܪܬܢ MS : corr Wright

67 ܘܒܩܠܗ ܗܘܢܘܬܗ] ܘܒܩܠܗ ܘܒܡܕܒܪܢܘܬܗ MS : corr Hoffmann

68 ܢܓܕܐ] ܢܓܕ MS : corr Wright

72 ܘܠܒܘܫܝ] ܘܠܡܐܢܝ MS : corr Wright (ܘܠܡܐܢܘܬܝ marg)

72 ܡܟܪܟܐ ܗܘܐ] ܡܟܪܟܐ MS : add Beyer

I took it, kissed it, and started to read the letter itself.
The words of my letter had been written on what was inscribed in my heart.
I remembered I was a son of kings, with my freedom checking on its nature.
I remembered the pearl I'd been sent to Egypt for,
And I began saying a spell to the fearsome, breathy snake.
I put it to sleep and made it slumber by recalling my father's name over it,
And the name of our second, and of my mother, queen of the East.
I snatched the pearl and turned to go back to my father's palace.
I took off the Egyptians' dirty, unclean clothes, left them in their country.
I directed my journey toward the light of our homeland, the East.
I found my letter, my awakener, in front of me on the road:
Just as it had awakened me with its voice, it was leading me with its light,
Shining to look like regal silk in front of me,
Encouraging me in my trepidation with its guiding voice,
And drawing me with its love.
I went out and crossed Sarbug, I left Babylon to my left,
And I eventually reached Mesene, the big city and haven of traders,
Situated across the sea.
My shining garment that I'd taken off, and my cloak it was covered with,

ܡܢ ܪܡܬܐ ܘܪܩܡ ܠܬܡܢ ܐܒܗ̈ܝ ܫܕܪܘܗ.
ܒܐܝܕܐ ܕܓܙܒܪ̈ܝܗܘܢ. ܕܒܫܪܪܗܘܢ ܠܗܘܢ ܡܗܝܡܢܝܢ.
ܘܠܐ ܥܗܕ ܗܘܝܬ ܠܐܝܩܪܗ ܕܒܛܠܝܘܬܝ ܫܒܩܬܗ ܒܒܝܬ ܐܒܝ
ܡܢ ܫܠܝ ܟܕ ܐܣܬܟܠܬܗ. ܠܡܚܙܝܬܝ ܠܒܘܫܐ ܕܡܐ ܠܝ.
ܟܠܗ ܒܟܘܠܝ ܚܙܝܬ. ܘܐܦ ܠܟܘܠܝ ܒܗ ܐܣܬܟܠܬ.
31vb ܕܗܘܝܢ ܬܪܝܢ ܒܦܘܪܫܢܐ. ܘܚܕ ܗܘܝܢ ܚܕܐ ܕܡܘܬ.
ܘܐܦ ܠܗܘܢ ܠܓܙܒܪ̈ܐ. ܕܠܝ ܐܝܬܝܘܗ ܗܟܢ ܚܙܝܬ.
ܕܬܪܝܢ ܐܢܘܢ ܚܕܐ ܕܡܘܬ. ܕܚܕ ܢܝܫ ܡܠܟܐ ܪܫܝܡ ܒܗܘܢ.
ܗܘ ܕܐܝܬܘܗܝ ܕܝܠܝ ܠܝ. ܠܓܘܡܠܟܝ ܘܡܠܘܐ ܒܐܝܕܝܗܘܢ.
ܟܬܘܢܬܝ ܡܪܟܒܬܐ. ܘܒܨܒܥ̈ܐ ܦܐܝ̈ܐ ܡܪܟܒܐ.
ܒܕܗܒܐ ܘܒܒܪ̈ܘܠܐ. ܘܟܪܟ̈ܕܢܐ ܘܦܠܐܬܐ.
ܘܣܪܕ̈ܘܢܐ ܦܪܝܫܝ ܓܘܢܐ. ܐܦ ܗܝ ܒܪܘܡܗ ܡܬܩܢܐ.
ܘܒܐܒܢ̈ܐ ܕܐܕܡܘܣ. ܟܘܠܗ ܥܪ̈ܣܬܗ ܡܣܡܟܢ.
ܘܨܠܡܗ ܕܡܠܟ ܡܠܟ̈ܐ. ܟܠܗ ܒܟܠܗ ܡܨܝܪ ܘܪܫܝܡ
ܘܐܦ ܟܐܦܐ ܕܫܦܝܠܐ. ܐܝܟ ܒܪܘܡܗ ܡܨܠܬܐ.
ܘܚܙܝܬ ܐܝܟ ܕܒܟܠܗ. ܙܘ̈ܥܐ ܕܝܕܥܬܐ ܪܦܦܝܢ.

---

75 ܘܠܐ] ܘܕܠܐ MS : corr Beyer
76 ܫܠܝ] ܥܠܝ MS : corr Hoffmann
76 ܠܒܘܫܐ] ܠܒܘܫܐ MS : corr Beyer
77 ܒܟܘܠܝ] ܒܟܘܠ MS : corr Bevan Hoffmann (cf. Nöldeke)
77 ܘܐܦ] ܘܐܦ ܐܢܐ MS : del Beyer
77 ܠܟܘܠܝ] ܠܟܘܠ MS : corr Bevan Hoffmann (cf. Nöldeke)
80 ܕܡܘܬ] ܕܡܘܬ ܐܢܘܢ MS : del Beyer
81 ܗܘ ܕܐܝܬܘܗܝ] ܕܐܝܬܘܗܝ MS : add Beyer
81 ܒܐܝܕܝܗܘܢ] ܒܐܝܕܝܗܘܢ MS : corr
82 ܟܬܘܢܬܝ] ܠܬܘܬܝ MS ܘ s.s. (ܠܬܘܬܝ)

These my parents sent to me from high Warkan
By their treasurers, entrusted with it for their reliability.
I didn't remember its quality: as a child I'd left it in my father's palace.
Suddenly, when I'd faced it, the garment seemed like my mirror:
I saw all of it in all of me, and in it likewise I faced all of me,
Because we're distinctly two, but still one, with one form.
I also saw that the treasurers who had brought it to me like this
Were both one form, with the one insignia of the king marked on them.
The king's hands returned my pledge and wealth to me through them:
My shining, decorated clothes, decorated with luxurious colors,
With gold, beryl, chalcedony, prismatic gems,
And sardonyx – a garment in a special color and decked out in its grandeur,
All of its seams studded with diamonds.
The entire image of the king of kings was embossed and depicted
On it entirely, along with sapphires and varied hues.
I saw, too, that the impulses of knowledge were writhing around in all of it.

ܘܐܝܟ ܕܒܡܡܠܠܗ. ܐܝܟ ܚܝܠܗ ܘܩܠ ܬܢܒܪܐ.
ܩܠ ܢܬܦܠܬܗ ܫܡܥܬ. ܘܩܡ ܡܚܝܠܘܬܗ ܡܢܫܢܬܡ.
ܘܗܘ ܐܝܬ ܐܘܪܚ ܟܬܒܐ. ܘܟܠܗ ܕܚܙܝܬ ܡܩܕܡܘܗܝ ܕܐܬܝ.
ܘܐܦ ܐܢܐ ܡܢܚܬ ܗܘܝܬ ܠܝ. ܘܦܘܡܝܬܐ ܐܝܟ ܟܬܒܘܗܝ ܕܪܘܚܐ.
ܘܒܪܘܚܗ ܡܠܒܫܐ. ܦܘܠܚܢܗ ܠܘܬܝ ܡܫܬܦܪܐ.
32ra ܘܥܠ ܐܝܟ ܕܡܫܘܚܢܗ ܡܫܬܪܪܐ ܐܝܟ ܕܐܫܬܟܚܗ.
ܘܐܦ ܟܝ ܚܘܝ ܐܢܬ ܗܘܐ. ܘܐܪܗܛ ܠܐܘܪܚܗ ܘܐܫܟܚܗ.
ܘܐܬܩܦܬ ܘܡܟܠܬܗ. ܒܦܘܩܕܐ ܕܒܪܢܫܗ ܐܪܙܝܬܐ.
ܘܚܛܦܬ ܢܚܝܫ ܟܦܬܐ. ܦܠܟܗ ܒܟܠܗ ܐܬܚܛܦܬ.
ܒܫܡܐ ܕܝܗ ܘܐܬܟܡܝܬ ܒܠܘܪ ܫܡܝܐ ܘܡܠܝܐ.
ܟܦܐ ܕܝܫܘܥ ܘܡܫܝܚܐ ܒܗ. ܒܩܘܗ ܘܐܬܐ ܒܝ ܥܒܕܗ.
ܘܟܬܒܐ ܒܦܩܕܢܘܗܝ ܘܐܦ ܗܘ ܕܐܫܬܘܝ ܒܟܝ.
ܘܒܠܘܪܐ ܕܡܣܦܪܘܗܝ. ܟܡ ܕܘܪܓܢܘܗܝ ܐܫܬܟܚܬ.
ܘܚܕܝ ܟܝ ܘܦܟܠ ܢܬܐ ܘܟܦܪܗ ܒܡܟܠܟܬܐ ܗܘܝܬ.
ܘܟܠܠܐ ܕܕܘܪܫܐ. ܦܘܠ ܦܟܝܢܘܗܝ ܠܗ ܡܡܟܢܫ.
ܘܐܬܠܘܝ ܕܠܠܘܪܐ. ܘܡܟܝ ܡܟܝܠܐ ܐܬܠܝܢ.
ܘܒܦܘܪܥ ܡܢܚܝܢܬܐ ܟܦܗ ܒܡܟܠܡ ܐܬܪܐ.

---

90 ܡܚܝܠܘܬܗ] ܬܚܣܝܠܘܬܗ MS : corr Beyer
90 ܡܢܫܢܬܡ] ܡܢܫܢܬܐ MS : corr
104 ܕܠܠܘܪܐ] ܕܠܬܪܥܐ ܗܘܬ MS : del Hoffmann
104 ܡܟܝܠܐ] ܡܠܟܐ ܒܟܡܗ MS : del Hoffmann
105 ܘܒܦܘܪܥ ܡܢܚܝܢܬܐ] ܘܒܦܘܪܥܢ ܡܢܚܝܢܬܝ MS : corr Hoffmann

Then I saw that it was ready to speak.
I heard the sound of its tones, whispering in its descent:
"I'm the swiftest servant's, for whom I was brought up before my father."
And I, too, felt my stature grow in accord with my father's efforts.
The garment was inundating me with its royal impulses
And rushing for me to take it from the hands of those giving it.
My love was likewise spurring me on to run to meet it and face it.
I reached out and took it, I dressed up in its beautiful colors,
I wrapped myself up completely in all my brightly colored cloak.
I put it on and I went up to the court of greeting and reverence:
I bowed my head and revered my father's splendor, who'd sent it to me.
Because I followed his commands, he also did as he had promised.
At the court of his nobles I joined his magnates,
Since he happily welcomed me, and I was with him in his reign.
His whole entourage was celebrating him with a gleeful sound,
And he agreed for me to go to the court of the king of kings,
That I might appear with him before our king with the offering of my pearl.

2.3 Transcription of Syriac Text

kaḏ ʔenå šḇar yalluḏ | w-ʕåmar b-malkuṯ bēṯ ʔåḇ
wa-ḇ-ʕuṯrå wa-ḇ-ḡēwåṯå | da-mrabbyån-ay mnåḥ-wēṯ
men maḏnḥå måṯ-an | zawweḏ ʔaḇåh-ay šaddru-n
w-men ʕuṯrå ḏ-ḇēṯ gazz-an | ʔaḵbar ṣammeḏ l-i mawblå
saggiʔå-y w-qallilå | d-ʔenå lḥoḏ-ay ʔešqli-h
dahḇå-y d-bēṯ ʕilammåyē | w-sēmå ḏ-ḡazzaḵ rabbṯå
w-qarkeḏnay hendu | wa-p̄ṯawtḵē d-men bēṯ qåšån
w-ḥazqu-n b-ʔåḏåmos | da-l-p̄arzlå hi šåḥqå
w-ʔašlḥu-n la-zhiṯå | da-ḇ-ḥubb-hon ʕaḇdu-h l-i
wa-l-ṭoḡ da-zḥoriṯå | d-ʕal qawmaṯ mmaššaḥ zqir
wa-ʕḇaḏ ʕam ḥurqånå | w-ḵaṯbu-y b-leḇ d-lå netṭʕē
w-ʔen teḥḥoṯ l-ḡaw meṣrēn | w-ṯaḥḥṯ-ih l-margåniṯå
håy d-ʔiṯ-ēh b-ḡaw yammå | ḥḏår-aw d-ḥewyå såyqå
telbš-ih la-zhiṯ-åḵ | wa-l-ṭoḡ-åḵ da-ʕl-ēh mnåḥ
w-ʕam ʔaḥu-ḵ trayyån-an | yåroṯ b-malkuṯ-an tehwē
šaḡreṯ maḏnḥå neḥteṯ | kaḏ ʕam trēn parwåqin
d-ʔurḥå ḏḥilå w-ʕaṭlå | w-ʔenå šḇar-nå l-merdy-åh
ʕeḇreṯ tḥumay mayšån | ṣawbå ḏ-ṯaggåray maḏnḥå
wa-mṭēṯ l-ʔaraʕ båḇel | w-ʕelleṯ b-šur-ēh d-sarbuḡ
neḥteṯ l-i l-ḡaw meṣrēn | wa-mlawwyån-ay men praš
terṣeṯ lwåṯ ḥewyå | ḥḏår-aw d-ʔašpåz-ēh šrēṯ
ʕaḏ nnum w-ʕaḏ neškaḇ | w-menn-eh l-margåniṯ ʔešqli-h
wa-ḏ-ḥaḏ-wēṯ mšawḥaḏ-wēṯ | la-ḇnay ʔašpåz nuḵråy-wēṯ
l-ḇar gens bar ḥērē | men maḏnḥåyē tammån ḥzēṯ
l-ṭalyå paʔyå ḥsiḏå
bar mšuḥt w-l-i ʔeṯå nqep̄
wa-ʕḇatt-eh bar ʕenyån | ḥaḇrå ḏ-ṯēḡurt l-eh šawtp̄eṯ
zahhart-eh men meṣråyē | w-men neqp-hon da-msayyḇē
w-ʔaḵ lḇuš-hon leḇšeṯ | d-lå nšakkru-n d-men l-ḇar ʔeṯēṯ
d-ʔessḇ-ih l-margåniṯå | wa-nʕirun-åy l-ḥewyå ʕl-ay
wa-ḇ-ʔaydå men ʕellåṯå | rḡaš b-i ḏ-lå hwēṯ bar måṯ-hom
wa-ḥlaṭ ʕam b-neḵlay-hon | ʔåp̄ ʔaṭʕmu-n mēḵult-hon
wa-ṭʕēṯ d-ḇar malkē-nå | w-p̄elḥeṯ l-malkå ḏil-hon
ṭʕēṯ-åh l-margåniṯå | da-ʕl-ēh ʔaḇåh-ay šaddru-n

wa-ḇ-yuqrå ḏa-ṭrop̄ē-hon | šeḵbeṯ b-šennṯå ʕammiqtå
wa-ḇ-hålēn kul-hēn d-ḡaḏš-an | ʔaḇåhay rḡaš w-ḥaš ʕl-ay
w-ʔeṯkrez b-malkuṯ-an | d-ḵul-nåš l-ṯarʕ-an neštḡar
malkē w-rēšay partaw | w-ḵul rawrḇånay maḏnḥå
wa-qṭar ʕl-ay ʔåp̄arsnå | d-ʔenå ḇ-meṣrēn lå ʔeštḇeq
wa-ḵṯaḇ l-i ʔeggartå | w-ḵul raḇ šm-eh b-åh ʔarmi
men ʔaḇu-ḵ mleḵ malkē | w-ʔemm-åḵ ʔaḥiḏaṯ maḏnḥå
w-men ʔaḥu-ḵ trayyån-an | l-åḵ br-ån da-ḇ-meṣrēn šlåm
naḏ w-qum men šennṯ-åḵ | w-mellē ḏ-ʔeggart-an šmaʕ
ʔeṯʕahd d-ḇar malkē ʔat | ḥzi ʕaḇduṯå l-man plaḥt
ʕhaḏ-ēh l-margåniṯå | da-ʕl-ēh l-meṣrēn ʔeštgart
ʔetdaḵr-ih la-zhiṯ-åk | wa-l-ṭoḡ-åḵ gaʔyå ʕhaḏ
d-ṯelbaš w-ṯeṣṭabbaṯ | d-ḇa-sp̄ar ḥliṣē šm-åḵ ʔeṯqri
w-ʕam ʔaḥu-ḵ pṣåḡriḇ-an | ʕamm-eh b-malkuṯ-an tehwē
w-ʔeggart eggartå-y | d-malkå ḇ-yammin-eh ḥaṯm-åh
men bišē ḇnay båḇel | w-ḏaywē marriḏē ḏ-sarbuḡ
perḥaṯ ba-ḏmuṯ nešrå | malkå ḏ-ḵul-åh pårahṭå
perḥaṯ w-šeḵnaṯ ṣēḏ-ay | w-ḵul-åh hwåṯ l-åh mellṯå
l-qål-åh wa-l-qål rḡešt-åh | neddeṯ w-qåmeṯ men šennaṯ
šqalt-åh wa-nšaqt-åh | w-šarriṯ ʔenå l-yåṯ-åh qrēṯ
w-ʕal haw da-ḇ-leḇ ršim | mell-ēh d-ʔeggart ʔeṯkṯeḇ
ʕehdeṯ d-ḇar malkē-nå | w-ḥēruṯ kyån-åh påqdå
ʕehdeṯ l-margåniṯå | da-ʕl-ēh l-meṣrēn ʔeštaddraṯ
w-šarriṯ mmaggeš-nå l-ēh | l-ḥewyå dḥilå w-såyqå
ʔanimt-ēh w-ʔaškeḇt-ēh | d-šem ʔåḇ ʕl-aw ʔeṯdaḵreṯ
wa-šm-ēh da-ṯrayyån-an | wa-ḏ-ʔem malkaṯ maḏnḥå
wa-ḥṭap̄t-åh l-margåniṯå | w-ʕeṯpeṯ d-ʔep̄nē l-ḇēṯ ʔåḇ
wa-lḇuš-hon ṣåʔå w-ṭamʔå | šelḥeṯ wa-šḇaqt-ēh b-ʔaṯr-hon
traṣt-åh l-mardiṯ d-ṯēṯē | l-nuhrå ḏ-måṯ-an maḏnḥå
wa-l-ʔeggart mʕiråniṯ | qḏåm-ay b-ʔurḥå ʔeškḥeṯ
w-ʔaḵ da-ḇ-qål-åh ʔaʕirṯ-an | tuḇ b-nuhr-åh l-i mḏabbrå
d-šēråyå basiliqon | qḏåm-ay b-ḥawr-åh map̄rḡå
wa-ḇ-qål haddåyuṯ-åh | tuḇån rhiḇuṯ mlabbḇå
wa-ḇ-ḥubb-åh nåḡdå l-i
nep̄qeṯ ʕḇart-åh l-sarbuḡ | šeḇqeṯ l-båḇel l-semmål
wa-mṭēṯ l-mayšån rabbṯå | la-lmēn-hon d-ṯaggårē

da-b-ʕebr-ēh d-yammå yåṯbå
w-la-zhiṯ d-šelḥeṯ-wēṯ | wa-l-ṭoḡ d-ḇ-åh mʕaṭṭp̄å-wåṯ
men råmtå warqån | l-ṯammån ʔaḇåh-ay šaddru-h
b-ʔiḏå ḏ-ḡēzaḇray-hon | d-ḇa-šrår-hon ʕl-ēh mhaymnin
w-lå ʕåheḏ-wēṯ teḡm-åh | da-ḇ-šaḇruṯ šḇaqt-åh bēṯ ʔåḇ
men šel kaḏ ʔaqbelt-åh | l-maḥziṯ lḇuštå ḏmåṯ l-i
kull-åh b-ḵull-i ḥzēṯ | w-ʔåp̄ l-kull-i ḇ-åh ʔaqbleṯ
da-ṯrēn-nan b-p̄uršånå | w-ḥaḏ tuḇ ḥnan ba-ḥḏå ḏmu
w-ʔåp̄ l-hon l-ḡēzaḇrē | d-li ʔaytyu-h håḵan ḥzēṯ
da-ṯrēn ʔennon ḥḏå ḏmu | d-ḥaḏ niš malkå ršim b-hon
haw d-ʔiḏ-aw ʔap̄ni l-i | l-ḡuʕlån w-ʕuṯr b-ʔiḏay-hon
la-zhiṯ mṣabbattå | da-ḇ-ḡawnē ḡʔayyå mṣabbṯå
b-ḏahḇå wa-ḇ-ḇērulē | w-qarkeḏnē wa-p̄ṯawtḵē
w-sardukkē prišåṯ gawnå | ʔåp̄ hi ḇ-rawm-åh matqnå
wa-ḇ-ḵēp̄ē ḏ-ʔåḏåmos | kul šåryåṯ-åh mqabbʕån
w-ṣalm-ēh da-mleḵ malkē | kull-ēh b-kull-åh massaq w-ṣir
w-ʔåp̄ kēp̄ē ḏ-sappilå | tuḇån krom-ēh mp̄attḵē
wa-ḥzēṯ tuḇ da-ḇ-ḵull-åh | zawʕay iḏaʕtå råp̄tin
w-ʔaḵ d-la-mmallålu | tuḇ ḥzēṯ-åh d-meṯʕattḏå
qål neʕmåṯ-åh šemʕeṯ | d-ʕam maḥḥṯån-åh mrattem
d-hu ʔenå zriz ʕaḇdē | d-l-ēh rabbyu-n qḏåm-aw d-ʔåḇ
w-ʔåp̄ ʔenå margeš-wēṯ b-i | d-qawmaṯ ʔaḵ ʕaml-aw råḇyå
wa-ḇ-zawʕ-ēh malkåyē | kull-åh lwåṯ meštappʕå
w-ʕal ʔiḏå ḏ-yåhoḇ-ēh | mestarhḇå ʔaḵ d-ʔešql-ih
w-ʔåp̄ l-i ḥuḇ zåqeṯ-wå | d-ʔerhaṭ l-ʔurʕ-åh w-ʔaqbl-ih
w-ʔeṯpaššṭeṯ w-qabbelt-åh | b-šup̄rå ḏ-ḡawnē ʔṣṭabbṯeṯ
wa-l-ṭoḡ naṣṣiḥ gawnē | kull-åh l-ḵull-åh ʔeṯʕaṭṭp̄eṯ
lebšeṯ b-åh w-ʔeṯʕalliṯ | la-ṯraʕ šlåmå w-segdtå
keppeṯ rēš w-segdeṯ l-ēh | l-ziw-ēh d-ʔåḇ l-i šaddr-åh
d-ʕeḇdeṯ l-p̄uqdån-aw | w-ʔåp̄ hu ḏ-ʔeštawdi ʕbaḏ
wa-ḇ-ṯarʕå ḏ-wåspr-aw | ʕam rawrḇån-aw ʔeṯḥallṭeṯ
da-ḥḏi ḇ-i w-qabbel yåṯ | w-ʕamm-ēh b-malkuṯ-ēh-wēṯ
wa-ḇ-qålå ḏa-ḏrusē | kul pålḥ-aw l-ēh mšabbḥin
w-ʔeštawdi ḏa-l-ṯarʕå | da-mleḵ malkē ʔeštgar
wa-ḇ-qurbån margåniṯ | ʕamm-ēh l-malk-an ʔeṯḥzē

2.4 Syriac-English Glossary and Concordance

The entries are arranged alphabetically according to the order of the Syriac writing system, but verbs are listed by root, and by *binyanim*/stems:

G	*pʕal*	tG	*ʔetp̄ʕel*
D	*paʕʕel*	tD	*ʔetpaʕʕal*
A	*ʔap̄ʕel*	tA	*ʔettap̄ʕal*
Q	[quadrilit.]	tQ	[*t*-quadrilit.]

I only give meanings for this text, not necessarily more generally in Syriac. Function words (pronouns, prepositions, etc.) and some very common nouns, adjectives, and verbs are not included, but I've tended toward inclusion rather than exclusion. For the concordance, which is complete for the included lemmas, occurrences are cited by line number at the end of each entry.

ʔ ܐ

ܐܶܓܰܪܬܳܐ, ܐܶܓܰܪܬܳܐ *ʔeggartå* letter (written document) 40 43 49 (2x) 55 64

ܐܳܕܳܡܳܣ *ʔåd̲åmos* adamant, diamond 8 85

ܐܳܦܰܪܣܢܳܐ *ʔåp̄arsnå* plot, plan (see below s.v. *qṭr*) 39

ܐܰܫܦܳܙܳܐ *ʔašpåzå* lodge, inn, house 21 23

b ܒ

ܒܹܪܘܠܠܳܐ *bērullå* beryl (emerald, aquamarine, etc.) 83

ܒܰܣܺܝܠܺܝܩܘܢ *basilikon* royal 66

g ܓ

ܓܐܘܬܐ *gēʔutā* (√gʔy) PL luxury/-ies 2
ܓܐܐ *gʔē* (√gʔy) luxurious, fancy, haute 46 82
ܓܕܫ *gdš* G happen 36
ܓܙܒܪܐ *gēzabrā* treasurer 74 79
ܓܘܥܠܢܐ *guʕlānā* (√gʕl) deposit, pledge 81
ܓܘܢܐ *gawnā* color 82, 84, 96, 97

d ܕ

ܕܒܪ *dbr* D direct, lead, guide 65
ܕܗܒܐ *dahbā* gold 6 83
ܕܚܝܠ *dḥil* (√dḥl) scary 17 58
ܕܝܘܐ *daywā* demon 50
ܕܟܪ *dkr* tG remember, call to mind 46 59
ܕܡܘܬܐ *dmutā* (√dmy) form, shape, appearance 78 80
ܕܡܐ *dmy* G seem like 76
ܕܪܘܣܬܐ *drustā*, PL (as here) ܕܪܘܣܐ *drusē* joy, delight, splendor 103

h ܗ

ܗܕܝܘܬܐ *haddāyutā* (√hdy) guidance, leading 67
ܗܝܡܢ *hymn* Q entrust 74

w ܘ

ܘܣܦܪܐ *wāsprā* noble, prince 101

z ܙ

ܙܗܝܬܐ *zhitā* (√zhy G.PTCP.PASS) s.t. shining 9 14 46 72 82
ܙܗܪ *zhr* D *men* warn s.o. about 28

ܙܘܕ *zwd* D provision, supply 3
ܙܘܥܐ *zawʕå* movement, (e)motion(s) 88 93
ܙܚܘܪܝܬܐ *zḥoriṯå* scarlet 10
ܙܝܘܐ *ziwå* splendor, radiance 99
ܙܩܪ *zqr* G weave 10
ܙܩܬ *zqt* G goad onward 95
ܙܪܝܙ *zriz* (√zrz) ready, swift, quick, willing and able, strong, eager 91

ܚ *ḥ*

ܚܐܪܐ *ḥērå* (√ḥrr) free person 24
ܚܐܪܘܬܐ *ḥēruṯå* (√ḥrr) freedom 56
ܚܒܪܐ *ḥaḇrå* colleague, associate 27
ܚܕܝ *ḥdy* G *b-* be happy with, be made happy by 102
ܚܘܒܐ *ḥubbå* (√ḥbb) affection, love 9 68 95
ܚܘܝܐ *ḥewyå* snake, serpent 13 21 30 58
ܚܘܪܐ *ḥawrå* appearance 66
ܚܘܪܩܢܐ *ḥurqånå* (√ḥrq) agreement 11
ܚܙܩ *ḥzq* D tighten, fasten, prep for a trip 8
ܚܛܦ *ḥṭp* G grab, snatch 61
ܚܠܛ *ḥlṭ* tD be mixed with, b/c part of 32 101
ܚܠܝܨ *ḥliṣ* (√ḥlṣ) strong, valiant, hero 47
ܚܣܝܕ *ḥsiḏ* (√ḥsd) charming, attractive 25
ܚܫܫ *ḥšš* G feel, sense, feel pain 36
ܚܬܡ *ḥtm* G seal 49

ܛ *ṭ*

ܛܘܓܐ *ṭoğa* outer garment associated with nobility or other distinction, cloak, “toga” 10 14 46 72 97
ܛܡܐ *ṭmē* dirty, defiled, unclean 62
ܛܥܝ *ṭʕy* G forget 33 34

tG be forgotten 11
ܛܥܡ *ṭʕm* A feed, have taste 32
ܛܪܘܦܐ *ṭropē* food, cuisine 35

y ܝ

ܝܕܥܬܐ *idaʕtå* (√ydʕ) knowledge 88
ܝܗܘܒܐ *yåhoḇå* (√yhb) giver 94
ܝܘܩܪܐ *yuqrå* (√yqr) weight 35
ܝܠܘܕܐ *yalluḏå* (√yld) baby, infant 1
ܝܡܝܢܐ *yamminå* right hand 49
ܝܪܘܬܐ *yåroṯå* (√yrt) inheritor, heir 15
-ܝܬ *yåṯ-* [old direct object marker], self, essence 54 102

k ܟ

ܟܦܦ *kpp* G bend s.t. 99
ܟܪܘܡܐ *kromå* color, appearance 87
ܟܪܙ *krz* tG be publicly announced 37
ܟܬܒ *ktb* G write 11 40
tG be written 55

l ܠ

-ܠܐܘܪܥ *l-ʔurʕ-* (+ set A SUFF) to meet ... 95
ܠܒܐ *lebbå* heart, mind 11 55
ܠܒܒ *lbb* D encourage 67
ܠܒܘܫܐ *ləḇušå* clothes 29 62 76
ܠܒܫ *lbš* G put on, wear 14 29 47 98
ܠܡܐܢܐ *lmēnå* port, harbor 70

m ܡ

ܡܐܟܘܠܬܐ *mēḵultå* (√ʔkl) food 32
ܡܓܫ *mgš* D charm, put a spell on 58
ܡܕܢܚܐ *maḏnḥå* (√dnḥ) the East, ≈ Parthia 3 16 18 38 41 60 63
ܡܕܢܚܝ *maḏnḥåy* (√dnḥ) eastern(er) 24
ܡܘܒܠܐ *mawblå* (√ybl) load, luggage 4
ܡܚܙܝܬܐ *maḥziṯå* (√ḥzy) mirror 76
ܡܚܚܬܢܐ *maḥḥṯånå* (√nḥt) descent 90
ܡܛܝ *mṭy* G arrive, reach 19 70
ܡܠܘܝܢܐ *mlawwyånå* (√lwy D) accompanier 20
ܡܠܟܐ *malkå* king 33 49 51 80 105 38 41 44 56 86 104
ܡܠܟܘܬܐ *malkuṯå* kingdom, realm 1 15 37 48
ܡܠܟܬܐ *malkṯå* queen 60
ܡܢܝܚ *mnåḥ* (√nwḥ A.PTCP.PASS) *b-* at ease in, living contently with 2
ܡܥܝܪܢܐ *mʕirånå*, F *mʕiråniṯå* (√ʕwr A) rouser 64
ܡܪܒܝܢܐ *mrabbyånå* (√rby D) rearer 2
ܡܪܓܢܝܬܐ *margåniṯå* pearl 12 22 30 34 45 57 61 105
ܡܪܕܝܬܐ *mardiṯå* (√rdy) trip, travel, journey 63
ܡܪܝܕ *marriḏ* (√mrd) rebellious, disorderly, chafing against authority 50
ܡܫܚ *mšḥ* D measure, fit, proportion 10
ܡܫܚܐ *mešḥå* oil, anointing 25
ܡܬܐ *måṯå* country, homeland 3 31 63

n ܢ

ܢܓܕ *ngd* G attract, draw 68
ܢܕܕ *ndd* G be awake(ned) 43 53
ܢܘܗܪܐ *nuhrå* light 63 65
ܢܘܟܪܝ *nuḵråy* foreign 23
ܢܘܡ *nwm* G sleep 22

A put to sleep, lull to sleep 59
ܢܚܬ *nḥt* G go down 12 20
A lower, bring down 12
ܢܝܫܐ *nišå* standard, mark, sign 80
ܢܟܠܐ *neḵlå* deceit 32
ܢܥܡܐ *neʕmå* sound, song 90
ܢܩܦ *nqp* G stick to, follow, stay close to 26
ܢܩܦܐ *neqpå* connection, close association 28
ܢܨܝܚ *naṣṣiḥ* (√nṣḥ) shining, bright 97
ܢܫܩ *nšq* G kiss 54
ܢܫܪܐ *nešrå* eagle, hawk 51

s ܣ

ܣܐܡܐ *sēmå* silver 6
ܣܓܕ *sgd* G bow down in deference 99
ܣܓܕܬܐ *seḡdṯå* reverence, deference, veneration 98
ܣܝܒ *syb* D make s.t./s.o. dirty 28
ܣܘܩ *swq* G breathe, inhale, puff 13 58
ܣܠܩ *slq* A overlay 86
ܣܡܠܐ *semmålå* left hand 69
ܣܦܝܠܐ *sappilå* sapphire 87
ܣܦܪܐ *sep̄rå* book 47
ܣܪܕܘܟܐ *sardukkå* sardonyx 84
ܣܪܗܒ *srhb* tQ hurry 94

ʕ ܥ

ܥܒܕܘܬܐ *ʕaḇduṯå* slavery, being enslaved 44
ܥܒܪ *ʕbr* G cross (a border, etc.) 18 69
ܥܒܪܐ *ʕeḇrå* crossing, bank, edge 71
ܥܗܕ *ʕhd* G remember 45 46 56 57 75

tG remember 44
ܥܘܪ *ʕwr* A wake s.o. up 30 65
ܥܘܬܪܐ *ʕutrå* (√ʕtr) wealth, riches 2 4 81
ܥܛܠ *ʕṭel* difficult 17
ܥܛܦ *ʕṭp* G go back, (co-verb) do again 61
D cover, clothe s.o. 72
tD wrap (o.s.) up in 97
ܥܠܝ *ʕly* tD ascend, go up 98
ܥܠܬܐ *ʕelltå* (√ʕll) cause 31
ܥܡܝܩ *ʕammiq* (√ʕmq) deep 35
ܥܡܠܐ *ʕamlå* (√ʕml) effort, labor, toil 92
ܥܢܝܢܐ *ʕenyånå* (√ʕny) concern, matter, business 27
ܥܬܕ *ʕtd* tD be prepared 89

p ܦ

ܦܐܐ *pʔē* (√pʔy) beautiful, appealing 25
ܦܘܩܕܢܐ *puqdånå* (√pqd) command 100
ܦܘܪܫܢܐ *puršånå* (√prš) difference, distinction, division 78
ܦܠܚ *plḥ* G work, serve 33 44
ܦܠܚܐ *pålḥå* attendant, member of royal staff/entourage 103
ܦܢܝ *pny* G turn, return 61
D *l-* return s.t. to s.o. 81
ܦܨܓܪܝܒܐ *pṣågribå* successor to the throne 48
ܦܩܕ *pqd* G look for, look after 56
ܦܪܓ *prg* A shine 66
ܦܪܘܩܐ *parwåqå* runner, messenger[10] 16
ܦܪܙܠܐ *parzlå* iron
ܦܪܚ *prḥ* G fly 51 52
ܦܪܚܬܐ *pårahtå* bird 51

[10]Not to be confused with ܦܪܘܩܐ *påroqå* savior!

ܦܪܫ *prš* G (*men*) leave, separate from 20 84
ܦܫܛ *pšṭ* tD stretch out (one's limbs, etc.), stand up 96
ܦܛܰܘܬܟܳܐ *pṯawtḵå* brocade, luxurious cloth interwoven with gold and various colors; a multicolored gem (?) 7 83
ܦܬܟ *ptk* D vary, mix 87

ܨ *ṣ*

ܨܳܐܐ̄ *ṣåʔē* dirty 62
ܨܒܬ *ṣbt* D decorate, adorn 82 (2x)
tD get dressed up in fancy clothes 47 96
ܨܰܘܒܳܐ *ṣawbå* gathering-place 18
ܨܘܪ *ṣwr* G form, draw, paint 86
ܨܰܠܡܳܐ *ṣalmå* (√ṣlm) image 86
ܨܡܕ *ṣmd* D bind, harness, tie on 4

ܩ *q*

ܩܒܠ *qbl* D receive 96 102
A face, be confronted by 76 77 95
ܩܒܥ *qbʕ* D fix together, set 85
ܩܘܪܒܳܢܳܐ *qurbånå* (√qrb) offering, a gift presented to royalty 105
ܩܰܘܡܬܳܐ *qawmṯå* size, physical stature 10 92
ܩܛܪ *qṭr* + *ʔåp̄arsnå* agree on a plan 39
ܩܳܠܳܐ *qålå* sound 53 (2x) 65 67 90 103
ܩܰܪܟܶܕܢܳܐ *qarkednå* chalcedony, agate 7 83
ܩܪܐ *qry* G read aloud 54
tG be read aloud 47

ܪ *r*

ܪܒܐ *rby* G grow, get bigger 92

D bring up, raise 91
ܪܓܫ *rgš* G (*b-*) notice, feel, be aware of 31 36 53
A *b-* notice, feel, be aware of 92
ܪܕܝ *rdy* G go, travel 17
ܪܗܛ *rhṭ* G run 95
ܪܗܝܒܘܬܐ *rhibuṯå* (√rb) fear 67
ܪܘܡܐ *rawmå* grandeur 84
ܪܦܬ *rpt* G wiggle around, writhe, squirm 88
ܪܡܝ *rmy* A put, place, provide 40
ܪܫܡ *ršm* G mark, incise, inscribe 55 80
ܪܬܡ *rtm* D whisper, mumble 90

š ܫ

ܫܒܩ *šbq* G leave behind, keep s.t. on a certain side (left, right) 62 69 75
tG be left behind 39
ܫܒܪܐ *šaḇrå* child 1 17
ܫܒܪܘܬܐ *šaḇruṯå* childhood 75
ܫܓܪ *šgr* D leave 16
tG *l-* go to, come to, be present at 37 45 104
ܫܕܪ *šdr* D send 3 34 57 73 99
ܫܘܕܝ *šwdy* tQ promise 100 104
ܫܘܚܕ *šwḥd* Q PASS.PTCP left alone, separate(d) 23
ܫܘܦܪܐ *šup̄rå* beauty 96
ܫܘܪܐ *šurå* wall 19
ܫܘܬܦ *šwtp* Q make s.o. a partner 27
ܫܚܩ *šḥq* G crush, grind 8
ܫܟܒ *škb* G lie down, go to sleep 22 35
A make s.o. go to sleep 59
ܫܟܢ *škn* G land, light 52
ܫܟܪ *škr* D suspect 29
ܫܠܚ *šlḥ* G take off one's clothes 62 72

A strip s.o. 9
ܫܠܳܡܳܐ *šlåmå* greeting(s) 42 98
ܫܶܢܬܳܐ *šennṯå* sleep
ܫܦܥ *špʕ* tD be poured out in a large amount 93
ܫܩܠ *šql* G pick up and carry, take away 5 22 54 94
ܫܪܐ *šry* G take position, stop and stay, camp 21
D begin 54 58
ܫܶܪܳܝܳܐ *šērāyå* silk 66
ܫܳܪܺܝܬܳܐ *šåriṯå* joint, seam 85
ܫܪܳܪܳܐ *šrårå* reliability 74

t ܬ

ܬܶܐܓܽܘܪܬܳܐ *tēḡurtå* business, dealings, mission 27
ܬܶܓܡܳܐ *teḡmå* rank, class, kind, type 75
ܬܰܓܳܪܳܐ *taggårå* merchant, trader 18 70
ܬܽܘܒܳܢ *tuḇån* further(more) (≈ ܬܽܘܒ *tuḇ*) 67 87
ܬܚܽܘܡܳܐ *tḥumå* border 18
ܬܩܢ *tqn* A fix, establish, prepare 84
ܬܪܰܝܳܢܳܐ *trayyånå* second (in command, rank, etc.) 15 42 60
ܬܰܪܥܳܐ *tarʕå* gate, door, royal court 98 101 104
ܬܪܨ *trṣ* G *lwåṯ* head for (someone's presence) 21 63

3 The Greek Texts

3.1 Introduction

There are two distinct versions of *The Pearlsong* known in Greek. One matches the Syriac closely, basically line for line, and can thus be considered a straightforward translation. Unlike the Syriac text, it's in prose, rather than anything resembling verse. The other Greek version, also prose, is an abridged paraphrase or retelling, but still told in the first person. This version is part of a homily and, in addition to the narrative, it includes a loose interpretive key, with the prince's story understood explicitly as reflecting lessons for Christian hearers. The two versions are distinct not only in their codicological settings – one hagiographic, like Syriac, the other homiletic – and the fact that the plain translation offers no interpretive recommendations, they are also distinct in their language: the homiletic version is written in a higher literary register, with a richer vocabulary, more varied syntax, etc. Among the marks of this more literary framing is Niketas' borrowing from the *Odyssey* (4.393) to describe the prince's difficult journey to Egypt.

There are scores of Greek manuscripts with the *Acts of Thomas*, but *The Pearlsong* appears in just a single one of them, which means that in both Syriac and in Greek there's just one known manuscript. The Greek manuscript, Vallicellanus B35, is thought to be from the eleventh century.[11] The Greek text of the *Acts of Thomas* was published in 1903 by Lipsius and Bonnet (*Acta Apostolorum Apocrypha*), notably with the Greek *Pearlsong* included in the main body of the saint's story, despite its slim scribal support. That is, if you're just casually reading the *Acts of Thomas* in Greek from Lipsius and Bonnet's edition, it's easy to read

[11]This is siglum U in Lipsius and Bonnet's edition.

§§108–112, where *The Pearlsong* is situated, without ever skipping a beat, unaware that so many manuscripts lack any hint of it. Poirier re-edited the text for his study.[12] In very general terms, the Greek translation lines up closely with the Syriac text as we have it, but the translator made attempts to reasonably render puzzling words, as noted, for example, in the discussion of the place-name, Sarbug.

Turning to the second version of *The Pearlsong*, this retelling of *The Pearlsong* narrative shows up in a Byzantine homily by Niketas of Thessaloniki, perhaps of the eleventh century, in a total of five manuscripts.[13] This text was published by Bonnet in 1901, and again by Poirier.[14] Given its homiletic context, it's not surprising that Niketas's version is also in prose, not verse. I don't call this version a translation, because it's clearly not following the same plan as either the Syriac or the other Greek version, skipping around and missing parts that those two earlier texts have. Nevertheless, Niketas's version is still told from the traveler-prince's perspective, like those other two texts, and the narrative doesn't differ in any major way. Niketas reads *The Pearlsong* allegorically in an unambiguously Christian way, as the preamble and epilogue to the paraphrase make explicit.

The Greek texts of both the plain translation and the later retelling are given below, along with a Greek-English glossary. The texts and minimal critical apparatus here are based on the aforementioned editions of Lipsius and Bonnet, alongside the re-editions and notes by Poirier.[15] While not the main focus of the commentary, both Greek texts are included in the discussion there.

[12] *L'Hymne*, 351–357.

[13] On the possible date and identity of Niketas, see Poirier, *L'Hymne*, 286–288.

[14] *L'Hymne*, 365–371.

[15] The variants for the Niketas text, which are given in full by Poirier, are more negligible (mostly spelling variants and obvious mistakes).

3.2 Greek Text and English Translation

προσευχόμενον δὲ πάντες ἔβλεπον αὐτὸν οἱ δέσμιοι καὶ ἐδέοντο αὐτοῦ ὑπὲρ αὐτῶν εὔξασθαι. προσευξάμενος δὲ καὶ καθεσθεὶς ἤρξατο λέγειν ψαλμὸν τοιοῦτον·

ὅτε ἤμην βρέφος ἄλαλον ἐν τοῖς τοῦ πατρός μου βασιλείοις ἐν πλούτῳ καὶ τρυφῇ τῶν τροφέων ἀναπαυόμενος, ἐξ Ἀνατολῆς τῆς πατρίδος ἡμῶν ἐφοδιάσαντές με οἱ γονεῖς ἀπέστειλάν με· ἀπὸ δὲ πλούτου τῶν θησαυρῶν τούτων φόρτον συνέθηκαν μέγαν τε καὶ ἐλαφρόν, ὅπως αὐτὸν μόνος βαστάσαι δυνηθῶ· χρυσός ἐστιν ὁ φόρτος τῶν ἄνω, καὶ ἄσημος τῶν μεγάλων θησαυρῶν, καὶ λίθοι ἐξ Ἰνδῶν οἱ χαλκεδόνιοι, καὶ μαργαρῖται ἐκ Κοσάνων· καὶ ὥπλισάν με τῷ ἀδαμάντι· καὶ ἐνέδυσάν με ἐσθῆτα διάλιθον χρυσόπαστον, ἣν ἐποίησαν στέργοντές με, καὶ στολὴν τὸ χρῶμα ξανθὴν πρὸς τὴν ἐμὴν ἡλικίαν.

σύμφωνα δὲ πρὸς ἐμὲ πεποιήκασιν, ἐγκαταγράψαντες τῇ διανοίᾳ μου τοῦ μὴ ἐπιλαθέσθαι με, ἔφησαν τε·

> ἐὰν κατελθὼν εἰς Αἴγυπτον κομίσῃς ἐκεῖθεν τὸν ἕνα μαργαρίτην τὸν ὄντα ἐκεῖ περὶ τὸν δράκοντα τὸν καταπότην, ὅπως ἐνδύσῃ τὴν διάλιθον ἐσθῆτα καὶ τὴν στολὴν ἐκείνην ἣν ἐπαναπαύεται· τοῦ εὐμνήστου καὶ γένῃ μετὰ τοῦ ἀδελφοῦ σου κῆρυξ τῇ ἡμετέρᾳ βασιλείᾳ.

ἠρχόμην δὲ ἐξ Ἀνατολῆς ἐφ᾽ ὁδὸν δυσχερῆ τε καὶ φοβερὰν μεθ᾽ ἡγεμόνων δύο, ἄπειρος δὲ ἤμην τοῦ ταύτην ὁδεῦσαι. παρελθὼν δὲ καὶ τὰ τῶν Μεσηνῶν μεθόρια ἔνθα ἐστὶν τὸ καταγώγιον τῶν ἀνατολικῶν ἐμπόρων, ἀφικόμην εἰς τὴν τῶν Βαβυλωνίων χώραν. εἰσελθόντος δέ μου εἰς Αἴγυπτον ἀπέστησαν οἱ συνοδεύσαντές μοι ἡγεμόνες, ὥρμων δὲ ἐπὶ τὸν δράκοντα τὴν ταχίστην καὶ περὶ τὸν τούτου φωλεὸν κατέλυον, ἐπιτηρῶν

---

23 Μεσηνῶν] conj Bonnet : Μοσάνων ms

3.2 Greek Text and English Translation

All the prisoners saw him praying and asked him to pray for them, and once he'd finished and sat down, he started reciting a song like this:

When I was a baby, an infant in my father's palace, resting in the wealth and luxury of my guardians, my parents got me ready for a trip and sent me off from the east, our homeland. They put my luggage together out of the wealth of their treasuries, an immense load, but still light enough that I could carry it by myself: it was gold from the upper regions, silver from vast treasuries, chalcedony stones from India, and pearls from Kushan. They armed me with adamant, and put a stone-studded outfit on me inlaid with gold, which they had made in affection for me, together with a yellow garment just my size.

They made an agreement with me, having inscribed it in my mind, so I wouldn't forget, and they said:

> If you go down to Egypt and carry off from there the one pearl that's near the snake-dragon there, the gorger, so that you can put on the stone-studded outfit and that garment it rests on, then you'll be an emissary in our kingdom with your mindful brother.

I began coming from the east on a difficult, frightful road, with two guides, but I wasn't experienced in traveling it. I passed by the borders of Mesene, where there's a stop for eastern traders, and I arrived in Babylonian country. As I entered Egypt, the guides traveling with me took their leave, but I rushed as quickly as possible for the snake-dragon, and I finished my journey there near its lair, waiting for it to doze off and sleep, so I could steal my pearl out from underneath it.

νυστάξαι καὶ κοιμηθῆναι τοῦτον, ὅπως μου τὸν μαργαρίτην ὑφέλωμαι.

μόνος δὲ ὢν ἐξενιζόμην τὸ σχῆμα καὶ τοῖς ἐμοῖς ἀλλότριος ἐφαινόμην. ἐκεῖ δὲ εἶδον ἐμὸν συγγενῆ τὸν ἐξ Ἀνατολῆς, τὸν ἐλεύθερον, παῖδα εὐχαρῆ καὶ ὡραῖον, υἱὸν μεγιστάνων. οὗτός μοι προσελθὼν συγγέγονεν, καὶ συνόμιλον αὐτὸν ἔσχον, καὶ φίλον καὶ κοινωνὸν τῆς ἐμῆς πορείας ποιησάμενος. παρεκελευσάμην δὲ αὐτῷ τοὺς Αἰγυπτίους φυλάσσεσθαι καὶ τῶν ἀκαθάρτων τούτων τὴν κοινωνίαν. ἐνεδυσάμην δὲ αὐτῶν τὰ φορήματα, ἵνα μὴ ξενίζωμαι ὥσπερ ἔξωθεν ἐπὶ τὴν τοῦ μαργαρίτου ἀνάληψιν, καὶ τὸν δράκοντα διυπνίσωσιν κατ᾽ ἐμοῦ οἱ Αἰγύπτιοι. οὐκ οἶδα δὲ ἐξ οἵας ἔμαθον προφάσεως ὡς οὐκ εἰμὶ τῆς χώρας αὐτῶν, δόλῳ δὲ συνέμειξάν μοι τέχνην, καὶ ἐγευσάμην τῆς αὐτῶν τροφῆς. ἠγνόησα ἐμαυτὸν υἱὸν ὄντα βασιλέως, τῷ δὲ αὐτῶν ἐδούλευσα βασιλεῖ. ἦλθον δὲ καὶ ἐπὶ τὸν μαργαρίτην, ἐφ᾽ ὃν οἱ πατέρες μου ἀπεστάλκασίν με, τῷ δὲ τῆς τροφῆς αὐτῶν βάρει εἰς ὕπνον κατηνέχθην βαθύν.

ταῦτα δέ μου παθόντος καὶ οἱ πατέρες μου ᾔσθοντο καὶ ἔπαθον ὑπὲρ ἐμοῦ. ἐκηρύχθη δὲ κήρυγμα ἐν τῇ βασιλείᾳ ἡμῶν ἵνα πάντες ἐπὶ τὰς ἡμετέρας ἀπαντῶσιν θύρας. καὶ τότε οἱ βασιλεῖς τῆς Παρθίας καὶ οἱ ἐν τέλει καὶ οἱ Ἀνατολῆς πρωτεύοντες γνώμης ἐκράτησαν περὶ ἐμοῦ ἵνα μὴ ἐαθῶ ἐν Αἰγύπτῳ. ἔγραψαν δέ με καὶ οἱ δυνάσται σημαίνοντες οὕτως·

> παρὰ τοῦ πατρὸς βασιλέων βασιλεὺς καὶ μητρὸς τὴν Ἀνατολὴν κατεχούσης καὶ ἀδελφοῦ σου τοῦ δευτέρου ἀφ᾽ ἡμῶν τῷ ἐν Αἰγύπτῳ υἱῷ ἡμῶν εἰρήνη. ἀνάστηθι καὶ ἀνάνηψον ἐξ ὕπνου, καὶ τῶν ἐπιστολιμαίων ῥημάτων ἄκουσον, καὶ ὑπομνήσθητι υἱὸς βασιλέων ὑπάρχων. δουλικὸν ὑπεισῆλθες ζυγόν· μνημόνευσον τῆς ἐσθῆτός σου τῆς χρυσοπάστου· μνημόνευσον τοῦ μαργαρίτου δι᾽ ὃν εἰς Αἴγυπτον ἀπε-

48 Παρθίας] conjeci : Παρθενίας ms
49 ἐαθῶ] conj Hilgenfeld: ἔλθω ms
52–53 ἀδελφοῦ σου τοῦ δευτέρου] conj Bonnet : ἀδελφοὺς αὐτῶν δευτέρους ms

Being by myself, I seemed a stranger in appearance, and I began to seem like a foreigner to my own people, but I saw a relative of mine there from the east: a free-born child, charming and handsome, and from an important family. When he came, he joined me, and I took him on as an associate, making him both a friend and a partner on my trip. I urged him to watch out for the Egyptians and for partnership with those impure people, but I wore their clothing, so as not to seem like a stranger, an outsider, while taking the pearl back, and so the Egyptians wouldn't rouse the snake-dragon against me. I'm not sure what pretense tipped them off that I wasn't from their country, but with a trick, in a scheme, they conversed with me, and I tasted their food. I was unaware that I myself was a king's son, but I served their king. I came even to the pearl, which my parents had sent me for, but I was weighed down by the heaviness of their food into a deep sleep.

While I was suffering these things, my parents took notice and felt for me. An announcement was made in our kingdom, that everyone should convene at our gates. Then the kings of Parthia, the magistrates, and the leaders of the east settled on a proposal for me, that I shouldn't be left alone in Egypt, and the authorities wrote to me, communicating as follows:

> From your father, king of kings, and your mother, who controls the east, and your brother, the second – from us to our son in Egypt: greetings! Get up, and come to from your sleep! Listen to the epistolary words, and remember you're a son of kings! You assumed a slave-yoke: remember your outfit inlaid with gold, remember the pearl you were sent to Egypt for – you and your brother, whom you succeeded in our kingdom, were named "book of life."

στάλης. ἐκλήθη δὲ τὸ ὄνομά σου βιβλίον ζωῆς καὶ τοῦ ἀδελφοῦ σου οὗ παρείληφας ἐν τῇ βασιλείᾳ ἡμῶν.

ὁ δὲ βασιλεὺς ὡς πρεσβευτὴς κατεσφραγίσατο διὰ τοὺς πονηροὺς Βαβυλωνίους παῖδας καὶ δαίμονας τυραννικοὺς Λαβυρινθίους.

ἐγὼ δὲ πρὸς τὴν ταύτης φωνήν τε καὶ αἴσθησιν ἐξ ὕπνου ἀνωρμησάμην, ἀναλαβὼν δὲ καὶ καταφιλήσας ἀνεγίνωσκον. ἐγέγραπτο δὲ περὶ ἐκείνου τοῦ ἐν τῇ καρδίᾳ μου ἀναγεγραμμένου· καὶ ὑπεμνήσθην παραχρῆμα ὅτι βασιλέων εἰμὶ υἱὸς καὶ ἡ ἐλευθερία μου τὸ γένος μου ἐπιζητεῖ.

ὑπεμνήσθην δὲ καὶ τοῦ μαργαρίτου ἐφ' ὃν κατεπέμφθην εἰς Αἴγυπτον· ἠρχόμην δὲ ἐπᾴσμασιν ἐπὶ τὸν δράκοντα τὸν φοβερόν, καὶ κατεπόνεσα τοῦτον ἐπονομάσας τὸ τοῦ πατρὸς μου ὄνομα. ἁρπάσας δὲ τὸν μαργαρίτην ἀπέστρεφον πρὸς τοὺς ἐμοὺς ἀποκομίσας πατέρας. καὶ ἀποδυσάμενος τὸ ῥυπαρὸν ἔνδυμα ἐν τῇ αὐτῶν κατέλειψα χώρᾳ, ηὔθυνον δὲ αὐτὸ καὶ τὴν ὁδὸν πρὸς τὸ φῶς τῆς κατὰ ἀνατολὴν πατρίδος.

καὶ εὗρον καθ' ὁδὸν διαιροῦσάν με· αὐτὴ δέ, ὥσπερ φωνῇ χρησαμένη ἀνέστησεν ὑπνωθέντα με, καὶ ὡδήγησέν με τῷ παρ' αὐτῆς φωτί. ἔστιν γὰρ ὅτε ἡ ἀπὸ σηρικῶν ἐσθὴς βασιλικὴ πρὸ τῶν ἐμῶν ὀφθαλμῶν. ἀγούσης δέ με καὶ ἑλκούσης τῆς στοργῆς τὴν Λαβύρινθον παρῆλθον· καὶ καταλείψας ἐπ' ἀριστερὰ τὴν Βαβυλῶνα εἰς τὴν Μεσήνην ἀφικόμην τὴν μεγάλην οὖσαν παραλίαν.

οὐκ ἐμνημόνευον δὲ τῆς λαμπρότητός μου· παῖς γὰρ ὢν ἔτι καὶ κομιδῇ νέος κατελελοίπειν αὐτὴν ἐν τοῖς τοῦ πατρὸς βασιλείοις· ἐξαίφνης δὲ ἰδόντος μου τὴν ἐσθῆτα ὡς ἐν ἐσόπτρῳ ὁμοιωθεῖσαν, καὶ ὅλον ἐμαυτὸν ἐπ' αὐτὴν ἐθεασάμην, καὶ ἔγνων καὶ εἶδον δι' αὐτῆς ἐμαυτόν, ὅτι κατὰ μέρος διῃρήμεθα ἐκ τοῦ αὐτοῦ ὄντες, καὶ πάλιν ἓν ἐσμεν διὰ μορφῆς μιᾶς.

62–63 *Λαβυρινθίους*] conj Poirier : *Λαβυρίνθους* ms
65 *ἀνωρμησάμην*] conj Bonnet : *ἀνερμησάμην* ms
70 *ἐπᾴσμασιν*] conj Bonnet : *ἐφ' ἅρμασιν* ms.
80 *Λαβύρινθον*] cod (Poirier) : *Βαβύρινθον* cod (Bonnet, conj *Λαβύρινθον*)
81 *Μεσήνην*] conj Bonnet : *Μέσον* ms

The king, like an ambassador, authorized it with a seal, on account of those perverse Babylonians and tyrannical Labyrinthine demons.

At the letter's sound and impression I jolted up from sleep, and I started reading it, after I'd picked it up and kissed it. It had been written about what was recorded in my heart, and I was reminded, at that moment, that I was the son of kings, and that my freedom was missing my family.

I also remembered the pearl that I'd been sent down to Egypt for, and I came to that terrifying snake-dragon with spells and I subdued it by reciting my father's name over it. I snatched the pearl and, carrying it away, I started heading back to my parents. I took off the filthy clothes I'd been wearing and left them in Egypt, and now directed my way toward the light of my homeland back east.

Down the road, I found something picking me up: just like it woke me with a voice when I was asleep, so it guided me with the light around it, since the royal silk outfit was then before my eyes. With affection leading and pulling me along, I passed by Labyrinth. I left Babylon behind on my left and reached Mesene, the big city by the sea.

I didn't remember my splendor, since I was still just a boy and pretty young when I had left it behind in my father's palace, but all of a sudden, when I saw the outfit like something in a mirror, I gazed upon my entire self in it. I both knew and saw myself through it, since we are each distinct from the other, and yet we are one through a single form.

οὐ μὴν ἀλλὰ καὶ αὐτοὺς τοὺς ταμειούχους τοὺς τὴν ἐσθῆτα κομίσαντες ἑώρων δύο, μορφὴ δὲ μία ἐπ' ἀμφοτέρων, ἓν σύμβολον βασιλικὸν ἐν ἀμφοτέροις ἔκειτο· τὸ δὲ χρῆμα καὶ τὸν πλοῦτον ἐν χερσὶν εἶχον, καὶ ἀπεδίδουν μοι τιμήν· καὶ τὴν ἐσθῆτα τὴν εὐπρεπεστάτην, ἥτις ἐν φαιδροῖς χρώμασιν χρυσῷ πεποίκιλτο καὶ λίθοις τιμίοις καὶ μαργαρίταις χροιᾷ πρεπούσῃ· ἵδρυντο ἐν ὕψει· καὶ ἡ εἰκὼν τοῦ τῶν βασιλέων βασιλέως ὅλη δι' ὅλης· λίθοις σαμπφειρίνοις ἐν ὕψει ἐπεπήγεισαν ἁρμοδίως.

§113 ἑώρων δὲ αὖθις ὅτι δι' ὅλων κινήσεις ἐξεπέμποντο γνώσεως, καὶ ἦν ἑτοίμη ἀφεῖναι λόγον· ἤκουον δὲ αὐτῆς ὁμιλούσης·

> ἐγώ εἰμι ἐκείνου τῶν πάντων ἀνθρώπων ἀνδρειοτάτου οὗ ἕνεκεν παρ' αὐτῷ τῷ πατρὶ ἐνεγράφην·

καὶ αὐτὸς δὲ ᾐσθόμην αὐτοῦ τῆς ἡλικίας. αἱ δὲ κινήσεις αἱ βασιλικαὶ πᾶσαι ἐπανεπαύοντό μοι αὐξανούσης πρὸς ταύτης ὁρμάς· ἔσπευδεν ἐκ χειρὸς αὐτοῦ ὀρεγομένη ἐπὶ τὸν δεχόμενον αὐτήν.

κἀμὲ ὁ πόθος διήγειρεν ὁρμῆσαι εἰς ὑπάντησιν αὐτοῦ καὶ δέξασθαι αὐτήν ἐκταθεὶς ἄνθῃ χρωμάτων ἐκοσμήθην, καὶ τὴν στολὴν μου τὴν βασιλικὴν ὑπερέχουσαν ἐστολισάμην δι' ὅλου· ἐνδυσάμενος δὲ ἤρθην εἰς χώραν εἰρήνης σεβάσματος· καὶ τὴν κεφαλὴν κλίνας προσεκύνησα τοῦ πατρὸς τὸ φέγγος τοῦ ἀποστείλαντός μοι ταύτην, ὅτι ἐγὼ μὲν ἐποίησα τὰ προσταχθέντα καὶ αὐτὸς ὁμοίως ὅπερ κατεπηγγείλατο· καὶ ἐν ταῖς θύραις τοῦ βασιλικοῦ τοῦ ἐξ ἀρχῆς αὐτοῦ κατεμειγνύμην. ἥσθη δὲ ἐπ' ἐμοὶ καὶ εἰσεδέξατό με μετ' αὐτοῦ ἐν τοῖς βασιλείοις· πάντες δὲ οἱ ὑπήκοοι αὐτοῦ εὐφήμοις φωναῖς ὑμνοῦσιν· ὑπέσχετο δέ μοι καὶ εἰς τὰς τοῦ βασιλέως θύρας σὺν αὐτῷ ἀποσταλεῖσθαι, ἵνα μετὰ τῶν ἐμῶν δώρων καὶ τοῦ μαργαρίτου ἅμα αὐτῷ φαινώμεθα τῷ βασιλεῖ.

---

95 βασιλέως] conj Bonnet : βασιλεὺς ms

Not only that, but I watched two treasurers themselves bring the outfit, both of them with a single form and a single royal mark between them. They had money and riches in their hands, they rendered me honor, and handed over the most beautiful outfit, which had been embroidered in bright colors with gold, valuable gems, and pearls of beautiful hue, all situated above. The image of the king of kings runs completely through the whole thing. Up high they had fastened it proportionately with sapphires.

I watched anew as impulses of knowledge were flowing throughout all of it, and it was ready to make an utterance, and I heard it speaking:

> I belong to the bravest of all people, which is why I was
> inscribed by the father himself.

And even I myself perceived his stature, and all the royal impulses were coming to rest on me as it grew with this surge: it rushed from his hand, stretching out to be taken.

Desire prompted me to rush to meet him and take it. Once I reached out, I was adorned with a full bloom of colors and entirely decked out in excellent royal attire. Clothed like this, I was lifted into the region of solemn peace. I bowed my head and worshipped the splendor of my father who had sent it to me, because I had done what I was told to, and he likewise had done the very thing he'd promised. I was re-assimilated at the gates of the palace, the same one that was there at the beginning. He was pleased with me, and he welcomed me into his presence in the palace, with all his subjects singing with beautiful voices. He also promised me I would be sent to the king's gates together with him, so that, with my gifts and pearl, we might appear together before the king himself.

3.3 The Byzantine Retelling and English Translation

οἵ τε ἐν τῇ φρουρᾷ ἅπαντες προσπεσόντες ἐδέοντο εὔξασθαι καὶ ὑπὲρ αὐτῶν· ὁ δὲ καθάπερ ἔνθους γενόμενος καὶ οἷα τραγῳδίαν τινὰ ἐξυφαίνων τοιοῖσδε λόγοις ἐξέθετο παραβολικῶς καὶ διέγραψε τὴν ἀνθρωπίνην εὐγένειαν, τὸν πλοῦτον τῶν χαρισμάτων ὃν ἐκ θεοῦ εἴληφεν, τὴν ἐκ ῥᾳθυμίας αὐτῶν καὶ παραβάσεως ἔκπτωσιν, τὰς διὰ τῶν θείων γραφῶν παραινέσεις, τὴν ἐκ δαιμόνων ἐπίθεσιν, τὴν διὰ μετανοίας ἀνάκλησιν, τὴν τοῦ βαπτίσματος χάριν καὶ αὖθις ἀποκατάστασιν, ἑαυτὸν ὑποθεὶς τῆς ἀνθρωπότητος πρόσωπον, καί φησιν·

υἱὸς γέγονα βασιλέως· στολῇ κεκόσμημαι χρυσοπάστῳ· θησαυρὸς ἐπεδόθη μοι θαυμαστός, οἷον προσῆκεν βασιλέας τοῖς τέκνοις χαρίζεσθαι· χρυσὸς ἦν καὶ ἄργυρος οὗτος καὶ λίθοι τῶν διαφανῶν καὶ τιμίων, ἡ δὲ τούτων ὁλκὴ κούφη καὶ ἀβαρὴς καὶ ῥᾴστη μόνῳ κουφίζεσθαι τῷ λαβόντι·[...] ᾧ πᾶς ἄλλος ὑπείκει καὶ διαπέφευγε σίδηρος.ἐφ' οἷς συνθέσθαι διησφαλίσατό μοι μὴ ἐκλαθέσθαι τῶν δωρεῶν καὶ τοῦ φύσαντος Αἴγυπτον διιόντα ποιητικῶς φάναι δολιχὴν ὁδὸν ἀργαλέην τε, ἀφ' ἧς κεκομικέναι ἀπέσταλμαι τὸν πολύτιμον μαργαρίτην δράκοντι κατ' αὐτὴν δεινῷ καλυπτόμενον, ὡς ἂν κἀκεῖνον ἔχων τῆς πρώτης στολῆς ἐπικόσμησιν τῆς πρότερας αὖθις ἀξιωθείην υἱότητος. τούτοις συνθέμενος καὶ δυσὶ συνταχθεὶς ὁδηγοῖς τὴν ἐξ ἀνατολῶν ἡλίου πρὸς δύσιν ἰοῦσαν πορείαν ἐστάλην.

ἀφικόμενος δὲ διὰ τῆς Βαβυλωνίων καὶ Λαβυρίνθου εἰς Αἴγυπτον πρὸς τῷ φωλεῷ τοῦ δράκοντος καταλέλυκα ὃς τὸν ἐπιζητούμενον μαργαρίτην περιεκάθητο. τοῦτον παρεφύλασσον ἀφυπνῶσαι, ὅπως αὐτὸς ἀκονιτὶ τοῦτον ἀφέλωμαι ὃν αὐτὸς φθόνῳ κατέχωσεν.εἶχον δ' ἐκεῖ καὶ τὸν ἐξ ἀνατολῶν μοι κατὰ γένος προσήκοντα τοῦ ἔργου συλλήπτορα, ὅς μοι ἀεὶ συμπαρῆν καὶ συνεβούλευεν τοὺς Αἰγυπτίους παραφυλλάττεσθαι καὶ τῆς αὐτῶν ζύμης καὶ τοῦ φυράματος.

3.3 The Byzantine Retelling and English Translation

Everyone in the prison fell down before him and asked him to pray for them, too, and he, as if becoming divinely inspired and weaving together a tragedy, and in the following phrases he symbolically depicted and described human nobility, the wealth of gifts they have received from God, the fall that came from their indifference and transgression, the advice of holy scripture, attacks from demons, the recalling that comes through repentance, the grace of baptism, and a future restoration, having put himself in the role of humanity. He says:

I was a king's son. I was decoratively dressed in an outfit inlaid with gold. I was given an amazing treasury, the kind that kings typically gift their children with: gold and silver, together with exquisite translucent gemstones – but the weight was light and not at all heavy, easy for just one person to take and it still feel light – [...], which everything else yields to, and iron avoids. By putting everything together for me, he made sure I wouldn't forget these gifts and my progenitor as I passed through Egypt, "a long and troublesome trip" (to use poetic language), on which I had been dispatched to get the priceless pearl, hidden down there by a fearsome snake-dragon, so that, because I held it to be the crowning ornament of my first outfit, I might once again become worthy of my former sonship. Set up with these things and assigned two guides, I was sent on the journey that goes east to west.

Reaching Egypt through Babylonian country and Labyrinth, I lodged by the lair of the snake-dragon that was sitting by the missing pearl. I was careful not to wake it, so that, without a fight, I myself could relieve it of the pearl that it had jealously covered up. An accomplice in the task was there with me, someone from the east and belonging to my family: he was always at my side and was counseling me to beware the Egyptians' leaven and dough.

ἀλλ᾿ οἱ δεινοὶ τῷ ὄντι Αἰγύπτιοι καὶ πέρα δεινότητος δόλῳ συνέμειξαν καὶ τέχνῃ παρέκλιναν καὶ τῆς τροφῆς αὐτῶν ἀπογεύσασθαι ὑπηγάγοντο· καὶ γευσάμενος, φεῦ μοι, τῆς ἄνωθεν εὐγενείας ἠλόγησα καὶ τὴν βασιλέως ἐπελαθόμην υἱότητα, καὶ τῷ αὐτῶν ἐδούλευσα βασιλεῖ, μακρὰ χαίρειν εἰπὼν τῇ φροντίδι τοῦ μαργαρίτου ὃν ἀνελέσθαι ἀπέσταλμαι.

τῷ βάρει γὰρ τῆς βρώσεως ἐκείνης κατενεχθεὶς καὶ ὕπνῳ καρωθεὶς θανάτου γείτονι τὸν τῆς Ἀνατολῆς ἄρχοντα καὶ τοὺς ὑπασπιστὰς αὐτοῦ οἳ τῆς Παρθίας κατάρχουσι παρελύπησα· οἵ γε καὶ δι᾿ ἐπιστολῆς τὰ δόξαντα διεσήμηναν ὧδέ πως ἔχοντα·

> πατὴρ καὶ βασιλεὺς βασιλέων καὶ μήτηρ ἡ τὴν Ἀνατολὴν κατέχουσα καὶ ἀδελφοὶ ἐξ αὐτῶν τὴν γένεσιν ἔχοντες τῷ ἐν Αἰγύπτῳ υἱῷ ἡμῶν καὶ ἀδελφῷ εἰρήνη. ἀνάνηψον, ἀνάστηθι, πόρρω στῆθι τῆς Αἰγυπτίων σκαιότητος καὶ σωτηρίων ῥημάτων ἐπάκουσον. υἱὸς ὢν μνήσθητι βασιλέως καὶ δούλειον ἕλκειν αἰδέσθητι ζυγὸν ἐπαυχένιον· μνήσθητι τοῦ πολυτίμου ὃν ἀπώλεσας μαργαρίτου δι᾿ ὃν παροδεῦσαι τὴν Αἴγυπτον κατελήλυθας. ἀντιποιήθητι τῆς πατρικῆς ἐσθῆτος τῆς χρυσοπάστου, καὶ τὴν εἰδεχθῆ ταύτην καὶ ἄμορφον τῶν Αἰγυπτίων ἀπόρριψον, καὶ τὸν μαργαρίτην ἀναληψάμενος δεῦρ᾿ ἀνάβηθι καὶ τοῖς ἀδελφοῖς τῶν ἄνω βασιλείων συμμέτοχος γένοιο.

Αὕτη ἡ ἐπιστολὴ φῶς γέγονεν ἐν ἐμοὶ καὶ πῦρ, καὶ τὸ ἐνόν μοι ζώπυρον ὥσπερ ἀνάψασα εἰς ὕψος ἦρεν καὶ ἀετοῦ δίκην ἀνῇξεν ὥσπερ ὑπόπτερον. ἐγκολπωσάμενος δὲ ταύτην καὶ ἀσπασάμενος ἐν μνήμῃ γέγονα τῶν προτέρων ἁπάντων, τοῦ γένους, τῆς υἱοτάτης, τῶν κόσμων, τῶν θησαυρῶν, τοῦ πολυτίμου καὶ ἀπαραβλήτου ἐκείνου μαργαρίτου δι᾿ ὃν ἡ ἀποδημία.

καὶ μνησθεὶς ἐπεστράφην, καὶ ἐπιστραφεὶς ἀντῆρα καὶ ἀντεπῆλθον τῷ πονηρῷ ἐκείνῳ δράκοντι, ἐπῳδαῖς τε καὶ θείοις κατακηλήσας ἐπᾴσμασι καταδαρθεῖν πέπεικα, καὶ οὕτω τὸν

60 πονηρῷ] προτέρῳ (!) Bonnet

But the Egyptians – genuinely crafty, and beyond craftiness in trickery – had me join them, cunningly diverted me, and seduced me into sampling their food. And once I tried it – dammit! – I disregarded the nobility from above and I forgot my kingly sonship: I became a servant to their king, bidding farewell in my mind to the pearl that I'd been sent to take away.

Dragged down by the weight of their food and plunged into sleep, death's neighbor, I grieved the leader of the east, and his shield-bearers who rule Parthia, and in a letter they told me their thoughts, as follows:

> Your father and king of kings, your mother, who rules the east, and your siblings, who owe their existence to them, to our son and brother in Egypt: greetings! Come to your senses, get up, and stay far away from the Egyptians' crookedness! Listen to words that'll save you! Remember that you are a king's son, and be ashamed to pull the yoke of slavery that's on your neck! Remember the priceless pearl you lost, which you came down for to Egypt for a while! Lay claim to your paternal gold-inlaid clothing, and throw away the Egyptians' ugly, misshapen clothes, and once you reclaim the pearl, come back home, so you might be a partner with your siblings in the palace above.

This letter became a light and a fire within me, and as if it were lit on fire, it lifted up the spark inside me, and it darted up like an eagle, like something with wings. Once I'd put the letter into my pocket and kissed it, I came to the recollection of everything from before: my people, sonship, decorative furnishings, treasures, that priceless and incomparable pearl, the reason I was away from home.

After I remembered all this, I turned around, and when I did, I rose up and marched against that evil snake-dragon. I recited charms and divine spells over it and lulled it to sleep, and this is how I stole the

μαργαρίτην ὑφήρπασα καὶ πρὸς τὸν πατέρα ὑπέστρεφον. ὁ δὲ ἡσθεὶς ὡς οὐκ ἄλλοτε οὔτε τὴν βραδυτῆτα προέφερεν καὶ τῇ πρώτῃ στολῇ κατημφίασε καὶ τοῖς βασιλείοις αὐτοῖς ἀποδέδωκεν ταῖς ἐν αὐτοῖς ἀγλαΐαις καὶ δωρεαῖς ἀϊδίως εὐφραίνεσθαι.

οὕτως, τοῖς παραβολικοῖς τούτοις ῥήμασιν εἴπερ ἔφθην, ὁ θεοφόρος ἀπόστολος τὸ εὖ γεγονὸς τοῦ κατ' εἰκόνα γένους διαγραψάμενος τὸν ἄφθονον πλοῦτον τῶν ὧν προσείληφε χαρισμάτων, τὰ νοητὰ ὅπλα οἷς πρὸς τοὺς νοητοὺς Αἰγυπτίους παρατετάγμεθα καὶ πρὸς τὸν ἐκείνων ἀρχηγόν τε καὶ πρόμαχον δράκοντα, τὰς ἐπιθέσεις αὐτῶν, τοὺς δόλους, τὰ φάρμακα, τὴν ἐκεῖθεν πτῶσιν τῶν αὐτοῖς πειθομένων, τὴν δι' αὐτὴν ἔκπτωσιν τοῦ θείου πλούτου, τὴν χρόνιον ὑπὸ τῶν ἁμαρτιῶν κάκωσιν, ἣν ὁ ὕπνος καὶ κάρος αἰνίττεται, τὴν εὐσπλαγχνίαν τὴν ἄνωθεν, τὴν διὰ τῶν θείων γραφῶν ὥσπερ ἐξ ἐπιστολῆς χορηγουμένην ἀντίληψιν, ἀφ' ἧς ἡ ἐπιστροφή, ἡ ἀνάνηψις, ὁ τοῦ βαπτίσματος φωτισμός, δι' οὗ καὶ τὸν πολύτιμον μαργαρίτην ἀπολαμβάνομεν, πρὸς τούτοις καὶ τὴν εὐφροσύνην τοῦ θεοῦ καὶ πατρὸς καὶ τῶν περὶ αὐτὸν θείων δυνάμεων, ἣν τῇ ἐπιστροφῇ καὶ τῇ ἀνακλήσει τῶν πεπτωκότων πεποίηται δηλαδὴ καθυπέδειξε, τέλος τὴν ἐπίτευξιν τῶν αἰωνίων γερῶν ἃ ἡτοίμασεν ὁ θεὸς τοῖς πρὸς αὐτὸν ὁλοσχερῶς ἐπιστρέφουσι, τούτοις τὸ περιδεὲς καὶ ἀμφίγνωμον τῶν ἡμετέρων ἀναρρώσας ψυχῶν καὶ διδάξας ὡς οἷόν τε καὶ ἡμᾶς τοῖς τρόποις τούτοις ἀναβιώσκειν, τοὺς νεκροὺς ἤδη γεγενημένους τοῖς ἁμαρτήμασιν, αἰωνίαν παράκλησιν οὐ μόνον τοῖς ἐν τῇ εἱρκτῇ τότε ἀλλὰ καὶ πᾶσι τοῖς δι' αἰῶνος ὀλιγοψύχοις κατέλιπεν. ἀλλὰ περὶ μὲν οὖν τῆς ἀποστολικῆς θεωρίας ἅλις· ἐπανιτέον δὲ πάλιν ἐπὶ τὴν ἱστορίαν τῶν πράξεων.

80 πεποίηται] πεποίηνται (!) Bonnet

pearl out from under it, and I returned to my father. And he, happier than ever before, didn't bring up my sluggishness, but covered me in my original outfit and restored me entry into the palace itself, forever to enjoy the splendors and gifts there.

In this way, with this figurative language (if indeed I've been successful), the god-carrying apostle, having described the noble birth of the image-bearing race – the bounteous wealth of the gifts that he'd received – the conceptual armor with which we array ourselves against the conceptual Egyptians and against their founder-champion, the snake-dragon – their attacks, tricks, drugs – the fall from there for those won over by them – the falling-away from divine riches – the temporal distress due to sins, which is signified by sleep and slumber – the compassion that comes from above – the perception supplied from the divine scriptures, as if from a letter, from which comes conversion, a coming to your senses, as well as the illumination of baptism, in which we also take back the precious pearl – in addition, also, the good disposition of God the Father and the divine powers around him, which has been brought about by the conversion and restoration of the fallen – all these things he clearly illustrated, and finally, the success of the eternal gifts God prepared for those who completely turn back to him. Having shored up what's timid and doubtful in our souls, and having taught how we're able, through these means, to bring back to life those who are now dead in their sins, he left an eternal exhortation, not only to those then in the prison, but to everyone faint-hearted across eternity. But that's enough for now on the apostle's vision, and we should return again to the narrative of events.

3.4 Greek-English Glossary

α a

ἀβαρής, -ές *abarēs* light, non-heavy
ἀγλαΐα, ἡ *aglaïa* splendor
ἀγνοέω *agnoeō* fail to recognize, be unaware, forget
ἄδαμας, -άντος, ὁ *adamas* adamant, steel
ἀετός, ὁ *aetos* eagle
Αἴγυπτος, ἡ *aiguptos* Egypt
Αἰγύπτιος, -α, -ον *aiguptios* Egyptian
αἰδέομαι *aideomai* be ashamed
ἀϊδίως *aïdiōs* forever, eternally
αἰνίττομαι *ainittomai* hint at, serve as a symbol for
αἴρω *airō* raise, lift
αἰσθάνομαι *aist*^{h}*anomai* perceive, sense, become aware of
ἀκάθαρτος, -ον *akat*^{h}*artos* unclean, impure, dirty
ἀκονιτί *akoniti* w/o effort/struggle, easily
ἄλαλος, -ον *alalos* unable to talk
ἅλις *halis* (it's/that's) enough, sufficient
ἀλλότριος, -α, -ον *allotrios* strange, foreign
ἀλογέω *alogeō* disregard, ignore
ἁμαρτία, ἡ *hamartia* failure, fault, sin
ἄμορφος, -ον *amorp*^{h}*os* misshapen, unsightly
ἀμφίγνωμος, -ον *amp*^{h}*ignōmos* doubtful
ἀναβαίνω *anabainō* go up
ἀναβιώσκω *anabiōskō* bring back to life, revive
ἀναγιγνώσκω *anagignōskō* read
ἀναγράφω *anagrap*^{h}*ō* record, register, describe
ἀναΐσσω *anaïssō* fly upward
ἀνάκλησις, ἡ *anaklēsis* restoration, revival
ἀναλαμβάνω *analambanō* pick up, recover, regain
ἀνάληψις, ἡ *analēp*^{s}*is* recovery, regaining, acquiring
ἀνανήφω *ananēp*^{h}*ō* b/c alert (from sleep), fully awake
ἀνάνηψις, ἡ *ananēp*^{s}*iss* return to one's senses, sobering up
ἀναπαύομαι *anapauomai* be at rest

ἀνάπτω *anaptō* be kindled, lit up (often TR, but INTR here)
ἀναρρώνυμι *anarrōnumi* strengthen
ἀνατολή, ἡ *anatolē* rising (of the sun), also PL; the east
ἀνατολικός, -ή, -όν *anatalolikos* eastern
ἀνδρεῖος, -α, -ον *andreios* strong, vigorous, courages
ἄνθη, ἡ *ant^hē* full bloom
ἀνθρώπινος, -η, -ον *ant^hrōpinos* human (ADJ)
ἀνθρωπότης, ἡ *ant^hrōpotēs* humanity
ἀνίστημι *anistēmi* wake up, get up
ἀντιποιέομαι *antipoieomai* lay claim to, seek out (+ GEN)
ἀνταίρω *antairō* rise against
ἀντεπέρχομαι *anteperk^homai* suddenly meet, encounter
ἀντίληψις, ἡ *antilēp^sis* exchange, receiving in turn
ἀνωρμάομαι *anōrmaomai* jolt upward
ἀξιόω *ak^sioō* make/consider worthy
ἀπαντάω *apantaō* convene, meet together
ἀπαράβλητος, -ον *aparablētos* incomparable
ἄπειρος, -ον *apeiros* inexperienced, not used to s.t.
ἀπογεύομαι *apogeuomai* taste, sample
ἀποδημία, ἡ *apodēmia* being abroad, a long journey
ἀποδίδωμι *apodidōmi* allow, permit
ἀποδύομαι *apoduomai* take off (clothes), strip
ἀποκατάστασις, ἡ *apokatastasis* restoration, return to previous state
ἀποκομίζω *apokomizō* carry back
ἀπολαμβάνω *apolambanō* get back, regain, recover
ἀπόλλυμι *apollumi* lose
ἀπορρίπτω *aporriptō* throw away, toss
ἀποστέλλω *apostellō* send (out, forth), dispatch
ἀποστρέφω *apostrep^hō* return, head back
ἀργαλέος, -α, -ον *argaleos* painful, troublesome
ἄργυρος, ὁ *arguros* silver
ἀριστερός, -ά, -όν *aristeros* left (≠ right)
ἁρμοδίως *harmodiōs* harmoniously
ἁρπάζω *harpazō* grab, snatch, carry off
ἀρχηγός, ὁ *ark^hēgos* founder
ἄσημον, τό *asēmon* silver

ἀσπάζομαι *aspazomai* welcome, greet, kiss, embrace
αὐξάνω *aukˢanō* increase, strengthen
ἀφαιρέομαι *apʰaireomai* deprive s.o. of s.t., take s.t. from s.o. (double ACC)
ἄφθονος, -ον *apʰtʰonos* plentiful, bounteous
ἀφίημι *apʰiēmi* emit, discharge
ἀφικνέομαι *apʰikneomai* reach, arrive
ἀφίστημι *apʰistēmi* leave, part ways
ἀφυπνόω *apʰupnoō* wake up (TR)

β b

Βαβυλών, -ῶνος, ἡ *babulōn* Babylon
Βαβυλώνιος, -α, -ον *babulōnios* Babylonian
βαθύς, -εῖα, -ύ *batʰus* deep
βάρος, τό *baros* weight
βασιλεία, τά *basileia* (PL) palace
βασιλεύς, ὁ *basileus* king
βασιλικόν, τό *basilikon* palace
βασιλικός, -ή, -όν *basilikos* royal, related to the kingdom
βαστάζω *bastazō* carry
βιβλίον, τό *biblion* book, document
βλέπο *blepō* see
βραδύτης, ἡ *bradutēs* sluggishness, slowness
βρέφος, τό *brepʰos* baby, infant
βρῶσις, ἡ *brōsis* food, eating

γ g

γείτων, -ον *geitōn* neighboring, bordering
γένος, τό *genos* family
γέρας, -ως, τό *geras* gift, honor, privilege
γεύομαι *geuomai* taste, sample, eat
γνώμη, ἡ *gnōmē* proposition, intention, motive

γνῶσις, ἡ *gnōsis* knowledge
γράφω *graphō* inscribe, write

δ *d*

δαίμων, -ονος, ὁ *daimōn* demon
δεινός, -ή, -όν *deinos* frightful, scary, terrible; crafty, tricky
δεινότης, ὁ *deinotēs* craftiness, trickery
δέσμιος, ὁ *desmios* prisoner
δηλαδή *dēladē* evidently, naturally
διαγράφω *diagraphō* delineate, describe, list
διαιρέω *diaireō* distinguish, separate
διαίρω *diairō* lift up, raise
διάλιθος, -η, -ον *dialithos* studded, fitted with stones
διανοία, ἡ *dianoia* thought, thinking
διασφαλίζομαι *diasphalizomai* secure firmly
διαφανής, -ές *diaphanēs* translucent, transparent
διαφεύγω *diapheugōi* escape, avoid
διασημαίνω *diasēmainō* clearly signal/indicate
διδάσκω *didaskō* teach
διεγείρω *diegeirō* rouse, stir
δίειμι *dieimi* pass through
διυπνίζω *diupnizō* wake up, rouse (TR)
δολιχός, -ή, -όν *dolikhos* long
δόλος, ὁ *dolos* bait, trick, deceit
δούλειος, -α, -ον *douleios* slave-
δουλεύω *douleuō* serve, be subject to
δουλικός, -ή, -όν *doulikos* slave-
δράκων, -οντος, ὁ *drakōn* giant, epic-sized, snake, "dragon"
δυνάστης, ὁ *dunastēs* ruler, authority
δύσις, ἡ *dusis* setting (of sun), west
δυσχερής, -ές *duskherēs* hard, difficult
δωρεά, ἡ *dōrea* gift, present
δῶρον, τό *dōron* gift, presnt

ϵ *e*

ἐάω *eaō* leave alone
ἐγγράφω *engrap*^{h}*ō* inscribe, engrave
ἐγκολπόομαι *enkolpoomai* put into the folds of one's clothes, pocket
εἰδεχθής, -ές *eidek*^{h}*t*^{h}*ēs* ugly, horrible, detestable
εἰρήνη, ἡ *eirēnē* peace (in a letter-greeting)
εἱρκτή, ἡ *heirktē* prison, enclosure
εἰσδέχομαι *eisdek*^{h}*omai* admit s.o. (into one's presence)
ἔκπτωσις, ἡ *ekptōsis* banishment, loss
ἐκτείνω *ekteinō* stretch out
ἐκτίθεμαι *ektit*^{h}*emai* set forth
ἐξυφαίνω *ek*^{s}*up*^{h}*ainō* weave together
ἐλαφρός, -ά, -όν *elap*^{h}*ros* light (≠ heavy)
ἐλευθερία, ἡ *eleut*^{h}*eria* freedom
ἐλεύθερος, -α, -ον *eleut*^{h}*eros* free
ἕλκω *helkō* pull, drag, draw
ἔμπορος, ὁ *emporos* trader, merchant
ἔνδυμα, τό *enduma* clothing, clothes
ἐνδύω *enduō* clothe | (MID) put on, wear
ἔνθους, -υν *ent*^{h}*ous* divinely inspired
ἔνειμι *eneimi* be in(side)
ἐπαναπαύομαι *epanapauomai* rest on, lie on
ἐπάνειμι *epaneimi* return to, resume
ἔπᾳσμα, τό *epa*$_{i}$*sma* charm, spell, magic formula
ἐπαυχένιος, -ον *epauk*^{h}*enion* on-the-neck, neck-
ἐπιδίδωμι *epididōmi* bestow, give
ἐπιζητέω *epizēteō* wish for, miss, lack
ἐπίθεσις, ἡ *epit*^{h}*esis* attack
ἐπικόσμησις *epikosmēsis* ornament, decoration
ἐπιλανθάνομαι *epilant*^{h}*anomai* forget
ἐπιστολιμαῖος, -α, -ον *epistolimaios* in a letter
ἐπιστροφή, ἡ *epistrop*^{h}*ē* turning around, change, turn, development
ἐπίτευξις, ἡ *epiteuk*^{s}*in* hitting the mark, success
ἐπιτηρέω *epitēreō* keep an eye out for, wait for
ἐπονομάζω *eponomazō* say/recite/pronounce a name over

ἐπῳδή, ἡ *epō$_{i}$dē* spell, charm

ἐσθής, -ῆτος, ἡ *est^{h}ēs* clothes, outfit, piece of clothing

ἔσοπτρον, τό *esoptron* mirror

ἑτοῖμος, -η, -ον *hetoimos* ready, prepared

εὐγενεία, ἡ *eugeneia* being well-born, nobility

εὐθύνω *eut^{h}unō* guide, direct straight

εὔμνηστος, -ον *eumnēstos* mindful, keeping in mind, with good memory

εὐπρεπής, -ές *euprepēs* good-looking

εὐσπλαγχνία, ἡ *eusplank^{h}nia* compassion

εὔφημος, -ον *eup^{h}ēmos* pleasant-sounding

εὐφραίνομαι *eup^{h}rainomai* enjoy, take pleasure in (+ DAT)

εὐφροσύνη, ἡ *eup^{h}rosunē* bliss, happiness, enjoyment

εὐχαρής, -ές *euk^{h}arēs* charming

εὔχομαι *euk^{h}omai* pray

ἐφοδιάζω *ep^{h}odiazō* prepare s.o. for a trip

ζ *z*

ζυγόν, τό *zugon* yoke

ζύμη, ἡ *zumē* leaven

ζώπυρον, τό *zōpuron* spark, flash

η *ē*

ἡγεμών, -όνος, ὁ *hēgemōn* leader, guide

ἥδομαι *hēdomai* be happy, enjoy o.s.

ἡλικία, ἡ *hēlikia* age, size

θ *t^{h}*

θαυμαστός, -ή, -όν *t^{h}aumastos* amazing, mind-blowing

θεάομαι *t^{h}eaomai* gaze at, watch

θησαυρός, ὁ *t*^{h}*ēsauros* treasure, treasury, store
θύραι, αἱ *t*^{h}*urai* (PL) gates

ι *i*

ἱδρύομαι *hidruomai* be seated, sit, be situated, reside
Ἰνδός, -ή, -όν *indos* Indian, from or related to India

κ *k*

καθέζομαι *kat*^{h}*ezomai* sit down
καθυποδείκνυμι *kat*^{h}*upodeiknumi* show clearly, illustrate
κάκωσις, ἡ *kakōsis* distress, suffering
καλέω *kaleō* call (w/ ὄνομα *onoma*), name
καλύπτω *kaluptō* cover, hide, conceal
καρδία, ἡ *kardia* heart, mind
κάρος, ὁ *karos* heavy sleep, drowsiness
καρόω *karoō* plunge into deep sleep
καταγώγιον, τό *katagōgion* residence, inn
καταδαρθάνω *katadart*^{h}*anō* fall asleep
κατακαλέω *katakaleō* summon
καταλείπω *kataleipō* leave behind
καταλύω *kataluō* take up residence, lodge
καταμίγνυμι *katamignumi* mix
καταμφιέννυμι *katamp*^{h}*iennumi* coat, cover s.o.
καταπέμπω *katapempō* send down
καταπονέω *kataponeō* subdue, beat down
καταπότης, ὁ *katapotēs* swallower, gulper
κατάρχω *katark*^{h}*ō* rule (+ GEN)
κατασφραγίζω *katasp*^{h}*ragizō* validate, authenticate w/ a seal
καταφέρω *katap*^{h}*erō* bring down, weigh down
καταφιλέω *katap*^{h}*ileō* kiss
καταχώννυμι *katak*^{h}*ōnnumi* bury, completely cover
κατεπαγγέλλομαι *katepangellomai* pledge, devote

κατέχω kat^{h}*ek*^{h}*ō* hold, possess, occupy
κήρυγμα, τό kērugma message
κῆρυξ, -κος, ὁ kēruk^{s} emissary, herald
κηρύσσω kērussō announce
κίνησις, ἡ kinēsis movement, motion
κοιμάομαι koimaomai sleep
κοινωνία, ἡ koinōnia association, partnership, joint relationship
κοινωνός, ὁ koinōnos companion, comrade, partner
κομιδῇ komidē$_{i}$ quite
κομίζω komizō carry off (as a prize), secure, bring
Κοσάνος, -η, -ον *kosanos* Kushan
κοσμέω kosmeō adorn, decorate
κόσμος, ὁ kosmos ornament, adornment, decoration
κουφίζομαι koup^{h}*izomai* feel light (when carrying something, etc.)
κοῦφος, -η, -ον koup^{h}*os* light (≠ heavy)
κρατέω krateō hold, support, keep, take possession of

λ l

Λαβυρίνθιος, -α, -ον *laburint*^{h}*ios* Labyrinthine, from or related to the Labyrinth (here a place-name)
Λαβύρινθος, ἡ *laburint*^{h}*os* Labyrinth (here a place-name)
λαμπρότης, ἡ lamprotēs splendor, brightness
λίθος, ὁ lit^{h}*os* stone

μ m

μανθάνω mant^{h}*anō* notice, perceive, learn
μαργαρίτης, ὁ margaritēs pearl
μεγιστᾶν, -ᾶνος, ὁ megistan leader, ruler
μεθόρια, τά met^{h}*oria* (PL) borders, territory, region
μέρος, τό meros part
Μεσήνη, ἡ *mesēnē* Mesene
Μεσηνός, -ή, -όν *mesēnos* Mesenian

μετάνοια, ἡ *metanoia* repentance, changing your mind
μνήμη, ἡ *mnēmē* memory
μνημονεύω *mnēmoneuō* remember
μορφή, ἡ *morp^hē* form, shape

ν *n*

νέος, -α, -ον *neos* young
νοητός, -ή, -όν *noētos* mental, intellectual, conceptual
νυστάζω *nustazō* doze off, go to sleep

ξ *k^s*

ξανθός, -ή, -όν *k^sant^hos* yellow, golden, light brown, tawny
ξενίζομαι *k^senizō* b/c (like) a stranger, be treated like a stranger

ο *o*

ὁδεύω *hodeuō* travel
ὁδηγέω *hodēgeō* guide
ὁδηγός, ὁ *hodēgos* guide
ὀλιγόψυχος, -ον *oligop^suk^hos* fainthearted
ὁλκή, ἡ *holkē* weight
ὁλοσχερῶς *holosk^herōs* completely
ὁμιλέω *homileō* speak, talk, converse
ὁμοιόω *homoioō* make s.t. like
ὅπλα, τά *hopla* arms, armor (PL)
ὁπλίζω *hoplizo* equip
ὁράω *oraō* see
ὀρέγομαι *oregomai* stretch, reach, grab
ὁρμάω *hormaō* rush at, start
ὁρμή, ἡ *hormē* onrush, surge, impuse

π *p*

παράβασις, ἡ *parabasis* transgression, overstepping, deviating
παραβολικός, -ή, -όν *parabolikos* figurative, symbolic
παράινεσις, ἡ *parainesis* encouragement, exhortation
παρακελεύομαι *parakeleuomai* urge, recommend, advise
παράκλησις, ἡ *paraklēsis* summons, address, exhortation
παρακλίνω *paraklinō* divert, turn aside
παραλαμβάνω *paralambanō* succeed, follow
παραλυπέω *paralupeō* grieve
παρατάσσομαι *paratassomai* stand side by side (in battle)
παραφυλάσσω *parap^hulassō* watch closely
παράλιος, -α, -ον *paralios* by-the-sea
Παρθία, ἡ *part^hia* Parthia
παροδεύω *parodeuō* pass through
πάσχω *pask^hō* experience, feel suffer, undergo
πατρικός, -ή, -όν *patrikos* related to or derived from one's father
πατρίς, -ίδος, ἡ *patris* homeland, home country
πείθω *peit^hō* persuade
περιδεής, -ές *perideēs* very afraid, timid
περικάθημαι *perikat^hēmai* sit around
πήγνυμι *pēgnumi* fix, set, fasten
πλοῦτος, ὁ *ploutos* wealth, riches
πόθος, ὁ *pot^hos* longing, desire
ποιητικῶς *poiētikōs* poetically, by quoting a poet
ποικίλλω *poikillō* embroider
πολύτιμος, -ον *polutimos* expensive, pricey, highly prized, precious
πονηρός, -ά, -όν *ponēros* bad, worthless, malicious, fiendish, degenerate
πορεία, ἡ *poreia* trip, journey, travel
πρεσβεύτης, ὁ *presbeutēs* agent, ambassador, legate
πρόμαχος, ὁ *promak^hos* champion
προσεύχομαι *proseuk^homai* pray
προσήκω *prosēkō* belong to, be right/suitable for
προσκυνέω *proskuneō* bow down in reverence to/before
πρόσωπον, τό *prosōpon* dramatic role, character

προσπίπτω *prospiptō* fall forward, fall down
προστάσσω *prostassō* command, order
πρόφασις, ἡ *prop^hasis* pretext, occasion, cause, suggestion, motive
προφέρω *prop^herō* bring up, allege, cite (as a problem/issue)
πρωτεύω *prōteuō* be first, hold first position
πτῶσις, ἡ *ptōsis* fall

ρ *r^h*

ῥᾳθυμία, ἡ *r^hat^humia* indifference, neglect, ignoring
ῥᾷστος, -η, -ον *r^haistos* SUP of ῥᾴδιος, -α, -ον *r^haidios* easy
ῥυπαρός, -ά, -όν *r^huparos* dirty, filthy

σ *s*

σαμπφείρινος, -η, -ον *sampp^heirinos* sapphire (ADJ)
σέβασμα, τό *sebasma* reverence, awe
σημαίνω *sēmainō* indicate, signal
σηρικός, -ή, -όν *sērikos* silk (ADJ)
σίδηρος, ὁ *sidēros* iron
σκαιότης, ἡ *skaiotēs* stupidity, awkwardness, crookedness
σπεύδω *speudō* hurry
στέλλω *stellō* send; PASS set out (on a journey)
στέργω *stergō* feel affection for, love
στολή, ἡ *stolē* clothes, garment, robe
στολίζω *stolizō* dress s.o.
στοργή, ἡ *storgē* affection, love
συγγενής, -ές *sungenēs* related
συγγίγνομαι *sungignomai* associate with, join
συλλήπτωρ, -ορος, ὁ *sullēptōr* accomplice, assistant
σύμβολον, τό *sumbolon* token, mark, seal, ID
συμβολεύω *sumboleuō* counsel
συμμέτοχος, ὁ *summetok^hos* partner, associate
συμμίγνυμι *summignumi* mix together

συμπάρειμι *sumpareimi* be present w/, stand by, assist
σύμφωνα, τά *sump^{h}ōna* (PL) agreement, pact
συνοδεύω *sunodeuō* travel together
συνόμιλος, -ον *sunomilos* partner, associate
συντίθημι *suntit^{h}ēmi* put together, construct
σχῆμα, τό *sk^{h}ēma* appearance, air, vibe

τ t

ταμειοῦχος, ὁ *tameiouk^{h}os* curator, administrator
τέλος, τό *telos* power, authority
τέχνη, ἡ *tek^{h}nē* cunning, craft
τιμή, ἡ *timē* honor, dignity
τίμιος, -α, -ον *timios* prized, valued, expensive, costly
τραγῳδία, ἡ *tragō$_i$dia* solemn song/poetry
τρόπος, ὁ *tropos* way, manner
τροφεύς, ὁ *trop^{h}eus* attendant, rearer, guardian
τροφή, ἡ *trop^{h}ē* food
τρυφή, ἡ *trup^{h}ē* luxury
τυραννικός, -ή, -όν *turannikos* despotic, tyrannical

υ u

υἱότης, ἡ *huiotēs* sonship, being someone's son
ὑμνέω *humneō* sing
ὑπάγω *hupagō* lead, draw, seduce
ὑπάντησις, ἡ *hupantēsis* encounter, meeting
ὑπαστπιστής, ὁ *hupaspistēs* shield-bearer, armed with a shield
ὑπείκω *hupeikō* yield
ὑπεισέρχομαι *hupeiserk^{h}omai* (gradually, slowly) assume, take on
ὑπερέχω *huperek^{h}ō* be above
ὑπήκοος, ὁ *hupēkoos* subject, subordinate
ὑπισχνέομαι *hupisk^{h}neomai* promise
ὑπνόομαι *hupnoomai* be asleep
ὕπνος, ὁ *hupnos* sleep

ὑπομιμνήσκομαι *hupomimnēskomai* remember
ὑπόπτερος, -ον *hupopteros* winged
ὑποστρέφω *hupostrep^{h}ō* return
ὑποτίθημι *hupotit^{h}ēmi* propose, suggest, present
ὑφαιρέω *hup^{h}aireō* steal out from under, filch
ὑφαρπάζω *hup^{h}arpazō* take from under, steal, filch away
ὕψος, τό *hup^{s}os* height, high position

φ *p^{h}*

φαιδρός, -ά, -όν *p^{h}aidros* bright, vibrant, gleaming
φαίνομαι *p^{h}ainomai* appear
φάρμακον, τό *p^{h}armakon* drug
φέγγος, τό *p^{h}engos* luster, sheen, brightness
φθάνω *p^{h}t^{h}anō* do first, arrive first
φθόνος, ὁ *p^{h}t^{h}onos* envy
φοβερός, -ά, -όν *p^{h}oberos* scary, frightening
φορήματα, τά *p^{h}orēmata* (PL) clothes
φόρτος, ὁ *p^{h}ortos* load, cargo
φυλάσσω *p^{h}ulassō* (MID) be on guard, beware
φροντίς, -ίδος, ἡ *p^{h}rontis* thought, care, attention
φρουρά, ἡ *p^{h}roura* guard, prison
φύραμα, τό *p^{h}urama* dough
φύω *p^{h}uō* produce, "beget"
φωλεός, ὁ *p^{h}ōleos* lair
φωτισμός, ὁ *p^{h}ōtismos* illumination

χ *k^{h}*

χαίρω *k^{h}airō* say "goodbye" | μακρὰ χαίρειν λέγω *makra k^{h}airein legō* dismiss from one's mind, completely ignore, renounce
χαλκεδόνιον, τό *k^{h}alkedonion* chalcedony (a mineral)
χαρίζομαι *k^{h}arizomai* graciously give
χάρις, ἡ *k^{h}aris* grace, gracious gift, gracious treatment

χάρισμα, τό *k*^{h}*arisma* favor
χορηγέω *k*^{h}*orēgeō* supply, furnish
χράομαι *k*^{h}*raomai* use (+ DAT)
χροιά, ἡ *k*^{h}*roia* surface, color
χρυσόπαστος, -η, -ον *k*^{h}*rusopastos* covered/inlaid/decorated with gold
χρυσός, ὁ *k*^{h}*rusos* gold
χρῆμα, τό *k*^{h}*rēma* money
χρῶμα, τό *k*^{h}*rōma* color
χώρα, ἡ *k*^{h}*ōra* region, country

ψ *p*^{s}

ψαλμός, ὁ *p*^{s}*almos* song

ω *ō*

ὡραῖος, -α, -ον *hōraios* attractive, in bloom, ripe

4 Commentary

1 **When I was just a little child** The narrator-traveler-prince is the subject and focus of the poem: it's he who tells the story, and it's his experiences and point-of-view we get throughout. The protagonist starts the story very young, and "does not seem to age" and "appears to go away and come back still in adolescence" – something Russell considers un-epic.[16] Joseph Campbell could have cited the prince's story as an instance of the monomyth: as Kuehn says, "The prince is represented not only in the traditional guise of a hero on a quest, but also as a seeker on a spiritual journey."[17]

The poem begins with a time marker, "when," and sets the stage during the narrator's childhood. The beginning of The Who's "Pinball Wizard" comes to mind: "Ever since I was a young boy ..." (Pete Townsend). In *Perle*, the Pearl-daughter says of the time she departed, "I was very young, at a tender age."[18]

As an indication that Ephrem might've known *The Pearlsong*, Adam[19] notes that a poem attributed to him – an attribution that's in doubt – has the phrase *men pum šaḇrē w-yalluḏē* instead of the Old Syriac (Curetonianus) phraseology of Matthew 21:16, *men pumå ḏa-ṭlåyē wa-ḏ-yalluḏē*. (The Peshitta has the same as the Old Syriac, while the seventh-century Harqlean revision has *men pumå ḏ-šaḇrē wa-ḏ-yånoqē*.) Whether or not this short poem is from Ephrem, the phrasing used is hardly proof that the poet knew *The Pearlsong*. The strange thing about *The Pearlsong*'s language here is not the vocabulary, or even the combination of the two synonyms, but that they're in the absolute state; *none* of

[16] Russell, "Epic," 75-77.

[17] *Dragon*, 203.

[18] 412: "I watȝ ful ȝong & tender of age."

[19] *Psalmen*, 75.

the double-lexeme versions of Matthew 21:16 given above are in the absolute, and neither is the pseudo-Ephrem line.

royally in my father's palace The prince recalls high living in kingly quarters. Here and twice more in the poem, the narrator uses this phrase, "my father's palace" (lines 61 and 75). A prince's reference to "my father's palace" may seem unremarkable enough at first glance, but the specific phrase has a long pedigree. A king called Bar Rakib, for example, uses <byt ʔby> in two eighth-century BCE inscriptions in Old Aramaic: "my family labored more than everyone ... I took possession of my father's palace and made it better than any palace the great kings have."[20] And again: "the gods of my father's palace."[21] Several centuries later, Jesus uses the same expression when he refers to his father's "many mansions" (John 14:2). Both the Old Syriac (Sinaiticus) and the Peshitta have *bēṯ ʔåḇ*, as here.[22]

My parents outfitted me and sent me off It's not the prince's 3
own decision to go to Egypt, and he doesn't just leave on a whim. Rather, he's dispatched by his parents, just as Hibil-Ziwa is dispatched by Manda aḏ-Heyyī (Manda of Life) in the Mandaic text that bears the former's name. "May there be for me, Hibil-Ziwa, thanks to the clemency of Life, a helper of Great-Life, since it was your will that I've traveled to the dark place."[23]

the East, our country In the famous words of eden ahbez, ("Nature Boy"): "There was a boy // A very strange enchanted boy // They say he wandered very far, very far // Over land and sea." The narrator-

---

[20]KAI 216/Bar-Rakib I 7-8, 11-14: 𐤅𐤁𐤉𐤕 · 𐤀𐤁𐤉 · 𐤏𐤌𐤋 · 𐤌𐤍 · 𐤊𐤋 ... 𐤅𐤀𐤇𐤆𐤕 · 𐤁𐤉𐤕 · 𐤀𐤁𐤉 · 𐤅𐤄𐤉𐤈𐤁𐤕𐤄 · 𐤌𐤍 · 𐤁𐤉𐤕 · 𐤇𐤃 · 𐤌𐤋𐤊𐤍 · 𐤓𐤁𐤓𐤁𐤍
<wbyt ʔby ʕml mn kl ... wʔḥzt byt ʔby whyṭbth mn byt ḥd mlkn rbrbn>.

[21]KAI 217/Bar-Rakib II 3: 𐤅𐤀𐤋𐤄𐤉 · 𐤁𐤉𐤕 · 𐤀𐤁𐤉 <wʔlhy byt ʔby>.

[22]Text in Kiraz, *Comparative Edition* 4, 264.

[23]*Baptism of Hibil-Ziwa* 1.57-58:

[illegible]

[illegible]

men aṯyābūṯa aḏ-heyyī tihwī al-Hibil Ziwa ašganda aḏ-heyyī rabbī aḏ-ab-ṣoḇyān-ḵon asgīt al-aṯar ahšuḵ.

Note, however, that at times in *The Baptism of Hibil-Ziwa*, the *uṯras* Manda aḏ-Heyyī and Hibil-Ziwa seem to be the same, at other times, to be father and son, respectively.

prince, "the intrepid traveler,"[24] names several places in the course of the story, starting here. The prince refers to his homeland with ܡܬܐ *måṯå* "country, homeland." The lexeme enters Aramaic languages from Akkadian *mātu* "land, country, region," more specifically "home country, native land."[25] Akkadian phrases with *mātu* and a possessive suffix may simply be translated by the adverbial "home," as in *kīma ina mātini nittallak ḫabullini nušallime* "as soon as we go home we will pay our debt," where *ina mātini* "to our homeland" ≈ "home." Outside of Syriac, the word is known in Aramaic also in JBA, where it's generally "town" (less "region"), and in Mandaic, where it may mean "town, city," but also "territory."[26] In Syriac, it's a bit less usual of a term, as noted already by Nöldeke, but its meaning in *The Pearlsong* is clear.[27]

"The East" is the prince's preferred way to refer to his royal homeland, with "Parthia" occurring just once. A geographically rich Manichaean text in Coptic also juxtaposes the East and Parthia:

> The lord Zarathustra came to Persia, to King Hystaspes;[28] he then revealed the law-established-in-truth in Persia. The Lord Buddha, the wise, the blessed, came to the land of India and of Kushans; he then revealed the law-established-in-truth in all of India and Kushan. After him, Aurentes and Pkedellos[29] came to the east; they then revealed the law-established-in-truth in the east, the center of the world, and Parthia; he revealed the law of the truth in all of these places. After that, Jesus Christ came in the Roman west to the land of all the west.[30]

[24] Ken Babbs' phrase in Tom Wolfe, *The Electric Kool-Aid Acid Test*, 65-66.
[25] AIOA 71, CAD M 414a, 419-420.
[26] DJBA 718a, MD 256b.
[27] Nöldeke, Rev. Wright, 678.
[28] Hystaspes = (the Avestan name) Vištāspa, the patron of Zarathustra.
[29] Aurentes and Pkedellos are disciples of the Buddha.
[30] Kph (Dublin) 299.2-12 (in Tardieu, "Diffusion"):

> ⲁ̣ ⲡ̣ϫⲁⲓ̈ⲥ ⲍⲁⲣⲁⲇ̣ⲏⲥ [ⲉⲓ ⲁ]ⲧ̣ⲡⲉⲣⲥⲓⲥ ϣⲁ <ϩ>ⲩⲥⲧⲁⲥⲡⲏⲥ ⲡ̣ⲣ̅ⲣⲟ ⲁϥ̣ⲟ̣ⲩⲱⲛϩ̅ ⲙ̅-
> ⲡⲛ[ⲟ]ⲙⲟⲥ ⲁ̣[ⲛ ⲁⲃ]ⲁⲗ ⲉⲧⲥⲙⲁⲛⲧ ⲙ̅ⲙ̣ⲏⲉ ϩⲛ̅ ⲧⲡⲉⲣⲥⲓⲥ ⲡϫⲁ[ⲓ̈ⲥ] ⲃⲟⲩⲇⲇⲁⲥ
> ⲡ̣ⲥ̣[ⲟⲫ]ⲟ̣ⲥ ⲡⲙⲁⲕⲁⲣⲓⲟⲥ ⲁϥⲉⲓ ⲁⲡⲕⲁϩ ⲙ̅ⲡϩ̣ⲛ̣ⲧ[ⲟⲩ] ⲙ̣ⲛ̅ ⲅⲟⲩϣⲁⲛ ⲁ̣ϥ̣ⲟⲩⲱⲛ-
> ϩ̅ ⲁⲛ ⲁⲃⲁⲗ ⲙ̅ⲡⲛⲟⲙⲟⲥ ⲉⲧⲥⲙⲁⲛⲧ̅ ⲙⲁⲙ̣ⲏⲉ ϩⲙ̅ ⲡϩⲛⲧ̣ⲟⲩ ⲧⲏⲣϥ̅ ⲙⲛ̅ ⲅⲟⲩϣⲁⲛ
> ⲙⲛ̅ⲛ̅ⲥⲱϥ ⲇⲉ̣ ⲁ ⲁⲩⲣⲉⲛ̣ⲧ̣ⲏⲥ ⲉⲓ ⲙⲛ̅ ⲡ̣ⲕⲏⲇ̣ⲏⲗⲗⲟⲥ ⲁⲧⲁⲛⲁⲧ̣ⲟⲗⲏ ⲁⲩⲟⲩⲱⲛ-

From a symbolic point of view, the prince's eastern homeland, the place he's left and to which he's to return – to echo the Plotinian lines quoted in the introduction – easily lends itself to being understood as some kind of other-than-earthly paradise, or as one interpreter vaguely adds, transcendence.[31]

on my own Even though the prince will initially have some traveling 5
guardians along the journey, his subsequent solitude on the trip is foreshadowed by this observation that what pricey baggage he's carrying, he can carry alone, however young he may be. He's already aware it's his journey, and it's his luggage, even if there are some temporary helpers at the beginning (and end) of the adventure. The narrator-traveler won't experience complete alienation until he's actually in Egypt, but there's a hint at it already, before he leaves. Like David Coverdale melodically shrieks in Whitesnake's 1982/7 ballad, "Here I go again on my own."

The gold of Elam For the obscure place-name *bēṯ ʕellåyē*, I have sug- 6
gested Elam as a possible reading. The text in the manuscript, referring to a region known for gold or golden products, has *bēṯ ʕellåyē*, something like "Highland," more literally "area of the upper people," which is roughly what the Greek translation has (*χρυσός …τῶν ἄνω*). The other places in the list of wealth and treasures are not difficult to identify, but this one isn't clear. There is indeed a "village" (Syriac *qriṯå*) called *bēṯ ʕellåyå* (i.e., with a singular second element, rather than plural), mentioned by Barhebraeus in his *Church History*, but there is no indication that this obscure, similarly named village is likely to be the same as the place named as a source of gold in *The Pearlsong*.[32]

ϩ̄ ⲁⲛ ⲁ̣ⲃ̣[ⲁ]ⲗ̣ ⲙ̄ⲡⲛⲟⲙ̣ⲟⲥ ⲉⲧⲥⲙⲁⲁⲛⲧ̄ ⲙⲁⲙⲏ̣ⲉ ϩⲛ̄ ⲧ̣ⲁ̣ⲛ̣ⲁ̣ⲧⲟⲗⲏ ⲧ̣[ⲙ]ⲏⲧ̣[ⲉ ⲙ̄ⲡⲕⲟⲥ]ⲙⲟⲥ [ⲙⲛ̄ ⲧ]ⲡⲁⲣⲑⲓⲁ ⲁϥⲟⲩⲱⲛϩ̄ ⲙ̄ⲡⲛⲟⲙⲟⲥ ⲛ̄ⲧⲙ̣ⲏⲉ ⲁ̣[ⲃⲁⲗ ϩⲛ̄ ⲛⲉⲓ̈ ⲧⲏ]ⲣⲟⲩ [ⲙ]ⲛ̄ⲛ̣̄[ⲥⲱⲥ] ⲁ ⲓ̄ⲏ̄ⲥ̄ ⲡⲭ̄ⲣ̄ⲥ̄ ϩⲙ̣̄ ⲡⲥⲁⲛϩⲱⲧⲡ ⲛ̣̄ⲛ̣̄[ϩ]ⲣ[ⲱⲙⲁⲓⲟⲥ] ⲉⲓ [ⲁ]ⲡ̣[ⲕⲁ]ϩ ⲙ̣̄ⲡⲥⲁⲛϩⲱⲧⲡ ⲧ̣ⲏⲣϥ̄

[31] "the East stands for paradise, or transcendence;" "… der Osten steht für das Paradies oder die Transzendenz" (Tubach, "Zur Interpretation," 243).

[32] The full sentence is (Abbeloos and Lamy, *Barhebraei Chronicon*, col. 119):
ܘܗܘ ܒܫܢܬܐ ܕܗܝ ܫܢܬ ܬܫܥܡܐܐ ܘܐܪܒܥܝܢ ܒܗ ܐܫܬܪܪ ܫܝܢܐ ܕܝܪܝ
ܐܬܐܢܣܝܘܣ ܦܛܪܝܪܟܐ ܕܐܢܛܝܘܟܝܐ ܒܥܠܬܐ ܠܡܬܢܝܚܘܬܗ ܘܢܣܩ ܡܢܗ̈ ܕܗܘ ܡܢ ܒܝܬܥܠܠܝܐ
ܩܪܝܬܐ ܠܘܬ ܡܠܟܐ ܕܦܪܣܝܐ ܡܛܠ ܫܠܡܐ ܡܫܬܪܪܬܐ ܕܥܠܡܐ

One possibility is to read ܒܝܬ ܥܝ̈ܠܡܝܐ *bēṯ ʕilam(m)åyē* "Elam."[33] This is a small change consonantally speaking, and Syriac regularly refers to countries with this construction, that is, the bound form *bēṯ* (home, residence, area) followed by a gentilic name. In addition to the place-name Kushan, discussed just below, examples abound. For example, Huzistan, Persia, and Mesene together are *bēṯ huzzåyē w-p̄årsåyē w-mayšånåyē*: "after he'd come up from the regions of Huzistan, Persia, and Mesene."[34] Similarly, *bēṯ rhomåyē* refers to Roman-controlled territories or regions, as here, from *The Martyrdom of Pusay*: "this victorious man, Pusay, was a descendent of the captives that Šapur son of Hormizd had brought from Roman territory."[35]

As for what Elam may have evoked, at least for later Syriac readers, for Bar Bahlul, there's a simple equation between "Elamites" and Iraq.[36] But in terms of its connection to gold and wealth, Elymais had long been well-known, as 1 Maccabees indicates:

> King Antiochus was passing through the upper regions and heard that Elymais, a city in Persia, was notable for wealth in silver and gold, with an extremely rich temple there, and golden helmets, breastplates, and armor that had been left behind there by Alexander, the son of Philip, king of Macedon, who had reigned first among the Greeks.[37]

> In the same year, i.e. 940 [628/9 CE], once peace had been established, Patriarch Athanasius, known as the cameleer, sent his student, John, a deacon from the village of *Bēṯ ʕellåyå*, to the Persian king for some personal business of his.

[33] See Payne Smith, *Thesaurus Syriacus*, cols. 2866-2867, for the place-name and its gentilic adjective.

[34] Bedjan, *Hist. Jabal.*, 225: ܘܡܢ ܒܬܪ ܕܣܠܩ ܗܘܐ ܡܢ ܐܬܪܘ̈ܬܐ ܕܒܝܬ ܗܘܙ̈ܝܐ ܘܦܪ̈ܣܝܐ ܘܡܝܫ̈ܢܝܐ

[35] AMS 2 208. ܗܢܐ ܗܟܝܠ ܢܨܝܚܐ ܦܘܣܝ ܐܝܬܘܗܝ ܗܘܐ ܡܢ ܬܘܠܕܬܐ ܕܫ̈ܒܝܐ ܫܒܝܬܐ ܕܐܝܬܝ ܫܒܘܪ ܒܪ ܗܘܪܡܝܙܕ ܡܢ ܒܝܬ ܪ̈ܗܘܡܝܐ

[36] BB 1430: العراق ܥܝ̈ܠܡܝܐ.

[37] 1 Maccabees 6:1-2:

> Καὶ ὁ βασιλεὺς Ἀντίοχος διεπορεύετο τὰς ἐπάνω χώρας καὶ ἤκουσεν ὅτι ἐστὶν Ἐλυμαΐς ἐν τῇ Περσίδι πόλις ἔνδοξος πλούτῳ ἀρ-

It's far from certain, but, since it's a small textual change, it's metrically allowable, and it makes sense geographically and in terms of the content, the reading "Elam" seems preferable to *bēṯ ʕellåyē*.[38]

the silver of Great Ganzak, Ganzak is named at the beginning of the poem in connection with silver in the list of riches prepared for the prince's trip. For this "silver of great Ganzak," the Greek has *ἄσημος τῶν μεγάλων θησαυρῶν* "silver from vast treasuries;" this takes the proper name Ganzak, spelled in Syriac with -zz- instead of -nz-, as the noun *gazzå* "treasure." Nevertheless the proper name is known in Greek, where, as in Syriac here, it's often spelled without -n-, but Ganzaka is also known.[39] Stephen of Byzantium cites Quadratus and Arrian, both of whom composed works on the Parthians, for Ganzak being known either as a "huge city," or "a big village," respectively.[40] According to Gēorgios Kedrēnos, when Heraclius captured Ganzak in 628, a fire-temple, and even the wealth of Croesus, the Lydian king, were there.[41] This "fire-temple" is mentioned in other sources as well, and Zarathustra is said to have come from Ganzak.[42] Finally, while it's not silver, some lines in the *Mani Codex* link Ganzak and another metal, tin. The titular hero visits comrades there, reflecting with a metallic tidbit in an aside: "I traveled from the country of the Medes to the

---

γυρίῳ τε καὶ χρυσίῳ καὶ τὸ ἱερὸν τὸ ἐν αὐτῇ πλούσιον σφόδρα, καὶ ἐκεῖ καλύμματα χρυσᾶ καὶ θώρακες καὶ ὅπλα, ἃ κατέλιπεν ἐκεῖ Ἀλέξανδρος ὁ Φιλίππου βασιλεὺς ὁ Μακεδών, ὃς ἐβασίλευσε πρῶτος ἐν τοῖς Ἕλλησι.

[38] Adam (*Psalmen*, 71) suggests Beth Lapat – that is, in the region of ancient Elam – as the home of the "circle" that produced the *Acts of Thomas*.

[39] E.g. Ptolemy 6.18.4: *Γάζακα ἢ Γάνζακα* (text at Oppenheimer, *Babylonia Judaica*, 122).

[40] Text at Oppenheimer, *Babylonia Judaica*, 122: *πόλις μεγίστη τῆς* Μηδίας, *ὡς* Κουάδρατος *ἐν ὀγδόῳ* Παρθικῶν. Ἀρριανὸς *δὲ κώμην μεγάλην αὐτήν φησιν ἐν* Παρθικῶν *τετάρτῳ* "a huge city in Media, as Quadratus says in book 8 of his *Parthica*, while Arrian says it's a big village in book four of his *Parthica*."

[41] "He took control of the city of Ganzak, where there was a fire-temple, as well as the wealth of Croesus, the Lydian king." *Patrologia Graeca* 121 789-790, text at Oppenheimer, *Babylonia Judaica*, 122: Καὶ *καταλαβὼν τὴν* Γαζακὸν *πόλιν, ἐν ᾗ ὑπῆρχεν ὁ ναὸς τοῦ* Πυρὸς *καὶ τὰ χρήματα* Κροίσου *τῶν* Λυδῶν *βασιλέως*.

[42] Oppenheimer, *Babylonia Judaica*, 124.

brothers in Ganzak, and there was tin there. When we'd reached the city of Ganzak, the people with the brothers were worried about[...]"[43]

7 **The chalcedonies of India** For India, the proper name *hendu*, and its derived gentilic adjective *hendwåy* "from or related to India," are well known in Syriac. In Middle Persian and Parthian inscriptions, it's *Hind* (and *Hindestān*).[44] Mentioned in *The Pearlsong* only once (line 7), India is nevertheless the main setting of the *Acts of Thomas*, including Thomas's recitation of *The Pearlsong* itself while he's in jail. Unlike Thomas – and Mani, who says, "I stirred up all of India"[45] – the narrator of *The Pearlsong* doesn't actually go to India. Rather, it's just the source of the precious stones called "chalcedonies" that the prince takes on his journey.

brocade from Kushan Kushan (Syriac *bēṯ qåšån*) refers to Bactrian territories of the Kushan empire (c. 30–c. 375 CE), which reached from Central Asia into northern India and Parthian and then Sasanian territories.[46] In *The Book of Laws of Countries*, it says: "among the Bactrians, who are called Kushans."[47] The spelling <kwšn> *Kušān* is found in Iranian inscriptions, and the name is *kuṣāṇa* or *koṣāṇa* in Kushan Prakrit (Brāhmī script) inscriptions.[48] The city of Bactra itself, capital of Bactria, "became a major commercial center. The city was one of the chief halts on the silk road and the crossroads of routes" reaching to Marv, Kāšgar, Bagrām, and eventually India.[49] "Kushan" occurs at the beginning of *The Pearlsong* (line 7) in reference to *pṯawtḵē*, which means either "brocade" or a kind of multi-colored gem.

[43] KMK 121.6-13: ἐκ δ[ὲ τῆς χώρας] τῶν Μήδων [εἰς τοὺς ἐν] Γουναζὰκ ἀδ[ελφοὺς] ἐπορεύθην. λί[θος δ' ἐκεῖ] ὑπῆρχεν κασσ[ιτέ]ρου. ὁπηνίκ[α δὲ εἰς] Γαναζὰκ τὴν π[όλιν ἐ]φθάσαμεν, οἱ σὺ[ν τοῖς ἀ]δελφοῖς μερ[ιμνῶντες] περὶ τῆς[...]

[44] Gignoux, *Glossaire* 23, 52.

[45] Kph 184.27: ⲁ̈ⲓⲕⲓⲙ ⲁⲡⲕⲁϩ ⲧⲏⲣϥ ⲙⲡϩⲛ̅ⲧⲟⲩ.

[46] See further Bivar, "Dynastic History;" Sims-Williams and Falk, "Inscriptions;" Leriche and Grenet, "Bactria;" and the essays gathered in Mairs, *Graeco-Bactrian and Indo-Greek World*.

[47] Col. 588: ܒܝܬ ܒܚܬܪ̈ܝܐ ܕܡܬܩܪܝܢ ܩܫܢ̈ܝܐ

[48] Gignoux, *Glossaire*, 55, and Sims-Williams and Falk, "Inscriptions."

[49] Leriche and Grenet, "Bactria."

The specific items of value in this list – gold, silver, chalcedonies, brocade, and diamonds – may not be especially significant, but they're recognized as marking wealth and royalty, thus suitable baggage for a traveling prince. These possessions and gifts, like the reference to his father's kingdom and palace, mark the narrator unquestionably as royal. As one of Bar-Rakib's inscriptions phrases it: "among the great kings, possessors of silver and possessors of gold."[50] Similarly, in Ephrem's *Hymns on the Pearl*, the famous poet sets pearls with other valued elements and minerals like family members or friends:

> Precious gems can be your siblings, together with beryls
> and pearls as your comrades.
> Gold can be your relative.
> A crown for the king of kings can be among your loved
> ones.[51]

The prince is about to be sent to Egypt to get *the* pearl, and, at least according to the Syriac, he doesn't have any other pearls besides, but the Greek translation, instead of "brocade" (Syriac *pṯawtkē*), has "pearls" *μαργαρῖται*. The Syriac word isn't well-known, and may refer to either a kind of multi-colored precious stone or, as I've taken it here, brocade or some other similarly decorative textile. Here is Bar Bahlul's description of the word:

> *pṯawtkå* acc. to Bar Srošway, a cloth coffin-covering, something exquisite, very colorful, sparkling. Job said it's *dībāǧ* (brocade), and in his discussion he calls it *peṯkå*, i.e. any colored clothing. Otherwise, it's deluxe cloth interwoven with gold. *pṯawtkå*, taken in another way, is a necklace, or a belt, and outer garments woven with various colors of

---

[50] KAI 216/Bar-Rakib I 9-11: 𐡁𐡌𐡑𐡏𐡕 • 𐡌𐡋𐡊𐡍 • 𐡓𐡁𐡓𐡁𐡍 • 𐡁𐡏𐡋𐡉 • 𐡊𐡎𐡐 • 𐡅𐡁𐡏𐡋𐡉 • 𐡆𐡄𐡁 • <bmṣʕt mlkn rbrbn bʕly ksp wbʕly zhb>.

[51] 6.1-5:

ܟܐ̈ܦܐ ܟܐ̈ܦܐ ܢܗܘܘܢ ܐܚ̈ܝܟܝ
ܥܡ ܒܪ̈ܘܠܐ ܘܡܪ̈ܓܢܝܬܐ
ܐܝܟ ܚܒܪ̈ܬܟܝ ܢܗܘܐ ܕܗܒܐ
ܐܝܟ ܒܪ ܛܘܗܡܟܝ ܠܡܠܟ ܡ̈ܠܟܐ
ܟܠܝܠܐ ܢܗܘܐ ܡܢ ܚܒ̈ܝܒܝܟܝ

> mixed dyes: anything that's particularly attractive and varied with a lot of color, with designs on the cloth, or with high-quality gems, something varied in attractive colors and emeralds. In Arabic it's called *dībāǧ*. "Shining *pṯawtḵå*," according to Bar Srošway, is a decorative shirt, used of an article of clothing with mixed colors, beautifully bright and shining, i.e. incomparable for the skill it requires to make. Colorful and exquisite cloth, cloth interwoven with gold, brocade.[52]

8 **iron-grinding diamonds** Under the lemma *ʔaḏamos*, "adamant, diamond," Bar Bahlul says:

> *ʔaḏamos* acc. to our teacher, "diamond(s)," it's the hardest rock there is, and pearls can be pierced with it; the unbreakable stone brass-smiths and copper-smiths strike on, called the solidest stone, and called [in Syriac] *šåmirå*.[53]

Still noting diamonds' extreme hardness, a *Physiologus*-inspired naturalist in Syriac also highlights their sparkle, using a verb that the poet of *The Pearlsong* later (line 66) uses for the garment:

> Diamonds are a mineral found in eastern regions, but it's not found in the daytime, only at night, since it naturally possesses a sparkling sheen. And since it naturally

---

[52]BB 1645-1646:
ܦܬܘܬܟܐ ܐܝܟ ܒܪ ܣܪܘܫܘܝ، ܬܠܒܫܬ ܡܨܒܬܐ وشي مرتفع كثير الالوان برّاق. ܘܐܡܝܪ ܐܦܘܕ ܕܡܬܚܫܒ ܐܢܬ̈ܐ. ܘܦܪܐ ܠܗ ܒܡܡܠܠܗ ܦܬܘܬܐ ܗܘ ܥܠ ܡܐܢܐ ܕܡܒܗܠ آخر الاستبرق الفاخر. ܦܬܘܬܟܐ ܒܢܝܐ ܐܝܟ ܚܡܐ ܐܘܨܝܬ ܙܗܝܐ ܘܢܗܝܪܬܐ ܘܥܒܕ̈ܝ ܡܢ ܚܘܒܐ ܡܫܟܠܦܐ ܕܐܘܡܢܘܬܐ ܦܬܘܬܐ. ܘܥܠ ܝܕܗ ܕܕܓܠܝܐ ܗܠܝܢ ܘܡܦܬܟܐ ܒܠܒܘܫܐ ܡܨܒܬܐ ܘܡܨܝܪܬܐ ܕܡܫܚܠܦܬܐ ܐܘ ܒܟܐܦܐ ܝܩܝܪܬܐ ܐܝܟ ܐܢܐ ܕܦܬܟܐ ܒܠܒܘܫܐ ܕܓܠܝܐ ܘܡܐܪܓܢܝܬܐ ܒܙܙܐ ܘܡܨܒܬܐ ܡܬܩܪܐ ديباج. ܦܬܘܬܟܐ ܙܗܝܐ ܐܝܟ ܒܪ ܣܪܘܫܘܝ ܗܘ ܢܗܝܪܐ ܠܡܐܢܐ ܕܡܦܬܟ ܒܠܒܘܫܐ ܘܢܨܚ ܘܗܢܐ ܥܣܩܘܬܗ ܗܘ ܕܠܝܬ ܡܕܡ ܕܦܣܩ ܠܡܦܬܟܘܬܐ الوشي المرتفع والديباج والاستبرق.

[53]BB 39:
ܐܕܐܡܘܣ ܐܝܟ ܪܒܢ الماس وهو اصلب الحجارة وبه يثقب اللؤلؤ. الحجر الذي يضرب عليه الصفّارون العني النحّاسون ولا ينكسر ويسمّى حجر الاصمّ ܘܡܬܩܪܐ ܕܫܡܝܪܐ܀

tops everything else in its hardness, nothing can best it: since, although iron is hard and can stand up to anything, against diamond it can be pounded down like clay. This is why it's called *ʔaḏamos*, "fortified strength."[54]

So diamonds find a fitting adjective in *The Pearlsong*'s "iron-crushing." Centuries later, Barhebraeus still specifically notes adamantine imperviousness to iron when he describes diamonds in his *The Cream of Wisdom: Book of Mineralogy*: "diamond, which is neither malleable nor softenable: rather, when when you strike it on an anvil, the diamond will penetrate the anvil, unaffected by the iron."[55]

they stripped me The Greek translation here has a verb with the 9
opposite meaning: "they clothed me" (ἐνέδυσάν με).

the shining garment they had lovingly made me The shining garment, mentioned throughout the poem, is typically referred to simply by *zhiṯå*, simply an adjective referring to something shiny or brightly glowing, without a specific word for the kind of clothes meant. As already mentioned, while the pearl is the goal of the prince's trip to Egypt, it's not the main point of the poem: "Really, the poem narrates how the prince obtains his light-garment forever, and stealing the pearl is the prerequisite for this."[56] Whatever the *zhiṯå* looked like beyond glowing, it's closely associated with the prince's cloak or "toga," as seen in the next line and beyond (lines 10, 14, 46, 72, 97).

Whether called clothes, clothing, garments, an outfit, uniform, or even raiment, the *zhiṯå* (with the cloak) is specifically the prince's; even more, it's identity-revealing, and enchantingly beautiful, as described

[54] Ahrens, *Naturgegenstände*, 66.1-8:
ܐܕܡܘܣ ܟܐܦܐ ܒܐܬܘܪ̈ܬܐ ܕܡܕܢܚܐ ܡܫܬܟܚܐ. ܘܠܐ ܒܐܝܡܡܐ ܡܫܬܟܚܐ. ܐܠܐ ܒܠܠܝܐ. ܟܐܦܐ ܕܝܢ ܡܦܪܟܐ ܡܠܝܐ ܒܚܝܠܗ. ܘܟܕ ܠܟܠ ܡܕܡ ܙܟܐ ܒܩܫܝܘܬܐ ܕܚܝܠܗ. ܠܗ ܕܝܢ ܠܝܬ ܠܗ ܡܕܡ ܕܙܟܐ ܢܩܫ ܠܗ. ܡܛܠ ܕܟܕ ܦܪܙܠܐ ܩܫܝܐ ܗܘ. ܕܚܣܝܢ ܠܟܠܡܕܡ ܡܬܒܪܐ ܡܢ ܡܕܡ ܒܟܐܦܐ ܗܕܐ ܕܐܕܡܘܣ. ܐܝܟ ܛܝܢܐ ܡܬܕܩܩ. ܡܛܠ ܗܕܐ ܩܝܡ ܠܗ ܐܕܡܘܣ ܚܣܝܢܐ ܚܝܠܐ܀

[55] III.i.2 (ed. Takahashi, p. 100): ܐܕܡܐܣ ܗܘ ܕܠܐ ܡܬܦܫܛܢܐ ܐܦܠܐ ܡܬܪܟܟܢܐ. ܐܠܐ ܟܕ ܡܬܡܚܝܢܐ ܥܠ ܩܘܕܢܐ ܚܕܪܐ. ܘܡܢ ܦܪܙܠܐ ܠܐ ܢܐܟܐ

[56] "In Wirklichkeit erzählt das Gedicht, wie der Prinz sein Lichtgewand für immer erlangt, und der Raub einer Perle ist die Bedingung dafür" (Beyer, 240). Cf. Poirier, 201-203.

at the end of the poem. A memorable line from the *Gospel of Philip* underscores the rank-giving power of the right clothes at the right time: “In this world, people wearing clothes are better than the clothes; in the sky-kingdom, the clothes are better than the people wearing them.”[57]

A proverbial remark in the Talmud serves as a reminder of how clothes mark you in the eyes of others when you’re away from home: “In my town, it’s my name; elsewhere, it’s my clothes.”[58] But the prince’s custom-fitting ensemble of toga and shining garment, unique and marking his rank, doesn’t make the prince’s traveling wardrobe: he does *not* have these special clothes on his trip to Egypt, so whatever identity or rank might have been indicated by them, he’s traveling under a different guise. (As we’ll see, he ends up dressing like the Egyptians once he gets there.) He doesn’t say why his parents have him leave his shining garment at home, but it will meet him again at a crucial point in the narrative, before he returns home.

Allegorically or symbolically, a garment may be a sign for the body, in relation to a soul or immaterial self, as in the *Sentences of Sextus*, a Greek text that was translated into several languages in Late Antiquity, including a Coptic translation known from the Nag Hammadi codices: “Note in your mind that the body is the garment of your soul, so keep it clean, since it’s sinless.”[59]

10 **my scarlet cloak, measured and woven to my size** The word translated “cloak” here is the Latin loanword *ṭoga*, quite rare in Syriac. From Latin, but also known in Greek (and English, of course), is ܛܘܓܐ *ṭoga*, the outer garment associated with nobility, “toga.”[60] It’s not a common word in Syriac and probably seemed foreign to a Syriac reader,

---

[57] 57.19–22 (ed. p. 154): ϩⲙ̅ ⲡⲉⲉⲓⲕⲟⲥⲙⲟⲥ ⲛⲉⲧϯϩⲓⲱⲟⲩ ⲛ̅ⲛ̅ϩⲃⲥⲱ ⲥⲉⲥⲟⲧⲡ̀ ⲁⲛⲛ̅ϩⲃ̅ⲥⲱ ϩⲛ̅ ⲧⲙⲛ̅ⲧⲉⲣⲟ ⲛⲙ̅ⲡⲏⲩⲉ ⲛ̅ϩⲃ̅ⲥⲱ ⲥⲉⲥⲟⲧⲡ̀ ⲁⲛⲉⲛⲧⲁⲩⲧⲁⲁⲩ ϩⲓⲱⲟⲩ.

[58] *Shabbat* 145b(42), text at DJBA 1200: במאת שמאי דלא במאי תותבאי

[59] *SentSext* §346, (XII 30.11–14, ed. p. 312): ϫⲟⲟ[ⲥ] ϩⲙ̅ ⲡ[ⲉⲕ]ϩⲏⲧ ϫⲉ ⲧϩⲃ̅ⲥⲱ ⲛ̅ⲧⲉⲕⲯⲩⲭⲏ̣ [ⲧⲉ] ⲡⲥⲱⲙⲁ· ⲁⲣⲏϩⲉ ϭⲉ ⲉⲣⲟϥ ⲉϥ[ⲟⲩ]ⲁⲁⲃ· ⲉϥⲟ ⲛ̅ⲁⲧⲛⲟⲃⲉ. The Coptic MS, which is far older than any Greek copy, differs from the Greek, which doesn’t refer to a garment (ed. Chadwick): *ἐκμαγεῖον τὸ σῶμά σου νόμιζε τῆς ψυχῆς· καθαρὸν οὖν τήρει* “consider your body the soul’s impressionable mass, so keep it clean.”

[60] Lampe, *Lexicon*, 1395a.

even more foreign than in English. (The word is not in Bar Bahlul's *Lexicon.*)

At home the young prince donned his shining garment and scarlet cloak, as though his caretakers knew Robert Hunter's lyric, "wrap the babe in scarlet covers, call it your own,"[61]. But ready for his voyage, he has to leave the outfit behind. Burkitt points to a description by John Malalas – who was from Antioch and knew Syriac – of togas as official or formal Byzantine clothing in the sixth-century to show how "scarlet" togas mark high rank.[62] Rather than a word meaning scarlet or red, the Greek translation calls it *ξανθός* "yellow, golden, light brown, tawny."

They made a pact with me and and inscribed it in my heart, lest it 11
be forgotten This line, wish unfulfilled, presages the letter that comes to the prince later in the story. When the letter reaches him, he realizes that its message matches what was recorded in his mind at this point before he leaves, a graphic way to portray an activated memory.

The common Syriac noun here translated "heart" (*lebbå*) may equally mean "mind," and the Greek translator follows the latter meaning more explicitly with *διανοία*.

If you go down into Egypt and you bring down the pearl For 12
the verb "bring down" (*w-ṯaḥtih*), some interpreters have preferred to emend to *w-ṯaytēh* "bring." The Greek has "carry (off), bring" *κομίσης*, which would agree with the latter Syriac reading. While it's a small change graphically – ܘܬܝܬܝܗ instead of ܘܬܚܬܝܗ – the emendation is not without its problems, since the proposed verb *ʔayti* doesn't typically include adverbial notions like "bring *back*, *off*, or *away*."

Egypt, from the point of view of the prince, is a dangerous, distracting, and deceiving place. From a symbolic point of view, Egypt has been interpreted as "the dark demonised world,"[63] or more simply just "the present world."[64] Especially if Egypt corresponds with some world of darkness, the prince and his journey to Egypt are seemingly

[61]From "St. Stephen," (Grateful Dead).
[62]Burkitt, "Toga."
[63]Kuehn, *Dragon*, 203.
[64]"Ägypten symbolisiert die diesseitige Welt ..." (Tubach, "Zur Interpretation," 243).

echoed in the Mandean story of Hibil-Ziwa and his journey to the darkness.

> Hibil-Ziwa – the great, the sweet, the delightful – why are you sitting there? Get up and start walking! Go down to the world of darkness! So Manda of Life, with his brothers, traveled to the world of darkness: they went down world upon world until they reached the world of Krun, the big flesh-mountain. Then passing the mysteries, the seal of Krun, they went up until they had reached the world of Qin, Anatan's spouse, to Gaf the great. Then he went to be with Qin the great.[65]

The manuscript has the numeral "one" with "pearl," but Beyer is probably right that this is a "Christian addition" – from the Gospels, see Matthew 13:46 – that "makes no sense."[66]

If we take titles like "Hymn of the Pearl" and "Pearlsong" seriously, the pearl is a major part of the story and text, but it really isn't much in the poem's story itself, despite such monikers. This seemingly minimal role may impact its meaning in any allegorical reading. As Beyer somewhat grandiloquently says, for example:

> Most notably, the pearl is much too insignificant in the context of the poem to be able to symbolize the central

---

[65] *Hibil-Ziwa* 1.44-50:

[illegible]

> *al-mā-hū yāṯb-īt, Hībīl-Zīwa, rabba helya u-bassīma, qūm asgī īzel {anhoṯ} al-ālma aḏ-ahšōḵa hāyzāk asgī Manda aḏ-heyyī u-ahh-ī al-ālma aḏ-ahšōḵa u-anheṯ ālma al-ālma aḏ-amṭā al-ālma aḏ-Akrun ṭūra rabba aḏ-besra u-hāyzāk āden-on' al-rāzī hāṯma aḏ-Akrun u-asleq alma aḏ-amṭon al-ālma aḏ-Qīn Anātan alwāṯ-ī aḏ-Gap̄ rabba u-hāyzāk azal alwāṯ-ī aḏ-Qīn rabtī*

[66] Beyer, "Perlenlied," 252-253: "ist hier sinnlos," "christlicher Zusatz."

> gnostic *mythologumenon* of the sparks of light secured from the darkness and belonging to the spiritual, to whom the gnostic message is directed and whose salvation is the goal of all gnostic salvation events.[67]

While it's not a poem in praise of the pearl, whether real or symbolic, the pearl is the focus of the travel-mission that the parents give their child. But even after he gets the pearl from the snake, which he couldn't have done without his parents' letter waking him up, there's more to the narrative, including his reunion with his shining garment and his arrival back home at the royal court. The narrator-prince sometimes refers to it as "my pearl," including in the last line of the poem.

Pearls are, of course, mentioned in ancient literature as the actual hard, shiny things found in oysters, and the origin of pearls, how they're produced in the sea, was a matter of curiosity for some writers. (See Appendix IV for some examples in Coptic, Syriac, and Arabic.) But aside from realia, some authors turned to the pearl as something more, as a metaphor for something extremely valuable, worth getting and hanging onto at all costs.

In the Gospels, in the parable of the pearl (Matthew 13:45–46), Jesus compares the kingdom of heaven to when someone is out shopping for pearls and, after finding a single, expensive pearl, they sell everything just to get that one pearl. The parable doesn't show up in Ephrem's *Commentary on the Diatessaron*, the lost Gospel harmony that predates and overshadows early Syriac translations of the "separate" Gospels.[68] Since it's hard to imagine Ephrem passing up an opportunity to talk symbolically about pearls, it presumably wasn't in the Gospel text he

---

[67] "Perlenlied," 240:

> Vor allem aber ist die Perle innerhalb des Gedichtes viel zu bedeutungslos, um das zentrale gnostische Mythologumenon der von der Finsternis festgehaltenen Lichtfunken der Pneumatiker symbolisieren zu können, an die sich die gnostische Botschaft richtet und deren Erlösung das Ziel aller gnostischen Heilsveranstaltungen ist.

[68] See Petersen, *Tatian's Diatessaron*; Barker, *Tatian's Diatessaron*; and Koltun-Fromm "Reimagining Tatian." Tatian's *Diatessaron* certainly existed in Syriac, but Greek cannot be ruled out of any early stages of composition. See Barker, 38–39, and Mills, "Zacchaeus."

was commenting on. This short parable isn't in the much later *Persian Diatessaron* either, but it is in the *Arabic Diatessaron*.[69]

Ephrem made pearls the specific focus, an object of theological reflection, in five of his *Hymns on the Faith*.[70] (Several excerpts from these hymns are translated below in Appendix IV.) Elsewhere in his hymns, Ephrem uses pearls as a metaphor for virginity.[71] Another kind of value is ascribed to a pearl in a line from the Palestinian Talmud:

> Ulla, an emigrant to Babylonia, was dying there and started to cry. They said to him, "Why are you crying? We'll bring you up to Israel." He answered them, "What good is that to me, if I lose my pearl in a polluted land?"[72]

With "my pearl" Ulla probably means "life," while "soul" may be going too far. In any case, this language of a "pearl" being in a "polluted land" shares a frequency with *The Pearlsong*. Most obviously, the prince's pearl, whatever it may mean, is in Egypt, and he refers to the Egyptians as "polluted," using the same root in Syriac as the Talmud text above has in Jewish Palestinian Aramaic.

Lexically speaking, both Aramaic and Greek forms of the regular word for "pearl" derive from an Iranian source, comparable lexemes including Pa *moryārīd*, MP *morwārīd*,and NP *morvārīd*. In Syriac, it's *margånitå*, and similarly in Mandaic and Jewish Babylonian Aramaic, but in western Aramaic (and Hebrew) there's an *-l-*, rather than *-n-*, e.g. Jewish Palestinian Aramaic *margāli*.[73] The Greek forms have nei-

---

[69]See Messina's edition of the Persian *Diatessaron* (with Italian translation). It's not the same as the Arabic Diatessaron, and not directly connected to Tatian's Diatessaron, but a translation, probably from the thirteenth century, into Persian from Syriac, copied in 1547. For the Arabic, see ed. Ciasca, p. 67. In general on the Arabic Diatessaron see Joosse, "Introduction."

[70]For the Syriac text, see Beck, *Hymnen de Fide*, 248-262 (nos. 81-85).

[71]McVey, *Ephrem*, 151n365, 326n198.

[72]Palestinian Talmud, *Ketubot* 35b, with some corrections based on the parallel passage in PT *Kilayim* 32c:

עולה נחותה הוה. אידמיך תמן. שרי בכי. אמרין ליה. מה לך בכי. אנן מסקין לך. אמי לון. ומה הנייה אית לי. ואנא מובד מרגליתי גו ארעא מסאבתא.

[73]DJPA 327b, and also known in CPA. It's unattested in Samaritan Aramaic, another kind of western Aramaic from this time period.

ther an *-n-* or an *-l-* here, but an *-r-*: *margaritēs*, etc. An Aramaic form like the Syriac becomes Arabic *marǧān* "small pearls, coral," a word which shows up twice in the Quran.[74] The Iranian>Aramaic>Arabic loanword eventually re-enters Persian (meaning "coral") and thus completes a circle.

Finally, even though it's on the fringes, one wonders whether any readers who knew both an Iranian and an Aramaic language might see some possible relationship, however fleeting, between the pearl-word *margånitå* and Iranian *mār* (MP, also NP) "snake." (This Iranian noun for snake even shows up in Syriac, Mandaic, and other Aramaics in ≈ *måragnå* "whip, staff.")[75]

The one that's in the sea With the previous line, this is the first 13
reference to the pearl, including its present location. The prince doesn't have it now, and even though it's described as belonging to him, we don't know that he's ever actually possessed it in his life. The prince, at least, can't say with the Middle English *Perle*-poet, "I didn't know where in the world it was."[76]

In both Syriac and the Greek version, the pearl is said to be "around" the snake, not literally, but in the sense of "near." Niketas refers to the snake as *τὸν ἐπιζητούμενον μαργαρίτην περιεκάθητο* "sitting around (i.e. by, near) the missing pearl." Nevertheless, *drakontes* are known to incorporate, literally, their treasure-items, like gold, into their bodies.[77]

The object in view here is the pearl: that's what's in the sea, but since it's also "around the breathy snake," the snake, like Puff, the Magic Dragon, "lives by the sea."[78] Giant serpents, generally speaking, whether of the land or water variety, are closely connected with water sources.[79] This is true of dragons in Iranian tradition, and the giant

74 55:22, 58. See Jeffery, *Foreign Vocabulary*, 261.

75 The Iranian etymon is *māragna-*; cf. Greek *μάραγνα*. See Hinz, *Altiranisches Sprachgut*, 160.

76 *Perle* 65: "I ne wyste in þis worlde quere þat hit wace."

77 Ogden, *Drakon*, 176–178.

78 Lyrics by Peter Yarrow, based on a poem by Leonard Lipton.

79 Ogden, *Drakon*, 165.

snake in *The Pearlsong* is a water-dweller.[80] In Greek, a giant snake-creature on land is a *drakōn*, but in the water, they're called *kētē* (the PL of *kētos*), whale-like sea-monsters.[81] (Whale skeletons may even have been an inspiration.) Aside from being big and serpentine, their faces may look like those of lions, dogs, boars, or horses; they may have leonine forearms, bristles down their backs, horns, tusks, and long ears, and their bodies may end in a fish-tail or flippers.

In the formulation of fifth-century author Eznik of Kołb "dragons" are indeed huge snakes, they can live primarily on either land or in the sea:

> It's obvious that "dragons" are just snakes, and in the scriptures huge snakes or sea-monsters are called dragons. Just like gigantic people are called giants, monstrous terrestrial snakes and sea-monsters the size of mountains – I'm talking about *kētē* and orcas – are called dragons. ...
>
> Dragons are hardly anything but huge land-snakes, or enormous fish that are said to be mountain-sized and huge, that eat smaller fish, like huge snakes eat any kind of smaller bug or animal.[82]

[80] "... in almost all of the stories in Iranian literature, the dragon's lair is close to either a source of water or the sea" (Kuehn, *Dragon*, 52). The list of Zoroastrian heroes includes dragon-slayers Θraētaona and Kərəsāspa, slayers, respectively, of the dragons Aži Dahāka – with three mouths, three heads, and six eyes – and Aži Śruuara, a horned dragon with a diet of humans and horses. But it's another giant serpent creature of Zoroastrian lore that's more like *The Pearlsong*'s serpent, Gandarəβa (or Gandarb), a kind of sea-serpent that comes out to devour any and all, but is slain by Kərəsāspa. "Of all the Iranian monsters Gandarəβa is the most reminiscent of Near Eastern, Semitic, sea monsters" (Skjærvø, Khaleghi-Motlagh, Omidsalar, and Russell, "Aždahā").

[81] See Ogden, *Drakon*, ch. 3.

[82] Mariès and Mercier, eds. *Eznik*, § 133:

> Զի վիշապի այլազգ ինչ բնութիւն չէ՝ եթէ ոչ աւձի, այն յայտ իսկ է: Եւ զաւձ յաղթանդամ, կամ զգազան ինչ ծովածին, կոչեն գիրք վիշապ: Որպէս զմարդ յաղթանդամ Հսկայ անուանեն, նոյնպէս և զաւձ ցամաքային անճոռնի, և զգազանն ծովական լեռնաձև, զկիտացն ասեմ և զդելփինաց, վիշապս անուանեն. …
>
> Եւ այլ ինչ ոչ են վիշապք՝ բայց կամ աւձք մեծամեծք ցամաքային, կամ ձկունք անարիք ծովականք, զորոց ասեն,

The Pearlsong's snake-dragon seems to live in or by the sea, but in any case, "The distinction between land- and sea-beast is often blurred,"[83] with giant serpent-creatures not necessarily stuck in just one specific domain or the other. And the sea is, in a way, the origin of giant land-snakes and other monstrous creatures. Like the monsters that Tolkien's Ungoliant birthed, "[m]ost of the great *drakontes* of Greek myth are descended from the archetypal sea monster Ceto in the influential genealogy of Hesiod's *Theogony*."[84]

the breathy snake The snake-dragon in the poem is called *ḥewyå* in Syriac. This is a generic Aramaic term for a snake, not especially big or distinctive in any way.[85] It's the context and the accompanying descriptions that render the serpent stupendous. Like Old Norse *ormr* and Old English *wyrm*, which is itself sometimes used in parallel with *draca* "dragon" (< Latin < Greek), Aramaic *ḥewyå* can refer to a regular, everyday snake, or to something more unique and remarkable.[86]

From what is said (lines 13, 58), *The Pearlsong*'s serpent-dragon is portrayed as menacing, at least to the traveler-prince, who describes the creature as "breathy" and "fearsome."[87] As discussed below, "breathy" does not mean "hissing," but refers to the massive serpent's power of in- and exhalation, that is, of blowing out noxious or toxic fumes and of powerfully sucking its prey in. At the very least, it's the image of a noisy creature with a voracious appetite – in the Greek translation it's called *καταπότης* "devouring" – huffing and puffing, loudly inhaling

---

Թէ լեռնաբերձք մեծամեծք են: Եւ որս և կերակուր նոցա մանր ձկունք են, որպէս աւձից մեծամեծաց մանր մանր ինչ ճճիք կամ անասունք:

[83] Kuehn, *Dragon*, 51.

[84] Ogden, *Drakon*, 117.

[85] Löw, "Aramäische Schlangennamen." Related Semitic-language snake-lexemes include Ugaritic *bṯn* (DUL 250), related to Akkadian *bašmu* and to both the rarer Hebrew *bāšān* and the more common *peṯen*, this last cognate with Syriac *paṯnå* (also known in other Aramaics), and possibly even Greek *Πύθων* (> English "python"), the serpent killed by Apollo. The "name" of the Hittite serpent Illuyanka is also just "snake" (Hoffner, *Hittite Myths*, 111).

[86] For *wyrm*, see Barney, *Word-hoard*, 59, no. 184, and Preston, *Animals*, 141-143.

[87] What would *The Pearlsong*'s story look like from the point-of-view of the serpent, like John Gardner's *Grendel*?

and exhaling. Nothing is said about the snake's size, but if it's like a typical mythical snake, it's abnormally big: "Whatever else they were, *drakontes* were fundamentally large snakes."[88]

The threatening nature of this Egyptian snake aligns with other traditions where a serpent is a human antagonist, from Genesis 3 and beyond, rather than those where the serpent-character may be a beneficial, non-threatening "revealer of saving gnosis."[89] Even though the serpent is menacing, as it turns out, it's susceptible to spells, at least the one the prince intones over it to incapacitate it with sleep. Further, the prince's serpent has the pearl in or near the sea. It's not explicitly said to be guarding or watching over the pearl, just that it's near it. This may mean that the pearl is somehow incorporated into the creature's body, as mentioned above. Exactly how the serpent and pearl are related isn't explained, but they are clearly connected, and the prince has to go through the serpent to get to the pearl. Whatever *The Pearlsong*'s serpent and pearl mean, as in other dragon-and-treasure narratives, "the dragon that was seen to guard a worldly treasure can readily be transformed by the mystic into the dragon that guards divine and heavenly treasures."[90]

Snake-dragons and demons may be considered related, with the former sometimes viewed as a kind of instantiation of the latter. In later hagiography (ninth century and after), snake-dragons become more prominent, while demons fade away, with dragon-episodes even pushing other miracle-stories to the side.[91] *The Pearlsong*'s serpent has no apparent demonic affiliation, but nevertheless it's still dangerous, if the narrator's adjectives are taken seriously.

Two episodes from the *Life of Symeon the Stylite* illustrate both serpentine danger and the hero's unexpected imperviousness to that danger. In the first episode, the hero-saint's divine protection from serpent-

[88]Ogden, *Drakon*, 2.

[89]For this kind of positive presentation of the serpent in some Nag Hammadi texts, see Pearson, *Ancient Gnosticism*, 119-122. For the "bronze serpent" – meant to be a remedy against *śərāpīm*, "burning snakes," themselves – see Numbers 21, 2 Kings 18:4, and John 3:14.

[90]Kuehn, *Dragon*, 203.

[91]White, "Rise of the Dragon," 150-151, 167.

power is especially evident: not only does the snake not scare Symeon, a divine messenger also decisively dispatches it.

> He had secretly experienced numerous conflicts with the hater of beauty. Then, when Symeon was standing and praying, Satan had a black snake, one especially fierce, come to him. It was blowing and hissing and threatening him and it coiled itself between his feet: several times it wrapped itself around the saint's leg, up to his knee, and it tightened like a rope, to scare him and make him stop praying.
>
> But the saint wasn't scared and endured throughout his prayer, and after he finished it, the snake uncoiled itself and went out to go away, but after it had gotten a little bit away, an angel of the Lord hit it and split it end to end.[92]

In the second episode from the same saint-story, Symeon's name in someone else's mouth has temporary power over an attacking snake, but a more permanent effect comes by telling the snake to leave in Jesus's name.

> After this, there was a deacon who had gone three miles outside the monastic precincts for the harvest, and a little boy was with him. While the deacon was busy harvesting and the kid was playing, a fierce, black snake came out and coiled around the boy's feet and it started tightening and the boy started yelling for help. When the deacon saw it, he said to it, "By the prayers of Symeon, who lives in Tell

[92] AMS 4 529:
ܟܣܝܐܝܬ ܓܝܪ: ܐܦ ܩܪ̈ܒܐ ܣܓܝ̈ܐܐ ܗܘܘ ܥܡܗ ܡܢ ܠܘܬ ܣܢܐܗ ܕܫܘܦܪܐ. ܗܝܕܝܢ ܐܝܬܝ ܥܠܘܗܝ ܩܕܝܫܐ: ܟܕ ܩܐܡ ܘܡܨܠܐ: ܣܛܢܐ ܚܕ ܐܘܟܡܐ ܕܥܙܝܙ ܗܘܐ ܠܒ: ܘܢܦܫ ܘܡܫܪܩ ܘܡܐܡ ܗܘܐ ܥܠܘܗܝ. ܘܐܬܟܪܟ ܒܝܬ ܪ̈ܓܠܘܗܝ: ܘܟܪܟ ܢܦܫܗ ܥܠ ܪ̈ܓܠܗ ܕܩܕܝܫܐ ܘܠܘܬ ܣܓܝ̈ܐܢ ܥܕܡܐ ܠܒܘܪܟܗ: ܘܐܝܟ ܚܒܠܐ ܐܬܚܒܨ ܥܠܘܗܝ: ܐܝܟ ܕܢܙܝܥܝܘܗܝ ܘܢܒܛܠܝܘܗܝ ܡܢ ܨܠܘܬܐ.
ܗܘ ܕܝܢ ܡܪܝ ܩܕܝܫܐ ܠܐ ܐܬܕܚܠ: ܐܠܐ ܐܓܪ ܗܘܐ ܦܘܫ ܒܨܠܘܬܐ. ܘܡܢ ܕܫܠܡ ܨܠܘܬܗ: ܦܫܛ ܢܦܫܗ ܘܢܦܩ ܕܢܐܙܠ. ܘܡܢ ܕܐܪܚܩ ܩܠܝܠ ܡܢ ܠܘܬܗ: ܡܠܐܟܐ ܕܡܪܝܐ ܡܚܝܗܝ ܘܦܠܓܗ ܡܢ ܪܫ ܠܪܫ.

> Nešil: don't hurt him!" Immediately the snake left the boy and then coiled itself up like a pile and hurt no one, but stayed like this for three days.
>
> The whole village came and saw it, and they went and told the blessed one about the snake. He told the deacon, "Go and say to it, 'In the name of our Lord Jesus Christ, go on! Get away, and don't hurt anybody!'" And after that the snake unwound itself and left.[93]

Similarly, in *The Pearlsong* the prince's power over the serpent-dragon lies especially in the names he charms it with, the names of each of his parents and of his brother.

The prince uses this power to bypass the dragon's watch and violence, rather than to confront it directly. He has no weapons, just the sleeping-charm, powered by the names of his family, knowledge activated by the letter he received from them. The serpent, as far as the poem relates, does not die, but, in a narrative twist, he goes to sleep, which means that the prince, now awakened from his own slumber by the letter, in a way, transfers sleep from himself to the serpent, thus making the pearl's theft possible. Even though *The Pearlsong*'s dragon-encounter is one of a spell and sleep, and not a clash ending in a dead dragon, the prince's encounter with the snake-dragon in Egypt still echoes such better known combat-encounters with dragons.

> In these contexts the mythical creatures are suited ideally to play the role of adversaries as they represent forces or

[93] AMS 4 533-534:
ܒܬܪ ܩܠܝܠ ܕܝܢ܆ ܡܫܡܫܢܐ ܚܕ ܐܬܐ ܗܘܐ ܥܠ ܬܠܬܐ ܡܬܠܝܢ ܡܢ ܩܪܝܬܐ܆
ܘܢܦܩ ܠܣܝܓܐ܆ ܘܐܝܬ ܗܘܐ ܒܒܝܬܗ ܛܠܝܐ ܚܕ ܙܥܘܪܐ. ܘܟܕ ܗܘ ܡܫܡܫܢܐ ܫܝܓ܆
ܘܛܠܝܐ ܗܘ ܡܫܬܥܐ܆ ܢܦܩ ܚܘܝܐ ܚܕ ܐܘܟܡܐ ܒܥܝܢܐ܆ ܘܐܬܟܪܟ ܥܠ ܪ̈ܓܠܘܗܝ
ܕܛܠܝܐ ܗܘ܆ ܘܥܨܪ ܣܓܝ܆ ܘܥܨܪ ܗܘ ܛܠܝܐ ܡܒܟܐ ܘܡܝܠܠ. ܗܘ ܕܝܢ ܡܫܡܫܢܐ ܟܕ ܚܙܝܗ̇
ܐܡܪ ܠܗ܆ ܒܨܠܘܬܗ ܕܡܪܝ ܫܡܥܘܢ ܕܩܐܡ ܒܬܠܢܫܝܠ܆ ܠܐ ܬܚܒܠܝܘܗܝ. ܘܡܚܕܐ ܫܒܩ
ܠܗ ܡܢ ܠܛܠܝܐ܆ ܘܐܬܟܪܟ ܘܗܘܐ ܐܝܟ ܡܘܟܪܐ܆ ܘܡܕܡ ܠܐ ܐܚܒܠ. ܐܠܐ ܬܠܬܐ
ܝ̈ܘܡܝܢ ܗܘ̣ܐ ܗܟܢܐ.
ܘܐܬܬ ܟܠܗ̇ ܩܪܝܬܐ ܚܙܬܗ܆ ܘܐܙܠܘ ܐܘܕܥܘܗܝ ܠܛܘܒܢܐ܆ ܐܡܪ ܠܗ ܠܗܘ
ܡܫܡܫܢܐ܆ ܙܠ ܘܐܡܪ ܠܗ܆ ܒܫܡܗ ܕܡܪܢ ܝܫܘܥ ܡܫܝܚܐ ܥܒܪ ܙܠ܆ ܘܠܐܢܫ ܠܐ
ܬܚܒܠ. ܘܡܢ ܒܬܪܟܢ ܐܫܬܪܝ ܚܘܝܐ ܗܘ ܘܐܙܠ.

elements that interfere with the correct order or functioning of the world, and they are defeated by deities, kings or heroes who shape and organise the cosmos. Through their victory the latter acquire authority and power over the newly ordered world. The iconography of the dragon combat or encounter, part of the Indo-Iranian literary theme of heroic mythological exploits, draws on the immemorially ancient epic theme of this quest, an ever-recurring motif even in cultures that are culturally and geographically far removed from one another.[94]

It goes without saying that snakes, especially mythically giant ones, can be scary. The Aramaic forbear of the Syriac word used here shows up among other creatures to be avoided in an Old Aramaic curse:

> May the serpent's mouth consume, and the mouth of the scorpion, the mouth of the wasp [or bear?], the mouth of the ant [or panther?], may moths, lice, and [?] become an adder's throat against it (the city of Arpad).[95]

Syriac *ḥewyå* regularly corresponds to Greek *drakōn*, while according to Bar Bahlul, a *drakōn* is a *tinnīn/tanninå*.[96] This last word, also used for biblical "sea monsters," is explained as:

> *tanninå* whale, sea-monster. *tanninē* snake/s, sea-monster/s. Big *tanninē*, acc. to Bar Srošway, are *ketoi*, big, dense fish. The Greeks call these sea-monsters big whales. A *tanninå* eating its tail is a thing with alchemists. Acc. to one expert: dry medicines are put in a nice brass pot with a perforated bottom, and it's hung in a cucurbit prepared with water in it; the alembic is put on top of it, and steam from the water goes up and passes through the dry medicines

---

[94] Kuehn, *Dragon*, 87.

[95] KAI 222/Sefire I A 30-32:
]𐤅𐤉𐤀𐤊𐤋 · 𐤐[𐤌 · 𐤇𐤅𐤄 · 𐤅𐤐𐤌 · 𐤏𐤒𐤓𐤁 · 𐤅𐤐𐤌 · 𐤃𐤁{𐤄}‹𐤓›𐤄 · 𐤅𐤐𐤌
· 𐤍𐤌{𐤓}‹𐤋›𐤄 · 𐤅𐤎𐤎 · 𐤅𐤒𐤌𐤋 · 𐤅𐤀]...𐤉𐤄𐤅𐤅 · [𐤏𐤋𐤄 · 𐤒𐤒 · 𐤁𐤕𐤍 ·
<[wyʔkl p]m ḥwh wpm ʕqrb wpm db{h}‹r›h wpm nm{r}‹l›h wss wqml wʔ[.. yhww] ʕlh qq btn>.

[96] BB 595: ܕܪܩܘܢ ܗ̄ التنّين

> and takes their effective force and makes it rise until it drips down.[97]

The snake is called "breathy" here. (Once again, cue "Puff the Magic Dragon.") It specifically does not mean "hissing," even though it may be tempting to read it that way.[98] The verb √swq G means "suck, inhale, breathe loudly." It's used earlier in the *Acts of Thomas* when Thomas commands a different giant snake to suck the venom from someone it had bitten.[99] What does it mean for our snake-dragon to be breathy? It's a common characteristic of giant serpents like this to have "poisonous and pestilential" breath, not as a by-product of venom or a bit, but a "blowing out of noxious and destructive fumes that could kill in their own right."[100] But breathing goes both ways, and with their toxic blowing they also have a sucking superpower: as Ogden puts it, "an inverse power of breath ... the ability to suck prodigiously."[101] In Iranian literature, dragons – *aždahā*, coming from the name of the Avestan demon Aži Dahāka – may inhale so energetically that large water-animals, birds in flight, and even horses and riders, aren't safe from their breathing.[102]

your brother, our second For second, second-in-command, the Greek has εὐμνήστος "well-remembering, mindful," etc.

---

[97]BB 2076:
ܬܢܝܢܐ حوت تنّين. ܬܢܝܢܐ الثعابين والواحد ثعبان. تنانين والواحد تنّين. ܬܢܝܢܐ ܪܘܪܒܐ ܐܝܟ ܒܪ ܣܪܘ ܗ̄ ܩܐܬܐ. ܝܘܢܝܐ ܒܬܢܝܢܐ ܪܘܪܒܐ التنانين اليوناني يقول بالتنانين يعني الحيتان الكبار. ܬܢܝܢܐ ܐܡܪ ܙܘܣܝܡܘܣ ܠܘܬ ܦܠܢܝ ܒܡܠܐܟܬܐ. ܐܝܟ ܐܢܐ ܕܡܣܒܪܐ قدر لطيفة من صُفر مثقّبة الاسفل تُجعل فيها الادوية اليابسة وتُعلّق في قرعة فيها مياه مدبّرة وتُجعل عليها الانبيق فيصعد بخار الماء فيمرّ بتلك الادوية اليابسة فياخد قوّتها ويرفعها حتّى تقطر ❖

[98]One way to say "hiss" is √šrq A, as in *mašreq ḥayyelṯånå?iṯ*, "hissing intensely," for example, from AMS 6 487.5. For hissing as a loud sound that *drakontes* make, amid their panoply of other armaments, see Ogden, *Drakon*, 240-241.

[99]See the second selection translated in Appendix III below. See AMS 3 34.13, 19 and 35.3 for the verb's occurrence.

[100]Ogden, *Drakon*, 226.

[101]*Drakon*, 230.

[102]Skjærvø, Khaleghi-Motlagh, Omidsalar, and Russell, "Aždahā."

In Sohravardī's *Western Exile* story, the brother travels with the narrator, at least at first: "When I traveled with my brother ʕāṣim from regions of Central Asia to the lands of the west ..."[103]

This mention of the brother, together with the parents at the beginning, fills out the royal family. Like the prince himself, none of their names are given, even though it's their names that actuate the sleeping-spell against the snake. All three members of the family are mentioned together, with the brother known as the "second" (15, 42), and once (48) referred to with the Parthian loanword *pṣåḡrib(å)*, "successor-to-the-throne." As noted by Stang, this is "a pair of brothers neither of whom is specified as elder."[104] The narrator-prince refers to both king/father and queen/mother together as "my parents" in line 36. The prince's mother is called "controller of the east" (41) and "queen of the east" (60), highlighting both her authority and her Parthian residence.

The prince's king and father is mentioned most often in the poem among the royal family, but even so, all three are typically mentioned together. The king explicitly seals the letter himself (line 49). He's mentioned solo in "my father's palace," which occurs three times (lines 1, 61, 75) and, as discussed in the above, may reflect a lingering Old Aramaic formula. Also three times (lines 41, 86, 104), he bears the august title, "king of kings" (*mlek̲ malkē*) – well known from Akkadian *šar šarrāni* to Parthian and Middle Persian *šāhān šāh*[105] to Armenian *tʿagawor tʿagaworacʿ* to Gəʕəz *nəgušä nägäšt* and elsewhere.

The poem ends with the prince's reunion with the royal family at the palace in "the East:" the king/father, queen/mother, and the brother. In line 99 the prince refers to "the splendor of my father," but is there one father here, or two? The father and "our king" may not be the same at the end of the poem, lines 99-105: "with him" (105) seems to mean "with my father," who is the third-person referent for all of

---

[103] §1, Arabic: لمّا سافرت مع أخي عاصم من ديار ما وراء النهر الى بلاد المغرب ; Persian: چون سفر کردم با برادر خود عاصم از دیار ماوراء النهر الی بلاد المغرب

[104] *Divine Double*, 138.

[105] Written both with Aramaeograms and a phonetic complement (<MLKYN MLKʔ>, <MLKʔ-n MLKʔ>), and plainly, as in Manichaean texts, <šʔhʔn šʔẖ>, the former orthographic garb even more clearly akin to the Syriac phrase. See Gignoux, *Glossaire*, 57; DMMPP 314.

these lines, which makes "our king" seem to refer to another person. In Sohrwavardi's exile-story, at the end (§§ 42–43), the protagonist learns from his immediate father that there is a succession of "fathers" back to the supreme, luminous king; it's possible that the end of *The Pearlsong* reflects a similar spectrum.

my heir The Greek has *κῆρυξ* "emissary, herald."

16 **with two guardians accompanying me** While he's alone for part of the journey to Egypt and back, given the prince's youth and royal status, guides and treasurers show up, respectively, right at the beginning, as he leaves the east, and then again as he nears home. In *The Pearlsong*, these two kinds of royal minister are both indicated by Iranian loanwords that are also known in other Aramaic languages besides Syriac. First, on the way to Egypt, the prince is temporarily accompanied by two guardian-guides, *parwåqē* (line 16), and then he encounters two stewards or treasurers, *gēzaḇrē* (74, 79), who deliver his garment to him. In each case, it's a pair of royal assistants – first two guides, and then two treasurers – that are temporarily with the prince, and he comments explicitly in the latter case on there being two of them, but still sort of the same.

Parwåqå "guide, messenger" comes from a form like MP *parwānag* "guide, leader."[106] The Iranian loanword also occurs in JBA, as in the proverb, "A letter's reader should be the messenger."[107] (Incidentally, MP *parwānag* is also the origin of the modern Persian word for "butterfly," پروانه *parvāne*!)

The Greek here has *ἡγεμόνες* "guides." They accompany the traveler-prince only briefly, but while they're there, they're there to make the trip less scary and hard. In the *Mani Codex*, Mani is watched over by "angels" and "powers:"

> I was guarded with the strength of the angels, and of the holy powers[108] entrusted with my protection: they brought

[106] ILS 237, CPD 65, DMMPP 280a.

[107] קריאנא דאיגרתא הוא ליהוי פרוונקא – The proverb appears in Sanhedrin 82a and 96a, and Bava Meṣia 83b. Cf. DJBA 929a.

[108] More exactly in Greek "powers of holiness," reflecting a well-known feature in some Aramaic and other Semitic languages where an abstract noun in a genitive relationship is descriptive, as in Syriac *ruḥå d-qudšå* "spirit of holiness," i.e. "Holy Spirit."

> me up, too, with visions and signs they would show me,
> minimal and super brief, so I could handle them.[109]

the road was scary and hard This is all the poet says, so readers are left to their imaginations to press these adjectives further, but Sohravardi's language shows how quickly the trip can become gloomy: "On the road I saw the skulls of ʕād and T̠amūd as I roamed through the region, *and they were empty on their thrones*."[110] As lines from the Old English *Seafarer* put it, from the perspective of non-travelers: "Those who have it easy have no idea what some people suffer, the ones that most widely travel exile-paths."[111] 17

Niketas takes the opportunity here to quote the *Odyssey*, a phrase occurring twice in book 4 (4.393, 483: δολιχὴν ὁδὸν ἀργαλέην τε). In the first instance, the phrase is Eidothea's, goddess-daughter of Proteus, used to describe Menelaus's long trip back home following the Trojan War. In the second, Menelaus uses the same phrase for the same thing. This is while Menelaus is kept from sailing away from Pharos, in Egypt, and Proteus knows why. Eidothea advises the Greek king how to capture her shape-shifting father while he's asleep, so he can learn the way out. While Menelaus and his crew attempt to seize the god, he not only becomes a lion, a leopard, a board, water, and a tree, but also a *drakōn*! While points of comparison between *The Pearl-song*'s story and this Homeric narrative may seem slim, they are worth

---

[109] KMK 3.2-12:

> *[διὰ σθ]ένους [τῶν] ἀγ[γέ]λων ἐφυλάχθην καὶ τῶν δυνάμεων τῆς ὁσιότητος τῶν ἐγχειρισθεισῶν τὴν ἐμὴν παραφυλακήν, οἳ καὶ ἀνέθρεψάν με δι' ὀπτασιῶν καὶ σημείων ὧν ὑπεδείκνυόν μοι μικρῶν καὶ βραχυτάτων καθὼς ἐδυνάμην ὑποφέρειν.*

[110] *Western Exile*, §24, Arabic: ورأيت في الطريق جماجم عاد وثمود وطفت في تلك الديار وهي خاويةٌ على عروشِها; Persian: و بديدم در راه كَلهاء سرِ عاد و ثمود تهى پوسيده بر تختهاء ايشان. The Quran reference is 22:45.

[111] 55b-57:

> þæt se beorn ne wāt
> sēftēadig secg, hwæt þā sume drēogað
> þe þā wræclāstas wīdost lecgað.

mentioning. Like the prince, Menelaus was stuck in Egypt, away from home. Like the prince, too, Menelaus took advantage of his antagonist's sleep to get what he wanted. Elsewhere in the same book of the *Odyssey* (4.219-232), Egypt is reputed as a land of drugs, as discussed further below.

17 **I was too young to travel it** The guardian-guides are presumably there to make up for the prince's youth, but, again, they don't hang around for very long.

18 **Mesene, the meeting-spot for eastern merchants** Mesene, mentioned twice (18, 70) in the narrative, on the prince's way to Egypt and then again on the way back, was an important city transmitting goods, information, languages, and more. It's called *Mayšān/Mēšān* in Aramaic languages, and similarly *Mēšān* in Iranian inscriptions, and referred to in Palmyrene inscriptions as *krak* and *(karkā dī) Mēšān*.[112] Founded by Alexander in 324 BCE and under Seleucid control until 129 BCE, when Antiochus VII died, the city is for a short time under the control of the erstwhile Seleucid satrap, Hyspaosines, for whom the place is then known as Spasinu Charax (Σπασίνου Χάραξ), i.e. the "*karkā* of Hyspaosines," and the region more widely as Characene (Χαρακηνή), both of these names using the Aramaic lexeme for "(walled) city," *karkā*, already seen in the Palmyrene designation.[113] (The first part of the name of the famous fortress, Crac des Chevaliers, is from the same Aramaic noun.)

From this time in the 120s BCE, Mesene is under Parthian control. As Oppenheimer explains, "The region was of vital interest because it controlled communications between Mesopotamia and the Persian Gulf. In Hellenistic, Parthian and Sassanian periods, that meant control of the trade with India, the Far East and South Arabia, which exported aromatics and spices."[114] Since Mesene was a trade nexus, different kinds of coins were in circulation there, as indicated by a hypothetical situation laid out in the Babylonian Talmud:

---

112 Gignoux, *Glossaire*, 59; Hillers and Cussini, *Palmyrene*, 374 and 380.
113 Schuol, *Charakene*.
114 Oppenheimer, *Babylonia Judaica*, 249; see also 251-252.

> Say someone gives a loan to someone using a currency, but it becomes obsolete. Rav says, "He should give them valid currency at the same time," while Samuel says, "He can tell them, 'Go, spend it in Mesene!'" R. Naḥman says, "Samuel's statement is reasonable, if they make trips to Mesene, but if they don't, it's not."[115]

As late as Bar Bahlul the spoken Aramaic of Mesene is still a distinct variety of the language; sometimes he uses the adverb *mayš(ån)åʔiṯ*, "in Mesenian" to indicate it.[116] Earlier evidence from the Talmud (*Qiddushin* 71b) has part of the city of Apamea "speaking Mesenian."[117]

Given its prominence at this time as a trade-spot, and consequently also a place where multiple languages are used, it's no surprise that a traveler like Mani stops there. (There's also a bonus reference here to another *Pearlsong* place, Kushan.)

> He didn't move until he got to Hormizdakšahr. He wanted to [...] to Kushan. He [...] to go, then he turned angrily, with his mind in distress, and he went to Susa. He went from Hormizdakšahr until he reached Mesene, and from Mesene he went to the Tigris River, and continued up to Ctesiphon.[118]

It's a minimal mention, to be sure, just a travel list, but, as in *The Pearlsong*, these lists reinforce the physical geography, real or conceptual, of a traveler's experience.

---

[115] *Bava Qamma* 97a-b. Text in Oppenheimer, *Babylonia Judaica*, 243 (cf. 255), but cited here from the manuscript Hamburg 165.

איתמר המלוה את חברו על המטבע ונפסל המטבע אמ׳ רב נותן לו מטבע היוצא באותה שעה ושמואל אמ׳ יכול שיאמר לו לך והוציאו במישן אמ׳ רב נחמן מסתברא מלתיה דשמואל דאית ליה אורחא למישן אבל לא אית ליה אורחא למישן לא

[116] See Duval, *Lexicon Syriacum*, vol. 3, p. xxv.

[117] דמישתעיא מישנית. The text is quoted at Oppenheimer, *Babylonia Judaica*, 29.

[118] MHm 44.10-16: ⲙ̄ⲡϥⲕ̣ⲓⲙ ϣⲁⲛⲧϥ̣ⲡ̣[ⲱϩ] ⲁ̣ϩⲟⲣⲙⲏⲥ̣[ⲇⲁⲕϣⲁ]ϩⲁⲣ· ⲁϥⲟⲩⲱϣⲉ ⲁ . . ⲁⲃⲁⲗ ⲁⲕⲟⲩϣ̣ⲁⲛ: ⲁ . [. . . . . . .]ⲱⲡ ⲁⲣⲁϥ ⲁⲃⲱⲕ· ⲧⲟⲧⲉ ⲁϥⲛⲁⲩϩϥ ϩⲛ̄ⲟⲩⲃⲗ[ⲕⲉ ⲉϥϩ]ⲏ̣ϣ ⲛ̄ϩⲏⲧ: ⲁϥⲉⲓ ⲁⲡⲕⲁϩ ⲛ̄ⲟⲍⲉⲟⲥ· ⲁϥⲉⲓ ⲁ[ⲃⲁⲗ ⲛ̄ϩ]ⲟⲣⲙⲏⲥⲇⲁⲕϣⲁϩⲁⲣ ϣⲁⲛⲧⲉϥⲡⲱϩ ⲁⲧⲙⲁ-ⲓ̈[ⲥⲁⲛ]ⲟⲥ: ϫⲛ̄ⲛ̄ⲧⲙⲁⲓ̈ⲥⲁⲛⲟⲥ ⲁϥⲉⲓ ⲁⲡⲓⲉⲣⲟ ⲛ̄ⲧ†[ⲅⲣⲓⲥ]· ⲁϥⲧⲉⲗⲟ ⲁϩⲣⲏⲓ̈ ⲁⲕⲧⲏⲥⲓⲫⲱⲛ:

From the *Mani Codex*: "... to the city of Perat, near the island of the Mesenians."[119] Mesene held a port where ships brought goods from India and elsewhere to the east, and from Mesene these products could travel north to Babylon on the Euphrates, or up the Tigris and on to Adiabene or to Nisibis and Edessa.[120] The presence of merchants is also indicated in inscriptions. A bilingual inscription in Palmyrene Aramaic and Greek dated 24 CE, for example, commemorates "all the merchants of Babylon" for setting up an honorary statue for a patron:

> Malikhos, son of Nesa, son of Bola, also known as Asas, of the Khomarene family, by the people of Palmyra, in affection.
>
> In the month of Kanūn, in the year 336 – this is the statue of Malik, son of Naša, son of Bolḥa, also known as Ḥašaš, of the Kumra family, which all the merchants of Babylon set up for him, since he treated them kindly in every kind of way, aided the building of the temple of Bel, and donated from his own funds, something no one else did. They have accordingly set up this statue for him in his honor.[121]

A much later Palmyrene inscription, dated 258 CE, also an Aramaic-Greek bilingual, is a commemorative marker set up by a guild of smiths.

---

[119] KMK 140.4-7: εἰς Φαρὰτ τὴν [πό]λιν πλησίον τῆς [νήσ]ου τῶν Μαϊσα[νῶν].

[120] Segal, *Edessa*, 68.

[121] Inv 9 11 (Hillers and Cussini, *Palmyrene*, 199), originally J. Cantineau in *Syria* 12 (1931): 122-123, no. 4; text also in Oppenheimer, *Babylonia Judaica*, 58: first Greek, Μάλιχον Νεσᾶ τοῦ Βωλάα τοῦ ἐπικαλουμένου Ἀσάσου, φυλῆς Χομαρηνῶν, Παλμυρηνῶν ὁ δῆμος, εὐνοίας ἕνεκα. And Palmyrene Aramaic:

𐡡[𐡩𐡴]𐡧 𐡪𐡮𐡥𐡭 𐡵𐡮𐡶 3.100+20+10+5+1 𐡲𐡫𐡬𐡠 𐡣𐡮𐡤 𐡣𐡩 𐡬𐡫𐡪𐡥 𐡡𐡴 𐡮𐡵𐡠 𐡡𐡴 𐡡𐡥𐡫𐡧𐡠
𐡣𐡩 𐡬𐡶𐡳𐡴𐡠 𐡧𐡵𐡵 𐡣𐡩 𐡬𐡭 𐡡𐡮𐡩 𐡪𐡬𐡴𐡠 𐡣𐡩 𐡠𐡳𐡩𐡬𐡥 𐡫𐡤 𐡶[𐡢]𐡴𐡩𐡠 𐡪𐡫𐡤𐡥𐡭 𐡣𐡩
𐡡𐡬𐡣𐡩𐡮𐡶 𐡡𐡡𐡫 𐡬𐡭 𐡣𐡩 𐡵𐡱𐡴 𐡫𐡤𐡥𐡭 𐡡𐡪𐡫 𐡢𐡮𐡯 𐡪𐡫𐡤 𐡥𐡰[𐡣]𐡴 𐡡𐡮𐡩𐡮𐡠 𐡣𐡩 𐡤[𐡩]𐡪𐡫𐡠
𐡣𐡩 𐡡𐡫 𐡥𐡩𐡤𐡡 𐡬𐡭 𐡪𐡩𐡯𐡤 𐡣𐡩 𐡫𐡠 𐡰𐡡𐡣𐡤 𐡠𐡮𐡵 𐡡𐡣𐡩𐡫 𐡪𐡥𐡶 𐡠𐡳𐡩𐡬𐡥 𐡫𐡤 𐡲𐡫𐡬𐡠 𐡣𐡮𐡤
𐡫𐡩𐡳𐡴𐡤

<b[yr]ḥ knwn šnt 3.100+2-+10+5+1 ṣlmʔ dnh dy mlkw br nšʔ br bwlḥʔ dy mtqrʔ ḥšš dy mn bny kmrʔ dy ʔqymw lh t[g]ryʔ klhwn dy bmdynt bbl mn dy špr lhwn bkl gns klh wʕ[d]r bnynʔ dy h[y]klʔ dy bl wyhb mn kysh dy lʔ ʕbdh ʔnš bdyl kwt ʔqymw lh ṣlmʔ dnh lyqrh>.

> The statue of Septimius Udaynat, the luminous consul, our lord, which the guild of gold-&-silver-smiths set up for him in his honor in the month of Nisan, in the year 569.[122]

External merchants – in this case, basket-sellers, דיקולאי *diqqulåʔe* – coming to Babylon (and other places) to sell their wares are mentioned at *Bava Batra* 22a.[123] Trader-groups like these are known in inscriptions from early in the first century CE, not only in Babylon, but also in Vologesias and Mesene, and their caravans made trade between here and Palmyra possible.[124] Mesene occurs in a list of nearby places in a Jewish Babylonian Aramaic incantation bowl from Nippur: "I hereby adjure you all: spirits of Babylon and Arabia, spirits of Iraq and Mesene, spirits of the Euphrates and the Tigris river."[125] Later, Bar Bahlul flatly equates Mayšån with Baṣra.[126] Generally in Arabic it can be called Furāt al-Baṣra or Furāt Maysān.[127]

Babylon The city of Babylon, on the Euphrates River in southern 19
Mesopotamia, is named three times in the poem (lines 19, 50, 69), always with the enigmatic "Sarbug." The first and last occurrences are during the prince's trip to and from Egypt, respectively, while in line 50 the pair of cities comes up as a would-be impediment to receiving the letter from his parents. Babylon, the ancient town, then massive city – the wider region of southern Mesopotamia is known as Babylonia – was the namesake of the Old Babylonian (1894-1595 BCE) and then New Babylonian (626-539 BCE) empires.[128] Following the latter, the city is

---

[122] D-H C3945 (p. 69); the Greek is more fragmentary, but where it survives it matches the Palmyrene Aramaic text exactly.

[illegible]
[illegible] 5.100+60+5+4

<ṣlm spṭmyws ʔdynt nhyrʔ hpṭyqʔ mrn dy ʔqym lh tgmʔ dy qynyʔ ʕbd‹y›{ʔ} dhbʔ wkspʔ lyqrh byrḥ nysn šnt 5.100+60+5+4>.

[123] Text in Oppenheimer, *Babylonia Judaica*, 46.

[124] Oppenheimer, *Babylonia Judaica*, 53.

[125] See Kaufman, "Appendix C," 151, where the text is reproduced in transliteration. For a photo, see fig. 89, no. 4. The lines translated above are: אשבעית עליכון רוחי בבל וערב רוחי אירג ומישון רוחי פרת ודגלת.

[126] BB 1077: ܡܝܫܢ ܐܘܦܪܬ البصرة.

[127] Oppenheimer, *Babylonia Judaica*, 253.

[128] Seymour, *Babylon*; Oppenheimer, *Babylonia Judaica*, 44-62.

under Achaemenid, Seleucid, and Parthian rule, which comes to the time of *The Pearlsong*'s events.

In some Christian contexts, like Revelation 17–18, "Babylon" is representative of supreme evil and satanic control, including one of the more enduring images of Christian scripture, the "whore of Babylon." While Babylon, along with its unidentified sidekick city, Sarbug, is not considered favorably in *The Pearlsong*, it's not the arch-evil city it is in Christian traditions like Revelation 17–18. (Note that the book of Revelation was unavailable in Syriac until the sixth century.) Nevertheless, the book of Revelation has language reminiscent of *The Pearlsong*'s descriptors for Babylonians and Sarbugians, "perverse" and "riotous devils:" "Babylon the great fell, it fell! It became a demon-residence, a garrison for every unclean spirit, a garrison for every unclean and hateful bird."[129]

Just how notorious a place was Babylon for Christian readers and hearers?[130] A picturesque case comes from a homily in Bohairic Coptic attributed to Theophilus of Alexandria and dedicated to the "the three young people of Babylon," that is, Shadrach, Meshach, and Abednego, of fiery furnace fame, from chapter three of the book of Daniel. Since it echoes the prince's own apprehensiveness of Babylon, it's worth quoting from this homily at length. Theophilus sends Abba John, archimandrite of Siout (Asyut), to Babylon for relics of Shadrach, Meshach, and Abednego (Daniel 3), and as John approaches the old city, he finds it desolate and dangerous, a den for demons and serpents.[131] Like the narrator-prince, this John feels insecure near the journey's start.

> I didn't know where to go, since I hadn't gone there before: I was walking around like wandering sheep, asking the Lord to be my guide. As it happened, the sun set while

[129] Revelation 18:2: ἔπεσεν, ἔπεσεν Βαβυλὼν ἡ μεγάλη, καὶ ἐγένετο κατοικητήριον δαιμονίων καὶ φυλακὴ παντὸς πνεύματος ἀκαθάρτου καὶ φυλακὴ παντὸς ὀρνέου ἀκαθάρτου καὶ μεμισημένου.

[130] See de Vis, *Homélies coptes*, vol. 2, 122, for additional similar stories about Babylon in Bohairic, Sahidic, Syriac, Arabic, and Gəʕəz.

[131] (ps-)Theophilus of Alexandria, *Sermon on the Three Young People of Babylon*, text in de Vis, *Homélies coptes*, vol. 2, 121 ff., here 136.10–144.4. The manuscript is Vat. copt. 62, ff. 143v–165v, from possibly the ninth or tenth century.

I was walking, and I came to some desert wastelands. I became very worried, and I said, "Where can I sleep here? There's no village or spring,[132] and I'm afraid the animals will kill me during the night."[133] ...

While I was walking, I looked in the distance and saw something like an abandoned, desolate thicket, and there I saw leopards, ostriches, centaurs, and huge, fearsome snake-dragons. When they saw me, they angrily rushed at me, intending to kill me, but for my part, I took courage and grabbed the Gospel of John and read in it. Suddenly I saw John the evangelist and the archangel Michael: they said to me, "Don't be scared! We're always with you! All these you see are demons, but don't be scared of them." When I was 14 miles from Babylon, I crossed the border of Dura field,[134] which was terribly difficult to pass through, given the mass of wild animals, reptiles, and snakes. The blessed John testified to me, "I have seen snake-dragons there so big that I said to myself, 'With such thick gullets and their faces like little crocodiles, just one of them will swallow a three-year-old child!'" As they got close to me, the holy archangel Michael and John the evangelist rebuked them, and the creatures dug up the ground and left, and I didn't see them anymore.[135] ...

[132] Assuming ⲡⲓⲅⲓⲟⲛ is *πηγίον*.

[133] [136.10–137.4]:

> ⲁⲛⲟⲕ ⲟⲩⲛ ⲙⲡⲓⲉⲙⲓ ϫⲉ ⲉⲓⲛⲁⲙⲟϣⲓ ⲉⲑⲱⲛ ⲉⲑⲃⲉ ϫⲉ ⲙⲡⲓϩⲱⲗ ⲉⲡⲓⲙⲁ ⲉⲧⲉⲙⲙⲁⲩ ⲉⲛⲉϩ ⲛⲁⲓⲙⲟϣⲓ ⲡⲉ ⲉⲓⲟⲓ ⲙⲫⲣⲏϯ ⲛϩⲁⲛⲉⲥⲱⲟⲩ ⲉⲩⲥⲟⲣⲉⲙ ⲉⲓⲧⲱⲃϩ ⲙⲡϭ̅ⲥ̅ ⲉⲑⲣⲉϥϣⲱⲡⲓ ⲛⲏⲓ ⲛϭⲁⲩⲙⲱⲓⲧ. ⲁⲥϣⲱⲡⲓ ⲇⲉ ⲙⲙⲟⲓ ⲉⲓⲙⲟϣⲓ ⲁⲫⲣⲏ ϩⲱⲧⲡ ⲉⲣⲟⲓ ⲁⲓⲓ ⲉϩⲣⲏⲓ ⲉϫⲉⲛ [137] ϩⲁⲛⲙⲁⲛϣⲁϥⲉ ⲉⲩⲟⲓ ⲛϩⲉⲣⲏⲙⲟⲥ ⲁⲓϣⲱⲡⲓ ⲉⲓⲟⲓ ⲛⲉⲙⲕⲁϩⲛϩⲏⲧ ⲉⲙⲁϣⲱ ⲉⲓϫⲟ ⲙⲙⲟⲥ ϫⲉ ⲉⲓⲛⲁϫⲱⲓⲗⲓ ⲉⲑⲱⲛ ⲙⲡⲁⲓⲙⲁ ⲙⲙⲟⲛ ϯⲙⲓ ⲟⲩⲇⲉ ⲡⲓⲅⲓⲟⲛ ⲉⲓⲉⲣϩⲟϯ ϧⲁⲧϩⲏ ⲛⲛⲓⲑⲏⲣⲓⲟⲛ ϫⲉ ⲛⲛⲟⲩϧⲱⲧⲉⲃ ⲙⲙⲟⲓ ϧⲉⲛ ⲡⲓⲉϫⲱⲣϩ

[134] The proper name Dura has been re-analyzed as "Ira" in Coptic. See De Vis, *Homélies*, vol. 2, 80n3.

[135] [138.11–139.14]:

After this I went a mile on ahead, and I looked in with the sight of my eyes and saw the city of Babylon with darkness overspreading it, and a stormy gloom like smoke from a fiery furnace. I came to the rivers of Babylon, and found them surrounding the entire city. I sat down under the willows growing by the rivers of Babylon, so I could rest from my exertion.[136] ...

I saw the walls surrounding Babylon, with high towers on them, and I saw legions of demons in the form of serpents on the walls of the towers. When they saw me, they rushed at me, eager to kill me, and a fiery flame was coming out their mouths because of their burning venom. The saints turned their faces toward them, so they all anxiously

---

ϩⲱⲥ ⲇⲉ ⲉⲓⲙⲟϣⲓ ⲁⲓϫⲟⲩϣⲧ ϩⲓ ⲫⲟⲩⲉⲓ ⲙⲙⲟⲓ ⲁⲓⲛⲁⲩ ⲙⲫⲣⲏϯ ⲛⲟⲩⲙⲁⲛϣϣⲏⲛ ⲉϥⲭⲏ ⲉⲃⲟⲗ ⲉϥⲟⲓ ⲛϣⲁϥⲉ ⲁⲓⲛⲁⲩ ϧⲉⲛ ⲡⲓⲙⲁ ⲉⲧⲉⲙⲙⲁⲩ ⲉϩⲁⲛⲡⲁⲣⲇⲁⲗⲓⲥ ⲛⲉⲙ ϩⲁⲛⲥⲧⲣⲟⲩⲇⲟⲥ ⲛⲉⲙ ϩⲁⲛⲟⲕⲉⲛⲧⲁⲩⲣⲟⲥ ⲛⲉⲙ ϩⲁⲛⲕⲉⲛⲓϣϯ ⲛⲇⲣⲁⲕⲱⲛ ⲉⲩⲟⲓ ⲛϩⲟϯ ⲉⲙⲁϣⲱ. ⲉⲧⲁⲩⲛⲁⲩ ⲉⲣⲟⲓ ⲁⲩϯⲙⲡⲟⲩⲟⲩⲟⲓ ⲉⲣⲟⲓ ϧⲉⲛ ⲟⲩϫⲱⲛⲧ ⲉⲩⲟⲩⲱϣ ⲉϧⲱⲧⲉⲃ ⲙⲙⲟⲓ ⲁⲛⲟⲕ ⲇⲉ ⲁⲓϭⲓ ⲛⲏⲓ ⲛⲟⲩⲙⲉⲧϫⲁⲣϩⲏⲧ ⲁⲓⲁⲙⲟⲛⲓ ⲙⲡⲓⲉⲩⲁⲅⲅⲉⲗⲓⲟⲛ ⲕⲁⲧⲁ ⲓⲱⲁⲛⲛⲏⲥ [139] ⲁⲓⲱϣ ⲛϧⲏⲧϥ. ϧⲉⲛ ϯⲟⲩⲛⲟⲩ ⲁⲓⲛⲁⲩ ⲉⲓⲱⲁⲛⲛⲏⲥ ⲡⲓⲉⲩⲁⲅⲅⲉⲗⲓⲥⲧⲏⲥ ⲛⲉⲙ ⲡⲓⲁⲣⲭⲏⲁⲅⲅⲉⲗⲟⲥ ⲙⲓⲭⲁⲏⲗ ⲡⲉϫⲱⲟⲩ ⲛⲏⲓ ϫⲉ ⲙⲡⲉⲣⲉⲣϩⲟϯ ⲧⲉⲛϣⲟⲡ ⲛⲉⲙⲁⲕ ⲛⲥⲏⲟⲩ ⲛⲓⲃⲉⲛ ⲛⲁⲓ ⲧⲏⲣⲟⲩ ⲉⲧⲉⲕⲛⲁⲩ ⲉⲣⲱⲟⲩ ϩⲁⲛⲇⲉⲙⲱⲛ ⲛⲉ ⲙⲡⲉⲣⲉⲣϩⲟϯ ⲟⲩⲛ ϧⲁⲧⲟⲩϩⲏ. ⲁⲥϣⲱⲡⲓ ⲇⲉ ⲉⲧⲁⲓϧⲱⲛⲧ ⲉϧⲟⲩⲛ ⲉⲃⲁⲃⲩⲗⲱⲛ ⲛⲓ̅ⲇ̅ ⲙⲙⲩⲗⲗⲓⲟⲛ ⲁⲓⲓ ⲉⲛⲓⲑⲱϣ ⲛⲧⲉ ⲧⲕⲟⲓ ⲛⲓⲣⲁ ⲕⲉⲅⲁⲣ ⲡⲓⲙⲁ ⲉⲧⲉⲙⲙⲁⲩ ϥϧⲟⲥⲓ ⲛⲥⲓⲛⲓ ⲛϧⲏⲧϥ ⲉⲙⲁϣⲱ ⲉⲑⲃⲉ ⲡⲁϣⲁⲓ ⲛⲛⲓⲑⲏⲣⲓⲟⲛ ⲛⲉⲙ ⲛⲓϭⲁⲧϥⲓ ⲛⲉⲙ ⲛⲓϩⲟϥ ⲉⲧϩⲱⲟⲩ. ⲁⲡⲓⲙⲁⲕⲁⲣⲓⲟⲥ ⲓⲱⲁⲛⲛⲏⲥ ⲉⲣⲙⲉⲑⲣⲉ ⲛⲏⲓ ϫⲉ ⲁⲓⲛⲁⲩ ⲉϩⲁⲛⲛⲓϣϯ ⲛⲇⲣⲁⲕⲱⲛ ϧⲉⲛ ⲡⲓⲙⲁ ⲉⲧⲉⲙⲙⲁⲩ ϩⲱⲥ ϫⲉ ⲛⲧⲁϫⲟⲥ ϩⲱ ϧⲉⲛ ⲡⲁϩⲏⲧ ϫⲉ ⲡⲓⲟⲩⲁⲓ ⲛϧⲏⲧⲟⲩ ⲛⲁⲱⲙⲕ ⲛⲟⲩⲕⲟⲩϫⲓ ⲛⲁⲗⲟⲩ ⲉϥϧⲉⲛ ⲅ̅ ⲛⲣⲟⲙⲡⲓ ⲉⲑⲃⲉ ⲡⲓϧⲑⲁⲓ ⲛⲧⲉ ⲧⲟⲩϣⲃⲱⲃⲓ ⲉⲣⲉ ⲡⲟⲩϩⲟ ⲟⲛⲓ ⲛϩⲁⲛⲕⲟⲩϫⲓ ⲛⲉⲙⲥⲁϩ. ϧⲉⲛ ⲡϫⲓⲛⲑⲣⲟⲩϧⲱⲛⲧ ⲅⲁⲣ ⲉⲣⲟⲓ ⲁⲡⲓⲁⲣⲭⲏⲁⲅⲅⲉⲗⲟⲥ ⲉⲑⲟⲩⲁⲃ ⲙⲓⲭⲁⲏⲗ ⲛⲉⲙ ⲡⲓⲁⲅⲓⲟⲥ ⲓⲱⲁⲛⲛⲏⲥ ⲡⲓⲉⲩⲁⲅⲅⲉⲗⲓⲥⲧⲏⲥ ⲉⲣⲉⲡⲓⲧⲓⲙⲁⲛ ⲛⲱⲟⲩ ⲁⲩϣⲱⲕⲓ ϧⲉⲛ ⲡⲓⲕⲁϩⲓ ⲁⲩϣⲉ ⲛⲱⲟⲩ ⲙⲡⲓⲛⲁⲩ ⲉⲣⲱⲟⲩ ϫⲉ

[136] [141.9-15]:

ⲙⲉⲛⲉⲛⲥⲱⲥ ⲁⲓⲙⲟϣⲓ ⲉⲧϩⲏ ⲙⲡϣⲓ ⲛⲟⲩⲙⲩⲗⲓⲟⲛ ⲁⲓϫⲟⲩϣⲧ ⲉϧⲟⲩⲛ ⲙⲫⲛⲁⲩ ⲛⲛⲁⲃⲁⲗ ⲁⲓⲛⲁⲩ ⲉⲃⲁⲃⲩⲗⲱⲛ ϯⲡⲟⲗⲓⲥ ⲉⲣⲉ ⲟⲩⲭⲁⲕⲓ ⲫⲟⲣϣ ⲉⲃⲟⲗ ϩⲓϫⲱⲥ ⲛⲉⲙ ⲟⲩⲛⲓϣϯ ⲛϫⲟⲥⲉⲙ ⲙⲫⲣⲏϯ ⲛⲟⲩⲕⲁⲡⲛⲟⲥ ⲛⲧⲉ ⲟⲩϩⲣⲱ ⲛⲭⲣⲱⲙ. ⲁⲓⲓ ⲟⲛ ⲉϫⲉⲛ ⲛⲓⲓⲁⲣⲱⲟⲩ ⲛⲧⲉ ⲃⲁⲃⲩⲗⲱⲛ ⲁⲓϫⲉⲙⲟⲩ ⲉⲩⲕⲱϯ ⲉϯⲡⲟⲗⲓⲥ ⲧⲏⲣⲥ ⲁⲓϩⲉⲙⲥⲓ ⲥⲁϧⲣⲏⲓ ⲛⲛⲓⲃⲱⲛⲑⲱⲣⲓ ⲉⲧⲣⲏⲧ ϩⲓϫⲉⲛ ⲛⲓⲓⲁⲣⲱⲟⲩ ⲛⲧⲉ ⲃⲁⲃⲩⲗⲱⲛ ϫⲉ ϩⲓⲛⲁ ⲛⲧⲁⲙⲧⲟⲛ ⲙⲙⲟⲓ ⲉⲑⲃⲉ ⲡⲓϧⲓⲥⲓ.

fled. When we got to the city-gate, there were seven gigantic walls surrounding it, as though six cities were built together in a single spot. When I entered the city, I saw it was deserted, with no people or domesticated animals, but instead just reptiles, demons, wealth – once like the sands of the sea and now owned by demons – and everything bad.[137]

This is, of course, much more than *The Pearlsong* says about Babylon, but the prince, explicitly apprehensive about the region, may have had such visions in mind when describing "the perverse Babylonians and the riotous devils of Sarbug."

Given *The Pearlsong*'s possible relationships to Manichaean writers and readers, it's worth mentioning that Babylon in Manichaean texts is known, not necessarily negatively, as a haunt for demons and monsters, but as Mani's home. A hymn in Parthian, for example, has Mani in autobiographic mode:

I am a grateful student
who is sprouted from the country of Babylon.
I am sprouted from the country of Babylon
and I stand at the truth-door.

I am a young student
who left the land of Babylon.

---

[137] [143.6–144.4]:

ⲁⲛⲟⲕ ⲇⲉ ⲁⲓⲛⲁⲩ ⲉⲛⲓⲥⲟⲃⲧ ⲉⲧⲕⲱϯ ⲉⲃⲁⲃⲩⲗⲱⲛ ⲉⲣⲉ ϩⲁⲛⲡⲩⲣⲅⲟⲥ ϩⲓϫⲱⲟⲩ ⲉⲩϭⲟⲥⲓ ⲉⲙⲁϣⲱ ⲁⲓⲛⲁⲩ ⲉϩⲁⲛⲛⲓϣϯ ⲛⲗⲉⲅⲓⲟⲛ ⲛⲇⲉⲙⲱⲛ ϩⲓϫⲉⲛ ⲛⲓⲥⲟⲃⲧ ⲛⲧⲉ ⲛⲓⲡⲩⲣⲅⲟⲥ ⲉⲩⲟⲓ ⲙⲡⲥⲙⲟⲧ ⲛϩⲁⲛⲇⲣⲁⲕⲱⲛ. ⲉⲧⲁⲩⲛⲁⲩ ⲉⲣⲟⲓ ⲁⲩϯⲙⲡⲟⲩⲟⲩⲟⲓ ⲉⲣⲟⲓ ⲉⲩⲟⲩⲱϣ ⲉϧⲱⲧⲉⲃ ⲙⲙⲟⲓ ⲛⲁⲣⲉ ⲟⲩϣⲁϩ ⲛⲭⲣⲱⲙ ⲡⲉ ⲛⲛⲟⲩ ⲉⲃⲟⲗ ϧⲉⲛ ⲣⲱⲟⲩ ϩⲓⲧⲉⲛ ⲡⲓⲣⲱⲕϩ ⲛⲧⲉ ⲧⲟⲩⲙⲁⲑⲟⲩⲓ. ⲛⲏ ⲉⲑⲟⲩⲁⲃ ⲇⲉ ⲁⲩⲕⲱϯ ⲙⲡⲟⲩϩⲟ ⲉⲣⲱⲟⲩ ⲡⲁⲓⲣⲏϯ ⲁⲩⲫⲱⲧ ⲧⲏⲣⲟⲩ ϧⲉⲛ ⲟⲩⲥⲑⲉⲣⲧⲉⲣ. ⲁⲥϣⲱⲡⲓ ⲇⲉ ⲉⲧⲁⲛⲫⲟϩ ⲉⲛⲓⲡⲩⲗⲏ ⲛⲧⲉ ϯⲡⲟⲗⲓⲥ ⲉⲣⲉ ⲍ ⲛⲥⲧⲩⲭⲟⲥ ⲕⲱϯ ⲉⲣⲟⲥ ⲉⲥⲟⲓ ⲛⲛⲓϣϯ ⲉⲙⲁϣⲱ ϩⲱⲥ ⲇⲉ ⲋ ⲙⲡⲟⲗⲓⲥ ⲉⲩⲕⲏⲧ ϧⲉⲛ ⲟⲩⲙⲱⲓⲧ ⲛⲟⲩⲱⲧ ⲉⲩⲥⲟⲡ. ϧⲉⲛ [144] ⲡϫⲓⲛⲑⲣⲓϩⲱⲗ ⲉⲣⲟⲥ ⲁⲓⲛⲁⲩ ⲉⲣⲟⲥ ⲉⲥⲟⲓ ⲛϣⲁϥⲉ ⲙⲙⲟⲛ ⲣⲱⲙⲓ ⲛϧⲏⲧⲥ ⲟⲩⲇⲉ ⲧⲉⲃⲛⲏ ⲓⲙⲏϯ ⲉϭⲁⲧϥⲓ ⲛⲉⲙ ⲇⲉⲙⲱⲛ ⲛⲉⲙ ⲭⲣⲏⲙⲁ ⲉⲩⲟⲓ ⲛⲫⲣⲏϯ ⲛⲡⲓϣⲱ ⲛⲧⲉ ⲫⲓⲟⲙ ⲉⲧ ⲁⲛⲓⲇⲉⲙⲱⲛ ⲉⲣϭ̅ⲥ̅ ⲉⲣⲱⲟⲩ ⲛⲉⲙ ϩⲱⲃ ⲛⲓⲃⲉⲛ ⲉⲧϩⲱⲟⲩ.

> I left the land of Babylon
> so I could call out at the world.[138]

Mani is known as the "interpreter of the country of Babylon the great."[139] According to the *Kephalaia*, Mani also returns to Babylon in the course of his preaching and travels:

> At the end of King Ardashir's time I went out to preach. I traveled to India and preached the hope of life to the people there: I chose a good elect-group there. In the same year that King Ardashir died, Shapur his son became king. He [...]. I traveled from India to Persia, and from Persia I went to Babylon, Mesene, and Susa. I appeared before King Shapur, and he received me with great honor and gave me permission to travel in [...], preaching the message of life.[140]

Babylon had long been famous for its buildings, like Nebuchadnezzar's summer-palace, the Esagila temple complex, and the old ziggurat, Etemenanki. In the Parthian period, the palace seems to have been in use as a fort, and the sanctuaries also survived, but not necessarily as temples. Parthian houses with courtyards and colonnaded streets from

---

[138] Boyce text cv, 21; p. 162:

abžīrwānag išnōhrag hēm
kē až bābel zamīg wisprixt hēm
wisprixt hēm až zamīg bābel
ud pad rāštīft bar awištad hēm

sarāwag hēm abžīrwānag
kē až bābel zamīg franaft hēm
franaft hēm až zamīg bābel
kū xrōsān xrōs pad zambūdīg

[139] MHm 61.16-17: ϩⲉⲣⲙⲏⲛⲉ̣[ⲩⲧⲏⲥ] ⲙ̅ⲡⲕⲁϩ ⲛ̅ⲧⲛⲁϭ̣ ⲛ̅ⲃⲁⲃⲩⲗⲱⲛ.

[140] Kph 15.24-33: ϩⲛ̅ ⲧϩⲁⲏ ⲛⲛⲣⲙⲡⲉⲩⲉ ⲛⲁⲣⲧⲁⳉ[ⲟⲟⲥ] ⲡⲣ̅ⲣⲟ ⲁⲉ̈ⲓ ⲁⲃⲁⲗ ⲁⲧⲁϣⲉⲁⲓ̈ϣ ⲁⲓ̈ϫⲓⲟⲣⲉ ⲁⲧⲭⲱⲣⲁ ⲛⲛ̅ϩⲛⲧⲟⲩ ⲁ[ⲓ̈]ⲧⲁϣⲉⲁⲓ̈ϣ ⲛⲉⲩ ⲛⲧϩⲉⲗⲡⲓⲥ ⲙ̅ⲡⲱⲛϩ ⲁⲓ̈ⲥⲱⲧⲡ ⲙⲡⲙⲁ ⲉⲧⲙⲙⲉⲩ ⲛ̅ⲟⲩⲙⲛⲧⲥⲱⲧⲡ ⲉⲥⲁⲛⲓⲧ ϩⲛ̅ ⲧⲣⲁⲙⲡⲉ ⲇⲉ ϩⲱⲱϥ [ⲉⲧⲁ ⲁⲣⲧⲁ]ⳉⲟⲟⲥ ⲡⲣ̅ⲣⲟ ⲙⲟⲩ ⲁ ⲥⲁⲡⲱⲣⲏⲥ ⲡⲉϥϣⲏⲣⲉ ⲣ̅ⲣⲣⲟ ⲁϥϫ . . . . . ⲁⲓ̈ϫⲓⲟⲣⲉ ϫⲛ ⲛⲧⲭⲱⲣⲁ ⲛⲛϩⲛⲧⲟⲩ ⲁⲡⲕⲁϩ ⲛⲛⲡⲉⲣⲥⲏⲥ ϫⲛ̅ ⲛⲡⲕⲁϩ ⲁⲛ ⲛⲧⲡⲉⲣⲥⲓⲥ ⲁⲉ̈ⲓ [ⲁ]ⲡⲕⲁϩ ⲛⲧⲃⲁⲃⲩⲗⲱⲛ ⲧⲙⲁⲓ̈ⲥⲁⲛ[ⲟⲥ] ⲙⲛ̅ ⲧⲭⲱⲣⲁ ⲛⲟⲍⲉⲟⲥ ⲁⲓ̈ⲟ[ⲩ]ⲱⲛϩ̅ ⲁⲥⲁⲡⲱⲣⲏⲥ ⲡⲣ̅ⲣⲟ ⲁϥϩⲩⲡⲟⲇ[ⲉ]ⲭⲉ ⲙⲙⲁⲓ̈ ϩⲛ̅ ⲟⲩⲛⲁϭ ⲛⲧ[ⲁⲓ̈]ⲟ ⲁϥϯⲙⲁ ⲛⲏⲓ̈ ⲁⲧⲁⲙⲁϩⲉ ϩⲛ [. . . . . . ⲉⲓ̈ⲧⲁ]ϣⲉⲁⲓ̈ϣ ⲙⲡⲥⲉϫⲉ ⲙⲡⲱⲛϩ

the first and second centuries CE have been found south of Esagila.[141] According to Strabo:

> Most of Babylon has now turned into an ample desert, so that you wouldn't hesitate to refer to it by quoting one of the comics on the big-city-folk in Arcadia, "The big city's a big desert!"[142]

When Trajan was there in 116, not only was Parthian control in enough disarray that entering Babylon was easy, but Babylon itself hardly met his expectations: "for indeed he had come there because of how famous it was, but all he saw indicative of this was mounds, stones, and ruins."[143] Almost three centuries later, Babylon is still known as a wild, deserted place. In his commentary to Isaiah 5:14, Jerome remarks:

> We've learned from a Persian colleague, who's from there and now leading a monk's life in Jerusalem, that there are royal hunts in Babylon and all kinds of beasts are all that's kept in the circuit of its walls. ... for with the exception of the burned out walls, now restored after many years to keep the animals in, the entire middle part is a wasteland.[144]

Sarbug At this first mention of Sarbug in the poem, the Greek doesn't have anything, but, elsewhere when it occurs, it uses the proper name Labyrinth. The otherwise unknown place-name, Sarbug, oc-

---

[141] Oppenheimer, *Babylonia Judaica*, 54.

[142] *Geography* 16.1.5 (text in Oppenheimer, *Babylonia Judaica*, 48): *καὶ δὴ καὶ νῦν ἡ μὲν γέγονε Βαβυλῶνος μείζων ἡ δ' ἔρημος ἡ πόλλη, ὥστ' ἐπ' αὐτῆς μὴ ἂν ὀκνῆσαί τινα εἰπεῖν ὅπερ ἔφη τις τῶν κωμικῶν ἐπὶ τῶν Μεγαλοπολιτῶν τῶν ἐν Ἀρκαδίᾳ «ἐρημία μεγάλη 'στὶν ἡ Μεγάλη πόλις»*

[143] Cassius Dio 68.30.1 (text in Oppenheimer, *Babylonia Judaica*, 51): *και γὰρ ἐκεῖσε ἦλθε κατά τε τὴν φήμην, ἧς οὐδὲν ἄξιον εἶδεν ὅ τι μὴ χώματα καὶ λίθους καὶ ἐρείπια*. See also Cassius Dio 68.26.4 (Oppenheimer, *Babylonia Judaica*, 50).

[144] *Patrologia Latina* 24 163, 168; text in Oppenheimer, *Babylonia Judaica*, 51–52:

> Didicimus a quodam fratre Elamita, qui de illis finibus egrediens, nunc Hierosolymis vitam exigit monachorum, venationes regias esse in Babylone, et omnis generis bestias murorum eius tantum ambitu coerceri. ... exceptis enim muris coctilibus, qui propter bestias concludendas post annos plurimos instaurantur, omne in medio spatium solitudo est

curs three times in the poem, every time together with Babylon. The Greek translator calls it "Labyrinth," which is as puzzling (pun intended), as Sarbug. While it could be a portmanteau, accidental or intentional, of the better known place-names Sarug <srwg> and Mabbug <mbwg> (not least for Syriac writers associated with them, Jacob and Philoxenos, respectively), another early suggestion is Borsippa, <bwrs(y)p>, as a possibility of the original.[145] Nöldeke notes that it occurs as a pair with Babylon in Mandaic sources, and we can add that they also appear together in the Talmud.[146] Burkitt suggested the ancient city of Shuruppak, but it's hard to imagine a poet or reader of the early first millennium CE who could really have been aware of its name as such.[147]

Another suggestion is Vologesias, established in the first century CE near Seleucia-Ctesiphon.[148] Vologesias was a major stopping-place for travelers and merchants between Babylon and Palmyra.[149] Some spe-

[145] Nöldeke, Rev., 679.

[146] For example, אף אנו נאמר בבל בורסיף בורסיף בבל "we also say, 'Babylon is Borsippa, and Borsippa is Babylon'" (*Shabbat* 36a//*Sukkah* 34a, in Jewish Babylonian Aramaic). See further Oppenheimer, *Babylonia Judaica*, 100.

[147] Burkitt, "Sarbog."

[148] On Vologesias, see Oppenheimer, *Babylonia Judaica*, 456-461, and Nöldeke, "Geographie," 93-98. The prices of the city's market could serve as an economic standard. Mentioned specifically with reference to its *parwåtå*, "market" (DJBA 930a, the plural of a word for "port, harbor"), the city's name is variously spelled in manuscripts of the Talmud, including <by(-)lšpṭ>, <wylšpṭ>, <lšpṭ>, <wlšpṭ>, <wwlšpṭ>, <by-ʔlšpṭ>.

[149] In Tubach's explanation ("Weg," 95):

> While the prince passed Mesene, and partly Babylon, on the way to Egypt, on his return he stuck strictly to the caravan route. Based on this, Sarbug, which is actually mentioned in the text three times, has to have been located on this route, a city that could have played an important role in trade. In the Palmyrene inscriptions, after Charax Spasinou, Vologesias is the most frequently mentioned. From these texts it is singularly apparent that Vologesias was the most important stop along the way for a caravan between the Persian Gulf and Palmyra. The Palmyrene merchants had a trade branch in Vologesias, and sometimes they took caravans only as far as there.
>
> Wahrend der Prinz auf der Hinreise nach Ägypten die Mesene und teilweise auch Babylonien passiert, hält er sich auf dem Rückweg strikt an die Karawanenroute. Aus diesem Grund muß an ihr das im Text gleich dreimal erwähnte Sarbūg gelegen haben, eine Stadt, die eine

cific quotations from the Palmyrene inscriptions will illustrate the city's connection to trade. First, from 142 CE, there's an honorific inscription set up for someone by "the caravan-group that went up from Forat and Vologesias with him."[150] From close to the same time (dated 150 CE) is an inscription that mentions "the caravan-group that went down from Palmyra to Vologesias with him."[151] A final similar example comes from a century and a half later, dated 297 CE: "the caravan-merchants who went down to Vologesias with him."[152] So, from a time around the setting of the events in *The Pearlsong* there's clear evidence at Palmyra for Vologesias as a notable city along the trade route to Egypt.

So, maybe "Sarbug" is a portmanteau of Sarug and Mabbug, maybe it's a garbled version of Borsippa, or even Shuruppak, but what about the word/name itself, as such?[153] A "tower" in Middle Persian is a *sarbūg*, and similarly Sogdian has *sārβā/ūγ*.[154] A place named after a word for tower isn't unusual – Magdala on the Sea of Galilee, for example – but one with this Iranian word for tower isn't known along the prince's possible route.

nicht geringe Bedeutung im Transithandel gespielt haben dürfte. In den palmyrenischen Inschriften wird nun nach Charax Spasinou am häufigsten Vologesias genannt. Aus den Texten ist eindeutig ersichtlich, daß Vologesias der wichtigste Etappenort einer Karawane zwischen dem Persischen Golf und Palmyra war. In Vologesias besaßen die palmyrenischen Kaufleute eine Handelsniederlassung, und manchmal zogen die Karawanen auch nur bis Vologesias.

[150] C3916 = PAT 0262, 2-3 (Hillers and Cussini, *Palmyrene*, 63):

𐡡𐡮𐡩 𐡵𐡩𐡴𐡶𐡠 𐡣𐡩 𐡯𐡫𐡳 𐡰𐡬𐡤 𐡬𐡭 𐡱𐡴𐡶 𐡥𐡬𐡭 𐡠𐡫𐡢𐡵𐡩𐡠

<bny šyrtʔ dy slq ʕmh mn prt wmn ʔlgšyʔ>. This corresponds to Greek lines 2-4, with the same sense: *οἱ συναναβάντες μετ᾽ αὐτοῦ ἔμποροι ἀπὸ Φοράθου κὲ Ὀλογασιάδος*.

[151] Inv 10 124 = PAT 1419, 3-4; Hillers and Cussini, *Palmyrene*, 209:

𐡡𐡮𐡩 𐡵𐡩𐡴𐡶𐡠 𐡣𐡩 𐡮𐡧𐡶𐡥 𐡰𐡬𐡤 𐡬𐡭 𐡶𐡣𐡬𐡥𐡴 𐡫𐡠𐡫𐡢𐡵𐡩𐡠

<bny šyrtʔ dy nḥtw ʕmh mn tdmwr lʔlgšyʔ>.

[152] C3933 = PAT 0279, 3-4; C3916 = PAT 0262, 2-3 (Hillers and Cussini, *Palmyrene*, 66-67):

𐡶𐡢𐡴𐡠 𐡡𐡮𐡩 𐡵𐡩𐡴𐡶𐡠 𐡣𐡩 𐡮𐡧𐡶 𐡰𐡬𐡤 𐡫𐡠𐡫𐡢𐡵𐡩𐡠

<tgrʔ bny šyrtʔ dy nḥt ʕmh lʔlgšyʔ>.

[153] Cf. Tubach, "Weg," 100.

[154] DMMPP 308b and Gharib, *Sogdian Dictionary*, nos. 8720 and 8724.

Adam cites Arabic *šarbūka*, meaning labyrinth (like the Greek), but without any lexical reference.[155] It's not a widespread lexeme, but it indeed means "complication, predicament, net."[156] Along these lines, we can also mention Syriac *šarbuqiṯå* "snare."[157]

Finally, the story of *The Martyrs of Karka d-Beth Slok* begins with a history of the successive building and rebuilding of the city and its walls and towers, beginning with the Assyrian king, Esarhaddon, son of Sennacherib. This text offers a comparative picture of how an established, royally built city later in the Seleucid and Parthian periods might have been envisioned. Even more to the point, it includes a watchtower named "Sarbuy," from the aforementioned Iranian word for "tower." Here is this part of the text:

> Seleucus, the king of the Greeks, who was listed above, came after Darius and turned the city-wall Darius had built into rubble and built a high wall on top of it. He constructed 65 towers for this wall that he had built, along with a southeastern gate and a northwestern gate. At the southeastern gate he installed a stone engraving on it matching its height. On the right and left of this gate were towers made of stone and quicklime. This was the king's gate, and the other gate was named for the person in whose governorship it was built: Tutay. Seleucus built a palace inside the city, and developed it and made it teem with streets and plazas: he built it up extensively not only inside the wall, but outside, too. He divided it by 72 streets, and he brought the five aforementioned families from Eṣṭahar and settled them there, along with other people he brought from various places. He gave these five families lands and vineyards there and he exempted the city from having to pay tribute. Twelve streets were named for twelve known families, and the rest were named after trades. And as a memorial to the name of king Esarhaddon, who had

[155] *Psalmen*, 64.

[156] Barthélemy, *Dictionnaire*, 384. Cf. also Arabic *šabbak* "entangle, intertwine," with dissimilation of the double *-bb-*.

[157] BB 2007.

first built the city, Seleucus built a watchtower beside his palace, which he built inside a fortress: it's now called Sarbuy.[158]

Whether it's a word related to a tower, to entanglement, or to a combination thereof, "Sarbug," along with Babylon, was a place of danger to be avoided. The letter that the royal family sends is marked as a royal missive and flies through the air eagle-like "because of the perverse Babylonians and the riotous devils of Sarbug" (line 50).

my attendants left me Time is up for the prince's guardians, and 20
here they leave both him and the narrative. The sentiments of the Old English *Wanderer*-poet fit here:

> Anyone who's experienced knows how cruel a comrade sorrow is for people who have little in the way of friendly protectors: an exile-path holds them, not the earth's bounty. ... Happiness has all depleted.[159]

---

[158] AMS 2 510-511:

ܘܟܕ ܬܪܘܨ ܐܬܐ ܣܠܘܩܘܣ ܡܠܟܐ ܗܘ: ܗܘ ܕܪܫܡ ܡܢ ܠܥܠ: ܘܠܘܬܗ ܫܘܪܗ
ܕܒܢܐ ܕܒܢܐ ܒܒܢܝܢܗ ܗܘ ܬܠܠܐ: ܘܒܢܐ ܠܥܠ ܡܢܗ ܫܘܪܐ ܪܒܐ. ܘܥܒܕ ܠܗ ܠܫܘܪܐ
ܕܒܢܐ ܦܘܪܩܣܐ: ܗܠܐ ܕܝܢ ܒܬܪܟܐ ܥܠܡ ܘܣܓܝܐ. ܘܥܒܕ ܠܗ ܠܬܘܟܡ ܡܒܢܝܢ ܬܪܥܐ
ܣܢ: ܘܠܒܢܝ ܡܒܢܝ ܬܪܥܐ ܐܣܝܢܐ. ܘܠܗܘ ܬܪܥܐ ܕܬܘܟܡ ܡܒܢܝܢ: ܐܬܘܡ ܒܠܘܗܝ
ܒܡܘܫܚܬܗ ܠܒܠܦܐ ܕܒܐܦܐ. ܘܡܢ ܡܟܝܠܗ ܘܡܢ ܗܫܟܠܗ: ܥܠ ܚܕ ܬܪܥܐ ܗܘܝܐ:
ܦܘܪܩܣܐ ܕܐܒܐܦܐ ܘܒܠܥܐ. ܘܗܢܐ ܬܪܥܐ ܐܬܘܡܗܝ ܗܘܐ ܕܡܠܟܐ. ܘܗܘ ܐܣܝܢܐ
ܐܬܘܪܝ ܗܘܐ: ܥܠ ܫܡܗ ܕܗܘ ܕܐܬܒܢܝ ܒܪܝܫܘܬܗ: ܠܦܠܦ. ܘܒܢܐ ܣܠܘܩܘܣ
ܒܓܘܗ ܒܝܬ ܡܠܟܘܬܐ: ܘܐܬܘܩܡܗ ܘܫܪܝܬܗ ܒܥܘܡܩܐ ܘܒܦܠܛܘܬܐ: ܠܐ ܒܠܘܫ.
ܠܟܗ ܡܢ ܫܘܪܐ: ܐܠܐ ܘܠܒܪ ܡܢ ܫܘܪܐ ܗܟܢ ܐܘܪܒܗ. ܘܫܠܟܗ ܠܥܒܕܝܢ ܘܬܘܪܝܢ
ܫܘܩܝܢ: ܘܐܢܬܝ ܫܪܒܬܐ ܢܬܒܬܐ ܣܓܝܐ ܡܢ ܐܢܛܝܘܟܝܐ ܘܐܘܬܒ ܒܗ: ܒܡ ܫܪܒܐ
ܕܐܢܫܐ ܕܐܢܬܝ ܡܢ ܐܬܪ ܐܬܪ. ܘܝܗܒ ܠܗܠܝܢ ܫܪܒܬܐ ܣܓܝܐ ܕܐܢܬܝ: ܐܪܒܬܐ
ܘܬܪܥܐ ܒܗ ܒܐܬܪܐ: ܘܫܡܗܘܢ ܠܬܪܥܐ ܕܠܐ ܡܕܐܬܐ. ܘܬܪܒܨܗ ܫܘܩܝܢ ܥܠ ܫܡ
ܬܪܒܨܗ ܫܪܒܐ ܢܬܒܡ ܐܬܒܢܝܘ ܗܘܘ. ܘܕܫܪܒܐ ܥܠ ܫܡ ܐܘܡܢܘܬܐ ܐܫܬܡܗܘ
ܗܘܘ. ܘܒܢܐ ܣܠܘܩܘܣ ܥܠ ܫܡ ܒܗܕܢܐ ܕܗܪܕܢܐ ܡܠܟܐ: ܗܘ ܕܒܢܝܗ ܠܟܪܟܐ
ܡܕܝܢܬܐ: ܒܢܐ ܕܘܟܐ ܥܠ ܓܒ ܒܝܬ ܡܠܟܘܬܗ: ܕܒܢܐ ܒܓܘܗ ܕܚܨܢܐ: ܗܘ
ܕܒܢܐ ܠܗܫܐ ܣܪܒܘܝ ܡܫܬܡܗ.

[159] 25-36:

Wāt se þe cunnað
hū slīþen bið sorg tō gefēran
þām þe him lȳt hafað lēofra geholena:

21 **its lair** The idea of giant serpents living in caves is an ancient one, "with the cave serving the function of a snake's hole writ large, and as an eloquent symbol of their bond with the earth."[160] As Kuehn lists their habitats, "They dwell not only in springs, wells, rivers, lakes or sea water, but also in mountains, forests, caverns, caves, crevices and other subterranean enclosures, hence lending themselves to association with the underworld and chthonic forces."[161]

The term *ʔašpåzå* "lodge, inn, house" is an Iranian loanword.[162] Bar Bahlul marks it as an Aramaic dialect word, and reports that the people of Mosul and Beth Garmay pronounced it without the initial syllable. He also calls the related noun *ʔašpizkånå* ("host, householder") a Syriac-Persian "stolen term," showing that it was considered as a loanword. Further, for Bar Bahlul, it just means something like "house, domicile, residence."[163]

22 **Waiting until it dozed and slept** Hero-monster encounters, including those with serpent-dragons, may at first conjure images of combat, like Ninurta and Anzu's:

> Weapons clashed in chilling shade,
> they both bathed in battle-sweat.
> Anzu got tired in the stormy conflict and let his wing drop
> ...
> A shaft penetrated the contours of his heart.

---

warað hine wræclāst, nalæs foldan blǣd.
... Wyn eal gedrēas!

[160] Ogden, *Drakon*, 161.

[161] Kuehn, *Dragon*, 52.

[162] ILS 118; cf. Pa/MP *ispenǰ* inn, hostel, place to stay (DMMPP 87b, *ašpinǰ* ([CPD 12]); NP سپنج *sepanǧ*.

[163] BB 310:

> ܐܫܦܙܐ ܒܠܫܢܐ ܐܪܡܝܐ البيت. ܐܫܦܙܗ ܐܝܟ ܒܪ ܣܪܘܫ دعايمه
> وعندي انّه مسكنه. ܐܫܦܙܐ َاقول انّه المنزل المسكن واهل الموصل
> وباجرمي يقولون ܫܦܙܐ܀

ʔašpåzå in Aramaic, it means house. *ʔašpåzēh* acc. to Bar Srošway, "his supports," but in my opinion it's "his residence." I think *ʔašpåzå* means "dwelling, residence." In Mosul and Beth Garmay they say *špåzå*.

He made the arrow penetrate pinion and wing,
the arrow penetrated heart and lung.
He smote the mountains, he troubled and overwhelmed their inside.
Ninurta smote the mountains, he troubled and rushed at their inside.
His anger rushed over the wide land,
he rushed into the heart of the mountains and smote evil Anzu.[164]

But there's no such contest for the prince and the dragon. As Niketas says, the prince planned on retrieving the pearl ἀκοντί "without a fight."

I was one person, left alone, I was a stranger As Moses says, also 23
referring to Egypt, "I was a sometime resident in a foreign country,"[165] a self-declaration that, as "stranger in a strange land," became the title of a novel by Robert Heinlein and songs by the Byrds (instrumental), Leon Russell, and Iron Maiden.

my fellow lodgers Where the Syriac has *bnay ʔašpåz*, "the 'children' of my *ʔašpåzå*," the Greek translation just has τοῖς ἐμοῖς "my ...." Given the polyvalence of *ʔašpåzå* – "home" or "inn" – the Syriac may refer to either the prince's fellow-lodgers, as I've translated it, or the prince's relatives or family; the Greek, too, may have either meaning.

---

[164] *Anzû* III 7-9, 14-20:

kakkū utta''irū ṣulūl ḫurbāši
zu'ʾt tamḫāri irtamukū kilallān
īnaḫ-ma anzû ina mitḫur meḫê abaršu iddi
šiltāḫu ībira būn libbīšu
abra kappa ušēbira šukuda
libba u ḫašî ībir šiltāḫu
inār ḫursānī qerbēssunu udalliḫ irḫiṣ
ninurta inār ḫursānī qerbessunu udalliḫ irḫiṣ
irḫiṣ uzzuššu erṣeta rapašta
irḫiṣ ina qereb ḫursānī lemna anzâ inār-ma

[165] Exodus 2:22: Hebrew גר הייתי בארץ נכריה, Syriac ܬܘܬܒܐ ܗܘܝܬ ܒܐܪܥܐ ܢܘܟܪܝܬܐ, Greek πάροικός εἰμι ἐν γῇ ἀλλοτρίᾳ.

24 **someone there from my people, freeborn from the East** A counterpart for the prince arrives, coming all the way from the prince's homeland and "free" like him. As with Mani, "he [...] sent me my counterpart."[166] And similarly in Coptic, "my counterpart's image came to me with its three angels and gave me the garment, the crown, the palm-frond, and the victory."[167]

While the prince's brother back in the east can be seen as some kind of correlate to the prince, so can this mysterious person from back home. Like the prince, he's from the Easterners (*men madnḥåyē*), born free (*bar ḥērē*), and young (*ṭalyå*). The prince also calls him good-looking and attractive (*paʔyå ḥsidå*).

26 **My age** The MS has *bar mešḥē*, lit. "son of oils," something like "oily man" or maybe a poetic way to say "anointed one." It's an example of the common Semitic usage of a word for son or child to express someone or something's close relationship to someone or something else, in this case, oil(s). Among the Semitic languages, Aramaic languages, including Syriac, show scores of examples of such phrases, as any Syriac dictionary will show; phrases like *bar ḥērå* "free(-born)," *bar ʔeskolå* "student," and *bar šmå* "with the same name." So does *bar mešḥē* have something to do with anointing? Possibly, but the import of anointing for the prince's new and momentary partner isn't obvious. With a cue from Beyer, I read the text as *bar mšuḥt*, replacing ܒܪ ܡܫ̈ܚܐ with ܒܪ ܡܫܘܚܬܝ, lit. "son of my age," i.e. someone the same age as the prince.[168] As Mani refers to "my close-fitting counterpart,"[169] the prince meets someone very much like himself: free-born, from the east, and contemporary in age.

This person and the prince team up, presumably to work together in getting the pearl, and also to avoid any unpleasant altercations with the Egyptians, whom the prince tells his new companion to shun. Then

---

[166]KMK 18.14-16: ἀπέστειλέν μοι [..... .....]υς σύζυγόν [μου].

[167]T. Kell. Copt. 2 120-123 (text in Gardner, *Kellis Literary Texts*, 14): ⲁⲑⲓⲕⲱⲛ ⲙ̄ⲡ[ⲁⲥⲁ]ⲉⲓϣ ⲉⲓ ϣⲁⲣⲁⲉⲓ ⲙⲛ̄ ⲡⲉⲥϣⲁⲙⲧ ⲛ̄ⲁⲅⲅⲉⲗⲟⲥ ⲁⲥϯ ⲛⲏⲓ̈ [ⲛ̄ⲧϩ]ⲃ̄ⲥⲱ ⲙⲛ̄ⲡⲕⲗⲁⲙ ⲙⲛ̄ ⲡⲃⲁⲉ ⲙⲛ̄ ⲡϭⲣⲟ.

[168]For the form ܡܫܘܚܬܝ *mšuxt*, see Nöldeke, *Syriac Grammar*, §145F; cf. *tešboḥt* my praise, *mēḵult* my food.

[169]KMK 23.5-6: ὁ σύζηγός μου ὁ ἀραρώς.

this associate is silently absent, and nothing more is said about him. He shows up in the story at a point when the prince is feeling especially lonely and strange, losing his grip on his former identity and becoming something else. His guides had just left him, he's in a new place after a long trip, and he's waiting on the snake-dragon to go to sleep so he can get the pearl (lines 22–23). This momentary and apparently inert partner, seemingly a kind of double for the prince, means that, during those moments, the prince is no longer really alone on the expedition.

**I made him my expedition partner and brought him in as asso- 27
ciate** These lines partly bring to mind the treasure-hunter who enlists the speaker in a failed expedition in Bob Dylan's "Isis" (written with Jacques Levy in 1975 and released the next year on *Desire*). Even more are they reminiscent of some lines from the *Mani Codex*:

> I reverently received him and took him as my own possession. I believed him to be and to exist as my own, and to be a good and helpful adviser. I recognized him and realized that I'm the one I was split from. I witnessed that I am the same one as him, being completely equal.[170]

**I warned him about the Egyptians and from joining these pol- 28
luted people** The Egyptians in the poem (lines 12, 20, 28, 39, 42, 45, 57) are a vague mass, not individuals. No specific Egyptian does anything at all in the story, and no Egyptian character is singled out except the king, who is mentioned merely to highlight the narrator-prince's dedicated assimilation to a foreign way of life and identity. They're described as "polluted" and, at least to the prince, they have some connection to the serpent, since he's afraid they'll incite the creature against him (line 30). They are tricky and deceptive, and their food can't be trusted (line 32). Indeed, after he samples their cuisine, he falls into an

[170] KMK 24.3–15:

> *εὐσεβ[ῶς δ' ἔλαβόν] τε αὐτὸν καὶ ἐκτησάμην ὡς ἴδιον κτῆμα. ἐπίστευσα δ' αὐτὸν ἐμὸν ὑπάρχοντά τε καὶ ὄντα καὶ σύμβουλον ἀγαθὸν καὶ χρηστὸν ὄντα. ἐπέγνων μὲν αὐτὸν καὶ συνῆκα ὅτι ἐκεῖνος ἐγώ εἰμι ἐξ οὗ διεκρίθην. ἐπεμαρτύρησα δὲ ὅτι ἐγὼ ἐκε[ῖ]νος αὐτός εἰμι ἴσος [ὅλω]ς ὑπάρχων.*

indeterminately long slumber, having forgotten his royal identity and his mission.

While connections between Parthia, the prince's home, and Egypt are known through trade routes, especially via Palmyra, Persian-Egyptian relationships are much older than this.[171] From 525-402 BCE, following the Battle of Pelusium, Egypt was under Achaemenid Persian rule, governed by a satrap.[172] This is the historical and sociolinguistic setting of the numerous documents and texts that constitute the subvariety of Imperial Aramaic – the empire in question being the Achaemenid – known as "Egyptian Aramaic." It's during this period, and partly in this place, that Iranian influence, both lexical and grammatical, especially becomes a factor in Aramaic, an influence that will reverberate through the continuing history of its languages.

After the visit of the Magi, Egypt is also where Jesus's parents flee with him when he's a baby to escape Herod's killing of infant male children (Matthew 2). Just like the prince is able to leave Egypt after receiving a message to wake him and bring back his memory, the family of Jesus leaves Egypt only after an angelic dream-message comes to Joseph with the news that Herod is no longer having babies killed and no longer looking for Jesus, so they re-enter Palestine and go first to Judah and then to Nazareth in the Galilee. This view of Egypt as a sojourning place to escape from in both the Exodus story and the Jesus story is linked in the Gospel of Matthew at 2:15, when Hosea 11:1 is cited: "I have called my son out of Egypt."[173] The prince, too, then stuck in Egypt and in service to the Egyptian king, will be called out of Egypt by his parents and their letter.

Niketas, like several modern interpreters, has the prince being warned, not doing the warning: "counseling me to watch closely for the Egyptians' leaven and dough." The reference to leaven (and dough?) in Nike-

[171] Heinen, "Egypt:" "Palmyrene traders and escorts played a crucial role in the commerce between Egypt and the east, despite tensions between the Roman empire and the Parthians and later the Sasanians. A steady flow of eastern products and ideas (especially Manicheism) had already reached the Nile valley and Alexandria long before Sasanian troops occupied Egypt in 618/19."

[172] Bresciani, "Persians in Egypt."

[173] *ἐξ Αἰγύπτου ἐκάλεσα τὸν υἱόν μου* (וממצרים קראתי לבני).

tas is from a remark by Jesus about Pharisees and, depending on the gospel, others, with "leaven" meaning hypocrisy or some other unwelcome characteristic (Matthew 16:6, Mark 8:15, Luke 12:1).

In any case, in the narrative, the counterpart seems to disappear from view and from any apparent influence. In the *Mani Codex*, Mani's counterpart leads him through a revelatory flight:

> So, then, my most happy, luminous [counterpart] raised me in the air and conveyed me to forbidden places which have escaped the notice of the human places here where we live, and he pointed everything there out to me.[174]

But no such panoramic co-flight occurs in *The Pearlsong*: the counterpart is there for a short, unreported conversation, then he's just gone.

and then rouse the serpent against me According to the prince, the 30
serpent is at least in some way under the potential influence or control of the Egyptians themselves, and so they're all the more dangerous and risky to interact with.

They tricked me into joining them The prince has already, of his 32
own initiative, tried to make himself look like the Egyptians. But now, at least as he tells it, they take this initiative and run with it, inviting and beguiling him further and further to look and act Egyptian. In the previous line, the Egyptians realize that the prince is not an Egyptian, but more than that, it seems, they're not aware of. The prince could for the most part have recited these lines from the Manichaean *Psalmbook*: "The foreigners I joined in with didn't recognize me. They tasted my sweetness, they wanted me to walk with them: I was life for them, but they, well, they were death for me."[175] Like Mani's, this relationship with these "others" will noticeably affect the prince.

accustomed me to their fare The prince has dressed like an Egyptian, joined in with them, and is now forced to eat Egyptian food,

[174] KMK 126.4-12: [*τότε τοί*]*νυν μετεωρίσας* [*με* …]*ς ὁ μακαριώτα*[*τός τε*] *καὶ φωτεινὸς* [*ἀπεκό*]*μισεν εἰς ἀπορ*[*ρήτου*]*ς τόπους οἳ λελή*[*θασιν*] *τούσδε τοὺς τό*[*πους τ*]*ῶν ἀν*(*θρώπ*)*ων καθ' οὓς* [*διάγομ*]*εν. ὑπέδειξεν* [*δέ μοι πάν*]*τα τὰ ἐκεῖσε.*

[175] II 54.19-23: ⲛ̄ϣⲙ̄ⲙⲁⲓ̈ ⲉⲧⲁⲓ̈ⲧⲱⲧ ⲛⲉⲙⲉⲩ ⲛⲉⲥ̣ⲉⲥⲁⲩⲛⲉ ⲙ̄ⲙⲁⲓ̈ ⲁⲛ̣ⲁⲕ̣ ⲉⲛ ⲁⲩϫⲓ ϯⲡⲉ ⲙ̄ⲡⲁϩⲗⲁϭ ⲁⲩⲟⲩⲱϣ ⲉⲙⲁϩⲉ ⲙ̄ⲙⲁⲓ̈ ⲛⲉⲙⲉⲩ ⲁⲓ̈ϣⲱⲡⲉ ⲛⲉⲩ ⲛ̄ⲟⲩⲱⲛϩ ⲛ̄ⲧⲁⲩ ϩⲱⲟⲩⲉ ⲁⲩϣⲱⲡⲉ ⲛⲏⲓ̈ ⲛ̄ⲟⲩⲙⲟⲩ.

sealing the deal. The food you make, acquire, and consume can be a crucial part of your identity. This may be all the more apparent when you're not at home anymore. Avoiding the local cuisine when you're in a strange place marks you out as conspicuously foreign, that is, it shows and preserves your foreign identity, as it did for Daniel and friends (cf. Daniel 1:8 and ff.).

Centuries later, in the 1830s, when the scribe of the Mandaic *Hibil-Ziwa* manuscript finished copying, he confessed to learning some other languages (English, Armenian), but nevertheless maintained a Mandean identity, reflected here in the language of food and table:

> When I was little, I learned the current forms of their language in its variety, but I didn't convert. I became literate, though weird and foreign, with my prayer and praise devoted to Life, and I didn't convert, and I didn't eat from their table.[176]

The prince, though, *does* eat from the Egyptians' table, and becomes more and more affected by the place he's in and the people he's mixing in with.

33 **I forgot I was a son of kings, and I served their king** Memory and forgetting come up at important points in the story. Here, the prince's forgetting is tied to his set and setting, including the place he's at, the people he's with, and, of course, the food he's ingesting. In "Memory," the first version of a script that became the film *Alien*, a space crew gradually loses their memory on the planet they've landed on. Similarly, this place somehow wears down the prince's memory of who he is. The facts of his situation combine to steal his self-awareness. Not only does he forget he's a prince, he even joins the local royal en-

[176] See the colophon in Al-Mubaraki, 61.25–28:

[illegible]

kaḏ zuṭa ahwīt hāyyī līgī yalpit men leššān-on gawnī g<aw>nī u-aznī aznī u-lā-šannīt yālofa ahwīt aḏ-šannāy u-amnakr<ay> u-būṯ-e u-tošbīṯ-e al-heyyī u-lā-šannīt u-l-āklīt men pāṯur-on.

(For *u-amnakr<ay>*, the text has <wmnʔkryʔ>, i.e. ending in *-ī*, the active, but the passive, as above, is presumably meant.)

tourage. As in Sohravardi's *The Red Intellect*, where a hawk-now-human says, "I forgot my nest, that country, and everything I'd known, now supposing that I'd always been this way,"[177] the narrator-prince, seemingly oblivious to his old identity, takes on a new one. Like Adam and Eve in the *Apocryphon of Adam*, the prince from the east forgets former ways and enters a new service and is the worse for doing so.[178]

---

[177]The entire context is worth quoting (text from Thackston, 20-21):

دوستی از دوستان عزیز مرا سؤال کرد که مرغان زبان یکدیگر دانند؟ گفتم بلی دانند. گفت ترا از کجا معلوم گشت؟ گفتم در ابتدای حالت چون مصوّر بحقیق خواست که بنیت مرا پدید کند مرا در صورت بازی آفرید و در آن ولایت که من بودم دیگر بازان بودند. ما با یکدیگر سخن گفتیم و شنیدیم و سخن یکدیگر فهم میکردیم. گفت آنگه حال بدین مقام چگونه رسید؟ گفتم روزی صیادان قضا و قدر دام تقدیر باز گسترانیدند و دانه ارادت در آنجا تعبیه کردند و مرا بدین طریق اسیر گردانیدند. پس از آن ولایت که آشیان ما بود بولایتی دیگر بردند. آنگه هر دو چشم من بردوختند و چهار بند مختلف نهادند و ده کس‌را بر من موکّل کردند، پنج‌را روی سوی من و پشت بیرون و پنج‌را پشت سوی من و روی بیرون. این پنج که روی سوی من داشتند و پشت ایشان بیرون آنگه مرا در عالم تحیّر بداشتند چنانکه آشیان خویش و آن ولایت و هرچه معلوم بود فراموش کردم و می‌پنداشتم که من پیوسته خود چنین بوده‌ام

> One of my close friends asked me, "Do birds know each other's languages?" "They do," I said. "How do you know?" he responded.
>
> I said, "In the beginning condition, when the former truly wanted to reveal me in intent, he created me in the form of a hawk. There were also other hawks where I lived, and we spoke together, and we heard and understood each other's speech."
>
> Then he said, "How'd the current state happen?" I said, "One day, the hunters, fate and destiny, laid open a trap and set the seed of will in it, and this way they imprisoned me. Then they took me from the country our nest was in to another country, and there they sewed over both of my eyes, attached four different chains, and set ten guards over me – five with their face toward me and their backs away, and five with their backs to me and their face away. Then the five who kept their face toward me and their backs away kept me in a world of bafflement, so that I forgot my nest, the original country, and everything I'd known, now supposing that I'd always been this way."

[178]*Apocryphon of Adam* V 65.9-25 (ed. p. 156): ⲙⲛ̄ⲛ̄ⲥⲁ ⲛⲓϩⲟⲟⲩ ⲉⲧⲙ̄ⲙⲁⲩ ⲁⲥⲟⲩⲉ ⲉⲃⲟⲗ ⲙ̄-ⲙⲟⲓ̈ ⲁⲛⲟⲕ ⲙⲛ̄ ⲧⲉⲕⲙⲁⲁⲩ ⲉⲩϩⲁ ⲛ̄ϭⲓ ϯⲅⲛⲱⲥⲓⲥ ⲛ̄ϣⲁ ⲉⲛⲉϩ ⲛ̄ⲧⲉ ⲡⲛⲟⲩⲧⲉ ⲛ̄ⲧⲉ ⲧⲙⲉ ϫⲓⲛ ⲡⲟⲩⲟⲉⲓϣ ⲉⲧⲙ̄ⲙⲁⲩ ⲁⲛϫⲓ ⲥⲃⲱ ⲉϩⲉⲛϩⲃⲏⲩⲉ ⲉⲩⲙⲟⲟⲩⲧ` ϩⲱⲥ ϩⲉⲛⲣⲱⲙⲉ· ⲧⲟⲧⲉ ⲁⲛⲥⲟⲩⲱⲛ

> After those days, the eternal knowledge of the god of truth was far from both me and your mother, Eve. Since that time we have learned about dead things, like people; then we recognized the god that created us, since we weren't strangers to his powers, and we served him in fear and slavery. After that, we were gloomy in our hearts, and I was asleep with the thought in my heart.

The last line here, referring to Adam's sleep, foreshadows the prince's own Egyptian sleep.

34 **I forgot the pearl my parents had sent me for** Not only does the prince exchange royal service, Parthian for Egyptian, he also loses sight of the object of his trip to Egypt, the pearl itself, a fact he brings up by specifically mentioning his parents in this line. Viewed actively, this forgetfulness, a kind of dis-knowledge, affects the prince, like it does the Mother in the *Apocryphon of John*: "A forgetfulness came over her in the darkness of ignorance, and she began to feel shame."[179]

The Manichaean *Psalmbook* also has Mani forgetting: forgetting divinity, in this case. It's a longer quotation, but I give the fuller context, since several other possible comparanda with the pearl-prince are also lurking here, such as specific reference to a high or royal status, non-conventional fighting or combat, leaving one's family, a counterpart-helper, becoming anti-self, and an eventual meeting with a lord (Jesus, in this case) amid music and singing.

> I am a chief, crowned with the kings.
> I didn't know how to fight, belonging to the city of the gods.
> From the time the enemy maliciously eyed my kingdom,
> I left my fathers at rest, and went and gave myself to death for them.
> I armed myself and went out with my first [...].
> He went out, and I fought;

ⲡⲛⲟⲩⲧⲉ ⲉⲧⲁϥⲧⲁⲙⲓⲟⲛ· ⲛ̄ⲛⲉⲛⲟ ⲅⲁⲣ ⲁⲛ ⲡⲉ ⲛ̄ϣⲙ̄ⲙⲟ ⲛ̄ⲛⲉϥϭⲟⲙ· ⲁⲩⲱ ⲁⲛϣⲙ̄ϣⲉ ⲙ̄ⲙⲟϥ ϩⲛ̄ ⲟⲩϩⲟⲧⲉ ⲙⲛ̄ ⲟⲩⲙⲛ̄ⲧ̀ϩⲙ̄ϩⲁⲗ· ⲙⲛ̄ⲛ̄ⲥⲁ ⲛⲁï ⲇⲉ ⲁⲛϣⲱⲡⲉ ⲉⲛⲉ ⲛ̄ⲛⲉⲃⲏ ϩⲙ̄ ⲡⲉⲛϩⲏⲧ̀· ⲁⲛⲟⲕ ⲇⲉ ⲛⲉⲓ̈ⲛ̄ⲕⲟⲧ̀ ϩⲙ̄ ⲡⲙⲉⲉⲩⲉ ⲛ̄ⲧⲉ ⲡⲁϩⲏⲧ̀·

[179] II 13.24–25, ed. p. 81: ⲁⲩⲃ̄ϣⲉ ϣⲱⲡⲉ ⲛⲁⲥ ϩⲙ̄ ⲡⲕⲁⲕⲉ ⲛ̄ⲧⲙⲛ̄ⲧⲁⲧⲥⲟⲟⲩⲛ ⲁⲩⲱ ⲁⲥⲁⲣⲭⲉⲓ ⲛ̄ϣⲓⲡⲉ.

he went in and protected me.
You agreed on it with me then, saying:
"If you win, you'll get your crown."
I won in the first contest, but another struggle still reared up at me.
From the time I was bound in flesh, I forgot my divinity.
They made me drink the cup of insanity, they made me a rebel to my own self.
The powers and authorities went in and armed themselves against me.
My lord, Jesus, don't take your hand from me!
Be a light-summoner and engage[180] them until I pass them by.
Take me into your wedding chamber,
and I'll make music with the ones singing to you.[181]

---

[180]The meaning of the verb isn't certain, but usually means "appoint, consecrate, fill" (Crum, *Coptic Dictionary*, 691a). Allberry translates "bewitch," with a note (117n26), "The original meaning seems to be to use magic upon a man, whether it be to help him or to harm him, by means of a potion." He doesn't elaborate on the evidence for the seemingly original meaning, but he may be thinking of ϩⲓⲕ "magic" (hk > hkn > (metathesis) > hnk?) and, since he mentions "a potion," maybe even ϩⲛⲕⲉ "beer," but who knows? In any case, Clackson also gives "charm" as the meaning of ϩⲱⲛⲕ, ϩⲁⲛⲕ⸗ here (Clackson, Hunter, and Lieu, *Dictionary*, 167a). Černý (*Coptic Etymological*, 288) uncharacteristically fails to mention a probable connection with Semitic languages, namely Hebrew and Aramaic √ḥnk G "dedicate," D "train," etc., which fit the usual Coptic meaning well. Neither Crum nor Černý hint at any connection to magic, charms, or bewitching, because there's probably none there to hint at.

[181]*Psalmbook* II 117.3-30. (This psalm has the invocation, ⲡⲭ̅ⲣ̅ⲥ̅ "Christ!" interspersed between each line, but I have not included it here.)

[ⲁⲛ]ⲁⲕ ⲟⲩⲙⲉⲅⲓⲥⲧⲁⲛⲟⲥ ⲉⲓ̈ϫⲓ ϭⲣⲏⲡⲉ ⲙⲛ̅ⲛ̅ⲣ̅ⲣⲁⲓ | ⲛ̣ⲉⲓ̈ⲥⲁⲩⲛⲉ ⲙ̅ⲙⲓϣⲉ ⲉⲛ ⲉⲓ̈ⲏⲡ ⲁⲧⲡⲟⲗⲓⲥ ⲛ̅ⲛ̅ⲛⲟⲩ[ⲧⲉ] | [ϫ]ⲙ̅ⲡⲥⲏⲩ ⲉⲧⲁⲡⲓⲙⲉⲥⲧⲟⲩ ⲣ̅ⲃⲁⲛⲓⲉⲓⲣⲉ ⲁⲧⲁⲙⲛ̅ⲧ[ⲣ]ⲣⲟ [ⲁⲓ]ⲕⲁ ⲛⲁⲓ̈ⲁⲧⲉ ⲉⲩϩⲁⲣⲕ ⲁⲓ̈ⲉⲓ ⲁⲓ̈ⲧⲉⲉⲧ ⲁⲡⲙⲟⲩ ϩⲁ[ⲣ]ⲁⲩ | [ⲁⲓϩ]ⲁⲕⲧ̅ ⲁⲓ̈ⲉⲓ ⲁⲃⲁⲗ ⲙⲛ̅ⲡⲁϣⲁⲣⲡ̅ ⲙ̣̅ [...] | [ⲁϥ]ⲣ̅ϩⲓⲃⲁⲗ ⲁⲓ̈ⲙⲓϣⲉ ⲁϥⲣ̅ϩⲓϩⲟⲩⲛ ⲁϥ̣ⲣ̅ⲛⲁϣⲧⲉ [ⲛ]ⲏⲓ̈ | ⲁⲕⲥⲙⲛ̅ⲧⲥ ⲛⲉⲙⲏⲓ̈ ⲙ̅ⲡⲓⲥⲏⲩ ϫⲉ ⲉⲣϣⲁⲛϭⲣⲟ ⲧⲉⲣⲁϫⲓ ⲡⲉⲕⲗⲁⲙ | ⲁⲓ̈ϭⲣⲟ ϩⲛ̅ⲡϣⲁⲣⲡ̅ ⲛ̅ⲁⲑⲗⲟⲛ ⲁⲕⲁⲓⲁⲅⲱⲛ ⲁⲛ ⲛⲉϩⲥⲉ ⲁⲣⲁⲓ̈ | ϫⲙ̅ⲡⲧⲟⲩⲙⲁⲣⲧ̅ ϩⲛ̅ⲧⲥⲁⲣⳍ ⲁⲓ̈ⲣ̅ⲡⲱⲃϣ̅ ⲛ̅ⲧⲁⲙⲛ̅ⲧⲛⲟⲩⲧⲉ | [ⲁ]ⲩⲧⲥⲁⲓ̈ ⲡⲉⲡⲁⲧ ⲙ̅ⲡⲗⲓⲃⲉ ⲁⲩⲧⲁⲃⲱϭⲥ ⲁⲣⲁⲓ̈ ⲟⲩⲁⲉ | ⲉⲧⲛ̅ⲁⲣⲭⲏⲩ ⲙⲛ̅ⲛ̅ⲉⲝⲟⲩⲥⲓⲁ ⲁⲩⲣ̅ϩⲓϩⲟⲩⲛ ⲁⲩϩⲁⲕⲟⲩ ⲁⲣⲁⲓ̈ | ⲡⲁϫⲁⲓ̈ⲥ ⲓ̅ⲏ̅ⲥ̅ ⲙ̅ⲡⲱⲣⲕⲁⲧⲟⲟⲧⲕ ⲁⲃⲁⲗ ⲛ̅ⲥⲱⲓ̈ | ⲁⲣⲓⲟⲩⲣⲉϥⲙⲟⲩⲧⲉ ⲛ̅ⲟⲩⲁⲓ̈ⲛⲉ ⲕϩⲁⲛⲕⲟⲩ ϣⲁⲛϯϫⲱⲃⲉ ⲙ̅ⲙⲁⲩ | ϫⲓⲧ ⲁϩⲟⲩⲛ ⲁⲛⲉⲕⲙⲁⲛϣⲉⲗⲉⲉⲧ ⲧⲁϭⲛ̅ϭⲛ ⲙⲛ̅ⲛⲉⲧϩⲱⲥ ⲁⲣⲁⲕ

The prince's own royal identity and the goal of his trip to Egypt now forgotten, in this oblivion and sated with foreign food, there's little he can do but sleep.

35 **weighed down with their food** The MS has the PL of *ṭurråp̄å* "anxiety, distress," but the slight correction to the Greek loanword τροφή, "food, meal, sustenance," makes more sense. The *syåmē* dots, normally a plural marker in Syriac, here indicate the final Greek vowel *-ē*.[182] This reading, with the Greek loanword, also matches the Greek translation itself, which means this is presumably how the Greek translator either saw or understood the word.

Bar Bahlul, explaining the Greek-now-Syriac word, seems to conflate the two words into one: *ṭrop̄ē* "food, nourishment." But *ṭrop̄ē* and, acc. to Bar Srošway, '*ṭrop̄ē* in the stomach' mean stress and anxiety in the stomach."[183]

I fell into a deep sleep The language is simple and familiar. In the book of Acts (20:9), for example, it says of someone named Eutyches, "he had sunk into a heavy sleep." The Syriac is *wa-ṭḇaʕ b-šennṯå yaqqirtå*, and the CPA translation of this verse even has the same Aramaic adjective as in *The Pearlsong* ("deep"): *šqaʕ day b-šennā ʕammiqā*. The Greek *Pearlsong*, too, with εἰς ὕπνον κατηνέχθην βαθύν, also echoes the language of Acts (καταφερόμενος ὕπνῳ βαθεῖ), while Niketas departs with his florid, "plunged into sleep, death's neighbor" (ὕπνῳ καρωθεὶς θανάτου γείτονι).

Less parallel linguistically, but with similar sentiment the Middle English *Wanderer*-poet refers to "when care and sleep work together to tie up depressed loners."[184] Thus in an altered state, the now slumbering prince is like the *Perle*-poet, too, although minus the Christ-consolation:

---

[182] Butts, "*Syāmē*."

[183] BB 822: ܛܪܘܦܐ ܡܬܪܣܝܬܐ. اغذية. ܛܪܘܦܐ ܕܝܢ ܘܐܝܟ ܒܪ ܣܪܘ ܛܪܘܦܐ ܕܒܐܣܛܘܡܟܐ كرب وغمّ في المعدة ❖

[184] Lines 39-40:

ðonne sorg ond slǣp somod ætgædre
earmne ānhogan oft gebindað

> I mourned my pearl that was trapped there, with staunch, hard-fought arguments; though Christ's nature made me know comfort, my wretched will kept whipping up my despair. I fell onto a flowery glade: such a scent had shot to my brain that I slid down, slumber-slammed, over that spotless pearl.[185]

In the concluding résumé of his retelling, Niketas includes a mention of the Egyptians' "drugs" (*τὰ φάρμακα*), presumably referring to the Egyptian cuisine the prince was made to consume. As mentioned above, Egypt is known as a land where powerful drugs are produced. It's worth quoting several lines from the *Odyssey* (4.219-232), here in Emily Wilson's excellent translation:

> Then the child of Zeus,
> Helen, decided she would mix the wine
> with drugs to take all pain and rage away,
> to bring forgetfulness of every evil.
> Whoever drinks this mixture from the bowl
> will shed no tears that day, not even if
> her mother or her father die, nor even
> if soldiers kill her brother or her darling
> son with bronze spears before her very eyes.
> Helen had these powerful magic drugs
> from Polydamna, wife of Thon, from Egypt,
> where fertile fields produce the most narcotics:
> some good, some dangerous. The people there
> are skillful doctors. They are the Healer's people.[186]

---

[185] Lines 53-60:

> I playned my perle þat þer watȝ penned,
> Wyth fyr[c]e skylleȝ þat faste faȝt;
> Þaȝ kynde of Kryst me comfort kenned,
> My wretched wylle in wo ay wraȝte.
> I felle vpon þat floury flaȝt,
> Suche odour to my herneȝ schot,
> I slode vpon a slepyng-slaȝte,
> On þat prec[i]os perle wyth-outen spot.

[186] The Greek text, from West's edition, is:

It's reasonable to assume from *The Pearlsong* narrative that the food the prince refers to may not be just regular food, given that, in combination with his forgetfulness and seeming Egyptianization, it triggers such serious sleep. As Beyer notes, later in the poem (line 75), the prince again mentions forgetting (actually, not remembering) his royal status, which he's not been aware of since his childhood. This would seem to portray the prince as at least not a child anymore, so it's apparently some years later.[187]

36 **My parents sensed everything happening to me and they hurt for me** In the *Hibil-Ziwa* story, Hibil-Ziwa's parents, too, after sending him on a journey, realize he's in a predicament: "Then Mana the great, the head, said to the great, hidden, first drop: 'Our son's gloomy in the dark, with no power to come back up. Call Manda of Life, who will

> ἔνθ' αὖτ' ἄλλ' ἐνόησ' Ἑλένη Διὸς ἐκγεγαυῖα·
> αὐτίκ' ἄρ' εἰς οἶνον βάλε φάρμακον, ἔνθεν ἔπινον,
> νηπενθές τ' ἄχολόν τε, κακῶν ἐπίληθον ἁπάντων.
> ὃς τὸ καταβρόξειεν, ἐπὴν κρητῆρι μιγείη,
> οὔ κεν ἐπημέριός γε βάλοι κατὰ δάκρυ παρειῶν,
> οὐδ' εἴ οἱ κατατεθναίη μήτηρ τε πατήρ τε,
> οὐδ' εἴ οἱ προπάροιθεν ἀδελφεὸν ἢ φίλον υἱόν
> χαλκῶι δηϊόωιεν, ὃ δ' ὀφθαλμοῖσιν ὁρῶιτο.
> τοῖα Διὸς θυγάτηρ ἔχε φάρμακα μητιόεντα,
> ἐσθλά, τά οἱ Πολύδαμνα πόρεν, Θῶνος παράκοιτις
> Αἰγυπτίη, τῆι πλεῖστα φέρει ζείδωρος ἄρουρα
> φάρμακα, πολλὰ μὲν ἐσθλὰ μεμιγμένα, πολλὰ δὲ λυγρά·
> ἰητρὸς δὲ ἕκαστος ἐπιστάμενος περὶ πάντων
> ἀνθρώπων· ἦ γὰρ Παιήονός εἰσι γενέθλης.

[187]"According to line 75 he slept for many years" ("Nach 75 hat er viele Jahre geschlafen," Beyer, 255).

send him that power to go up and come here out of the dark to us.'"[188]

Kings and leaders of Parthia and all the magnates of the East *The Pearlsong*'s single explicit reference to Parthia has the name like the Parthian form, which is *parθaw*, distinct from the Middle Persian form, *pahlaw*.[189] Around the tenth century, Bar Bahlul cites two traditions equating Parthians and Edessans: "Parthians ... according to Bar Srošway, Edessans, ... and according to others: people who live on the Euphrates coast, i.e. in Edessa."[190] While Parthia itself is only named once in the poem, the preferred way to refer to the prince's home is nevertheless with the generic moniker, "the East" (lines 3, 16, 18, 38, 41, 60, 63). ("The East" in Parthian and Middle Persian is *xwarāsān*.)

The four ranks of Parthian nobility are:

1. *šahryār* king, dynast
2. *wispuhr* prince, royal family member
3. *wuzurg* prominent, magnate
4. *āzād* free, noble[191]

These four titles are juxtaposed, for example, in the Ḥājīābād inscription (Middle Persian-Parthian bilingual), describing an archery feat by Shapur and the subsequent moving of a cairn-target: "When we shot

188 *Hibil-Ziwa* 1.58-60:
ࡅࡄࡀࡉࡆࡀࡊ ࡀࡌࡀࡓ ࡌࡀࡍࡀ ࡓࡀࡁࡀ ࡓࡉࡔࡀࡉࡀ ࡀࡋࡍࡉࡈࡅࡐࡕࡀ ࡓࡀࡁࡕࡉ ࡊࡀࡎࡉࡕࡀ ࡒࡀࡃࡌࡀࡉࡕࡀ ࡏࡁࡓࡀࡉࡀࡍ ࡏࡕࡊࡀࡌࡀࡓ ࡀࡁࡀࡄࡔࡅࡊࡀ ࡅࡋࡉࡕࡋࡉ ࡄࡀࡉࡋࡀ ࡀࡋࡌࡉࡎࡀࡒ ࡀࡒࡓࡅࡋࡉ ࡀࡋࡌࡀࡍࡃࡀ ࡖࡄࡉࡉࡀ ࡖࡀࡌࡔࡀࡃࡓࡋࡉ ࡄࡀࡉࡋࡀ ࡖࡎࡀࡋࡉࡒ ࡅࡀࡕࡉ ࡌࡍ ࡀࡄࡔࡅࡊࡀ ࡀࡋࡅࡀࡕࡀࡉࡀࡍ

u-hāyzāk amar māna rabba rīšāya al-neṭṭup̄ta rabṯī kasīṯa qaḏmāyta: ebrayan itkammar ab̄-ahšōḵa u-lēt-lī hayla al-missaq. aqrō-lī al-Manda aḏ-heyyī, aḏ-amšaddar-lī hayla aḏ-sāleq u-ātī men ahšōḵa alwāṯ-ayan

189 Gignoux, *Glossaire*, 61.

190 BB 1639:
ܦܪܬܘܝܐ ... ܘܐܝܟ ܒܪ ܣܪܘ ܐܘܪܗܝܐ الرهاويّون ... ܘܐܢܫ̈ܐ ساكني شاطي الفراة وهي الرها

191 Chaumont and Toumanoff, "Āzād;" Harnack, "Parthische Titel," 525-528.

the arrow, it was shot in the presence of *šahryār*s, *wispuhr*s, *wuzurg*s, and *āzād*s."[192] This four-part grouping often shows up reduced to just two, as in this liturgical poem on the church: "Who is this, actually wrapped completely in purple, // With earth's kings and authorities bowing down to her master?"[193] Similarly, the *Mani Codex* has "the king and his leaders."[194] The *Kephalaia*, referring to pearls, says: "Divers give them to merchants, and merchants in turn give them to kings and chiefs."[195]

39 **They devised me a plot** The Syriac word ܐܦܪܣܢܐ *ʔåp̄arsnå* "plot, plan" occurs together with the verb √qṭr G in the meaning "agree on a plan, devise a plot" or something similar. This noun *ʔåp̄arsnå* has the feel of a loanword, and an Iranian origin has been suggested, but it's not certain.[196] Both in terms of meaning and consonantal building blocks (i.e. p-r-s), a possible connection to the common Syriac word *purså* "method, strategy" – itself from Greek (< πόρος) – also comes to mind.

40 **They wrote me a letter** Based on their long-range awareness of what their child was experiencing, the parents act by gathering their entourage and writing a letter. This letter is the catalyst for the prince's awakening and re-memory. Mentioned specifically in lines 40, 43, 49 (2x), 55, and 64, the letter is a major part of the story. Erik Davis's characterization is spot-on:

> Though ostensibly an action-packed tale of serpents and treasure, the 'Hymn' is really a story about messages and communication; the hero's information processing takes up far more lines than the battle with the beast or the description of the prized pearl.[197]

[192] From the Middle Persian version; MacKenzie, "Shooting," 499-500 (lines 4-6): *u-n ka ēn tigr wist, ēg-in pēš šahryārān ud wispuhrān ud wuzurgān ud āzādān wist.*

[193] Zingerle, "Syrische Poesien," 734.13-18: ܡܢ ܗܿܝ ܗܕܐ ܕܗܘܐ ܡܬܥܛܦܐ ܟܠ ܐܪܓܘܢܐ // ܘܡܠܟܐ ܕܐܪܥܐ ܘܫܠܝܛܢܐ ܠܡܪܗ ܣܓܕܝܢ

[194] KMK 133.15-16 (ὁ δὲ βασ[ιλεὺς καὶ οἱ] μεγ[ιστᾶνες αὐτοῦ]), and similarly other times in this part of the *Mani Codex*.

[195] Kph 204.3-4: ϣⲁⲣⲉ ⲛ̄ϫⲁⲗⲕⲙⲥⲉ [ⲧ]ⲉ̣ⲉⲩ ⲛ̄ⲛⲉϣⲁⲧⲉ ⲛ̄ⲧⲉ ⲛⲉ[ϣⲁ]ⲧⲉ ϩⲱⲩ ⲧⲉⲉⲩ ⲛ̄ⲛ̄ⲣ̄ⲣⲁï ⲙⲛ̄ ⲙⲙⲉⲅⲓⲥⲧⲁⲛⲟⲥ.

[196] ILS 115.

[197] *Techgnosis*, 117.

Similarly, Stang sees the letter and the garment as much more important in the story than the pearl, despite the attention given the pearl in the conventional title (and the one used here, admittedly!).[198] The letter results from an active link between the prince and his family, who, aware of his distant predicament, convene a gathering of the kingdom's upper crust, and together they consult and write an imperative-laden letter to wake up and remind the prince, then asleep and unaware in Egypt. The imperatives reach the prince staccato-like and wake him. Once he's awake, he's reminded not only that he's royal and shouldn't be subject to the Egyptian king, but the letter brings to mind the pearl and his shining-garment and toga. A reference to the enigmatic *Book of Heroes* closes out the letter, with a future view of the prince's royal co-inheritance with his brother.

With the letter now written, and sealed by the king himself, it's too important and too urgent to go by even the swiftest courier. In one of the most enchanting parts of the poem, the letter physically flies "like an eagle" to reach the prince, and reach him it does, landing right beside him. There's a physicality and presence to the letter: it makes noise as it moves, and it even has a voice, reciting its own message like a missive in *Mission: Impossible!*, only without the self-destruction. The words of the letter have their intended effect: the prince awakens, and then remembers, finding that the contents of the letter "had been written on what was inscribed in my heart."

We don't have to look far to find letters as major agents or supernatural instruments in narratives. In this passage from the *Kephalaia of the Teacher*, a divine Call and Response are each depicted as letters:

> He spoke further like this about the Call and Hearing: As for the Call that was sent out by the Living Spirit in the beginning, it was sent to the First Person: it's a letter of peace and of kiss-greeting, one he wrote and sent to his brother, one in which all the announcements are written down, together with everything that will happen for them to establish them in that Call. That Call of the First Person [...] is provided to be. The Response sent out by

[198] *Our Divine Double*, 137.

> the First Person went up to the Living Spirit: it's the letter sent by the First Person to the Living Spirit, in which all the announcements are written down, together with all the wars and battles he waged [...] in the Answer that the First Person [...] in everything that was, everything that will be, everything he did, together with what's prepared for them to do with it.[199]

The parents' letter-writing is again similar to what happens with Hibil-Ziwa: "Then an address came to Manda of Life: Go write a letter of Truth, secure it with a seal, and send it to him."[200] Another Mandaic text also supplies the language for a special, life-giving letter:

> A sealed letter that goes out from the world.
> A letter written with *kušta* and sealed with the great ones' ring.
> The perfect wrote it, the faithful made it firm.
> They hung it on the soul's neck and sent it to the door of life.[201]

---

[199] 182.1-17:

> ⲡⲁϫⲉϥ ⲁⲛ ⲁⲣⲁⲩ ⲙ̅ⲡⲓⲣⲏⲧⲉ ⲉⲧⲃⲉ ⲡⲧ[ⲱϩ][ⲙ]ⲉ ⲙⲛ̅ ⲡⲥⲱⲧⲙⲉ ϫⲉ ⲉⲕⲓⲁ ⲡⲧⲱϩⲙⲉ ⲉⲧⲁⲩⲧⲛ̅ⲛⲁⲩ[ϥ ⲁ]ⲃⲁⲗ ⲙ̅ⲡⲡ̅ⲛ̅ⲁ̅ ⲉⲧⲁⲛϩ ⲛ̅ⲧϩⲟⲩⲓ̈ⲧⲉ ⲁϥϫⲁⲩϥ [ⲁⲡϣⲁⲣⲡ] ⲛ̅ⲣⲱⲙⲉ ⲟⲩⲉⲡⲓⲥⲧⲟⲗⲏ ⲧⲉ ⲛ̅ⲉⲓⲣⲏⲛⲏ ϩⲓ ⲁⲥⲡⲁⲥ[ⲙⲟⲥ] ⲧⲉⲧⲁϥⲥⲁϩⲥ ⲁϥϫⲁⲩⲥ ϣⲁ ⲡⲉϥⲥⲁⲛ [ⲧ]ⲉⲧⲉⲣⲉ ⲛ̅[ⲁⲅⲅⲉ] ⲗⲓⲁ ⲧⲏⲣⲟⲩ ⲥⲏϩ ⲁⲡⲓⲧⲛⲉ ⲁⲣⲁⲥ ⲙⲛ̅ ϩⲱ̣ⲃ̣ ⲛ̣ⲓⲙ ⲉⲧⲛ̣ⲁ̣[ϣⲱⲡ]ⲉ ⲁⲣⲁⲩ ⲁⲥⲙⲛⲧⲟⲩ ϩⲙ̅ ⲡⲓ̈ⲧⲱϩⲙⲉ [ⲉⲧⲙ]ⲙⲉⲩ [ⲡⲓ][ⲧⲱ]ϩⲙⲉ ⲉⲧⲙⲙⲉⲩ ⲛ̅ⲧⲁ ⲡϣⲁⲣⲡ ⲛ̅ⲣⲱⲙ[ⲉ . . . . ⲥ]ϩⲛⲏⲩⲧ ⲁϣⲱⲡⲉ ⲡⲟⲩ[ⲱϣⲃ ⲉⲧⲁⲩϫⲁⲩϥ ⲁⲃⲁⲗ] [ⲙⲡ]ϣⲁⲣⲡ ⲛ̅ⲣⲱⲙⲉ ⲁϥⲉⲓ ⲁⲡϫ̣ⲓ̣ⲥ[ⲉ ϣⲁ ⲡⲡ̅ⲛ̅ⲁ̅ ⲉⲧⲁⲛϩ] [ⲟ]ⲩ̣ⲉⲡⲓⲥⲧⲟⲗⲏ ϩⲱϥ ⲁⲛ ⲡⲉ ⲡⲉⲧⲙⲙⲉⲩ [ⲉⲧⲁⲩⲧⲛⲛⲁⲩϥ ⲁⲃⲁⲗ ⲙ]ⲡϣⲁⲣⲡ ⲛ̅ⲣⲱⲙⲉ ϣⲁ ⲡⲡ̅ⲛ̅ⲁ̅ ⲉⲧⲁⲛϩ [ⲉⲧⲉⲣⲉ ⲛⲁⲅⲅⲉⲗⲓⲁ] ⲧⲏⲣⲟⲩ ⲥⲏϩ ⲁⲡⲓⲧⲛⲉ ⲁⲣⲁⲥ ⲙⲛ̅ ⲛ̅ⲡⲟ[ⲗⲉⲙⲟⲥ ⲧⲏⲣⲟⲩ] ⲙ̣ⲛ̅ ⲛ̅ⲙ̅ⲗⲟⲟϩ ⲉⲧⲁϥⲉⲓ̈ⲧⲟⲩ ⲛ̅ⲧⲁⲥⲧⲁ .[. . . . .] ϩⲙ̅ ⲡⲟⲩⲱϣ̣ⲃ̣ ⲉⲧⲁ ⲡϣⲁⲣⲡ ⲛ̅ⲣⲱⲙⲉ [. . . . .]ⲧ̣ . . ϩⲛ ϩⲱⲃ ⲛⲓⲙ ⲉⲁϥϣⲱⲡⲉ ⲙⲛ̅ ϩⲱ̣ⲃ ⲛⲓⲙ [ⲉϥⲛⲁϣⲱⲡⲉ] [ⲡ]ⲉⲧⲁ̣ⲩ̣ⲉ̣ⲓ̣̈ⲧ̣ϥ̣ ⲧⲏⲣϥ̅ ⲙⲛ̅ ⲡⲉⲧⲥⲃ̅ⲧⲁⲓ̈ⲧ ⲁ̣ⲧⲟⲩⲉⲉϥ ⲛ̅ϩⲏⲧϥ

[200] *Hibil-Ziwa* 1.60:

ࡅࡄࡀࡉࡆࡀࡊ ࡀࡕࡀࡋࡉ ࡌࡀࡌࡓࡀ ࡋࡌࡀࡍࡃࡀ ࡖࡄࡉࡉࡀ ࡖࡒࡅࡌ ࡀࡊࡃࡅࡁ ࡏࡂࡉࡓࡕࡀ
ࡖࡊࡅࡔࡈࡀ ࡅࡁࡄࡀࡕࡌࡀ ࡆࡀࡓࡆࡉ ࡅࡔࡀࡃࡓࡋࡉ

u-hāyzāk aṯā-lī mēmra al-Manda aḏ-heyyī: aḏ-qum akḏoḇ eggirta aḏ-kušṭa u-aḇ-hāṯma zarrz-ī u-šaddar-lī.

[201] *Left Ginza*, 3.27 = *Qolasta* prayer 73, based on Lidzbarski's edition of the latter (111.4-10)

In Hibil-Ziwa's case, even after a letter is sent and he's trying to return home, he remains in the dark region he was sent to, and his parents remain concerned. In the next series of lines, his parents arrange for an ascension-ritual to be performed for him, and sixty beings bring sixty letters and a passport, all to bring him back up from the land of darkness:

> Then Mana, the great and mighty, whose name is Adam As'haq the great, went to be with the great, hidden, first drop, and said: Our son's still in the dark, with no one responding to him. ... Come, make an assembly, and from the Father's upper world bring sixty beings, not any less, and read an ascension-ritual for him, and send Hibil-Ziwa the sixty letters, and send him the power for them to go and leave the seven worlds of darkness. ... They should have a passport: the Father's treasure that I have deposited with you, and the mysteries of darkness. Hibil-Ziwa then said to the king of darkness: honor the passport, the soul for their souls, which will lead them in it.[202]

[illegible]
[illegible]
[illegible]
[illegible]

engirta ambhattamta / ad-nāpqa min-ī min ālma
engirta ab-kušta akdība / u-htīma ab-esqat rawrbī
kedbū šālmānī / u-zarrzū gubrī ambaymnī
telyū-∅ ab-ṣawar nišma / u-l-bāba d-heyyī šaddrū.

[202] 1.67-80:

[illegible]
[illegible]
[illegible]
[illegible]
[illegible]
[illegible]
[illegible]
[illegible]

and each of the leaders signed it with their name The Greek translation lacks this sentence, but it further signals that their parents' effort to save their child is not unilateral.

41 **From your father, the king of kings, and your mother, ruler of the East** The letter begins with the mention of the members of the royal family, the prince's father referring to himself with the ubiquitous Iranian title, "kings' king/king of kings/kingliest king" (*šāhān šāh*).

42 **greetings to you in Egypt, son!** The simple, quotidian greeting makes the short letter feel more real, composed on the spot. In a more wordy literary context, a heavier, more grandiose opening, like the Parthian greeting of the so-called "Zarathustra fragment" is equally imaginable: "From your home to you: a greeting of the strength of the living and the peacefulness of the highest world!"[203]

43 **Wake up! Get up from your sleep, and listen to the words of our letter!** A string of imperatives opens the letter, following the salutation. The first two are orders to wake up from the sleep he's fallen into.[204] In the two Greek versions, the imperatives have an inverse order: in the translation it's "get up, and come to from your sleep" ἀνάστηθι καὶ ἀνάνηψον ἐξ ὕπνου, and in Niketas's sermon, it's "come to your senses, get up" (ἀνάνηψον, ἀνάστηθι). The "come to (your senses)" verb (ἀνάνηφειν) in both texts marks a change in awareness, including "from sin or ignorance."[205] In Christian Scripture, the same

u-hāyzāk qām Māna rabba kabbīra aḏ-hū Āḏām Ashaq rabba šum-ī u-azal alwāṯ-ī aḏ-niṭṭup̄ta rabṯī kasīṯa qaḏmāyta u-amar eḇr-ayan u-āp̄ aḇ-ahšōḵa lēt-lī gaḇra aḏ-ānī … u-aṯon u-kanap kanpa u-aṯon men ālma ellāya aḏ-aba aḏ-šītīn lā<-lˀ>-hon hasīr u-abṣīr, u-aqrā-lī masseqta u-šaddar-lī šītīn eggiryāṯa al-Hībīl Zīwa u-šaddar-lī hayla aḏ-āzlīn u-āṯī men šobba ālmī aḏ-ahšōḵa … nīhwī prudqa al-hāzen ginza aḏ-aba aḏ-anā armeṯ-ī alwāṯ-āḵ u-rāzī aḏ-ahšōḵa u-hāyzāk amar-lī Hībīl Zīwa al-malka aḏ-ahšōḵa: kahdū-lī prudqa, hātmā al-nap̄s-ēhon aḏ-aḇ-hānāṯī al-midabbr-īnon.

[203] M7 = Boyce 108(ay): *žīwandagān zāwar ud masišt gēhān drōd abar tō až padišt wxēbēh.*

[204] MacRae, "Sleep and Awakening."

[205] See Lampe, *Lexicon*, 114b for references.

verb occurs at 2 Timothy 2:26, speaking of opponents of (τοὺς ἀντιδιατιθεμένους) of the letter-writer and recipient, "that they might come to from the devil's snare, caught by him for his will."[206] One more example that helps illustrate this graphic verb comes from the *Tablet of Cebes* 9.[207] Here, a scene is being described where women adorned like courtesans – they're named Intemperance, Profligacy, Insatiability, and Flattery – try to tempt those they meet to stay there and enjoy a sweet, luxury-filled life. As explained there, "If, then, someone is convinced by them to enter luxury, for a time the amusement will seem sweet to them, as long, that is, as they're being titillated, but no more. For when they come to, they're aware that they weren't eating, but rather, they were being devoured and assaulted."[208] A sleep of the senses and unawareness may, as here, mean progressive annihilation, which makes the beckoning out of this oblivion life-changing, and even life-saving.

This call to a new state of consciousness and awareness shows up as a common exhortation both in old and in more recent texts. Musically, this includes Bach's biblically inspired cantata "Wachet auf, ruft uns die Stimme," Rage against the Machine's "Wake up," and "Wake up, Everybody" by Harold Melvin and the Blue Notes, with Teddy Pendergrass.

In the *Apocryphon of Adam*, the title character is roused by a command to wake up and then, as in *The Pearlsong*, is also told to listen:

> Get up from the sleep of death, Adam, and listen to this about the æon and the sowing of that person to whom life has come, who has from you and from Eve, your counterpart.[209]

---

[206] ἀνανήψωσιν ἐκ τῆς τοῦ διαβόλου παγίδος, ἐζωγρημένοι ὑπ᾽ αὐτοῦ εἰς τὸ ἐκείνου θέλημα.

[207] Greek text edited by Parsons, *Cebes*. See a complete translation in Seddon, *Guides*, 188–189.

[208] *Tab. Cebes* 9.2: ἐὰν οὖν τις πεισθῇ ὑπ᾽ αὐτῶν εἰσελθεῖν εἰς τὴν ἡδυπάθειαν, μέχρι μέν τινος ἡδεῖα δοκεῖ εἶναι ἡ διατριβὴ ἕως ἂν γαργαλίζῃ τὸν ἄνθρωπον· εἶτ᾽ οὐκέτι. ὅταν γὰρ ἀνανήψῃ, αἰσθάνεται ὅτι οὐκ ἤσθιεν, ἀλλ᾽ ὑπ᾽ αὐτῆς κατησθίετο καὶ ὑβρίζετο.

[209] *Apocryphon of Adam* V 66.1–8 (ed. p. 158): ⲧ[ⲱⲟⲩ]ⲛ̣ⲅ̄ ⲙ̄ⲙⲁⲩ ⲁ̄ⲇ̄ⲁ̄ⲙ̄ ⲉⲃⲟⲗ ϩⲙ̄ ⲡⲓⲛ̣̄ⲕⲟⲧ` ⲛ̄ⲧⲉ ⲡⲙⲟⲩ· ⲁⲩⲱ ⲥⲱⲧⲙ̄ ⲉⲧⲃⲉ ⲡⲓⲉⲱⲛ ⲙⲛ̄ ϯⲥⲡⲟⲣⲁ ⲙ̄ⲡⲓⲣⲱⲙⲉ ⲉⲧⲙ̄ⲙⲁⲩ· ⲡⲏ ⲉⲧⲁⲡⲓⲱⲛϩ̄ ⲡⲱϩ ϣⲁⲣⲟϥ· ⲡⲏ ⲉⲧⲁϥⲉⲓ ⲉⲃⲟⲗ ⲛ̄ϩⲏⲧⲕ̄· ⲁⲩⲱ ⲉⲃⲟⲗ ϩⲛ̄ ⲉ̄ⲩ̄ϩ̄ⲁ̄ ⲧⲉⲕⲥⲩⲛⲍⲩⲅⲟⲥ .

The double command, wake up and listen, is paralleled in a Manichaean Coptic text, where someone newly roused is told to expect some incoming news: "Wake up, you who are asleep, who doze in the mine, and you'll be told the news! / Here's the news-bringer, sent with news from the land of light to tell us the news of heaven!"[210] This language and imagery of being awakened to a new reality is also known from Manichaean hymnody in Parthian. A list of agent-nouns in one hymn runs, "savior of friends, awakener of the sleeping, healer of wounded souls, awakener of loved ones, our guardian, helper, rescuer, awakener and resurrector from death-sleep."[211] An incipit to a Manichaean hymn in Parthian runs: "Wake up, dear soul, from the drunken slumber you're asleep in!"[212] And again similarly from the Zarathustra fragment, cited just above: "You're asleep in a deep drunken stupor:[213] wake up and look at me! / From the land of peace, where I've been sent from for you: I hope you're well!"[214] This combination of letter-language at the end and the command to wake up are especially reminiscent of *The Pearlsong*.

44-46 **Remember ... Remember ... Recall ..., and remember ...** More commands follow: after waking up and preparing to hear the letter, the prince now has to remember what, as we've just learned, he's forgotten. In the letter's iterative, "remember!," you can almost hear the Shangri-Las whisperingly order the same in their 1964 hit, "Remember (Walkin' in the Sand)."

Some Manichaean language also resonates here. In the *Psalmbook* it is narrated, "He woke those who had fallen asleep, he reminded

[210] MPb II 197.16-19: [ⲛ]ⲉϩⲥⲉ ⲛⲉⲧϩⲓⲛⲏⲃ ⲛⲉⲧⲛ̅ⲕⲁⲧⲉ ϩⲛ̅ⲧⲗⲁⲛⲟⲩⲧ ⲛ̅ⲥⲉⲧⲉⲟ̣ⲩ̣ⲟ̣ ⲡϣⲓⲛⲉ ⲁⲣⲱⲧⲛ̅ / [ⲉⲓ]ⲥ ⲡⲃⲁϊϣⲓⲛⲉ ⲁⲩⲧⲛ̅ⲛⲁⲩϥ ⲙⲛ̅ⲡϣⲓⲛⲉ ⲙ̅ⲡⲕⲁϩ ⲙ̅[ⲡ]ⲟⲩⲁïⲛⲉ ⲁⲧⲉⲟⲩⲟ ⲡϣⲓⲛⲉ ⲁⲣⲁⲛ ⲛ̅ⲙ̅ⲡ̅(ⲏⲩⲉ)

[211] M5785/I/, §677b in Durkin-Meisterernst and Morano, *Mani's Psalms*, 215: *šīrgāmagān bōžāgar, xuftagān wiɣrānag, gyānān xastagān društgar, friyānagān wiɣrānag, amāh [parwarāg], aδyāwar, abdāžag, wiɣrāngar ud ahrādgar až maran xwamr.* Where I have *parwarāg*, the text has <przwng>; another alternative is *parwarzag* "nurturer."

[212] M4 = Boyce text cv, line 5: *wiɣrās, frih gyān, až xwamr mastīft, kū xuft ištē.*

[213] For an extended (Buddhist-inspired) Manichaean consideration of drunkenness, see the Old Turkic text published by van Tongerloo, "Nobleman."

[214] M7 = Boyce 108(ay): *garān mastīft kū xuft ištē, wiɣrāsā ud ō man wēnā drōd abar tō až šahr rāmišn kē až wasnāδ-tō frašūd hēm*

those who had forgotten."[215] As Philip K. Dick says, "to remember and to wake up are absolutely interchangeable."[216] Similarly, rousing and reminding are linked in a Manichaean text from Kellis: "... for him to perfect you, my friend, in his holy spirit, so it will be an awakener, a guardian, a memory-giver for you."[217]

As Erik Davis points out, it's the letter that undoes the forgetting: "Memory loss sets in until a letter arrives, a piece of writing that unleashes all the consciousness-bending powers of the alphabet."[218] The letter – a piece of writing inside another piece of writing (inside another, if you count the *Acts of Thomas*) – is thus one of many examples where writing, or the reading of it, serves to remind, from a grocery-list to a work schedule to a manuscript colophon or an ancient inscription, as here in Old Aramaic:

> We have spoken and written all this, and what I, Mati'el,
> have written, is for a reminder to my son and my grandson
> who will go up after me.[219]

look whom you've served! The combination of *ʕab̲duṯå* "enslave- 44
ment" and the verb √plḥ is not at all unusual.[220] All four Syriac versions of Luke 15:29, for example, have this same expression – ܦܠܚ ܐܢܐ ܠܟ ܥܒܕܘܬܐ – for the simple Greek verbal phrase δουλεύω σοι.[221]

you are named in *The Book of Heroes* While the Syriac text has the 47
appropriately epic-sounding "book of heroes," the Greek translation has the biblical-sounding "book of life." As to why the Greek has this

[215] MPb II 213.10-11: ⲁϥⲛⲉϩⲥⲉ [ⲛ̄ⲛ]ⲉⲧⲁⲩϩⲓⲛⲏⲃ· ⲁϥϯ ⲡⲣ̄ⲡⲙⲉⲉⲩ ⲛ̄ⲛⲉⲧⲁⲩⲣ̄ ⲡⲱⲃϣ̄.

[216] *Exegesis*, xxi, quoted in Davis, *High Weirdness*, 353.

[217] K. Copt. 53 12.16-19 (text in Gardner, *Kellis Literary Texts* II, p. 34): ⲁⲧⲣⲉϥϫⲱ ⲙ̄ⲙⲁⲕ̣ [ⲡⲁ]ⲙ̣ⲉⲣⲓⲧ ϩⲛ̄ ⲡⲉϥⲡⲛⲁ ⲉⲧⲟⲩⲁⲃⲉ [ϫ]ⲉ̣ [ϥⲛ]ⲁϣ̣ⲱ̣ⲡⲉ ⲛⲉⲕ ⲛ̄ⲟⲩⲣⲉϥⲛⲉϩⲥⲉ̣ [ⲛ̄ϩⲟ]ⲩ̣ⲣ̣ⲓⲧ ⲛ̄ⲣⲉϥϯ ⲙ̄ⲡⲣ̄ⲡⲙⲉⲩⲉ

[218] *Techgnosis*, 117.

[219] KAI 222/Sefire I C 1-4:
𐤊𐤄 · 𐤀𐤌𐤓𐤍 · [𐤅𐤊𐤄 · 𐤊]𐤕𐤁𐤍 · 𐤌𐤄 · 𐤊𐤕𐤁𐤕 · 𐤀[𐤍𐤄 · 𐤌𐤕𐤏]𐤀𐤋 ·
𐤋𐤆𐤊𐤓𐤍 · 𐤋𐤁𐤓𐤉 · [𐤅𐤋𐤁𐤓] · 𐤁𐤓𐤉 · 𐤆𐤉 · 𐤉𐤎𐤒𐤍 · 𐤁[𐤀𐤔𐤓]𐤉 ·
<kh ʔmrn [wkh k]tbn mh ktbt ʔ[nh mtʕ]ʔl lzkrn lbry [wlbr] bry zy ysqn b[ʔšr]y>.

[220] Less usual is the combination using a different verb with similar meaning, √šmš D, as in this line from Isaac of Nineveh: ܡܥܣܐ ܗܝ ܠܡܫܡܫܘ ܥܒܕܘܬܐ ܠܦܓܪܐ "it's hard to serve enslavement to the body" (Brock, *Wisdom*, no. 38).

[221] See Kiraz, *Comparative Edition*, vol. 3, 321. On the language of a "yoke" in the Greek versions, see Betz on Galatians 5:1 in *Galatians*, 258, with n. 45.

different reading, a misreading of Syriac <ḥlyṣʔ> as <ḥyʔ> is, of course, possible, but it involves more than a slight change. Perhaps it's just that it was well-known from the Bible.[222] This reference to a book, whether of heroes or of life, also recalls the verses from 2 Chronicles mentioned in the introduction, where *maḏråše* occurs. Not much can be said about what the poet meant by the title, but, especially with "book of heroes," it's reasonable to imagine an Iranian epic or mini-epic dedicated to heroic feats.[223]

The Greek, in addition to "life" instead of "heroes," strangely has "you were named 'book of life.'" That is, the prince is not named "in" the book, but he is named the book itself, which, admittedly, does not make much immediate sense.

48 **So that with your brother, you'll be our successor in our kingdom** *pṣågriḇå* "successor (to the throne)," used to refer to the prince's brother, is known from an Iranian form like Manichaean Middle Persian *pasāgrīw* "deputy, representative."[224]

This explicit linking of fates between the protagonist and his brother is echoed in a line from Sohravardī's *Western Exile* (§12): "If you want to be saved with your brother, then don't delay in your determination to travel!"[225]

49 **my letter was a letter that the king had sealed with his right hand** How do you know it's a royal document, and that the queen or king endorses it? By a royal seal. Even better if the sender does the sealing themselves. The document, or letter, as here, is then specially marked,

---

[222] See Philippians 4:3, Revelation 3:5 and 20:12; cf. Exodus 32:32 and Psalm 69:29. The Psalm verse in Hebrew has "book of life/living" (ספר חיים), and the Old Greek has *βίβλου ζώντων*, following the latter option, "living." The Exodus verse, in both Hebrew (ספרך אשר כתבת) and Greek (*τῆς βίβλου σου ἧς ἔγραψας*), just has "your book, which you wrote," but when this verse is paraphrased in *1 Clement* 53:4, the Psalm phrase, "book of the living," appears (*βίβλου ζώντων*).

[223] For more on this Iranian epic possibility, and the "book within a book" theme, see Russell, "Epic," 77-81.

[224] Gershevitch, "A Parthian Title;" Harnack, "Parthische Titel," 516-519; ILS 235-236; DMMPP 284a.

[225] Arabic: إن أردت أن تتخلص مع أخيك فلا تنيا في عزم السفر / Persian: اگر خواهی که با برادرت خلاص یابی در عزم سفر سستی مکن

a fact that appears in a line from the Manichaean *Homilies*: "It [Error] killed the representatives running with the king's documents."[226]

the perverse Babylonians and the riotous devils of Sarbug The 50
Syriac phrase for Babylonians here is *bnay båḇel*, "the 'children' of Babylon," a regular way to refer to the citizens or inhabitants of a place, not just in Syriac, but in other Semitic languages, too, like this geographically resonant Akkadian line: *mārū* (DUMU.MEŠ) *Bābili u Barsip* "the 'children' of Babylon and Borsippa."[227] In the Coptic Manichaean *Homilies*, too, the same phrase, with the same city, occurs: "to Babylon and all its 'children.'"[228]

I have changed the manuscript's ܡܪ̈ܝܪܐ *marrirē* to ܡܪ̈ܝܕܐ *marriḏē* "rebellious, disorderly" – cf. the Greek. The identically spelled ܡܪ̈ܝܕܐ *mriḏē* fits the meter slightly better, but fits the sense less, meaning "secure, impregnable." Beyer reads as *mriḏē*, but only after turning to Mandaic for the meaning of "'wild."[229] This recourse to Mandaic seems unnecessary here, since *marriḏē* "rebellious" makes sense and still fits well within the poem's metrical range.

As mentioned above, instead of having Sarbug, the Greek translation uses "Labyrinth," here as an adjective. What these "riotous demons" are more specifically isn't said, but as in the case of Babylon, it's presumably just a generic moniker. Borsippa was mentioned alongside Babylon in Akkadian just above. If Sarbug is Borsippa, as suggested by Nöldeke, maybe it's worth mentioning that, according to Strabo, Borsippa was known for having large numbers of giant bats, which they salted and ate.[230]

It flew like an eagle This and the following line are missing from 51
the Greek: there the letter doesn't explicitly fly, which also means no eagle, and it doesn't "become speech," but there is, as in Syriac, a noise

[226] MHm 12.18-20: ⲁ̣[ⲥ]ϩⲱⲧⲃⲉ ⲛ̄ⲛ̄ⲡⲣⲉⲥⲃⲉⲩⲧⲏⲥ· ⲛⲉⲧⲡⲏⲧ ⲙ̄ⲛ̄ⲛ̄ⲥϩ̣[ⲉⲓ ⲙ̄]ⲡⲣ̄ⲣⲟ. The fem. subject is ⲧ-ⲡⲗⲁⲛⲏ "Error."

[227] CAD M 1 315b.

[228] MHm 8.10: ⲁⲧⲃⲁⲃⲩⲗⲱⲛ ⲙⲛ̄ⲛⲉⲥϣⲏⲣⲉ ⲧⲏⲣⲟⲩ.

[229] Beyer, "Perlenlied," 256.

[230] *Geography* 16.1.7 (text in Oppenheimer 102): *πληθύουσι δὲ ἐν αὐτῇ νυκτερίδες μείζους πολὺ τῶν ἐν ἄλλοις τόποις ἁλίσκονται δ' εἰς βρῶσιν καὶ ταριχεύονται.* "There are lots of bats there, much bigger than in other places, and they're captured and preserved in brine for food."

(φωνή) alongside the sound of its movement. Both Syriac *qålå* and Greek *φωνή* can mean either "voice" or "sound," but without the line about becoming speech, the Greek probably means "sound," as I've translated it, whereas "voice" makes better sense in Syriac, since there we've just been told that the letter "became speech."

Flying or soaring "like an eagle" is a catchy, well-used metaphor from Akkadian to the Steve Miller Band (1976), and more. Akkadian has the adverb *arāniš* and prepositional phrases like *kīma erî*, both meaning "like an eagle."[231] Ugaritic has a cognate word to Syriac *nešrå* in *km/k nšr* "like an eagle."[232] And Hebrew uses a relative of the same word in places like Isaiah 40:31 "they'll take flight like eagles" and Psalm 103:5 "so that your youth is renewed like an eagle."[233] More enigmatic, but still worth mentioning for the way it stretches the metaphor, something the poet is also willing to do (the flying letter also lands, or perches, bird-like beside the prince), is the following line from the *Apocryphon of John*: "I appeared in the form of an eagle on the tree of knowledge."[234] Finally, from 2 Baruch (in Syriac), there's a clear letter-eagle connection, although different from the one in *The Pearl-song*. Baruch writes a letter and sends it via an eagle:

> [18]On the 11th day of the 8th month I, Baruch, came and sat under the shade of an oak tree's branches, with no one else with me: I was completely alone. [19]I wrote these two letters: one I sent by an eagle to the nine and a half tribes, and the other I sent to those in Babylon by three human messengers. [20]I called the eagle and told it the following:
>
> > [21]The most-high has made you to be superior to every bird, [22]so go, now, and don't stop anywhere! Don't go in a nest and don't perch on any tree until you cross the breadth of the abundant waters of the Euphrates River and

[231]CAD A 231a and CAD E 325a.

[232]del Olmo Lete and Sanmartín, *Dictionary*, 641. Among the attestations cited is <bn nšrm ˀarḫ̮p ˀan[k]> "let me fly among the eagles."

[233]יעלו אבר כנשרים and תתחדש כנשר נעוריכי, respectively.

[234]II 23.26-28, ed. p. 135: ⲁϊⲟⲩⲱⲛϩ ⲁⲛⲟⲕ` ⲉⲃⲟⲗ ⲙ̅ⲡⲥⲙⲁⲧ` ⲛ̅ⲟⲩⲁⲉⲧⲟⲥ ϩⲓϫⲛ̅ ⲡϣⲏⲛ ⲙ̅ⲡ-ⲥⲟⲟⲩⲛ.

come to the people who live there, and deposit this letter with them.[235]

In Sohravardī's *Western Exile* story, too, a letter comes *not* as a bird, but it's a bird (a hoopoe) that brings the letter:

> In its beak was a letter originating *from the right bank of the river-valley, in a sacred spot, from the tree*. I grasped your deliverance and I've brought you *definite news from Sheba*, and it's what's explained in your father's letter.[236]

In the Manichaean *Psalmbook* the soul, addressed here, floats up like an eagle: "He will set your foot on the truth-path and furnish you with your light-wings, like an eagle lightly floating, rising up within its air."[237] Similarly, later in the book come the lines, "The convocation of eagles, those that pull my heart to the sky," and "Lift me onto your wings, eagle: put my white clothes on me and take me in as a gift to your father!"[238]

---

[235]77.18-22 (ed. Gurtner):
18 ܘܗܘܐ ܒܚܕ ܘܥܣܪܝܢ ܒܝܪܚܐ ܕܬܡܝܢܝܐ ܐܬܝܬ ܐܢܐ ܒܪܘܟ. ܘܝܬܒܬ ܬܚܝܬ ܒܠܘܛܐ ܒܛܠܠܐ ܕܣܘ̈ܟܐ. ܘܐܢܫ ܠܐ ܗܘܐ ܥܡܝ. ܐܠܐ ܐܢܐ ܒܠܚܘܕܝ. 19 ܘܟܬܒܬ ܗܠܝܢ ܬܪ̈ܬܝܢ ܐܓܪ̈ܬܐ. ܚܕܐ ܫܕܪܬ ܒܝܕ ܢܫܪܐ ܠܬܫܥܐ ܫܒ̈ܛܝܢ ܘܦܠܓܗ. ܘܐܚܪܬܐ ܫܕܪܬ ܠܗܠܝܢ ܕܒܒܒܠ ܒܝܕ ܬܠܬܐ ܐܢ̈ܫܝܢ. 20 ܘܩܪܝܬ ܠܢܫܪܐ ܘܐܡܪܬ ܠܗ ܡ̈ܠܐ ܗܠܝܢ. 21 ܠܟ ܒܪܐ ܡܪܝܡܐ ܕܬܗܘܐ ܡܥܠܝ ܡܢ ܟܠܗ ܦܪ̈ܚܬܐ. 22 ܗܫܐ ܙܠ ܘܠܐ ܬܬܟܬܪ ܒܐܬܪܐ. ܘܠܐ ܬܥܘܠ ܠܩܢܐ. ܘܠܐ ܬܬܩܘܡ ܥܠ ܚܕ ܐܝܠܢ ܥܕܡܐ ܕܬܥܒܪ ܦܬܝܘܬܗ ܕܡ̈ܝܐ ܣܓܝ̈ܐܐ ܕܢܗܪܐ ܦܪܬ. ܘܬܐܙܠ ܠܘܬ ܥܡܐ ܗܘ ܕܥܡܪ ܬܡܢ. ܘܬܪܡܐ ܠܗܘܢ ܐܓܪܬܐ ܗܕܐ.

[236]The parts in italics are from the Quran (28:30 and 27:22, respectively). §§9-10, Arabic: وفي منقاره رقعة صدرت من شاطئ الواد الأيمن في البقعة المباركة من الشجرة إنّي أحطت بوجه خلاصكما وجئتكما من سبأٍ بنبأٍ يَقينٍ وهو ذا مشروح في رقعة ابيكما / Persian: ودر منقارش رقعه‌ئی که صادر شد از وادی ایمن آوردم شمارا از سبا بخبر یقین و در نامه پدرتان مشروح است

[237]MPb II 100.29-31: ϥⲁϯ ⲣⲉⲧⲉ ⲁⲡⲙⲁïⲧ ⲛ̄ⲧⲙⲏⲉ ⲛ̄ϥϭⲁⲣϭⲉ ⲁⲃⲁⲗ ϩⲛ̄ⲛⲉⲧⲛ̄ϩ ⲛ̄ⲟⲩⲁïⲛⲉ ⲛ̄ⲑⲉ ⲛ̄ⲟⲩⲁϩⲱⲙ ⲉϥⲁⲥïⲱⲟⲩ ⲉϥⲧⲁïⲗⲉ ⲁⲃⲁⲗ ϩⲛ̄ⲡⲉϥⲁⲏⲣ.

[238]155.6: ⲧⲥⲁ[ⲩ]ϩⲥ ⲛ̄ⲛⲁⲉⲧⲟⲥ· ⲛ̄ⲧⲁⲩ ⲉⲧⲥⲱⲕ ⲙ̄ⲡⲁϩⲏⲧ ⲁⲙⲡⲏⲩⲉ, and 188.21-22: ⲧⲉⲗⲁï ⲁϫⲛ̄ⲛⲉⲕⲧⲛϩ ⲡⲁⲉⲧⲟⲥ ϩⲱⲗ ⲛⲉⲙⲏï ⲁⲙⲡⲏⲩⲉϯ ⲡⲁⲗⲉⲩⲕⲟⲛ ϩⲓⲱⲱⲧ ϫⲓⲧ ⲁϩⲟⲩⲛ ⲛ̄ⲇⲱⲣⲟⲛ ⲙ̄ⲡⲕⲓⲱⲧ.

52-53 **the whole thing became speech. Waking at its voice and the noise of its movement** The sleeping prince cannot, of course, read the letter without waking up, and the catalyst for his awakening is the *sound* the letter makes, sound both from actual talking and from landing and settling at the prince's side. The sleeper begins stirring from sleep at "a noisy bit of rustling (whether of the papyrus or the bird's wings remains unclear)," and then the letter's startling transformation from script to sound decisively arrests his waking attention.[239] Using language from Philip K. Dick critic Lorenzo DiTomasso, Davis also recognizes the letter as an "in-breaking information vector," and an "instrument of narrative disruption."[240] For the prince, the letter is like the Manichaean light-mind, pulling him out of sleep and bringing him to the right place: "the light-mind, which is the rouser of those who sleep, the gatherer of those who are scattered."[241]

54 **I took it** The next lines show the prince wholeheartedly accepting the letter, first by physically taking and kissing it, and then, in reading the letter's text himself, recognizing that its message lines up with what's already there. With this anamnesis, like Hibil-Ziwa, once he's read the letter, he gets moving: "When Hibil-Ziwa had opened the letter sent to that darkness where he was, he went up and continued on."[242]

I … kissed it The verb √nšq occurs in both G and D stems, and the manuscript's consonantal text allows for either. Both fit here in meaning, but the former reading (*wa-nšaqt-åh*) yields a five-syllable line, and the latter (*w-naššqt-åh*) only a four-syllable line, making the G verb more probable.

I … started to read the letter itself The letter has a voice and speech, but the narrator-prince now turns to read it himself, whether

[239] Davis, *Techgnosis*, 117.

[240] *High Weirdness*, 349.

[241] Kph 44.11-12: ⲡⲛⲟⲩⲥ ⲛ̄ⲟⲩⲁⲓⲛⲉ ⲉ̣ⲧⲉ ⲛⲧⲁϥ ⲡⲉ ⲡⲣⲉϥⲛⲉϩⲥ̣[ⲉ ⲛ̄ⲛⲉ]ⲧⲛ̄ⲕⲁ̣ⲧⲉ ⲡⲣⲉϥⲥⲱⲟⲩϩ ⲁϩⲟⲩⲛ ⲛ̄ⲛⲉⲧϫ̣[ⲣⲁ]ⲣ̣ⲁ̣ⲧ̣ ⲁⲃⲁⲗ.

[242] *Hibil-Ziwa* 1.63-64: *kaḏ peht-ā Hībīl-Zīwa al-eggirta šīhla al-hānāṯī ahšōḵa aḏ-ahwā-ḇī u-asleq*
u-aṯā

to ingest its content by another means, or just to re-encounter the letter's contents.

The words of my letter had been written on what was inscribed in my heart The letter resets the prince's thinking, bringing him back to another message, this one also written (see line 11), but inscribed in his mind, rather than in a material letter. The re-connecting of the prince with his prior "inscribed" message, by means of the letter presently in his hands and on his voice, brings him back, as we're about to see, to his identity and his mission in Egypt. As Erik Davis notes, "Then the letter triggers the knowledge already written in the heart of our hero – a classic media metaphor for the Platonic recollection of true origins and true destiny."[243] Touching on the twinning-counterpart theme seen elsewhere in the poem, Stang sees the letter as the prince's "textual double, as it were: it mirrors back to him his inner inscription, which text had been obscured by exile. The young man is something of a palimpsest, and his textual double renders his inner inscription again legible."[244] 55

I remembered I was a son of kings The letter said, "Remember!" and the now awake prince does so. As it says in the Manichaean *Psalm-book*, "The bliss, my lord, of your sweet call has made me forget life; the sweetness of your voice has made me remember my city."[245] 56

my freedom was looking for its nature The phrase – Syriac *ḥēruṯ kyån-åh påqdå* – is a bit obscure. The verb √pqd G means "look after, care for, check on, visit," as well as "command" (also D). Maybe the prince has "dropped in to see what condition his condition was in."[246]

I began saying a spell How do you get what you want from a dragon, and come out unscathed? Dialog? Stealth and deception? A weapon and direct confrontation? In a Hittite text, the storm-god Teššub has his sister seduce the sea-serpent Ḫedammu, "beguiling him with, in turn, 58

[243] Davis, *Techgnosis*, 117.

[244] Stang, *Our Divine Double*, 139.

[245] MPb II 53.27-28: ⲁⲡⲟⲩⲛⲁϥ ⲡⲁϫⲁïⲥ ⲙ̄ⲡⲕϩⲣⲁⲩ ⲉⲧϩⲁⲗϭ ⲧⲁⲣ̄ⲡⲱⲃϣ̄ ⲙ̄ⲡⲃⲓⲟⲥ ⲁⲡϩⲗⲁϭ ⲛ̄ⲧⲉ̣ⲕ̣ⲥⲙⲏ ⲧⲁⲣ̄ⲡⲙⲉⲉⲩ ⲛ̄ⲧⲁⲡⲟⲗⲓⲥ.

[246] To paraphrase "Just Dropped In (To See What Condition My Condition Was In)," written by Mickey Newbury and recorded by The First Edition in Memphis in 1967.

music, her naked body, a love-potion, and some beer."[247] In another, it's a land-serpent, not a water-denizen, but in both, the storm-god doesn't confront the serpent directly, whether on land or sea, but needs human help and trickery to overcome the giant snake.[248]

In *The Pearlsong*, the story again turns on the effective use of the power of language.[249] The prince opts for a spell, rather than an attempt at a martial solution, which assumes both the effective power of the recited spell and the serpent's susceptibility to sound, whether that means intoned words, names, or phrases as such, or also includes rhythm and melody, too.[250] Just as the prince was susceptible to the flying letter's sound and voice, the serpent is susceptible to the sounds of the spell. The prince *begins* saying the spell, just as he *began* reading the letter just above (line 54).

This verb, √mgš D "say a spell," can be associated with Magians and Zoroastrianism, as Bar Bahlul indicates: "In *The Book of Paradise*, the mumbling of Magians, i.e. when they pray at meal-time: when they finish, they make a creaky noise with their nostrils while forcefully speaking."[251] In this case, the verb probably just indicates the reciting of an audible spell, even if it's mumbled or nasal. As noted by Russell, this Aramaic verb migrates to Ibn Khaldun to Franz Rosenthal's English translation of Ibn Khaldun to Brion Gysin, eventually reaching William S. Burroughs.[252] Ibn Khaldun (writing in Arabic) cites chant instructions in an Aramaic language for dream divination, possibly something like *tmaggeš b-ʕeddån swådå wa-g̱daš nawmṯå gådeš* "You should say the spell at conversation-time, and when it has happened, sleep will happen."[253] It's notable that here, too, the verb is associated with uttering a sleep-spell, just like in *The Pearlsong*.

[247] Ogden, *Drakon*, 13.

[248] Hoffner, *Hittite Myths*, 11.

[249] The story is "all about the saving power of incorporeal communications" (Davis, *Techgnosis*, 116).

[250] For snake-dragons and sound, see further Kuehn, *Dragon*, 191-193.

[251] BB 1008: ܡܓܫܐ ܒܟܬܒܐ ܕܦܪ̈ܕܝܣܐ ܪ̈ܛܢܐ ܕܡܓܘ̈ܫܐ ܗ̄ ܕܡܨܠܝܢ ܒܥܕܢ ܠܚܡܐ. ܘܟܕ ܫܠܡܝܢ: ܢܚܪܝܢ ܠܗ ܡܩܫܩܝܢ ܒܢܚܝܪ̈ܝܗܘܢ ܟܕ ܡܡܠܠܝܢ ܐܠܝܨܐܝܬ܀

[252] See Russell, "Epic," 79-80n80.

[253] My reading and translation differ slightly from Rosenthal's: see *Muqaddimah*, 213n311.

I put it to sleep and made it slumber In the Greek translation, there's no mention of what kind of effect the spell will have on the serpent, that is, it's not said to be a sleeping-spell, but in his Greek retelling, Niketas explicitly states it: "I recited charms and divine spells over him and lulled it to sleep, and this is how I stole the pearl out from under it" (ἐπῳδαῖς τε καὶ θείοις κατακηλήσας ἐπᾴσμασι καταδαρθεῖν πέπεικα, καὶ οὕτω τὸν μαργαρίτην ὑφήρπασα). 59

Ogden's analysis of incantations used against giant serpents yields four typical outcomes on the creatures:[254]

1. putting them to sleep
2. making them explode
3. summoning them forth
4. rendering them non-poisonous

For *The Pearlsong*'s serpent, it's option one. The prince, who was just asleep himself, uses the spell to render the serpent effectively unconscious. Making a giant serpent go to sleep takes magic since they don't normally really sleep all the way, always keeping their eyes open, just like regular snakes: serpents like the one in *The Pearlsong* "make the most ideal guardians, be it of springs, treasure, or anything else."[255] Medea, in differing traditions, sidelines the *drakōn* in Colchis with sleep, using a combination of incantation and drugs and prayer, while Orpheus, in the *Orphic Argonautica*, can dispense with drugs and just use music to lull a *drakōn* to sleep.[256] The traveling prince just has a spell or incantation, no drugs or music, and while the exact verbal content of the spell is unknown, it's based on the names of the prince's royal family.

While it's not for a serpent-dragon, but a primal water deity (Apsu), a scene from the Babylonian creation epic, *Enūma eliš*, also shows the use of a sleep-inflicting incantation against an opponent. The subject is the god Ea/Enki:

---

[254] *Drakon*, 242–243.
[255] Ogden, *Drakon*, 238.
[256] Ogden, *Drakon*, 239 and 242.

> He concocted him a plan and set everything up,
> masterfully making his pure incantation the best.
> He recited it to him and pacified the water,
> he doused him with slumber – he's comfortably asleep!
> He sedated Apsu – he's doused with slumber ...[257]

59-60 **by recalling my father's name over it, // And the name of our second, and of my mother, queen of the East** As far as we know anything of the "content" of the spell, it's the recited names of the prince's brother, mother, and father, names apparently all brought back to mind thanks to the letter.[258] In Syriac, it's not only the name of the father, but also of the brother and mother. The Greek translation only has the father's name.

The MS has *ʔenå ʕl-aw ʔeddaḵreṯ*, with marks signaling the transposition of the first two words, indicating the reading *ʕl-aw ʔenå ʔeddaḵreṯ*, but the pronoun *ʔenå*, unnecessary grammatically, adds two syllables to the metrical line, so its omission makes for a viable alternative reading.

61 **I snatched the pearl** If the pearl is the point, not just of the mission, but of the poem, then this is a critical point in the story. The traveler-prince's taking of the pearl while the serpent sleeps is akin to Hibil-Ziwa's retrieval of treasures unbeknownst to Qin, goddess of land of darkness:

> Then Qin went down, with a mystery: the gem, the mirror, and the bitter herbs, with the power of all darkness in them. Then Manda of Life took these mysteries from the great well, without her having seen him.[259]

[257] I 61-65:

> *ibšimšum-ma uṣurāti kalâ ukīnšu*
> *unakkilšu šūtura tâšu ella*
> *imnūšum-ma ina mê ušapšiḫ*
> *šitta irteḫīšu ṣalil ṭūbātiš*
> *ušaṣlil-ma apsâ reḫi šitta*

[258] "Besides shaking the prince out of his stupor, the letter also provides him with the magic data–the true names of his father and mother–which he uses to spellbind the serpent while he plucks the pearl from its scaly grasp." (Davis, *Techgnosis*, 117)

[259] *Hibil-Ziwa* 1.51-52:

Or in the Akkadian *Epic of Anzu*, too, when Ninurta steals back the tablet of destinies from the bird Anzu:

> Warlike Ninurta brought back the god's destiny-tablet in his hand.
> The wind carried Anzu's wings as a sign of his good tiding.[260]

Or like Ea, mentioned just above, gets away with Apsu's "awesome radiance:" "Ea carried away his awesome radiance and arrayed himself in it."[261]

and turned back to head toward my father's palace Pearl in hand, the mission over, the prince's sojourn in Egypt has come to an end, and he sets his sights for home. Hibil-Ziwa has to extricate himself from the world of darkness and asks, "How can we go up to be with my parents?"[262] For Hibil-Ziwa and for the prince, "with my parents" equals "home." And they both, too, hear and feel something like this line from a Manichaean hymn in Parthian: "Reach your home, the word-created land, where you were at the start."[263] But before the prince can really make his way home, he has one more thing to do.

I took off the Egyptians' dirty, unclean clothes, left them in their country The prince first disguised himself as an Egyptian so as not to spark their suspicion, then joined in with them and dined on Egyptian food, but now it's time to divest himself, literally, of any associations 62

ࡅࡄࡀࡉࡆࡀࡊ ࡍࡄࡉࡕࡀࡕ ࡒࡉࡍ ࡅࡀࡄࡅࡀࡕࡀࡋࡀࡄ ࡓࡀࡆࡀ ࡅࡂࡉࡌࡓࡀ ࡅࡍࡀࡅࡓࡀ
ࡅࡀࡌࡓࡀࡓࡀ ࡖࡄࡀࡉࡋࡀ ࡖࡊࡅࡋࡀࡉ ࡀࡄࡔࡅࡊࡀ ࡁࡂࡀࡅࡉ ࡀࡄࡅࡀ ࡅࡄࡀࡉࡆࡀࡊ
ࡄࡅ ࡌࡀࡍࡃࡀ ࡖࡄࡉࡉࡀ ࡀࡍࡎࡀࡁࡉࡍࡍࡅࡍ ࡀࡋࡄࡀࡋࡉࡍ ࡓࡀࡆࡉࡀ ࡌࡉࡍ ࡀࡉࡍࡀ
ࡓࡀࡁࡕࡉ ࡖࡊࡖ ࡋࡀ ࡄࡆࡀࡕࡋࡉ

u-hāyzāk nehtaṯ Qīn u-ahwāṯ-al-āh rāza u-gemra u-nawra u-amrāra aḏ-hayla aḏ-kull-ī ahšōḵa ab-gaww-ī ahwā. u-hāyzāk hū Manda aḏ-heyyī ansab-innon al-hālēn rāzī men ayna rabṯi aḏ-kaḏ lā-hzāṯ-lī

[260] *Anzû* III 21–22:

> *qarrādu ninurta tuppi šīmāti ilī qātuššu uttīr*
> *[a]na itti ša busratīšu kappī anzî ubil šāru*

[261] *Enūma eliš* I 68: *melammīšu itbala ea ūtaddiq*.
[262] 1.55: ࡀࡋࡌࡀࡄࡅ ࡍࡉࡎࡀࡒ ࡀࡋࡅࡀࡕ ࡀࡁࡀࡄࡀࡕࡀ *al-māhū nissaq alwāṯ abāhāṯ-e* .
[263] M4 (Boyce text cv) 5: *haxsā ō padišt, wāžāfrīd zamīg, kū būd-ē až nox.*

other than those of home.[264] As it says in the Manichaean *Psalmbook*: "I've left my clothes on earth, the old age of illness that I experience, and I've put on the outfit of undeath."[265] A body as an implicit or explicit garment for the soul is a feature of Manichaean (and other) anthropology. Such passages will appeal to those who read *The Pearl-song* allegorically. Again from the Manichaean *Psalmbook*, for example:

> I will rise up to the skies, and leave this body on earth.
> I hear the trumpet sounds: they call me up to the undying!
> I will throw my body onto the ground from which it was gathered.
> Since I was in my infancy, I have learned to walk the divine path.[266]

62 **I directed my journey toward the light of our homeland, the East** Now shed of his Egyptian clothes, the prince clearly and decisively sets his course back home. He's as far from home now as he's ever been, but at this point he can actually see where the end of his trip leads, just where it started.[267] This echoes the line from the Plotinus paragraph in the introduction, "Our homeland is where we came from, with the Father there."[268]

As it says in the Manichaean *Psalmbook* (addressing the soul): "The road to travel is right in front of you: don't forget your departure!"[269] And centuries earlier, in the first person, from an Old Aramaic inscrip-

[264] Young, "Divesting and Vesting."

[265] MPb II 81.8-9: [ⲁⲓⲕⲱ] ⲛ̅ⲑⲃ̅ⲥⲱ ⲁϫⲛ̅ⲡⲕⲁϩ· ⲧⲙⲛ̅ⲧϩⲗⲗⲟ ⲛ̅ⲛ̅ϣⲱⲛⲉ ⲉ[ⲧϣⲟ]ⲟⲡ ⲛⲉⲙⲏⲓ̈· ⲧⲥⲧⲟⲗⲏ ⲛ̣̅ⲁ̣ⲧ̣ⲙⲟⲩ ⲁⲓ̈ⲧⲉⲉⲥ ⲁϫⲱⲓ̈.

[266] MPb II 75.13-18: ϯⲛⲁⲡⲱⲛⲉ – read -ⲧⲱⲛⲉ (a common form of ⲧⲱⲟⲩⲛ) "rise"? – ⲁϩⲣⲏⲓ̈ ⲁⲙⲡⲏⲩⲉ ⲛ̅ⲧⲁⲕⲱ ⲁϫⲛ̅ⲡⲕⲁϩ ⲙ̅ⲡⲓⲥⲱⲙⲁ· ⲥⲱϣ ⲛ̅ϫⲓ ⲧⲥⲁⲗⲡⲓⲅⲝ ϯⲥⲱⲧⲙⲉ ⲥⲉⲧⲱϩⲙⲉ ⲙ̅ⲙⲁⲓ̈ ⲁϩⲣⲏⲓ̈ ϣⲁⲛⲓⲁⲧⲙⲟⲩ ϯⲛⲁⲛⲟⲩϫⲉ ⲁⲃⲁⲗ ⲙ̅ⲡⲁⲥⲱⲙⲁ ⲁϫⲛ̅ⲡⲕⲁ[ϩ ⲉ]ⲧⲁⲩⲥⲁⲩ̣ϩϥ̅ ⲁⲃⲁⲗ ⲛ̣̅ϩⲏⲧϥ̅· ϫⲛ̅ⲉⲓ̈ϣⲟⲟⲡ ϩⲛ̅ⲧⲁⲙⲛ̅ⲧϣⲏⲣⲉ̣ ϣⲏⲙ [ⲁ]ⲓ̣̈ϫⲓ ⲥⲃⲱ ⲁⲙⲁϩⲉ ϩⲛ̅ⲡⲙⲁⲓ̈ⲧ ⲙ̅ⲡⲛⲟⲩⲧⲉ.

We can also add 82.15-16, addressing ⲧⲁⲯⲩⲭⲏ "my soul:" ⲛ̅ⲧⲉ ⲟⲩϣⲙ̅ⲙⲱ ⲉⲣⲉϭⲉⲗⲓⲧ ⲁⲩⲥⲱⲙⲁ ⲛ̅ⲧⲉ ⲡⲕⲁϩ ⲉ̣[ⲧ]ϫⲁϩⲙ̅, "you're a foreigner lodging in a body that belongs to the polluted earth."

[267] "Gnosis is exactly the revealer of the identity between beeginning and end, joined together in a single point" ("La gnose est précisément la révélatrice de cette identité du commencement et de la fin, se rejoignant en un point unique," Corbin, *En Islam iranien*, 263).

[268] *Enneads*, 1.6.8: Πατρὶς δὴ ἡμῖν, ὅθεν παρήλθομεν, καὶ πατὴρ ἐκεῖ..

[269] MPb II 82.25-26: ⲉⲓⲥ ⲧϩⲓⲏ ⲙ̅ⲙⲁϩⲉ ϩⲓⲑⲏ ⲙ̅ⲙⲟ ⲙ̅ⲡⲱⲣϣⲃϣ ⲁⲧⲉϭⲓⲛⲉⲓ ⲁⲃⲁⲗ.

tion: "The road is open for me."[270] The Greek translation here recalls John 1:23, Εὐθύνατε τὴν ὁδὸν κυρίου "Straighten the Lord's road!"

Just as it had awakened me with its voice, it was leading me with 65
its light The letter, as if it were not already amazing enough, now lights up and acts as a glowing guide for the homeward-bound hero.

like regal silk in front of me The Syriac word *basilikon* seems just to 66
be the adjective βασιλικόν "royal," and this meaning fits the context, but it's nevertheless neither a regular Syriac word nor a regular way to derive vocabulary from Greek in Syriac: just a straight-up transliteration (with a neuter singular ending), rather than an actual Syriac adaptation. It may refer to a royal banner.

Encouraging me in my trepidation with its guiding voice Along 67
with its light, the letter presses the traveler, again using sound and voice. "Hurry, boy, it's waiting there for you," in the language of Toto's "Africa" (1982).[271] Here and in the following line the letter feels alive and sentient.[272]

Sarbug ... Babylon ... Mesene, the haven of traders Other than 69-71
repeating the same places as for the trip west, the narrative is silent about the return trip home.

My shining garment that I'd taken off, and my cloak it was cov- 72-74
ered with, // These my parents sent to me there from high Warkan, // By their treasurers, entrusted with it for their reliability Syriac lines 72-74 are absent from the Greek translation. This omission matches the Greek version's replacement of "stripped" with "put on" above in line 9.

Warkan, or Hyrcania, a region located southeast of the Caspian sea in the confines of the Alborz and Köpet Dag mountain ranges, is mentioned only here in the poem, as the place from which the prince's parents send his garment to him. Already named in the Bisotun inscription in Old Persian as *Varkâna*, it's known as *Warkān* in Parthian and *Gurgān* in Middle Persian, all meaning something like "wolf-country."[273] While it plays a minor role in the narrative, Warkan

---

[270] KAI 224/Sefire III 8-9: 𐤐𐤕𐤉𐤇𐤄 · 𐤋𐤉 · 𐤀𐤓𐤇𐤀 · / <ptyḥh ly ʔrḥʔ>.

[271] Lyrics by David Paich.

[272] Cf. Ménard, "Chant," 321.

[273] Gignoux, *Glossaire*, 66; Bivar, "Gorgān."

serves to locate the prince's family and home far away from both Egypt and the southern Mesopotamian locales he passes through on the way there. Warkan had long been treated as a sub-province of Parthia, both sometimes governed by a single satrap, and if the prince's family is meant to be ruling in Parthia, their presence in Warkan isn't unusual.

74 **treasurers** Syriac *gēzaḇrâ* "treasurer" reflects an early Iranian loanword in Aramaic.[274] Known from Old Persian *ganzabara-* and later,[275] the word was also "loaned" into Akkadian (*ganzabaru*),[276] and its pre-Syriac Aramaic form occurs in Artaxerxes' letter in Ezra 7:21.[277] Bar Bahlul defines the Syriac word in Arabic simply as *al-ḫāzin* "treasurer."[278]

76 **Suddenly, when I'd faced it, the garment seemed like my mirror** Stang marks the parallel between the letter and the garment: "Just as the letter reflected the prince's inner inscription, so the garment reflects his outer appearance back to him."[279]

For the very rare noun-form *lḇuštâ* (*lḇušâ* is more usual), see Mark 14:63 in the Old Syriac (Sinaiticus) version.[280]

77 **I saw all of it in all of me, and in it likewise I faced all of me** While it may not be entirely clear, this is one of the most remarkable lines in the poem. The prince, it seems, reflects the garment-mirror, just as it reflects him. It changes his vision and insight, as we see in the next line. In the Manichaean *Psalmbook*, the Holy Spirit (Paraclete), too, brings a revealing mirror: "He brought us a mirror: we looked, we saw the universe inside it."[281] And again, from the same book:

> You've left us lacking nothing, so we have a defense before the judge of truth.
> You brought a mirror for us from your kingdom.

[274] ILS 142.

[275] For later inscriptions, for example, see Gignoux, *Glossaire*, 51.

[276] CAD G 43.

[277] לכל גזבריא די בעבר נהרה "for all the treasurers west of the Euphrates."

[278] BB 478.

[279] Stang, *Divine Double*, 140.

[280] Cf. Beyer, "Perlenlied," 258.

[281] MPb II 9.6-7: ⲁϥⲉⲓⲛⲉ ⲛⲉⲛ ⲛ̄ⲟⲩⲓ̈ⲉⲗ ⲁⲛϭⲱϣⲧ̄ ⲁⲛ̣ⲛⲉⲩ ⲁⲡⲓⲧⲏⲣϥ̄ ⲛ̄ϩⲏⲧⲥ.

We looked, we saw the universe inside it:
All that has been, will be, and is.[282]

This imagery recalls the Guardian of Forever's time portal in the *Star Trek* episode, "The City on the Edge of Forever."[283] Finally, another Coptic text gives a reminder that reflection can be recursive. Here the object is the self, rather than *The Pearlsong*'s "everything:" "Seeing himself inside himself in a mirror, he appears, looking like himself."[284]

Because we're distinctly two, but still one, with one form This 78
partly obscure line reflects the language of logic, as explained, for example, by Sergius of Rēšʕaynå in his *Treatise on Genus, Species, and Individuality* in Syriac:

> Species are different from one another by distinctions, because not everything that one species has is had by its counterpart, for if they were to have everything equally, it would then be just one species in question, but where there are two, or however many, species that have something equally among those that are different from each other, these are species, but that which the species, whether two or many, have equally is called genus.[285]

the impulses of knowledge were writhing around in all of it The 88
noun translated "impulses," *zawʕå*, is a generic word in Syriac for movement and motion of all kinds, from psychological tremors and human

---

[282] 21.17-21: ⲙ̄ⲡⲉⲕⲕⲁⲁⲛ ⲉⲛϣⲁⲁⲧ ⲛ̄ⲗⲁⲩⲉ ϫⲉ ⲉⲛⲁϭⲛ ⲁⲡⲟⲗⲟⲅⲓⲁ ⲙ̄ⲡⲙ̄ⲧⲟ ⲙ̄ⲡⲕⲣⲓⲧⲏⲥ ⲛ̄ⲧⲙⲏⲉ· ⲁⲕⲉⲓⲛⲉ ⲛⲉⲛ ⲛ̄ⲟⲩⲓ̈ⲉⲗ ⲁⲃⲁⲗ ϩⲛ̄ⲧⲕⲙⲛ̄ⲧⲣ̄ⲣⲟ ⲁⲛϭⲱϣⲧ̄ ⲁⲛⲛⲉⲩ ⲁⲡⲧⲏⲣϥ ⲛϩⲏⲧⲥ ⲛⲉⲧⲁⲩϣ̣ⲱ̣ⲡ̣ⲉ̣ ⲙ̣ⲛ̣ⲛ̣ⲉ̣[ⲧⲁϣⲱⲡⲉ ⲙⲛ̄]ⲛⲉⲧϣⲟⲟⲡ ⲧⲏⲣⲟⲩ.

[283] Written by Harlan Ellison; airdate April 6, 1967.

[284] *Sophia of Jesus Christ/Eugnostos* BG 91.4-7 (ed. pp. 72-73): ⲉϥⲛⲁⲩ ⲉⲣⲟϥ ⲙ̄ⲙⲓⲛ ⲙ̄ⲙⲟϥ ϩⲣⲁ̈ⲓ ⲛ̄ϩⲏⲧϥ ϩⲛ ⲟⲩⲉⲓⲁⲗ ϣⲁϥⲟⲩⲱⲛϩ ⲉⲃⲟⲗ ⲉϥⲉⲓⲛⲉ ⲙ̄ⲙⲟϥ ⲙ̄ⲙⲓⲛ ⲙ̄ⲙⲟϥ.

[285] Text in BL add. 14658, ff. 125v-126r. *The Pearlsong*'s *puršånå*, which has the same root as the adjective *priš* here, has a synonym in Sergius's *šuḥlåpå*:

ܐܠܐ ܐܕܫ̈ܐ ܦܪ̈ܝܫܝܢ ܡܢ ܚܕ̈ܕܐ ܒܫܘ̈ܚܠܦܐ. ܕܠܘ ܟܠܡܕܡ ܕܐܝܬ ܠܚܕ
ܐܕܫܐ: ܐܝܬ ܐܦ ܠܚܒܪܗ. ܐܠܘ ܓܝܪ ܟܠ ܡܕܡ ܫܘܝܐܝܬ ܐܝܬ ܗܘܐ
ܠܗܘܢ. ܚܕ ܗܘܐ ܒܠܚܘܕ ܐܕܫܐ. ܐܝܟܢܐ ܕܝܢ ܕܐܝܬ ܐܕ̈ܫܐ ܬܪ̈ܝܢ ܐܘ
ܟܡܐ ܕܗ̈ܘ: ܕܐܝܬ ܠܗܘܢ ܡܕܡ ܫܘܝܐܝܬ ܒܗܠܝܢ ܕܦܪ̈ܝܫܝܢ ܡܢ ܚܕ̈ܕܐ.
ܐܝܬܝܗܘܢ ܐܕܫ̈ܐ. ܗܘ ܕܝܢ ܕܫܘܝܐܝܬ ܐܝܬ ܠܗܘܢ ܠܐܕ̈ܫܐ: ܐܘ
ܠܬܪ̈ܝܢ ܐܘ ܠܣܓܝ̈ܐܐ. ܓܢܣܐ ܡܬܩܪܐ.

emotions to earthquakes. The corresponding Greek word in the translation is equally general in meaning. This picturesque line shows how vivid and dynamic the garment is. It's hard not to think of a mass of slithering snakes or worms (cf. Acts 12:23 in Syriac, where the same verb as here is used). Out of these lively impulses, or motives, of knowledge – *gnosis*, if you like – come yet another instance of unexpected speech.

89-90 **it was ready to speak. / I heard the sound of its tones, whispering in its descent** Now that he's met his shining garment on the road, after having been awakened by a talking letter, the clothes also talk, or gently chant. (Would the prince be surprised to hear anything inanimate talking now?) Once again, sound, and even speech, irrupts into the prince's world.

91 **"I belong to the swiftest servant, for whom I was brought up before my father."** This line is apparently in the voice of the garment, that is, the garment is saying self-referentially that it is the prince's. The reference to "*my* father" may seem strange, and the Greek lacks a possessive pronoun, but it further gives the sense of the king-father's sway and ownership over everything.

93 **I, too, felt my stature grow in accord with my father's efforts** I take the first words in Syriac (*w-ʔåp̄ ʔenå*) to mark the change in speaker back to the prince. The prince takes the verb that the speaking letter has just used ("brought up"), and uses it for his own size or stature. The prince and the garment were last together in his childhood, and now they are both grown, as the identical verb highlights.

93 **its royal impulses** The phrase is similar to "impulses of knowledge" above (line 88).

98 **the court of greeting and reverence** For "court" (*traʕ*), the Greek has "country" (χώρα). This is a common word in Syriac for door or gate (large or small), which in royal contexts may also mean "court" or "antechamber." Beyond this "court," it seems there are two other explicit courts, too: "the court of his nobles" (101) and "the court of the king of kings" (101). At this first court, the prince is welcomed like the soul in the Mandaic *Qolasta* when it receives a welcome as it's returning to "the house of life."

The soul flew and continued until it got to the house of life.
They reached the house of life, it shouted to the house of life.
Life, which heard its voice, sent a guide to meet it.
He took it by its right hand and guided it, supported by the image of life.[286]

I joined his magnates As the prince had previously joined in and 101
mixed with the Egyptians (line 32), now he does so with his father's nobles. *wåsprå* "noble, prince," like the name of the Armenian province and kingdom of Vaspurakan, comes from a form like MP *wāspuhr*, known in Manichaean Pa/MP as *wispuhr*.[287] It only appears once in the poem (here), referring to the Parthian nobility that greet the prince when he arrives back home.

The picture is a bit like Ninurta's return in *Epic of Anzu*:

Go to him, and he can come here to us!
Let him be happy, dance, and celebrate!
Let him stand together with his brother-gods, and hear secret knowledge!
Let him hear the god's secret knowledge!
Let [...] go with him and give him responsibilities![288]

---

[286] 113.9-12:

[illegible]
[illegible]
[illegible]
[illegible]
[illegible]

pāhra u-āzel nišma / alma al-bīt heyyī amṭā
maṭṭūy-ī bīt heyyī / qāl-ī al-bīt heyyī armā
heyyī aḏ-šimūī al-qāl-ī / šaddar al-anp-ī parwānqa
legṭ-ī ab-prās yammīn-ī / u-adbar b-admū heyyī asmkū-ī

[287] ILS 166; Harnack, "Parthische Titel," 519-525; Gignoux, *Glossaire* 49; CPD 88; Boyce, *Wordlist*, 97; DMMPP 358a.

[288] III 27-31:

alikšum-ma lillikannâši
liḫdi limmelil nigûta līpuš

Sohravardi gives a different kind of homecoming in the *Western Exile*, complete with music and violent pleasure:

> With the distance cut and the road stopped, ... I saw the upper celestial bodies: I joined in with them and I heard their melodies and songs and learned their anthems. ... And my tendons almost severed, and my joints almost got disjointed, because of the pleasure I was receiving![289]

103 **with a gleeful sound** ܕܪ̈ܘܣܐ *drusē* has been read as a Greek loanword. Brockelmann, for example, emended it to ܐܕܪܘܪܣܐ and took it as a derivative of Greek ὕδραυλις "hydraulic organ."[290] Payne Smith ventures no guess.[291] Without emending, though, it makes sense to read *drusē* just as the plural of ܕܪܘܣܬܐ *drustå* "joy, delight, splendor."[292]

104–105 **for me to go to the court of the king of kings / That I might appear with him before our king** These final two lines present two apparent kings, with the third person pronoun of this and the previous lines referring to the prince's father, and "our king" (and maybe "king of kings") referring to another king of higher rank. The prince's father

lizziz itti ilī aḫḫīšū-ma pirišta lišme
[lišmē-m]a ša ilī pirišta
[... lil]lik itti ilī aḫḫīšū-ma liqīssu parṣī

[289] 36, Arabic:

ولمّا انقطعت المسافة وانقرض الطريق ... فرأيت الأجرام العلوية اتّصلت بها وسمعت نغماتها ودستاناتها وتعلمت انشادها ... فتكاد تنقطع أوتاري وتنفصل مفاصلي من لذة ما انال

Persian:

وچون مسافت بريده شد و راه بپايان رسيد ... پس جرم هاء علوى را بديدم، بدانها پيوستم و نغمه ها و دستانهاء آنها بشنودم و خواندن آن آهنگها بياموختم ... پس نزديك آمد كه از لذت آنچه بدو رسيده بودم رگ ها و پى هاء من از هم فرو گسلد و مفصل هاء من جدا گردد

[290] *Lexicon Syriacum*, 167b. The actual Syriac word derived from this Greek *does* occur in the *Acts of Thomas* at AMS III 6.9, among the selections translated in Appendix III.
[291] *Thesaurus Syriacus*, col. 947: "Quid sit nescio," that is, "I'm not sure what it might be."
[292] For this Syriac word Bar Bahlul (592) gives Arabic بهجة *bahǧa*ʰ.

and “our king” are not the same. In the Greek translation, too, there seem to be two kings: the king that is the prince’s father and another king.

5 Appendix I: Syriac Meter and *The Pearlsong*

Let my inspiration flow
in token rhyme suggesting rhythm
that will not forsake me
till my tale is told and done
– Robert Hunter, "Terrapin Station" (Grateful Dead)

The Pearlsong's metrical pattern isn't as obvious as it is in the rest of Syriac verse generally. It's closest to a well-known form of Syriac verse called a *memra*. As we will see, *The Pearlsong* has a baseline rhythm of six syllables per line or stich, arranged in distichs or couplets, but the underlying hexasyllabic pattern actually varies from five to seven syllables per line. But before looking in more detail at the poetic form of *The Pearlsong* itself, let's go over Syriac poetry more generally.[293]

Where Syriac literature is known, it's often known at the very least for its poetry, in particular the poetry composed and chanted or sung in churches and monasteries.[294] Poetry is of course hardly the sole possession of Syriac among the Aramaic languages, or among the Semitic languages more widely.[295]

[293] Brock and Kiraz, *Ephrem*, xiii-xvi; Brock, "Poetry" (esp. 657-658, 661-662 for meter, 659-660 for terminology); Brock, "Later Syriac Poetry;" Macuch, *Geschichte*.

[294] "Religious poetry, however, may be the most original contribution of Syriac writing to world literature." (Gzella, *Cultural History*, 377).

[295] "All Mesopotamian myths were phrased as epical poems having a strophic structure and were designed to be sung, as indicated by the fact that they were referred to as "songs" (*zamāru*)." (Parpola 183n14). Cf. West, "Akkadian Poetry." For non-Syriac

Syriac poetry regularly follows one of two main patterns: the *madraša* (PL *madraše*), which has a line-varying stanzaic pattern, and the *memra* (PL *memre*), which has a consistently syllabled repeating couplet or quatrain pattern. Both of these technical terms for kinds of poetry have additional broader meanings, as noted above under the discussion about "hymns." The term *memra*, for example, can also be applied to prose, where it can mean "treatise, essay, section (of a written work)," etc.

name	*metrical structures*
mēmrå ܡܐܡܪܐ	repeating couplet pattern with the same number of syllables each, most commonly 7+7 or 12+12[296]
madråšå ܡܕܖܫܐ	stanzas of a repeating pattern of syllables-per-line, e.g. with stanzas of 6+5 5+5 5+5, repeated as long as necessary

The unit for measuring line-length is the syllable, pure and simple, whether long or short, open or closed. Unlike metrical patterns in some languages, in Syriac it's not based on stress patterns or particular sets of long and short syllables. Where there's a full vowel, that counts as a syllable. A *šəvå*, the ultrashort, unwritten vowel ə, which is commonly the result of vowel reduction, does not count as a full, real syllable in poetic terms. While these rules are followed closely, especially with some authors (e.g. Jacob of Serug), Syriac poets may treat them with some license:

- the *šəvå* sometimes *does* count as a syllable
- an actual vowel, esp. those with ʔ- at the beginning of verbs like *ʔek̲al* "he ate," may elide

Rhyme isn't a typical productive feature of Syriac poetry until later examples, such as with ʕab̲dišoʕ bar Brik̲å at the turn of the fourteenth century.

Aramaic, cf. Greenfield, "Early Aramaic Poetry;" Tal, "Samaritan Literature;" Lieber, *Jewish Aramaic Poetry*; and Pereira *Studies in Aramaic Poetry*. For Hebrew see Watson, *Classical Hebrew Poetry* and Carmi, *Hebrew Verse*.

[296] That is, couplets of 4+4+4 each.

When we talk about a "line" of Syriac poetry, this is according to patterns of regular word junctures and syllable counts. In Syriac manuscripts, punctuation dots provide some guidance for divisions into longer or shorter clauses, but Syriac poetry is *not* typically laid out by line: it's all written continuously, like Syriac prose.

Both *madraše* and *memre* can be acrostics, like other Aramaic poetry, and there's a subset of *memra* that are dialogue poems (called *sogīṯå*, PL *soḡyåṯå*), where a conversational debate of some kind is carried out between characters like Death and the Devil.

Madraše, with their repeating stanzaic (+refrain) patterns, may last for a few or several pages, but *memre*, with their repeating line-by-line syllable-count, may typically be even longer, theoretically with no limit. *The Pearlsong*, at 105 lines, is a relatively short Syriac poem.

It's appropriate to think of *memre* as spoken poems – they're recited or chanted – *madraše* are songs, that is, people have sung and do sing them.[297] As such, they're associated with particular tunes, just as we might say, "Let's sing ______, to the tune of ______." Scribes indicate the tune (*qålå*) that goes with a particular *madraša*, and *madraše* of the same meter can share the same *qålå*. (A *madraša* can go with more than one *qålå*, too, though.) Each stanza of a *madraša* may end with a refrain.

The *memra* has had a much longer half-life in Syriac literature than the *madraša*. The *memra* is known from at least the fourth century on, with much later examples – into the twentieth century – available, although they're still mainly unpublished.[298] Many pieces of Syriac poetry are anonymous, but among named authors, Ephrem "the Syrian" is the one poet par excellence of the *madraša*. Authors associated with the *memra* form a much longer list.[299] To name a few from the fifth century: Jacob of Serug, Narsai, Isaac of Antioch, Balai, and Cyrillona. Later well-known *memra*-poets include George, bishop of the Arabs (d. 724), Emmanuel bar Šahhårē (d. 980), Yuhanon bar Maʕdānī (d. 1263), Barhebraeus (d. 1286), Gewargis "Warda" and Khamis bar

[297] "Whereas *memre* were evidently recited, *madrashe* were sung" (Brock, "Poetry," 658).

[298] See, for example, Macuch, *Geschichte*.

[299] See the respective entries in Brock, Butts, Kiraz, Van Rompay, eds., *Gorgias Encyclopedic Dictionary*.

Qardåḥē (both thirteenth century), ʕabdišoʕ bar Brikå (d. 1318), and Sargis bar Waḥlē (fl. ca. 1500).

Given the greater variety of possibilities with the arrangement of syllables in a *madraša* line, readers (and editors) may metrically analyze the same line in different ways. Here's an example of a *madraša* with a stanzaic pattern of 5+5 three times, with the occasional measure of 6+5 instead, as with the first distich of this stanza:[300]

b-ʕubbå dakyå d-nahrå	In the river's pure womb
ilap l-bat-nåšå	learn of the human daughter,
d-betnat d-lå gabrå	Who got pregnant without a man
w-yeldat d-lå zarʕå	and gave birth without "seed."
rabbyat b-mawhabtå	With a gift, she reared
l-mår-åh d-mawhabtå	the lord of the gift.

Here's a more complicated metrical pattern:[301]

mannu mṣē-wå d-neḥzē	Who could see
zawgå d-yaqqirē	the honored couple
d-ʔetparsiw men šely	suddenly exposed?
qåm bišå hwå lēh	The bad one got up and became
ḥazzåyå pṣiḥå	a beaming spectator
ḥzåy ṭåbå w-naṭr-ēh l-ēh	but the good one saw and closely watched him.
mannu mṣē-wå	Who could see
d-lå nebkē-wå	and not cry,
kad ḥåzē l-ʔådåm	Seeing how the great Adam
rabbå d-ʔeštappal	is laid low,
w-nakpå da-mdabbeq ṭarpē	And how he's modestly attaching leaves
l-taksitå d-ṣaʕr-ēh	as a covering for his shameful behavior?

300 Ephrem, *Eccl* 36.4 (Brock and Kiraz, *Ephrem*, 72).

301 Ephrem, *Ieiun* 3.2 (Brock and Kiraz, *Ephrem*, 98). I've analyzed the meter as 6+5+5 / 5+5+6 / 4+4 / 5+5 / 7+5 / 4+4+4+4.

brik-u d-ḥann-ēh	Blessed is the one who showed him grace
b-ṭarp-aw w-šaddar	with the leaves and sent him
ʔesṭel šubḥå	a garment of glory
la-šliḥut-ēh	for his nakedness.

Finally, here is a straightforward example of a *memra*, in this case 4+4+4 (dodecasyllabic):[302]

tahhir-wå b-hon ʔåp såṭånå b-pagrē nakpē	Satan was also amazed at their modest bodies,
da-kmå yuqrå ṭʕan b-ʔulṣånå d-la ruʕʕåmå	How much weight they bore under pressure without complaining,
pṣiḥin-waw dēn ʔåp malʔakē b-haw ḥumsånå	But the angels were beaming at their endurance,
da-kma ʔaggar haw ʔågonå dḥilå da-hwå	How it outlasted that scary struggle that ensued.

From these representative examples of *madraša* and *memra*, let's turn now to *The Pearlsong*'s metrical possibilities. The syllable counts per line vary slightly, but not to the extent that *madraša*-lines typically do, and the predominant measure is six syllables, but with an overall range of 5-7 syllables. If it is a *memra*, the hexasyllabic meter is nevertheless not

[302]Jacob of Serug, ed. Bedjan, AMS 1 138.1-4. This kind of poetry is often printed (as in Bedjan's editions of Jacob's work) line by line, all twelve syllables together, but it's occasionally printed as in Syriac manuscripts, that is, just like prose, continuously and without end-of-line breaks. Finally, it can also be printed in three groups of four syllables (as in Ryssel, "Poemi"). This text printed in the last style would be:

ܬܗܝܪ ܗܘܐ ܒܗܘܢ   ܐܦ ܣܛܢܐ   ܒܦܓܪ̈ܐ ܢܟܦ̈ܐ
ܕܟܡܐ ܝܘܩܪܐ   ܛܥܢ ܒܐܘܠܨܢܐ   ܕܠܐ ܪܘܥܡܐ
ܦܨܝܚܝܢ ܗܘܘ ܕܝܢ   ܐܦ ܡܠܐܟ̈ܐ   ܒܗܘ ܚܘܡܣܢܐ
ܕܟܡܐ ܐܓܪ   ܗܘ ܐܓܘܢܐ   ܕܚܝܠܐ ܕܗܘܐ

particularly common, and in any case the variation of syllables-per-line is much more than usual for a *memra*.

According to the conventional arrangement, there are four half-lines, in addition to the 101 full lines in the poem. (Since these half-lines are even in number, they could, of course, be arranged differently and just make two more full lines.) Again, the number of syllables per line hovers closely to six, with the following breakdown out of a total 101 lines (105 minus the four half-lines):[303]

- 6+6 49 lines
- 6+7 16 lines
- 5+6 13 lines
- 5+7 11 lines
- 7+6 8 lines
- 7+7 4 lines

(The counts are based on my edited text, but with or without emendations the text doesn't show a consistent pattern matching those of other Syriac poetry.) Three of the half-lines are six-syllable (25a, 26a, 68a), and 71a is seven-syllable.

So, is this a hexasyllabic *memra*? Again, if it is a *memra*, of any measure, there's much more variation in line-length than usual. And even

[303]The specific distribution of syllable patterns by line:

6+6	1 5 10 11 12 13 15 16 17 19 20 32 38 40 42 44 45 46 48 52 56 58 59 60 63 64 67 69 70 74 76 78 80 81 83 85 87 90 91 93 94 95 96 98 99 102 103 104 105
6+7	4 18 23 27 30 34 39 41 50 51 53 57 75 86 88 97
5+6	8 9 14 21 33 37 43 55 72 77 79 89 100
5+7	3 7 22 24 29 47 49 54 73 82 101
7+6	2 6 28 36 61 65 66 84
7+7	31 35 62 92

if it were consistently hexasyllabic, this is an uncommon meter. As an example of a *memra* that has a real and consistent six-syllable pattern, here's the second stanza from a dialogue poem:[304]

> *b-åḵ taħħir-nå ṭalyå | kmå marrirå nap̄š-åḵ*
> *wa-ḵmå ʕayyiq lebb-åḵ | wa-ḵmå šåp̄ʕån demʕ-ayk*
> I'm astonished at you, kid, how bitter your soul is,
> how pained your heart, how your tears overflow!

The Pearlsong, then, while it may hew more closely to a hexasyllabic *memra* pattern than to anything more obvious, that's not what it really seems to be. Poirier proposes a kind of "rhythmic prose," rather than verse pure and simple, in distichs.[305] Calling it prose, even metrical or rhythmic, is misleading. Whatever kind of fluid metrical pattern it follows, the clause-lines are still short, compared to Syriac prose, and they're *very* close to the same syllabic lengths, something that never happens in Syriac prose. Rather than "rhythmic prose," you could, therefore, call it "verse in varied meter" or something similar. This pattern, similar to a *memra* in *mostly* having the same number of syllables per line, nevertheless is different in deviating from that number much more than a *memra* in Syriac normally does. And yet, *The Pearlsong* doesn't follow an obvious stanzaic pattern like a *madraša* either. This strange poetic form may well reflect an Aramaic existence prior to and other than its Syriac shape. This strangeness in poetic form matches a strangeness in the poem's Syriac itself, as discussed in Appendix II.

---

[304] Brock, *Sogyåṯå*, no. 4.

[305] "The hymn, then, isn't constructed on a strict metrical basis, but is nevertheless still measured and rhythmic;" "L'hymne n'est donc pas construit sur la base d'une métrique stricte, mais il n'en est pas moins mesuré et rythmé" (Poirier, *L'Hymne*, 196).

6 Appendix II: Some Linguistic Features of *The Pearlsong*

Secret hymnal with the words
in a version of the mother tongue
– John Darnielle, "Parisian Enclave"
(The Mountain Goats)

The odd character of the Syriac may correspond to an early date of composition (i.e. prior to the Sasanian empire), a judgement voiced as early as Nöldeke.[306] A more recent formulation comes from Tubach:

> It is occasionally assumed that the song is older than the time the *Acts of Thomas* come from and belongs to the Parthian period. This is only possible if one reckons with a prehistory in the form of an oral, and then a literary, tradition, prior to the song taking its present form in Edessa. Had the hymn been translated from Middle Parthian (or Middle Persian), the translator would have had to dedicate more attention to the meter. If an already available text had been adjusted from a form of southeastern Aramaic to Edessan Syriac, then the metrical inconsistency,

[306] 677: "the very idiosyncratic language agrees with this dating," "zu dieser Zeitbestimmung stimmt die sehr eigenthümliche Sprache."

> together with the grammatical peculiarities, is more easily explained than in the case of a genuine translation or a proper poetic rendering.[307]

Similarly, as Beyer notes, readers of Syriac eventually have a poem they can read and understand as Syriac, even with some remaining non-Syriac features.[308]

Among these not-so-usual features are the particle *yåṯ-* and the high frequency of absolute and bound forms. Further, there's "the strong Iranian influence"[309] noticeable in the text, from Iranian loanwords, highlighted below, to the settings and place-names discussed in the commentary. The Parthian titles and settings, the Iranian loanwords more broadly, and the prince's homeland and travel-route would seem to point to an eastern Aramaic from the early first millennium CE, but all this really points to is "the East ≈ Parthia" as the origin of the prince and the story; this may include the language, too, but that language doesn't have to be an Aramaic, so some kind of "eastern Aramaic" is not so obvious a given as it might be at first glance. Indeed, some of the features discussed below point to a kind of western Aramaic, rather than eastern. (It's customary in Aramaic studies to classify Aramaic

[307]Tubach, "Zur Interpretation," 237: "Gelegentlich wird angenommen, dass das Lied älter als die Entstehungszeit der Thomas-Akten ist und in die parthische Zeit gehört. Dies ist nur dann möglich, wenn man mit einer Vorgeschichte in Gestalt einer oralen und dann literarischen Tradition rechnet, ehe das Lied in Edessa seine jetzige Form erhielt. Wäre der Hymnus aus dem Mittelparthischen (oder Mittelpersischen) ins Syrische übertragen worden, hätte der Bearbeiter dem Metrum mehr Aufmerksamkeit widmen müssen. Wurde ein bereits vorhandener Text aus einer südostaramäischen Sprachform dem edessenischen Syrisch angepasst, lässt sich die metrische Inkonsequenz nebst den grammatikalischen Besonderheiten leichter erklären als bei einer echten Übersetzung oder regelrechten Nachdichtung."

[308]"Although it was certainly increasingly adapted by scribes to the orthographic and grammatical rules of Syriac, after reaching Syrophone regions and eventually being incorporated into the *Acts of Thomas*, it still includes some non-Syriac features ..." "Obwohl es von den Abschreibern sicher zunehmend den Schreib- und Sprachregeln des Syrischen angepaßt wurde, nachdem es in das syrische Sprachgebiet gelangt und schließlich den Thomasakten einverliebt worden war (vgl. ATTM S. 156 unten), enthält es noch verschiedenes Unsyrische ..."(Beyer, "Perlenlied," 237).

[309]"der starke iranische Einfluß" (Beyer, "Perlenlied," 238).

languages after Imperial Aramaic as either eastern or western, a geographic binary that also corresponds to several distinguishing phonological, morphological, syntactical, and lexical features.)[310] While there are peculiarities in *The Pearlsong*'s Syriac, I want to emphasize that the poem as we know it in the manuscript, and as presented here, is very definitely "in Syriac," even if it has some features aligning more with other Aramaics. These things may reflect something about its origin or its translation or scribal transmission history, but they are more hints and possibilities than clear evidence.

6.1 The Particle *yåṯ-*

Two times in *The Pearlsong* (lines 54 and 102) the particle *yåṯ-* occurs. It's well known from other Aramaic languages, but in Syriac its use is anything but regular, so why is it here? Let's first look at the particle in some non-Syriac Aramaic languages. In the widely used Aramaic translation of the Pentateuch known as Targum Onqelos, the book of Genesis begins, "in the beginning YWY created the sky and the earth," with the particle *yāt* marking the (definite) direct objects "sky" and "earth."[311] There's nothing particularly special about the Genesis verse: *yāt* is regular throughout Targum Onqelos as well as its companion translation of the Hebrew Bible Prophets, Targum Jonathan. Elsewhere, for example, you can read (Jonah 1:5):[312] "they threw the cargo on the ship into the sea." As we will see momentarily, this *yāt* continues to be used in western Aramaic languages – Jewish Palestinian, Samaritan, and Christian Palestinian, and the end of the Genesis verse given above in Targum Neofiti, in JPA, has a distinct verb ("completed"), but still with that object-marking *yāt*.[313] (Neither the Samaritan Targum, nor the early CPA translation, for Genesis 1 survives, so those western Aramaic translations of the verse are uncheckable.)

---

[310] See an excellent overview of approaches to Aramaic "dialectology" in Pat-El, *Syntax*, 9-16.

[311] בקדמין ברא יוי ית שמיא וית ארעא. These Onqelos-Jonathan texts are cited from Sperber, *Bible*.

[312] ורמו ית מניא דבאלפא לימא

[313] שכלל ית שמיא וית ארעא

Something like this earlier *yāt* form famously shows up in the Syriac translation of Genesis 1, and Ephrem comments on it briefly in his commentary to the book. While *yåṯ-* in the Syriac Genesis is probably the same as in Onqelos and the Palestinian Targums, Ephrem seems to take it as a noun in a bound (construct) form.[314] Since it's in Genesis 1, Syriac-writing exegetes continue to refer to it, but it's also known in its full noun form in Syriac philosophical circles. Jacob of Edessa noted the apparent non-Syriac character of this *yåṯ-*, at the same time correctly pointing to its regular use in western Aramaic languages (alongside the Hebrew direct object marker *ʔēṯ*):

> This noun *yåṯå* is not regularly in use in the Syriac, or Mesopotamian, language, but in Syro-Palestinian, it's regular and preferred, and more so in Hebrew, the first language, since using this word is a characteristic feature of Hebrew.[315]

A couple of centuries later, Ishodad of Merv still felt it worth commenting on, also noting its western feel, but he also specifically mentions possible confusion when used as a technical philosophical term:

> Some people think *yåṯ-* means individual essence [*qnomå*], and is a Palestinian usage. They should realize that it doesn't mean that: rather, just like there's one *yåṯå* of the father, the son, and the spirit, they are one individual essence

[314] Mathews and Amar, *St. Ephrem*, 74n20. Similarly: ≈ "the substance of the sky and the substance of the earth" in the Armenian translation of Ephrem's commentary, with Armenian *hastatut'iwn* corresponding to Syriac *yåṯ-* (Mathews, *Armenian Commentary*, 534n2).

[315] From Jacob of Edessa's *Encheiridion*; see Furlani, "L'Ἐγχειρίδιον," 236:
ܗܘ ܕܝܢ ܗܢܐ ܫܡܐ ܕܝܬܐ. ܠܠܫܢܐ ܡܢ ܗܢܐ ܣܘܪܝܝܐ ܐܘ ܒܝܬ ܢܗܪܝܐ. ܠܐ
ܗܦܝܟ ܐܝܬܘܗܝ، ܒܚܒܝܒܐ ܘܡܠܝܐ. ܠܗܘ ܕܝܢ ܣܘܪܝܝܐ ܘܦܠܣܛܝܢܝܐ. ܠܒ ܡܚܒܝܒܐ
ܐܝܬܘܗܝ، ܘܪܫܝܡܐ. ܝܬܝܪ ܕܝܢ ܠܠܫܢܐ ܗܘ ܥܒܪܝܐ ܘܩܕܡܝܐ. ܕܝܠܗ ܓܝܪ ܐܝܬܘܗ̈ܝ
ܫܡܫܬܗ ܕܗܢܐ ܫܡܐ ܬܐܪܬܐ.

> [*qnomå*]. But *yåṯå* means thing and being. "God will judge the *yåṯå* of the just." "He granted the *yåṯå* of the world in their hearts." "*yåṯå* of wisdom," "*yåṯå* of love," etc. In Hebrew it agrees here.[316]

Finally, for lexicographer Bar Bahlul, the word is used as a specifier or intensifier, "the essence of a thing, the thing itself." In the entry for *yåṯå*, he basically equates it with Arabic *ḏāt*:[317]

> *yåṯå* the essence of a thing, the thing itself; its essence, itself; our *yåṯ* ≈ we ourselves; *yåṯ* self; *yåṯ*-sky ≈ the sky itself; but according to Bar Srošway *yåṯ* means *qnomå* [*hypostasis*] individual essence.

This *yāt/yåṯ-* is an old particle well known from Aramaic and Semitic languages much older than Syriac, from Phoenician and Punic 𐤀𐤕, 𐤀𐤉𐤕 ≈ **ʔiyyāt* (?) to Old Aramaic and even to Hebrew את.[318] It's not especially common in Imperial Aramaic. In so-called "biblical Aramaic," Daniel 3:12 has it: "there are Judeans whom you've appointed."[319] It's not in Hatran Aramaic, but it shows up in Palmyrene (rare) and Nabatean. From an inscription at Palmyra, dated 242, for example: "when

[316] *Commentary on Genesis*; see Vosté and Van den Eynde, *Commentaire d'Išoʿdad*, 13:
ܝܬ ܐܝܟ ܐܢܫܝܢ ܩܢܘܡܐ ܗܘ ܘܣܝܡܘܬܐ ܗܝ، ܠܡ ܦܝܠܣܘܦܝܐ. ܐܠܐ ܢܕܝܘܢ ܗܠܝܢ ܕܝܬ ܠܗ ܩܢܘܡܐ ܗܘ ܘܐܠܐ ܐܝܟ ܕܣܒܪܐ ܗܘ، ܝܬܐ ܕܐܡܪܐ ܘܕܪܘܚܐ: ܐܠܐ ܚܕ ܐܝܠܝܢ ܩܢܘܡܐ. ܐܠܐ ܝܬܐ ܣܘܟܢܐ ܗܘ ܘܐܝܬܘܬܐ. ܘܝܬ ܙܕܝܩܐ ܐܠܗܐ ܢܕܘܢ. ܘܝܬ ܥܠܡܐ ܝܗܒ ܒܠܒܗܘܢ. ܘܝܬ ܚܟܡܬܐ. ܘܝܬ ܪܚܡܬܐ. ܘܕܙܒܢܐ. ܐܦ ܒܥܒܪܐܝܬ ܐܟܢܐ ܫܘܐ.

[317] BB 853:
ܝܬܐ ذات الشيء نفس الشيء. ܝܬܗ ذاته نفسه شخصه. ܘܝܬܢ ܚܢܢ ذاتنا. ܝܬ ذات ܝܬ ܫܡܝܐ ذات السماء ܘܐܝܟ ܒܪ ܣܪܘܫܘܝ ܝܬ ܗܘ ܩܢܘܡܐ شخص ذات ❖

[318] For Phoenician, see Friedrich, Röllig, and Amadasi Guzzo, *Grammatik*, § 255. For Old Aramaic and other early northwest Semitic evidence for this particle, see Garr, *Dialect Geography*, 115–116.

[319] איתי גברין יהודאין די מנית יתהון

he brought the legions here."[320] A Nabatean Aramaic tomb inscription reads: "No one is allowed to sell this tomb, rent it out, or have any kind of document drawn up for the tomb."[321]

This *yāt* is still in use at the time of Syriac in western Aramaic languages as a definite direct object marker, occurring with nominal and with pronominal objects, in all three western Aramaic languages (Samaritan Aramaic, Christian Palestinian, and Jewish Palestinian).[322] In JPA, it's especially common in the Palestinian Targums.[323] An example from Genesis in Targum Neofiti was given at the beginning of this section. Examples abound in Christian Palestinian Aramaic, such as "thanks to the sailors who had brought them,"[324] "he saw me,"[325] and "I saw him going out with a large entourage."[326] And similarly from Samaritan Aramaic: "he opened his mouth and started asking,"[327] and "he bound his son, Isaac, and put him on the altar."[328] The second example has the object-marker two times: once before a noun, and once with a pronominal suffix.

So this is an old particle, known here and there from Old Aramaic on, and especially in JPA, CPA, and Samaritan Aramaic, the card-carrying members of the western Aramaic club. And yet, it's not so simple to say it's just a western lexeme and assume it has no place in "eastern" Aramaic. In its regular use as an accusative marker a form of

320 PAT 0278.4: <wkdy ʔty lkʔ yt lgynyʔ>. As mentioned above, *yāt* is rare in Palmyrene. Does the fact that the object begins with *l-* have anything to do with the option for *yāt* here?

321 CIS 224.9-10:
[illegible]
<wlʔ yhwh ʔnwš ršy dy yzbn kprʔ dnh ʔw yʔgr yth ʔw ytʔlp bkprʔ dnh ktb klh>.

322 Fassberg, *Palestinian Targum*, 252.

323 See DJPA 246b for numerous citations.

324 Müller-Kessler and Sokoloff, *Forty Martyrs*, 39: [illegible]

325 Müller-Kessler and Sokoloff, *Forty Martyrs*, 60: [illegible]

326 Müller-Kessler and Sokoloff, *Forty Martyrs*, 85: [illegible]

327 *Tibat Marqe* 191b (Tal, *Dict.*, 366a): [illegible]

328 Genesis 22:9 (Tal, *Dict.*, 366a): [illegible]

yāt- shows up in certain related strata of Babylonian Aramaic, namely the non-standard tractates of the Talmud, the language of the Geonim, and of the incantation bowls.[329] (This dialect cluster is noticeably distinct from the regular, everyday language of the Bavli.)[330] Here are some examples, the first from a Geonic responsum, the others from non-standard language in the Babylonian Talmud: "we've commanded him to repay him,"[331] "roast it over the fire,"[332] "I asked my teacher,"[333] and "he dressed them in purple garments."[334]

So, to sum up, *yāt* or a similar form is an old direct object marker in Aramaic, in regular use from Old Aramaic and here and there in Imperial Aramaic, continuing in western Aramaic languages, and in a dialect cluster of Babylonian Aramaic. In Syriac, as in Eastern Aramaic languages generally, the particle is not regularly used for direct-object-marking, with *l-* and other prepositions (*b-*, *men*, *ʕal*) having this function. In Syriac the noun *yåṯå*, meaning "self, essence, individuality," develops from this old object marker.

This *yåṯ-* occurs twice in *The Pearlsong*, in both places with a pronominal suffix, but it's used in slightly different ways. Let's take line 102 first. The usage here is straightforward and agrees exactly with this particle's use in earlier Aramaic and in western Aramaic languages.

ܩܒܠ ܝܬܗ

qabbel yåṯ

329 The non-standard tractates are Nedarim, Nazir, Meʿila, Keritot, and Tamid, which were not studied in the Geonic schools and are the latest of the Talmud's tractates.

330 Harviainen characterizes these dialects of Babylonian Aramaic as a rural "cluster of similar idioms," with the standard language of the Talmud being "the more changed (i.e. developed or distorted) urban vernacular (augmented with trends of an academic slang)" (Harviainen, "Diglossia," pp. 17-19). This group of Babylonian dialects is referred to as Standard Literary Babylonian Aramaic by Müller-Kessler ("Earliest Evidence"), who proposes that what became this kind of Babylonian Aramaic arrived from Palestine after the destruction of the Second Temple but before the breakup of Nehardea academy in 259 CE.

331 Harkavy 84.11 (DJBA 545b): ופקידנא יתיה למפרעיה

332 *Sanhedrin* 100b (DJBA 544b): טוי יתיה על נור

333 *Pesaḥim* 37a (DJBA 544b): שאילית ית ר׳

334 *Tamid* 32a (DJBA 544b): אלביש יתהון לבושין דארגוון

he received me

The first singular suffix – unpronounced, but spelled <-y> – is attached to *yåṯ-*, the combination thus indicating the object of the verb *qabbel*.

Line 54 is a bit more complicated: the particle seems to be marking a pronominal direct object, only this time, there's also an *l-*, in effect, doubly marking the object. In this case, it's preferable to read the form here not as the old object marker, but as the noun *yåṯå* discussed above. Alternatively, deleting the *l-* as a superfluous object marker would mean taking the remaining *yåṯ-åh* simply as the old object marker just as in line 102. In either case, the sense seems to be either "to read the letter itself," or simply "to read it."

ܫܪܝܬ ܐܢܐ ܠܝܬܗ ܩܪܝܬ
šarriṯ ʔenå l-yåṯ-åh qrēṯ
I started to read the letter itself

Neither of its two appearances in *The Pearlsong*, which may just be vestiges of a pre- or non-Syriac Aramaic form, are at all difficult to understand from a broader Aramaic perspective, but at the same time, they mark the poem as a little bit strange, when it's taken as Syriac.

6.2 Unusual Instances of Absolute Forms

Nouns in Aramaic languages have three different functional forms called states: absolute, bound (or construct), and determined. Syriac, along with Jewish Babylonian Aramaic, and Mandaic, uses the absolute state in a more limited way than other Aramaic languages: it no longer marks indefiniteness, something now included in the uses of the determined state. The absolute does still do things in Syriac – it's used with numbers, for example – but beyond a few specific uses, it's unusual to see nouns in the absolute state in Syriac. A few occurrences in *The Pearlsong* stand out, especially in the first quarter of the poem.

Two nouns in the absolute state meet us in the very first line, two nouns the narrator uses as a self-identification, both referring to very young children. According to normal Syriac usage and syntax, there's no reason either of these should be in the absolute state, and they're wrong from the point of view of typical Syriac grammar. The poem begins, *kaḏ ʔenå šḇar yalluḏ*, the last two words being the absolute nouns in question. The first, *šaḇrå* in its more usual Syriac form, means "newborn, infant, baby, little child, child," and the second, *yalluḏå*, means "little child."[335] The indefinite sense, it seems, lexically and grammatically is clear, even if the use of the absolute here doesn't fit regular Syriac grammar; it *does* agree with the usage of earlier, and more westerly, Aramaic languages.

Another similar use, and even with one of the same nouns, appears in line 17: *w-ʔenå šḇar-nå l-merdy-åh*. This construction is completely usual in Syriac: a nominal sentence with a first-person pronoun as subject – "I am a [*insert noun*]" – using a shortened form of the pronoun as an enclitic copula (in this case expanded by an infinitive verb at the end). But again, the noun *šaḇrå* is in the absolute state, where the determined state would be more usual in Syriac.

6.3 Frequency of Bound Constructions

The Aramaic languages have more than one way to indicate a close, genitive relationship between two nouns. In Syriac, one way is to use the bound or construct state for one noun, followed by the other noun in the determined state. Another way is to join the two nouns with an intervening *d-* "of," both in the determined state. For example, with the two nouns *malkṯå* "queen" and *kalbē* "dogs" to say "dog-queen" or "queen of the dogs" in Syriac, you can say *malkaṯ kalbē*, or you can say *malkṯå ḏ-ḵalbē*. Either is possible and grammatically normal, but Syriac writers show a decided preference for the second construction.

[335] For the noun pattern of *yalluḏå*, see Brockelmann, *Grundriss*, 363, and Fox, *Semitic Noun Patterns*, 271-273. Brockelmann includes *yalluḏå* among lexemes of this pattern that indicate diminutives.

In general, bound constructions may show up more often in Syriac poetry than prose, but even so, compared to other Syriac texts, *The Pearlsong* shows a high frequency of bound constructions. A random sample gives the ratio of bound phrases to total genitive phrases (i.e. both bound and *d*-phrases) as 31:209, or about fifteen percent.[336]

The Pearlsong includes no less than eighteen of these bound constructions across its 105 lines.

- *malkuṯ bēṯ ʔåḇ* (1) "the kingdom of the house of my father"
- *qarkeḏnay hendu* (7) "chalcedonies of India"
- *tḥumay mayšån* (18) "borders of Mesene"
- *ṯaggåray madnḥå* (18) "traders of the East"
- *ʔaraʕ båḇel* (19) "land of Babylon"
- *rēšay partaw* (38) "leaders of Parthia"
- *rawrḇånay madnḥå* (38) "the magnates of the East"

[336] I took random pages from several Syriac prose and poetic texts from different periods and places, and I counted the bound forms over against both kinds of constructions. (I excluded fixed and still productive constructions with *bar/baṯ-* or *bēṯ-*, the specific phrase *mleḵ malkē* (itself also three times in *The Pearlsong* 41, 86, 104), or prepositions that are grammaticalized nouns, e.g. *l-ḡaw* "into" and *ba-ḏmuṯ* "like.") The texts and pages are as follows: Harris and Mingana, *Odes*, 41, 56-59, 78; Beck, *Hymnen de fide*, 104, 116-117, 131, 140, 253; Gignoux, *Narsaï*, 530, 532, 618, 660, 662, 682; Brock, *Mar Maʿin*, 19, 21, 23, 45, 47, 49; Schulthess, *Kalila und Dimna*, 3, 23-24, 61-62, 115; and Budge, *Laughable Stories*, 75-77, 99-100, 118. And here are the counts:

	bound	*d*-
Odes of Solomon	1	28
Ephrem	3	7
Narsai	20	51
Mar Maʕin	0	41
Kalila wa-Dimna	4	16
Barhebraeus	3	35

Granted, page sizes vary and it's a small sample size, but these thirty-six pages have only thirty-one bound constructions (by far most of them in Narsai), and *d*-phrases are clearly preferable: there are 178 of them.

- *ʔaḥidat madnḥå* (41) "controller of the East"
- *spār ḥliṣē* (47) "the book of heroes"
- *qål rḡešt-åh* (53) "the sound of its movement"
- *šem ʔåb̲* (59) "the name of my father"
- *malkat̲ madnḥå* (60) "queen of the east"
- *qål haddåyut̲-åh* (67) "its guiding voice"
- *niš malkå* (80) "insignia of the king"
- *zawʕay id̲aʕtå* (88) "the impulses of knowledge"
- *qål neʕmåt̲-åh* (90) "the sound of its tones"
- *traʕ šlåmå* (98) "the court of greeting"
- *qurbån margånit̲* (105) "the offering of my pearl"

They are less marked, in general terms of Syriac, but, as a sample, here are several *d*-phrases from *The Pearlsong*:

- *ʕut̲rå d̲-b̲ēt̲ gazz-an* (4) "the wealth of our treasury"
- *šur-ēh d-sarbuḡ* (19) "the walls of Sarbug"
- *mell-ēh d-ʔeggart* (55) "the words of my letter"
- *lmēn-hon d-t̲aggårē* (70) "the haven of traders"
- *kēp̄ē d̲-ʔåd̲åmos* (85) "diamonds"
- *tarʕå d̲-wåspr-aw* (101) "the court of his nobles"

In all *The Pearlsong* has eighteen *d*-phrases, so the ratio of bound to total genitive phrases is 18:36, or fifty percent, compared to the fifteen percent for the sample selection of other Syriac texts.

Whatever else can be said of the style of the Syriac *Pearlsong*, its composer inordinately favored bound phrases, thus making this one of the text's most striking formal characteristics.

6.4 Vocabulary, Loanwords in Particular

Among the notable Syriac lexemes in the poem is the verb √šgr, which occurs four times in the poem (lines 16, 37, 45, 104).[337] This is not a common verb, and to appear so many times across just 105 lines is a remarkable feature. The meaning of the verb root here is not in question, whether in the lone occurrence of the D form (line 16), "leave," or the three other occurrences (tG) "go to, come to, be present at." It's cognate with the CPA verb √šgr D "send."[338]

A larger category of distinctive vocabulary is that of loanwords. Loanwords are terms that are "loaned" or "borrowed" (but usually not returned) from one language to another.[339] They're a regular lexical feature, no matter the language, and language users may or may not recognize them as foreign in any way. Of the loanwords that show up in the Syriac text, some are usual suspects in Syriac and in Aramaic languages more generally; these do not characterize *The Pearlsong* in any special way. On the other hand, Syriac readers almost never encounter some of the loanwords here.

Common loanwords in Aramaic languages generally may have origins in Akkadian, in Iranian languages (earlier from Old Persian [OP], later from Parthian [Pa] or Middle Persian [MP]), and Greek. Among these more regular, apparently naturalized, loanwords are

Syriac	gloss	analog
ʔeggartå	letter	Akk *egirtu*[340]
ziwå	splendor, radiance	Akk *zīmu*[341]
måṯå	country, homeland	Akk *mātu*[342]
šawtep̄	make s.o. a partner	Akk *šutappu*[343]

337 Nöldeke, Rev. Wright, 678.

338 The homonymous verb root in Syriac, which has meanings related to heating and warming, is clearly something different.

339 Haspelmath, "Lexical Borrowing."

340 AIOA 48.

341 AIOA 113.

342 AIOA 71.

343 AIOA 105.

taggårå	merchant, trader	Akk *tamkaru*[344]
gawnå	color	OP *gauna-*, MP *gōn*[345]
daywå	demon	MP *dēw*[346]
nišå	mark, sign	Pa/MP *nīšān*[347]
kromå	color	Grk χρώμα
lmēnå	port, harbor	Grk λιμήν
teḡmå	rank, class, kind	Grk τάγμα

Again, generally speaking, these terms from Akkadian, Iranian languages, and Greek are not especially unusual in Syriac (and other Aramaic languages).

A few terms in the text for minerals and gems are also recognizable from Greek, whether they are direct loanwords or more widely ranging, and difficult to trace, "culture words."

Syriac	gloss	Greek analog
ʔåḏåmos	adamant, diamond	ἀδάμας
bērullå	beryl	βήρυλλος
sappilå	sapphire	σάπφειρος
sardukkå	sardonyx	σαρδόνυξ (σαρδόνυχ-)
qarkednå	chalcedony, agate	χαλκηδών

These same Greek-derived terms for gems and stones in Syriac are also, of course, Greek loanwords in English.

It is the more unusual loanwords in Syriac that characterize *The Pearlsong* in a unique way. As highlighted above, Iranian languages are among those Aramaic speakers and writers took and adapted a long list of vocabulary from. Beyond more widespread Iranian vocabulary in Syriac, *The Pearlsong* includes a few lexemes – titles and roles known

344 AIOA 107.

345 ILS 137.

346 ILS 151.

347 Cf. Boyce, *Wordlist*, 65; DMMPP 254b.

from Parthian, in particular – that are considerably rarer. These are discussed in more detail in the commentary, but here's a list:

- *ʔašpåzå* "lodge, inn, house" (lines 21, 23)
- *gēzaḇrå* "treasurer" (lines 74, 79)
- *wåsprå* "noble, prince" (line 101)
- *pṣågriḇå* "successor (to the throne)" (line 48)
- *parwåqå* "guide, messenger" (line 16)

The following loanwords, also not very common in Syriac, are from Greek and Latin:

- *basilikon* "royal" (line 66)
- *ṭrop̄ē* "food, meal, sustenance" (line 35)
- *ṭoḡa* "toga" (lines 10, etc.)

Finally, Syriac *ʔåp̄arsnå* "plot, plan" (line 39) may be a loanword, possibly of Iranian origin, but it's uncertain. And *drusē*, occurring at the end of the poem (line 103), has been considered as a Greek loanword (ὕδραυλις "hydraulic organ"), and as a candidate for emendation, but it seems just to be the plural of *drustå* "joy, delight, splendor."

7 Appendix III: Excerpts from the *Acts of Thomas*

7.1 The Beginning of the *Acts of Thomas*, with the Wedding-song

Translation based on the Syriac text in AMS 3 3-11, with the page numbers marked in the margins.

When all the apostles had been in Jerusalem a while – Simon Peter, Andrew, Jacob and John, Philip and Bartholomew, Thomas and Matthew the tax-collector, Jacob, son of Alphaeus, and Simon the Canaanite, and Judas, son of Jacob – they divided the countries among
them so that each one could preach in the region that fell to them, [4]
and in the country the Lord sent them to. In the allotment and division, India fell to the apostle Judas Thomas, but he didn't want to go, remarking, "I can't do this task, since I'm the most insignificant of all the apostles, and I'm a Hebrew: how can I teach the Indians?"

While Judas was thinking about this, the Lord appeared to him in a night-vision, and said to him, "Don't be afraid, Thomas, because my grace is with you," but he wasn't at all persuaded, responding, "Lord, send me wherever you want, I'm just not going to India." While Thomas was thinking about this, an Indian trader came from the south, whose name was Habban, who had been sent by king Gondophar to bring him back a skilled carpenter. Our Lord saw him walking around in the market and said to him, "Do you want to buy a carpenter?" Habban replied, "Yes." The Lord said, "I've got a carpenter I'll sell you," and he showed Thomas to him from a distance, and agreed with him on a price of twenty[348] pieces of silver. He drew up a document, as follows:

[5] I, Jesus, son of Joseph, a carpenter from the village of Bethlehem in Judea, affirm that I have sold Judas Thomas, my slave, to Habban, the trader of king Gondophar.

When he'd finished the document, Jesus led Thomas over and presented him to Habban the trader. Habban saw him and said, "Is this your master?" Judas Thomas said, "Yes, he's my master." Habban the trader said to him, "Well, he's sold you to me," and Judas was silent.

In the morning he got up and prayed and asked the Lord and said, "Look, Lord, however you want it, may your will happen!" He went to be with Habban the trader, having taken with him nothing except his payment, since the Lord had given it to him. So Judas went and found Habban the trader loading his merchandise onto a boat, and he started to board with him. When they'd boarded and sat down, Habban the trader said to Judas, "What skill are you able to do?" Judas answered him, "Carpentry and finish carpentry." Habban the trader said, "What do you know how to make with wood or with cut stone?" Judas told him, "With wood I've learned to make plows, yokes, oxgoads, rudders
[6] for pontoons, and masts for boats. With stones, tomb-monuments and shrines, and temples and palaces for kings." Habban the trader said to him, "I'm also looking for skills like this." They started traveling, since the wind had picked up, and they continued traveling smoothly until they reached the port of Sandruk.

When they'd disembarked to land, as they were entering and walking the city, they heard the sound of bagpipes, organs, and lots of singing. Judas was asking and saying, "What are these good times happening here in the city?" They said to him, "The gods have brought you, too, to have fun in the city! The king's got just one daughter, and he's

[348] The Berlin manuscript has "thirty."

having her marry someone: this sound of good times is from the party. Heralds have also been assigned by the king to announce that everyone should come to the party – poor and rich, slave and free, foreigner and citizen – and that whoever doesn't come to the party will be liable to the king for the insult." Habban the trader said to Thomas, "We should go, too, so as not to be noncompliant, especially since we're foreigners."

Once they'd gotten a room at an inn and rested a bit, they went and [7]
sat down to eat at the party: Thomas sat down right in the middle, and everyone was staring at him, like they were looking at a stranger who'd come there from some other place, while Habban the trader, his master, was sitting in another spot. When people had eaten and drunk some, Judas still hadn't sampled anything at all, and the people beside him were saying, "Why'd you come here, if you're not able to eat or drink anything?" Thomas answered them, "I've come here for something better than eating and drinking, also to please the king, and so I might fulfill his wish. And because the heralds are saying that whoever hears and doesn't come will be capitally punished."

When they had eaten and had drunk, oil and snacks were brought in and taken up: some people anointed their faces, some their beards, some other places, but Thomas was praising God and marking a seal in the middle of his head. He oiled his nostrils, put some on his ears, and signed his heart. A myrtle-crown was put on his head, and he held reed-leaves in his hand. Then a singer, a woman there at the dinner, was going around them all, and when she got to Thomas, she was
standing there and singing over him. This singer was Hebrew by race, [8]
and when she had stood there over him a long time, Thomas hadn't lifted his face up, but was staring at the ground. One of the servers came and lifted his hand and hit him on the cheek. Thomas looked at him and said, "May my God forgive this thoughtlessness of yours in the world to come, but in the present world may he demonstrate his marvels using this hand that hit me, and may I see a dog come to this dinner-party dragging it along."

Thomas started singing this song:

1 The church, daughter of light, has the king's splendor.

2 People are happy and eager to look at her, with her lovely appearance, decorated with every good work.

3 Her clothes are like blossoms with a sweet, fragrant odor.

4 The king lives at her head and sustains his residents below.

5 Truth is fixed at her head, happiness wiggles at her foot.[349]

6 Her mouth is open and well-suited for reciting praises with it.

7 The Son's twelve apostles and the seventy-two sing thunderously in her.

8 Her tongue is the front of the door which the priest lifts and then enters.

9 Her neck is the various stairways the first architect built.

[9] 10 Both her hands herald the place of life and her ten fingers open heaven's gate.

11 Her wedding-room is lit up and full of her saving scent.

12 Her incense-tray inside is ready, spreading the perfume of love, hope, and faith to everyone.

13 Trustworthiness is embedded in her, her doors decorated with truth.

14 All the men of her wedding party that she invited surround her,

15 And the holy wedding-party women are speaking praise in front of her.

16 Life serves before her and waits for the groom to arrive.

17 Let them shine with his glory and be with him in the kingdom which never passes away.

18 May they share in that glory all the just are gathered for.

19 May they share in that enjoyment that each of them enters.

349 From Bedjan's note, reading *ḥaḏwå ḇ-reḡl-åh råp̄tå*.

20 May they wear luminous clothes and wrap themselves up in their lord's glory.

21 Let them praise the living father whose luxuriant light they've received.

22 They shone with their splendor of their lord, whose ever-endless provision they have received from.

23 They have drunk from the living water that fills its drinkers with desire and thirst.

24 They praised the father, lord of all, and the single son who's from him, and they praised the spirit of his wisdom.

While Thomas was singing, everyone beside him was staring at him,
seeing that his color had changed, but they weren't really listening to
what he was saying, since he was speaking Hebrew, which they didn't [10]
know. The singer, though, was listening to everything, since she was
Hebrew, and staring at him. Even when she'd moved from where he
was and she was singing to other people, she kept staring at him. She
liked him, since he was a man from her own country, but also better
looking than anyone else there. When she finished her song, she sat
down across from him, and didn't take her eyes off him. He didn't lift
up his eyes and stare at her, but kept staring at the ground until getting
up and leaving the dinner.

The server from before had gone down to the spring to get some water, and a lion jumped out there and ripped and cut him to pieces. Then some dogs were carrying off the pieces of his body, with a black dog carrying off the server's right hand, which he'd raised against Judas, and the dog brought it right into the middle of the dinner-party. Everybody was shocked, when they saw it. As everyone was asking which of them had wandered off, it was discovered that it was the hand of the server who had hit Judas. Then the singer smashed her flutes, and went and sat down at the apostle's feet, and she was saying, "This guy's either god or god's apostle, because I heard him say something in Hebrew to the server, and right then it happened to him, because he said to him, 'May I see the hand that hit me being dragged by a dog,' and look here! You've seen how a dog dragged it in." Some of them believed the singer, but some didn't.

7.2 Thomas's Encounter with a Giant Snake

Translation based on the Syriac text in AMS 3 30–35.

While Thomas was asleep at night, the Lord came and stood over him and said, "Thomas, get up and go out in the morning, following the service, and go on the eastern road about two miles, and I will demonstrate my glory in you, since, because of the event you're going out for, lots of people may come to my refuge and live, and you can put the enemy's power and nature in its place." When he woke up, he said to the brothers there with him, "Sons, the Lord wants to do something today, but let's pray and ask him that nothing impede us from him. But as he always wants to demonstrate his glory in us, let's do his will now, too." After he'd said this, he lay his hand on them, celebrated the eucharist and gave it to all of them and said, "May this eucharist be clemency and mercy for you, and not judgment and punishment." And
[31] they said, "Amen."

The apostle left to go where our Lord had shown him, and after he'd gone two miles, he turned off the road a little bit and saw a corpse lying there, the corpse of a good-looking boy. He said, "Lord, did you bring me out here for this temptation? May it be as you wish." Then he started praying: "Our Lord, lord of the dead and the living – the living who are standing here, and the dead lying here – Lord, lord of the souls that are in bodies and father of all the souls that leave bodies, come, my Lord, right now, for the dust that your holy hands have formed! Look down from the sky, because I'm calling to you, and show your glory in this one lying here." He said further, "This couldn't have happened without the instigation of the enemy, who does such things. But that enemy doesn't dare do them with someone foreign to him, unless they've submitted to his will."

After he'd said this, a black snake came out of a hole, with its head and tail slamming and slapping the ground, and it loudly said to the
apostle, "I'm gonna say before you why I killed this boy. There's a good- [32]
looking woman in this village in front of you. As she was passing by me, I saw her and fell in love with her. I went after her, and I saw this boy kissing her, and he actually even slept with her and did other nasty stuff with her! It would be easy for me, but I don't dare tell them to you, since I know you're an apostle of Christ, the annihilator of our nature. So as not to disturb her, I didn't kill him right then, but I kept an eye on him, and in the morning, when he passed by me, I struck him and killed him. (Especially since he'd dared to do this on a Sunday!)"

Thomas said to him, "Tell me: what seed do you come from?" The snake answered, "I'm a reptile, descendant of a reptile. I'm a harmer, descendant of a harmer. I'm the son of the one authority over creation was given to and he gave it trouble. I'm the son of the one who makes himself like god to those who submit to him, so they might do his will, and he takes what's his from what they've borrowed from him. I'm the son of the one with authority over every created thing under the sky. I'm the son of the one outside the ocean with his mouth open. I'm a son of the family of the one who talked with Eve, with whom he
made Adam break God's command. I'm the one who incited Cain to [33]
kill his brother. Because of me – since this is why I was created – the ground has been cursed and thorns have sprouted in it. I'm the one who dared to throw down the just from their height, and I wounded them with lust for women, and I caused the birth of children with gigantic bodies and I accomplished my will through them. I'm the one who made Pharaoh noncompliant, so he would slaughter the Israelites and subjugate them with hard labor. I'm the one who made the people wander lost in the wilderness, having subjugated them into making themselves a calf. I'm the one who incited Caiaphas and Herod with lying slander against the equitable judge. I'm the one who made Judas take the bribe, once he'd subjugated himself to me, to hand Christ over to death. I'm the one who was given authority in this world, but Mary's son led me away by force, and led his own away from me. I'm a son of

the family of the one who came from the east, since he'd been given authority."

Since Judas Thomas had asked the Lord that a spoken response be given to him, and that the snake be made to speak contrary to snake's nature, once the snake had said all this and had finished speaking, the
[34] crowd of people was attentive to everything, and fear and faith rested on everyone there. When they had seen and heard these miracles, they shouted together in a single voice, "This man who has shown us about his god, his god is one! With his word he commanded this scary animal, and it showed its nature." They were asking Thomas to kill the snake with his word, like he'd commanded it to talk like a person with his word. Then Thomas signaled them with his hand, raised his voice, and said, "You're brazen, even though your nature's laid bare and you've been killed and your destruction has come – not that you should say what's been done by you with those subjugated to you! – and you're not afraid that your end has come. But in the name of our Lord Jesus, who will contend with your nature for his slaves until the end, I tell you to suck in the venom you injected into the boy, because my God sent me to kill you, and raise him alive in front of this crowd of people, so they'll believe that he is the true God, and no other."

The snake said to him, "Contrary to what you've said, our end hasn't come yet. Why are you pressing me to take something I gave this boy?
[35] My father, too, when he sucks in and takes something he's thrown into creation, his end happens." The apostle said to him, "So demonstrate your father's nature." The snake came and put his mouth on the boy's wound and was sucking the venom out of him. Little by little, as the venom was extracted, the boy's color, which had turned purple, became white, and the snake swelled up. Once all the venom had been extracted from him, he jumped up and ran to the apostle's feet, and fell down before him in reverence. The snake then burst open at the saint's word, and a giant chasm appeared where the snake's venom had fallen. Thomas ordered the king and his brother to fill the place up, lay foundations, and construct lodging rooms for foreigners.

7.3 Part Ten of the *Acts of Thomas*

Translation based on the Syriac text in AMS 3 101–110, 115–119. This is the context surrounding The Pearlsong. *The excerpt below reaches up to* The Pearlsong *itself, which is followed immediately by a long* tešboḥtå, *a praise-song, after which point the hagiographic narrative continues.*

Kariš spent the whole night sighing and wringing his hands to-
gether, wanting to go that night to tell King Mezdi about the violence
he'd been dealt. He thought to himself, "If I go to King Mezdi in my
current distress, who's going to let me in? Because I know that, even
had fate not knocked me down and thrown me from my pomps and
pride and prominence to a lowly littleness, and separated Mygdonia,
my darling, from me, there's no one to let me in to the king at this [102]
hour. (If he were standing at my door, I wouldn't go out and answer.)
So I'll wait until dawn, and I'm sure that whatever I tell King Mezdi,
he'll bend his will my way. I can tell him about the foreigner's magic,
how he uses violence and throws the heights down to the deep. It's not
that I'm sad that I'm separated from my partner, Mygdonia: rather,
I'm upset for her honor, since her prominent standing has lessened,
her free status has collapsed, and her elevated soul has been lowered.
And a woman never seen with shabby clothes on by anyone in her
household is running naked from her bedroom outside. I don't know
where she's gone. Maybe she went out to the market-street under the
influence of the foreigner's magic. But I don't know where she's gone,
since not a thing has been seen of her."

When he'd said all this, he started crying and talking again: "I'm
done for, thanks to you, my true partner, whom I'm now deprived of!
I'm done for, thanks to you, my darling, my love, who has meant more
to me than my whole family, and I have neither a son nor a daughter
from you to take any relief in. You didn't finish a whole year with
me, and I've been robbed of seeing you. If only the violence of death [103]
had lead her away from me, and I could count myself among kings,

leaders, and magnates, and not some stranger, maybe a slave who'd run away from his owners and come here – thanks to my bad fortune! I'll brook no rest nor restraint, until I destroy him, punish him, and have vengeance on him. How about I not appear before King Mezdi tonight, but if he won't bend his will my way by punishing the foreigner, I can also tell him about General Ṣipor, who was the reason for her ruin? There he is, sitting in his house, with lots of people going in and out to be with him, and he doles out a new teaching about being holy, teaching and saying that people won't live unless they've parted ways with what is theirs and they have become a loner and a wandering beggar like he is. He's just trying to get some companions."

As he was thinking about all this, dawn came, and he first got dressed and put shoes on: what he wore was repulsive, and his face was nasty and especially gloomy, and he went in to greet King Mezdi. When the king saw him, he said, "Why have you come here to me with this broken look? Why is your appearance so gloomy and your face so messed up?"

[104] Kariš said to him, "King Mezdi, I've got some new action to tell you about, and some new havoc brought by Ṣipor to India. There's this Hebrew sorcerer staying at his house, and he never leaves his side, and lots of people go in to see him. He's teaching them a new god and instituting new laws we've never heard of before. He says, 'You can't belong to the eternal life I teach unless you've separated from each other, husbands from wives, and wives from husbands.' And it happened that my evil, weak wife went to see him, listened to his talk, believed it, and got up in the night and ran away from me – she who couldn't last a single hour without me, and couldn't exist apart from me! But now send word and bring Ṣipor and the foreigner ensconced there by him in his house, and punish them! If you don't, all our country's people are gonna die due to his talk."

Once King Mezdi had heard all this from Kariš, his relative, he told him, "Don't worry, and don't be sad: I'm going to send word and bring him, and I'll punish him, and you'll enjoy possession of your wife again, for if I avenge foreigners, isn't it even more the right thing to do for you?" Then the king went out to the law-court and ordered
[105] General Ṣipor to be summoned. So they went to his house and found

him sitting to the right of the Apostle Thomas, with Mygdonia sitting down at his feet, together with a big crowd, all listening to him. The people who'd come after General Ṣipor spoke up and said, "You sit there listening to useless talk, with King Mezdi angry and wanting to kill you, because of this sorcerer and seducer whom you've welcomed into your home?!"

When General Ṣipor heard this, he was worried – not because the king was threatening him, but because the king had become aware of the Apostle Thomas. So Ṣipor said to Thomas, "I'm worried about you: I told you a day ago that that woman's the wife of Kariš, a relative of King Mezdi, and he's not gonna let her do what she's promised, and whatever he says to the king, the king will bend his will that way."

Thomas said to Ṣipor, "Don't be afraid, but trust in Jesus, who will speak in defense of me and of you, and of anyone who's taken refuge in him and come to his meeting-place." When General Ṣipor had heard this, he got dressed and went to King Mezdi.

Thomas was asking Mygdonia, "What's the reason your husband's [106]
angry and thinking this way?" She said, "Because I didn't give up myself to destruction with him: in the evening he wanted to enslave me and throw me down under the one he serves, but the one I've entrusted myself to gave me an escape from his hands, and I ran away from him naked and went to sleep beside my nanny. But I don't know what happened to him to make him plot an ambush against you."

The apostle said to her, "This stuff's not gonna hurt us, daughter. Trust in Jesus, and he'll keep Kariš's aggression away from you and save you from destruction and shameless behavior. He will become a guide for you on a scary trip, and a leader toward his and his father's kingdom. He'll bring you into eternal life, and give you the kingdom that doesn't pass away or change."

As for Ṣipor, when he was standing before King Mezdi, the king was asking him, "What's his story? Where's he from, and what's he teaching, that sorcerer you've ensconced in your house?" Ṣipor answered, "Maybe you are unaware, my lord, what heavy suffering I and all my friends were experiencing because of my wife, whose worthiness, as you know, many people have been captivated by, and my daughter, whom I
consider comparable with nothing I possess, and the fate and trial that [107]

has met them, and how they've become a joke and a curse throughout the country."

"Well," Ṣipor continued, "I heard about this man, and I went to see him. I asked him for help, led him away, and we came here. I saw some unusual miracles as I was traveling with him on the road. Here, too, a lot of people have seen and heard what the ass said and what the demon communicated about him. He healed both my wife and daughter, and, yes, they're still healthy! He didn't want any payment but belief, and he also wanted holiness, so they all might become participants in what he's doing. He says: 'Fear the one god, lord of everything, and Jesus Christ, his son, and you can live forever.'"

"He doesn't ingest anything at all except bread and salt from evening to evening, and he just drinks water. He prays a lot, and whatever he asks of God, God gives it to him. He prescribes that his God is holy, good, sweet, gentle, and life-giving, which is why those who trust in him approach him in purity, holiness, and love."

When King Mezdi heard Ṣipor, he sent several of his attendants
[108] to General Ṣipor's house to fetch the Apostle Thomas and whoever was there with him. When they went in, they found him sitting and teaching a big group of people, with Mygdonia sitting there at his feet, too. When they saw the big group of people around him, they were scared, and they left to tell King Mezdi, "We don't dare tell him a thing, because of the big crowd there with him. Also, Mygdonia's sitting at his feet and listening to what he says."

Mezdi and Kariš heard this, and Kariš jumped up from King Mezdi's presence and took the lead of a group of attendants, and said, "I'm gonna go bring him myself, and Mygdonia, too, whose mind he's taken control of." He quickly went to General Ṣipor's house, and he found Thomas sitting and teaching there. Once he'd gone in, he[350] saw Judas, but he didn't find Mygdonia there, since she had gone to her house, because she was aware that people were telling her husband that she was there. Kariš said to Judas, "Get up, you evil, destructive foe, unless

[350]The Berlin MS has: *He saw that Mygdonia had gone out, and didn't say anything to her, and he went in and said to the apostle, 'Evil, … '"*

– what can your magic do to me? Because I'm gonna send your spells right back on your head!"

Once he'd said this, Thomas looked at him and said, "You can have
your threats back, since you can't hurt me at all, because the lord Jesus [109]
Christ, whom I take refuge in, is better than you, than your king, and
than all your forces." Then Kariš took a hood from one of his house-
staff and put it on Judas's neck and said, "Drag him away! I'm gonna
see whether Jesus saves him from my grasp!" And they kept dragging
him on and on all the way to King Mezdi.

Judas stood before King Mezdi, and the king said, "Tell me your story. And whose power are you working these feats with?" But Thomas was quiet, and didn't respond at all. Mezdi ordered his attendants, and they beat Thomas with 120 spikes.[351] He ordered them to bring him bound to the prison, which they did, and once he was in prison, King Mezdi and Kariš were thinking about how they could kill him, since all the people were worshiping him like a god. They thought about claiming that he'd cursed the king and practiced magic.

As for Thomas, once he'd gone to the prison, he was happy and
ecstatic, saying, "Thank you, Lord Jesus Christ, since you've made me
worthy, not only to trust in you, but also to suffer a lot for you!" He [110]
continued, "I thank you, Lord, for making me worthy of all this. I
thank you that your attentive care has been on me. You have made me
worthy to suffer many evils for you. I thank you, Lord, that for you
I have become a sorcerer, a bum, poor, and a beggar. So let me take
something from the good things the poor have, from the relief of the
weary, and from the good things of those who people may hate, chase
off, despise, and say nasty things about! Here I am, hated and singled
out among many because of you: they say who-knows-what about me
because of you!"

While he was praying, all the prisoners were watching him do so and asking him to pray for them, too, and when he had prayed and sat down, he began to recite this poem.[352]

351 Reading <kwbyn> for <kwkyn>. The Berlin MS has "eight whips," using an uncommon Greek loanword for "whip," *ʔesqṭå* (< Greek *skutos*).

352 The BL MS has *maḏråšå*, often translated "hymn," here, followed by *The Pearlsong*. The Berlin MS lacks *The Pearlsong*, and instead of *maḏråšå*, has *tešboḥtå*, "praise-song." This

In the BL MS, The Pearlsong *appears here across two folios, while otherwise (represented by the Berlin* MS*), there is no* Pearlsong, *and the narrative jumps immediately into the following conventional Christian praise-song. This praise-song, missing in Greek, occurs in both Syriac manuscripts, but it's much shorter in the Berlin copy. The praise-song's language, even though the Holy Spirit is almost absent from it, is more conventionally and explicitly Christian than* The Pearlsong*'s language.*

[115] Now, Thomas the Apostle's Praise-song[353]

1 You are given glory, Father, lord of all, essence that's unspeakable, hidden from every æon in the splendor of his glory.

2 You are given praise, Son, firstborn of the living, who's from the lofty Father and is the Word of Life.

3 You are given glory, one-of-a-kind Father, who skillfully depicts himself in every created thing and in every æon.

4 You are given praise, Son of light, wisdom, power, and knowledge, who exists in every æon.

[116] 5 You are given glory, lofty Father, who has dawned, from covert to overt, at the hand of all his prophets.

6 You[354] are given praise, Son of mercy, in whom everything is completed, in wisdom and silence.

7 You are given glory, splendid Father, whose firstborn was born in the silence and stillness of thought.

8 You are given praise, worshiped Son, who has dawned in his appearance from the Father in stillness and praise.

is followed in both manuscripts – in the Berlin MS in this spot, and in the BL MS after *The Pearlsong* – by a praise-song, but it's much longer in the latter.

[353]This rubric is only in the BL MS, since in the Berlin MS's absence of *The Pearlsong*, the narrative's mention of a "praise-song" (*tešboḥtâ*) there (instead of the *madrâšâ* of the BL copy) flows smoothly and immediately right into the praise-song.

[354]This is where the praise-song ends in the Berlin MS.

9 You are given glory, good Father, who revealed the secret of his firstborn to his prophets by the holy spirit.

10 You are given praise, chosen Son, who revealed the Father's glory to his apostles among all nations.

11 You are given glory, sincere Father, forever making his greatness holy by his firstborn, the life-giver for his creation.

12 You are given praise, beautiful Son, who shone forth in the Father's splendor and saved our souls with his innocent blood.

13 You are given glory, omnipotent Father, who dwells in his splendid light, hidden in his glory, but openly visible to all in his grace.

14 You are given praise, perfect Son, sown in the living ground, yet you exist before the æons in your holy Father.

15 You are given glory, all-nourishing Father, who exists in every æon on high and down below, and there's nowhere empty of you.

16 You are given praise, Son, the worshiped fruit, who has dawned on everyone in mercy, put on our humanity, and killed our enemy.

17 You are given glory, unlimited Father, who made his angels a spirit, and his servants his burning fire.

18 You are given praise, Son of light, who rides on the wind, wrapped up in the Father's light, on holy clouds.

19 You are given glory, all-enlivening Father, who gathered the
æons for his glory with his precious one's hand, so they would send [117]
praise up to him.

20 You are given praise, Son of life, with whose gifts the Father satisfies the saints, and they travel out from him and arrive via the road of peace.

21 You are given glory, all-enlivening Father, who, by the spirit, revealed the Son's secrets to the saints in stillness and gentleness.

22 You are given praise, Son, fruit of the Father, hiding his elect under his wings, who completed his Father's will and saved his precious ones.

23 You are given glory, good Father, keeping all creation alive with his precious one's hand: by mercy, by grace, and by his murder on the cross.

24 You are given praise, firstborn Son, nourishing the æons with his body and wiping away our sins with the sign of his wounds and the sprinkling of his blood on us.

25 You are given glory, good Father, who resides in a clean heart, in the knowledge of his worshipers: concealed from all in his appearance, but openly visible to us in his Christ.

26 You are given praise, Son, the Logos who announces his coming in stillness: he put on our humanity and saved us with his living, innocent blood.

27 You are given glory, living Father, who brought life to our mortality as we were wandering from your road – we were dead and lost! – and your mercy came upon us.

28 You are given praise, dear Son, who brought life to our mortality, and redirected our wandering: you became our life-medicine with your life-giving body and the sprinkling of your living blood.

29 You are given glory, Father, loftier than any mouth or tongue, who thought of us with your Christ: we tasted you through your fruit and became people of your peace.

30 You are given praise, peace-making Son, you who healed our wounds, persuaded our obstinacy, gathered in our going astray, and
[118] made us walk in your truth, and we recognized your Father in you.

31 You are given glory, omnipotent Father, who sent us your living and life-giving fruit, and made peace between your mercy and your creatures with the blood of his crucifixion.

32 You are given praise, Son, Logos of light, you who shone forth from on high, satisfied us with your knowledge, cleaned our filth, and brought life to our mortality with your standard, the cross of light.

33 You are given glory, Father of all praises, with your name exalted in every æon, you who haven't held our faults against us, but made us alive in your Christ of life, of your will.

34 You are given praise, Son, the voice born of knowledge, our holy priest, you who spared us with your pure and holy offering and poured out your living blood for sins.

35 You are given glory, lofty Father, hidden from all the æons, and yet openly visible, as you wish, to all your worshipers.

36 You are given praise, Son of life, accomplisher of the Father's will, you who made peace among your creatures, so that they might worship your sender in you and become participants in your secrets.

37 You are given glory, Father, loftier than every knee that may bend to you through your precious one, both in the sky and on the earth.

38 You are given praise, worshiped Son of perfect mercy, through whom peace and hope came to creatures, that they might know the creator.

39 You are given glory, all-enlivening Father, the wealth of whose mercies doesn't wane in the flow of your gifts: you always need to give to us.

40 You are given praise, Son, fruit, you who are the door of light and the road of truth, and you have made us walk in your footsteps, so that we can reach your lofty Father's mansion.

41 You are given glory, sweet Father, you who gave us peace through
our life-giver and revealed your glorious and holy secrets through hear- [119]
ing his teaching.

42 You are given praise, only Son of the Father, you whose mercy has come upon us, you who have sealed us with your living and life-giving cross.

43 Every mouth and every tongue, æons and created things both hidden and out in the open, they glorify the Father, worship the Son, and praise the holy spirit.

44 Your angels give you praise on high through your Christ, because peace and hope have come to Sheol, upon the dead, who've come to life and been resurrected.

45 We ask you, our Lord and life-giver: [accomplisher][355] of everything that you have said and promised, complete[356] your grace with us, and bring us into your peaceful country, because you're our life-giver, you're our Paraclete, you're our life-medicine, you're our victorious standard!

---

[355]Assuming a now missing word such as *gåmorå*. The sentence seems incomplete otherwise.

[356]This ("complete") is where the Berlin MS picks up.

46 How fortunate we are to have known you, how fortunate are we to have trusted in you, how fortunate we are because of your wounds and your blood for us, how fortunate we are that you're our great hope, how fortunate we are that you're our God, and forever and ever, amen!

8 Appendix IV: Some Texts on Pearls

8.1 Manichaean Coptic Texts

8.1.1 From the *Kephalaia*

ⲉϣⲁⲣⲉ ⲙ̅ⲙⲁⲣⲅⲁⲣⲓⲧⲏⲥ ϣⲟ̣[. . . . .][357] ϩⲛ̅ ⲙⲁ ⲛⲓⲙ ϩⲛ ⲑⲁ- 202.10-13
ⲗⲁⲥⲥⲁ ⲟⲩⲧⲉ ⲉⲩⲡⲗ̣ⲁ̣ⲥ̣ⲥ̣ⲉ̣ [ⲙⲙⲁⲩ ϩⲛ ⲑⲁ]ⲗⲁⲥⲥⲁ ⲧⲏⲣⲥ ⲁⲗⲗⲁ
ϩⲙ ⲙⲁ ⲙⲁ ⲛⲉⲧϣⲟⲟ̣ⲡ̣ ϩ̣ⲛ̣ ϯⲑⲁ[ⲗⲁⲥⲥ]ⲁ ⲉⲩⲡⲗⲁⲥⲥⲉ ⲛ̅ϩⲏⲧⲥ
ⲛⲙ̅ⲙⲁⲣⲅⲁⲣⲓⲏⲥ

Pearls exist [… not?] everywhere in the sea, nor are they formed in the entire sea, but in each place where they exist in the sea, that's where pearls are made.

ⲥⲡⲱϣⲉ ⲛⲥⲥⲱⲣ ⲁⲃⲁⲗ ⲁϩⲛ̅ⲧⲗϯⲗⲉ [ⲉ]ⲛⲁϣⲱⲩ ⲛⲥϫⲓ ⲟⲩⲁïϣ 203.1-16
ⲇⲉ ⲁⲩⲧⲗϯⲗⲉ ⲙ̅ⲙⲁⲩ ⲉⲥϩⲁⲗϭ [. . .]ⲛ̣ⲥⲉⲓ ⲁϩⲣⲏï ϩⲛ̅ ⲧϩⲁⲗⲁⲥ-
ⲥⲁ ⲛ̅ⲧⲉ ⲡⲙⲟⲩⲛϩⲱⲩ ⲉⲧⲣ[. . . ⲙ]ⲛ̅ ⲡⲙⲟⲩⲛ̅ϩⲱⲗϭ ⲛ̅ⲥ̣ⲉ̣ⲱⲙⲥ
ⲁϩⲟⲩⲛ ⲁⲧⲃ̣ⲏⲧⲉ ⲉⲧⲉ[ϣⲁ]ⲥⲟ ⲛ̅ϩⲃⲏⲧⲉ ⲛ̅ϣⲁⲣⲡ̅ ϣⲁⲩⲙⲟⲩ-
ϫⲧ ⲙ̅ⲛ ⲛⲉⲩⲉⲣⲏⲩ ⲙ̅[ⲡⲓ]ⲛⲉⲩ ⲛ̅ⲥⲉⲡⲗⲁⲥⲥⲉ ⲙ̅ⲙⲁⲩ ⲛ̅ⲥⲉⲣ̅ⲟⲩ-
ⲛⲁϭ ⲙ̅ⲙⲁⲣⲅⲁⲣⲓ̣[ⲧⲏⲥ] ⲟⲩⲛⲁϭ ⲛ̅ⲉⲓⲇⲟⲥ ⲉϥⲧⲁïⲁïⲧ ⲉϣⲱⲡⲉ
ⲇⲉ ϩⲱⲱϥ ⲛ̅ⲧⲉ ⲟⲩⲧⲗϯⲗⲉ ⲙ̅ⲙⲟⲩⲛ̅ϩⲱⲟⲩ ⲉⲓ ⲁⲡⲓⲧⲛⲉ ⲛ̅ⲧⲉ
ϯⲧⲗϯⲗⲉ ⲉⲧⲙ̅ⲙⲉⲩ ⲡⲱϣⲉ ⲁϩⲛⲧⲗϯⲗⲉ ⲉⲛⲁϣⲱⲩ ⲁϩⲛϫⲗⲁϣ
ϫⲗⲁϣ ϣⲁⲩⲡⲗⲁⲥⲥⲉ ⲙ̅ⲙⲁⲩ ⲛ̅ⲥⲉⲧⲁϣⲟⲩ ⲁϩⲙ̅ⲙⲁⲣⲅⲁⲣⲓⲧⲏⲥ

357 Poss. ϣⲟⲟⲡ ⲉⲛ

[ⲉ]ⲛⲁϣⲱⲩ ϩⲛ̄ ⲧⲃⲏⲧⲉ ⲙⲛ ⲡϫⲉⲕ ⲟⲩⲛ̄ ⲟⲩⲁⲛ ⲉϥⲁ̣[ⲡⲗⲁⲥ]ⲥ̣ⲉ̣ ⲙ̄ⲙⲁⲣⲅⲁⲣⲓⲧⲏⲥ ⲥⲛ̄ⲧⲉ ⲟⲩⲁⲛ ⲉϥⲁⲡⲗⲁⲥⲥⲉ ⲛ̄ϣⲁⲙⲧⲉ ⲟⲩⲁⲛ ⲉϥⲁⲡⲗ̣ⲁⲥⲥⲉ ⲛ̄ϯⲉ ⲟⲩⲁⲛ ⲉϥⲁⲙⲟⲩⲛⲕ ϩⲟⲩⲟ̣ ⲁ̣ⲛⲉⲓ ⲟⲩ[ⲁⲛ ⲉϥⲁ]ϭⲱϫⲃⲉ ⲁⲛⲉϊ ⲡⲥⲁⲡ ⲙⲉⲛ ⲉⲕⲁ̣[ϭⲛ ⲟⲩ]ⲧⲗϯⲗⲉ ⲉⲥⲟⲩⲁϫ ⲛⲧⲉ ⲧ{ϩ}<ⲃ>ⲏⲧⲉ ϫⲓⲧⲥ ϣⲁⲥⲣ̄ⲟⲩⲛⲁϭ ⲙ[ⲙⲁⲣ]ⲅⲁⲣⲓⲧⲏⲥ ⲉⲥⲧⲁïⲁïⲧ ⲉⲣⲉ ⲧⲉⲥⲉⲥⲟⲩ ϫⲏⲕ

It divides and spreads out into several other drops and it takes time to become a sweet drop of water [...] and it goes down into the sea, and the rainwater, which [...], together with the sweet-water, they sink down into a shell – which originally comes from foam – and they're mixed together at this time and as a result a large pearl is formed, one of the big, valuable kind. If a drop of rainwater comes down and that drop divides into several other drops, into various droplets here and there, they form together there and are arranged into as many pearls in the shell or carapace, some forming two pearls, some forming three, some forming five, some fashioning more than these, some less. When you find a drop intact and the shell[358] takes it, it makes a big, valuable, priceless pearl.

203.24-204.4 ⲉⲓⲥⲧⲉ ⲁ̣[ⲛⲁⲕ] [ⲁⲓ]ⲧⲥⲉⲃⲉⲧⲏⲛⲉ ⲁⲧϩⲉ ⲉⲧⲉϣⲁⲩⲡⲗⲁⲥⲥⲉ ⲛⲙ̄-ⲙⲁⲣⲅⲁⲣⲓ[ⲧⲏⲥ] ⲛ̄ⲑⲁⲗⲁⲥⲥⲁ ⲁⲓ̈ϫⲟⲟⲥ ⲁⲣⲱⲧⲛ̄ ϫⲉ ⲉϣⲁⲣⲉ ⲟ̣ⲩ-ⲙⲁⲣ[ⲅⲁ]ⲣⲓⲧⲏⲥ ϣⲱⲡⲉ ϩⲓⲧⲛ̄ ⲡⲙⲟⲩⲛϩⲱⲟⲩ ⲉⲧⲉϣⲁϥϫⲓ [ⲟⲩ]ⲁ̣ⲓϣ ⲁⲧϩⲃⲏⲧⲉ ⲉϣⲁⲣⲉ ⲡϫⲉⲕ ϣⲱⲡⲉ ϩⲓⲧⲛ̄ ⲧϩⲃⲏⲧⲉ ⲛⲧⲉ ⲧϩⲃⲏⲧⲉ ϩⲱⲱϥ ϣⲱⲡⲉ ϩⲓⲧⲛ ⲡϫⲱⲃⲉ ⲙⲛ ⲡ . . . . ⲛ̣ⲑⲁⲗⲁⲥ-ⲥⲁ ⲧⲟⲧⲉ ϯⲛⲟⲩ ⲙ̄ⲡⲕⲁⲓⲣⲟⲥ ⲉⲧⲥⲟⲩ [. . . . . .] ⲉⲣⲉ ⲛϫⲁⲗ-ⲕ̣ⲙ̣ⲥⲉ ⲥⲁⲩⲛⲉ ⲁⲣⲁϥ ϣⲁⲩⲡ[. . .] ⲛ̄ⲥⲉ [. . . . .]ⲡⲓⲧⲛ̄ ⲁⲛⲓ-ⲙⲁ ⲉⲧⲙⲙⲉⲩ [ⲛⲥ]ⲉⲛ̄ ⲙⲁⲣⲅ̣ⲁ̣ⲣⲓⲧⲏⲥ ⲁϩⲣⲏⲓ ⲁⲃⲁⲗ ⲙ̄ⲡϣⲓⲭϩϥ̄

[358] A mistake possibly due to the similarity between ⲃⲏⲧⲉ "shell" and ϩⲃⲏⲧⲉ "foam," both of which occur immediately above. Acc. to Crum (384b), the gender of ϩⲃⲏⲧⲉ is M, but it's F at least sometimes, as in 203.28 below. "Shell" ⲃⲏⲧⲉ is also F, so the article above would fit either word.

ⲛⲑⲁⲗⲁⲥⲥⲁ ⲛⲧⲉ [ⲡ]ϫ̣ⲁⲗⲕⲙ̅ⲥⲉ ⲡϫⲁⲗⲕⲙ̅ⲥⲉ ϭⲓⲛⲉ ⲕⲁⲧⲁ ⲧⲉ-
ϥⲧⲩⲭⲏ ⲕⲁⲧⲁ ⲡⲉⲧ[ⲧⲏ]ϣ ⲛⲉϥ ϣⲁⲣⲉ ⲛ̅ϫⲁⲗⲕⲙⲥⲉ [ⲧ]ⲉ̣ⲉⲩ
ⲛ̅ⲛⲉϣⲁⲧⲉ ⲛ̅ⲧⲉ ⲛⲉ[ϣⲁ]ⲧⲉ ϩⲱⲩ ⲧⲉⲉⲩ ⲛ̅ⲛⲣ̅ⲣⲁⲓ̈ ⲙⲛ̅ ⲙⲙⲉⲅⲓ-
ⲥⲧⲁⲛⲟⲥ

Ok, so I've taught you all the way pearls are formed in the sea. I told you that a pearl comes into existence through rainwater which takes time to become foam, the shell coming into existence through the foam, and the foam itself coming into existence through the transfer and the [...] of the sea. Then, right at the time [...], with the divers recognizing it, they [...] and they [...] down there and bring a pearl up out of the depth of the sea, and each diver finds something according to their luck and what's ordained for them. The divers give them to merchants, and the merchants in turn give them to kings and chiefs.

8.1.2 From the Manichaean *Homilies*

ⲁⲥϩⲱⲧⲃⲉ ⲛ̅ⲙ̅ⲡⲣⲁⲅⲙⲁⲧⲉⲩⲧⲏⲥ ⲙⲛ̅ ⲙ̅ⲉⲙ[ⲡ]ⲟⲣⲟⲥ· ⲛⲉⲧⲣ̅ⲓ̈ⲉⲡ- 12.14-17
ϣⲱⲧ ϩⲛ̅ⲛⲭⲣⲏⲙⲁ ⲙ̅ⲡⲣ̅ⲣⲟ: ⲁ̣ⲥ̣ϣ̣ⲱϭⲧ ⲁⲛ ⲛ̅ⲛ̣ϫⲁⲗⲕⲙ̅ⲥⲉ· ⲛ̅ⲉ-
ⲧⲉⲓⲛⲉ ⲁϩⲣⲏⲓ̈ ⲛ̅ⲛⲙ̣[ⲁⲣ]ⲅ̣ⲁⲣⲓⲧⲏⲥ:
It [Error] killed the merchants and traders who deal in the king's assets. It strangled the divers who bring up pearls.

8.2 From Ephrem's Hymns on the Pearl

These hymns are part of the larger collection, *Hymns on the Faith*.[359]

[359] See Beck, *Hymnen de Fide*, 248-262.

8.2.1 Hymn no. 81

1.1-2

ܒܚܕ ܡܢ ܝܘ̈ܡܝܢ   ܡܪܓܢܝܬܐ
ܢܣܒܬ ܐܚ̈ܝ   ܚܙܝܬ ܒܗ ܐܪ̈ܙܐ

One day, I took a pearl, brothers, and I saw mysteries in it.

2.1-5

ܣܡܬܗ̇ ܐܚ̈ܝ   ܥܠ ܦܣܬ ܐܝܕܝ
ܕܐܬܒܩܐ ܒܗ̇   ܐܙܠܬ ܕܐܚܙܝܗ̇
ܡܢ ܚܕ ܓܒܐ   ܗܘܬ ܠܗ̇ ܐܦ̈ܐ
ܡܢ ܟܠ ܓܒ̈ܝܢ

I put it in my palm, brothers, so I could inspect it.
I went to see it from one side:
It had a face on every side

6.1-5

ܚܙܝܬ ܒܗ̇ ܩ̈ܠܠܐ   ܕܠܐ ܡ̈ܠܠܐ
ܕܒܪ̄ܬ ܢܘܗܪܐ ܗ̄ܝ   ܠܘܦܩܐ ܬ̈ܠܝܠܐ
ܕܠܐ ܠܫ̈ܢܐ   ܠܒܢܐ ܕܐܪ̈ܙܐ
ܕܠܐ ܣܦܘ̈ܬܐ   ܟܢܪ ܫܬܩܐ
ܕܕܠܐ ܩܠܐ   ܝܗܒ ܩ̈ܠܝܬܐ

I saw inner recesses in it, without shadows, since it's something luminous:
Discursive "types" without tongues,
The language of mysteries without lips.
A quiet, soundless lute produced melodies

ܚܙܝܬ ܒܡܥܡ̈ܕܐ   ܕܢܚܬܘ ܒܬܪܝ 11.1-5
ܟܕ ܡܬܒܠܗܝܢ   ܕܡܢ ܠܓܘ ܝܡܐ
ܠܝܒܫܐ ܢܦܩܘܢ   ܠܦܘܪܐ ܘܒܘܪܐ
ܠܐ ܡܣܝܒܪܘ ܗܘܘ   ܡܢܘ ܢܣܒܪ
ܢܒܨܐ ܒܥܘܡܩܗ̇   ܕܐܠܗܘܬܐ

I have seen the divers who came down after me terrified they wouldn't come back from inside the sea to dry ground.
They couldn't stand it a little while – who can expect to investigate the depths of divinity?

8.2.2 Hymn no. 82

ܐܘ ܒܪܬ ܝ̈ܡܐ   ܕܐܫܡܘܬ ܝܡܐ 9.1-5
ܕܝܠܕܐ ܒܗ   ܠܝܒܫܐ ܫܠܡܬ
ܕܪܚܡܐ ܒܗ   ܘܪܚܡܘ ܢܩܦܘܗ̇
ܘܐܨܛܒܬܘ ܒܗ̇   ܐܝܟ ܗ̇ܘ ܡܠܟܐ
ܕܪܚܡܘ ܒܝ̈ܡܐ   ܘܐܬܟܠܠܘ ܒܗ

Water-child, who left the sea, where it was born, and went up to dry land, where it was loved!
They loved it and snatched it and adorned themselves with it, like the child the gentiles loved and crowned themselves with.

10.2-4 ܫܠܚܘ ܒܡ̈ܘܕܐ
ܘܠܒܫܘ ܡܫܚܐ ܒܐܪ̈ܙ ܡܫܝܚܐ
ܓܢܒܘܟܝ ܘܣܠܩܘ

Divers stripped and just wore oil.
As a mystery of Christ they stole you and went up.

8.2.3 Hymn no. 84

3.1-5 ܘܐܦ ܒܡܘܕ̈ܐ ܠܒܨܝܢܘܬܗ̇
ܠܐ ܚܙܐ ܠܗ̇ ܒܗ̇ ܗܘ ܚܕܝܢ
ܟܠ ܬܓܪ̈ܐ ܟܕ ܠܐ ܚܙܝܢ
ܕܐܡܬܝ ܐܝܬܘܗ̇ ܠܐ ܡܥܩܒ ܒܗ̇
ܐܦ ܠܐ ܡܠܟܐ ܕܡܬܟܠܠ ܒܗ

Even divers won't scrutinize their pearl.
Every merchant likes a pearl, yet without scrutinizing when it's there.
Not even a king who's crowned with it will dare to scrutinize it.

ܡܐܢܐ ܡܠܝܐ ܕܡܠܐ ܢܘܗܪܐ 8.1-5
ܡܪܓܢܝܬܐ ܗܝ ܘܠܝܬ ܐܘܡܢܐ
ܕܢܓܢܘܒ ܡܢܗ ܕܫܘܪܗ ܫܘܦܪܗ
ܐܦ ܢܛܘܪܗ ܠܐ ܚܣܝܪܐ
ܐܝܟܐ ܕܐܝܬܝܗ ܫܠܡܬ ܟܠܗ

A pearl's a full object,
Since it's full of light,
And there's no artisan who can steal from it,
Since its beauty's its bulwark and protector.
It lacks nothing: wherever it is, all of it's complete

8.2.4 Hymn no. 85

ܐܝܬܝ ܗܝ ܕܪܒܐ ܒܙܥܘܪܘܬܗ 4.1-5
ܡܪܓܢܝܬܐ ܒܨܝܪܐ ܡܫܘܚܬܟܝ
ܘܙܥܘܪ ܟܝܠܟܝ ܥܡ ܡܬܩܠܟܝ
ܪܒ ܕܝܢ ܫܘܒܚܟܝ ܠܬܓܐ ܗܘ ܒܠܚܘܕ.
ܠܝܬ ܕܫ̈ܘܝܐ ܘܒܗ ܗܘ ܣܝܡܬܝ

You're something big in its smallness, pearl:
Your size is diminutive, your measurements and your weight small, but your acclaim's big acclaim.
A crown is singularly priceless, and you've been placed in one.

6.1–5

ܐܢܫܐ ܫ̈ܠܝܚܐ ܥܡܕܘ ܘܐܣܩܘܟܝ
ܡܪܓܢܝܬܐ ܠܐ ܗ̄ܘܐ ܡ̈ܠܟܐ
ܝܗܒܘܟܝ ܠܘܩܕܡ ܠܒ̈ܢܝ ܐܢܫܐ
ܐܠܐ ܥܪ̈ܛܠܝܐ ܐܪܙܐ ܡܩ̈ܕܡܐ
ܘܕܡܣ̈ܟܢܐ ܘܕܓ̈ܠܝܠܝܐ

People who'd stripped dove in and pulled you out, pearl. It wasn't kings who first offered you to humanity, but naked people: a mystery pointing to the poor, Galilean fishermen.

7.1–5

ܠܐ ܡܨܝܢ ܗ̄ܘܘ ܠܟܝ ܓܘܫ̈ܡܐ ܠܒ̈ܝܫܐ
ܕܢܐܬܘܢ ܥܐܕܝܢ ܐܬܘ ܕܫ̈ܠܝܚܝܢ
ܐܝܟ ܝܠܘ̈ܕܐ ܛܡܪܘ ܦܓܪ̈ܝܗܘܢ
ܢܚܬܘ ܥܐܕܝܢ ܘܩܒܠܬܝ ܠܗܘܢ
ܘܛܫܝܬܝ ܒܗܘܢ ܕܣܓܝܐ ܪ̇ܚܡܘܟܝ

Bodies with clothes can't come to you, but bodies stripped naked have come to you like babies:

They buried their bodies deep and came down to you,
And you welcomed them and found refuge with them,
since they loved you so much.

ܣܒܪܬܐ ܢܗܒܘ   ܠܟܝ ܠܫ̈ܢܝܗܘܢ 8.1-5
ܩܕܡ ܟ̈ܝܣܝܗܘܢ   ܦܬܚܘ ܡܣ̈ܟܢܐ
ܘܐܦܩܘ ܚܘܝܘ   ܒܬܘܪܐ ܚܕ̈ܬܐ
ܒܝܬ ܠܓܪ̈ܐ   ܒܘܪ̈ܝܗܘܢ
ܕܐܢܫܐ ܣܦܩܘܟܝ   ܐܝܟ ܣܡ ܚ̈ܝܐ

Their tongues shared your message before their pockets,
Poor people opened their things and brought out and showed a new kind of wealth among traders.
They furnished you to people by the fistful, like a life-giving drug.

ܘܕܗܐ ܦܗܝܬ ܒܟܝ   ܡܪ̈ܓܢܝܬܐ 11.1-5
ܐܟܢܫ ܡܕ̈ܥܝ   ܘܕܚܙܝܬ ܒܟܝ
ܐܬܕܡܐ ܒܟܝ   ܕܟܢܝܫܬܝ ܗ̄ܘ
ܒܟܠܟܝ ܠܐܕܝܟܝ   ܘܕܟܠ ܙܒܢ̈
ܚܕܐ ܐܝܬܝܟܝ   ܚܕ ܐܗܘܐ ܒܟܝ

Since I'm pretty lost in you, pearl, let me collect my thoughts.
Since I've looked at you, let me be like you, because you're completely collected with yourself.
And since at every moment you're a single thing, let me be single in you.

8.3 From the Palestinian Talmud

From Bikkurim 65d.

שמעון בר ווא הוה בדמסקוס ואיתמנון דקיקין
מיניה והוא לא איתמני. שמעון בר ווא הוה בקי
במרגליתא בכל מילה ולא הוה ליה עיגול מיכליה

When Simeon b. Aba was in Damascus, people less than him were appointed and he wasn't. Simeon b. Aba was a pearl-expert in every way, but he didn't have a loaf of bread to eat.

8.4 From a Syriac Fragment on Herakles

These two parallel texts were published together in Brooks, Guidi, and Chabot, Chronica Minora, *363.*[360]

The BL text:

ܘܗܢܐ ܗܪܩܠܝܣ. ܗܘ ܚܘܝ ܗܘܐ ܨ̈ܒܥܐ ܕܟܠܗܘܢ
ܓܘ̈ܢܐ ܫܦܝ̈ܪܐ. ܘܐܝܟܢܐ ܣ̈ܠܩܢ ܬܘܒ ܡ̈ܪܓܢܝܬܐ ܡܢ
ܝܡܐ. ܗܘ ܚܘܝ ܘܐܠܦ ܠܒ̈ܢܝܢܫܐ.

Herakles showed how to dye every lovely color, and he taught people how pearls come up from the sea.

[360]The British Library (BL) text had been previously published in Lagarde, *Analecta Syriaca*, 202.

The "Nöldeke" text:

ܘܗܘܐ ܗܢܐ ܗܪܩܠܝܣ ܚܟܝܡܐ ܚܘܝ ܠܟܠܗܘܢ ܒܢ̈ܫܐ
ܕܨܒ̈ܥܐ ܫܦܝܪ̈ܐ. ܕܦܘܪܦܘܪܘܢ ܘܕܙܘܣܪܝܬܐ
ܘܕܐܪܓܘܢܐ ܘܕܟܘܠܬܘܢ ܘܕܦܪܣܝܘܢ. ܘܟܠ ܓܢ̈ܣܐ
ܘܕܙ̈ܢܘܬܐ ܕܐܝܬ ܒܐܪܥܐ. ܘܗܘܐ ܥܒܕ ܘܝܕܥ ܐܦ
ܠܟܐܦܐ ܘܡܪ̈ܓܢܝܬܐ. ܕܐܝܟ ܐܝܟܢ ܣܠܩܝܢ ܡܢ ܝܡܐ
ܕܦܘܢܛܘܣ. ܘܗܘܐ ܐܠܦ ܠܒ̈ܢܝܢܫܐ. ܡܛܠ ܕܓܒܪܐ ܗܘܐ
ܚܟܝܡܐ.

Herakles the wise showed people all lovely dyed colors: purple, scarlet, reddish purple, blue, green, and all kinds and types on earth. And he also made and recognized gems, and he taught people how pearls come up from the Black Sea, because he was a wise man.

8.5 From *The Book of Natures*

Syriac text in Ahrens, Naturgegenstände, *64–65. Paragraph numbers added.*

ܥܠ ܡܪ̈ܓܢܝܬܐ. I ܡܪ̈ܓܢܝܬܐ ܡܬܝܠ ܕܐܝܟܢܐ ܡܬܝܠ̈ܕܢ.
ܡܬܐܡܪ ܕܝܢ ܕܬܐܘܡܣܛܐ ܪܒܐ ܐܘܣܛܘܣ ܒܟܬ̈ܒܐ ܕܟ̈ܝܢܐ ܠܡܪܐ
ܪܘܚܐ ܠܡܠܘܗܝ. ܘܡܢܐ ܕܐܝܬܐ ܒܡܠܠܐ ܚܕ ܠܥܒ̈ܐ ܗܠܝܢ ܕܢܦܩܝܢ
ܡܢܗ ܘܡܬܩܠܩܠܝܢ ܒܝܡ̈ܡܐ. ܥܦܠ ܡܢܗ ܐܝܟ ܕܙܘܦܬܐ
ܕܡܬܦܠܓܐ ܒܠܘܦܐ ܘܢܦܠܐ ܒܡܝ̈ܐ ܕܝܡ̈ܡܐ ܘܒܕܡܘܬ ܕܒܪܐ
ܕܙܪܥ ܒܢܡܘܣܐ. ܡܚܝܠܐ ܡܬܥܒܕܐ ܡܢܗ ܐܒܢܐ ܕܙܪܥܐ.
ܘܡܬܩܠܩܠܝܢ ܒܗ

2 ܢܘ̈ܦܠܬܐ ܕܝܢ ܗܠܝܢ ܕܪ̈ܘܩ ܡܢܗ. ܕܐܝܟ ܬܬܡܬܠ ܚܕܐ ܚܕܐ
ܒܠܗܘܢ ܒܐܝܕܐ ܕܐܢܫ. ܗܟܢܐ ܕܝܢ ܙܒܢܐ ܒܐܝܕܗ. ܐܝܟ
ܡܬܦܫܛܬܐ ܕܡܐܡܪܐ ܕܡܦܪܫ. ܗܟܢܐ ܗܫܬܝܢ ܘܕܒ̈ܝܢ: ܘܟܕ ܢܦܠ
ܒܛܝܢܐ ܕܡܛܪ̈ܬܐ ܠܐ ܡܬܬܠܝܠ ܒܚܒܠܗܘܢ. ܐܠܐ ܢܫ̈ܬܠ ܒܚܒܠܗܘܢ.
ܚܕ ܒܠܚܘܕܝܢ. ܐܝܟ ܥܠܝܬܐ ܕܫܘܩ ܡܢ ܨܒ̈ܘܬܐ ܥܪ̈ܝܪܬܐ ܘܡܬܬܪܝܡ
ܒܡܐܢܐ ܕܦܫܪܐ.

3 ܘܡܚܡܣ ܠܗ̇ ܕܝܢ ܠܗܕܐ ܐܣܛܐܪܘܣ ܗ̇ܘ ܕܐܡ̈ܓܪܢ ܒܠܗܘܢ، ܡܢ
ܟܠ. ܘܚܠܒ ܠܗ̇. ܘܕܡܐ ܗ̇ܘ ܗܢܐ ܐܣܛܐܪܘܣ ܠܫܠܘܚܐ ܒܠܠܝܐ
ܘܣܝܦܐ ܐܝܬ ܠܗ ܐܝܟ ܙܠܝܩܬܐ. ܘܗܟܢܐ ܕܒܠܥܗ̇ ܠܗ̇، ܠܦܩܬܐ.
ܦܬܚ ܒܪܡ ܨܦܪܐ ܦܘܡܗ ܠܘܩܒܠ ܫܡܫܐ ܘܚܠܒ ܡܢ ܙܠܝܩ̈ܐ
ܕܫܡܫܐ. ܘܟܠ ܨܦܪܐ ܗܟܢܐ ܚܒܪ. ܒܪܡܐ ܕܡܬܬܥܝܩܐ ܒܗ̇
ܡܢ ܒܝܫܬܐ. ܘܡܥܪܢܐ ܠܗ̇ ܕܬܬܒܥܐ ܐܝܟ ܕܒܡܪܒܥܐ. ܘܗܘܝܢ
ܡܢܐ ܕܡܬܚܝܣܢܐ ܢܫܬ ܠܐܫܬܗ ܕܡܢܐ ܘܡܢܐܬܐ ܒܡܪܐ ܐܝܟ
ܐܠܗܐ ܘܡܬܬܠܝܢ ܬܡܢ ܒܪ ܡܪ̈ܬܐ ܘܡܬܒܥܐ ܠܗ̇. ܒܡܫܪܘܬܐ
ܒܪܡܐ ܕܦܫܩ ܠܗ̇ ܠܡܪܓܢܝܬܐ.

4 ܚܙܘܬܐ ܕܦܐܪܐ ܐܝܬ ܠܗ̇ ܒܡܢܐ ܕܒܗ̇ ܡܬܪܒܝܐ. ܘܗܘܝܢ ܦܠܓܐ
ܐܦ ܡܪܓܢܝܬܐ. ܘܗܟܢܐ ܕܐܬܡܠܝܬ ܬܪܒܝܬܗ ܡܬܓܠܝܐ ܡܢ
ܚܙܘܬܗ ܐܝܟ ܦܐܪܐ ܕܓܒܠ ܘܡܛܐ ܠܡܠܦܐ. ܘܡܬܐܡܪ ܕܐܝܟ
ܚܬܡܐ ܒܗ ܠܐ ܡܬܡܠܝܐ. ܫܦܝܐ ܒܗ ܡܬܚܙܝܐ. ܐܝܟ ܦܐܪܐ
ܒܐܝܠܢܐ.

5 ܒܥܘܕܪܐ ܕܝܢ ܟܕ ܡܬܚܣܝܢ ܠܗ. ܒܡܚܘܫܐ ܦܫܩܝܢ ܠܗ ܠܫܠܘܚܐ
ܡܢ ܒܣܪܗ. ܘܢܦܩܝܢ ܠܗ ܒܬܪܥܝܗܘܢ. ܘܗܟܢܐ ܕܐܣܩܘܗ̇ ܠܟܠ.
ܚ̈ܝܝܢ ܘܡܬܚܣܝܢ ܠܗ̇ ܠܡܪܓܢܝܬܐ. ܘܚܕܐ ܠܚܕܐ ܡܬܚܣܝܢ
ܡܪܓܢܝܬܐ ܡܫܬܠܡܬܐ. ܗܝܡܢܘܬܐ ܬܡܢ ܒܪ ܡܬܚܫܠ ܡܢ ܢܚܫܐ.
ܘܐܝܬ ܬܘܒ ܕܠܐ ܒܕܚܠ ܒܡܪܢܝ ܬܪܒܝܬܗ̇. ܘܐܝܬ ܕܗܘܩܡ ܒܗܘܢ
ܩܠܦܬܐ ܡܢ ܒܣܪܗ ܕܫܠܘܚܐ ܐܝܟ ܨܐܬܐ ܘܡܚܫܠܐ ܠܗ
ܠܒܗܝܢ.

6 ܗܢܐ ܕܝܢ ܐܣܛܐܪܘܣ ܟܕ ܒܡܕܒܪܬܐ ܚܙܘܬܐ ܘܡܪܓܢܝܬܐ
ܩܢܐ. ܡܢܐ ܕܝܢ ܕܓܠܚ ܡܪܓܢܝܬܐ ܢܨܝܚܘܬܐ ܒܠܚܘܕ ܕܐܝܠܢܐ
ܫܘܐ ܒܗ ܘܡܬܠܗܕܐ ܒܡܚܘܫܐ ܦܫܩܝܢ ܠܗ ܒܥܘܕܪܐ ܐܝܟ
ܕܠܒܫܪܐ ܕܠܐ ܪ̈ܓܝܬܐ܀

On pearls 1 How do pearls come about? It's said that at certain times the wind strikes the waters of the great deep of the ocean, and when the ocean moves in waves through the arms[361] that go out from it and mix with smaller seas, from the wind it takes a kind of rainstorm which divides into drops and falls into the waters of the seas, and something like semen is ejaculated from it, like a male inseminating a female, and the sea-waters mix with it.

2 The drops sprinkled from this are so transparent and pure, if each drop were taken in someone's hand, they would seem like a drop of melted silver, and although the drops fall into the seas, they don't mix in with them, but they go down as the waters gather together, like some solid flakes of something[362] tossed into a clay jar.

3 The oyster (*ʔesṭåros*), which we mentioned before, finds this drop and swallows it. (This "oyster" is like a round murex that has shells, like a *zlap̄ṯå* in Syriac.)[363] Once it has swallowed that drop, it opens its mouth in the morning toward the sun and swallows the sun-rays, something it does every morning until the pearl inside it is polished and it begins turning into a body, like in a womb. Then when it firms up, the oyster goes down to the ocean floor and plants a root like a tree and it stays fixed there while it carefully helps the pearl grow and get its body, until it cuts the pearl loose.

4 While it's growing, a pearl has life like a fruit does, then it also has perception, and when it's completely grown, it's removed from this life-source, like a fruit that has ripened and is ready to be picked. It's said that if the pearl ages inside the oyster without being removed, it will wither and decompose, like fruit on a tree.

---

361 The Syriac word is "tongues."

362 The phrase is obscure; this is an attempt at making sense of it.

363 That is, the Greek>Syriac word *ʔesṭåros* and the Syriac word *zlap̄ṯå* refer to the same creature.

5 When divers find one, they use a pruning knife and cut the "murex" from its root and put it in their bags, and when they've brought them to the surface, they look for and find a pearl. Once in a while they find a whole pearl, but a lot of pearls are blemished. Sometimes it hasn't completely grown to maturity, and sometimes there are scaly pieces from the oyster-meat, like waste that discolors them.

6 While oysters at first have a life-source and sensation, once they're pregnant with a pearl, they are only ensouled like trees, and this is why divers cut them with a pruning knife, like a root with no feeling.

8.6 From Abū Zayd al-Sīrāfī, *Accounts of China and India*

Arabic text (and another English translation) in Mackintosh-Smith and Montgomery, Two Arabic Travel Books, *128-131.*

2.17.1 [٢]فاللؤلؤ يبتدئ في مثل قدر الأنجذانة وعلى لونها وفي هيئتها وصغرها وخفّتها ورقّتها وضعفها فيطير على وجه الماء طيرانا ضعيفا ويسقط على جوانب مراكب الغاصّة [٣]ثم يشتدّ على الايام ويعظم ويستحجر فإذا ثقل لزم قعر البحر ويغذو بما الله أعلم به [٤]وليس فيه إلّا لحمة حمراء كمثل اللسان في أصله ليس لها عظم ولا عصب ولا فيها عِرق [٥]وقد اختلفوا في بدء اللؤلؤ فقال قوم إنّ الصدف إذا وقع المطر ظهر على وجه البحر وفتح فاه حتى يقطر فيه من المطر فيصير حَبّا [٦]وقال اخرون إنّه يتولّد من الصدفة نفسها وهو أصحّ الخبرين لأنّه

ربّما وُجِد في الصدفة وهو نابت لم ينقلعْ فيُقلَع وهو الذي تسمّيه تجّار البحر اللؤلؤ القِلع والله أعلم

[2]Pearls start out about the size of an asafetida leaf, of a similar color and shape, and just as small, light, thin, and fragile. They float lightly on the surface of the water and come into contact with boats divers use. [3]Then they get stronger, bigger, and harder, and once they've gotten heavy, they stick to the sea-floor. God knows what they feed on! [4]There's nothing in them but a tongue-like red muscle at the root, with no bones or tendons, and no veins on the inside. [5]People have disagreed about how pearls start out, but some people say that, when it rains, oysters come to the surface of the sea and open their mouths, until some rain drips in, and then that becomes a pearl-grain. [6]Other people say pearls are produced from an oyster itself, and this report is better, since pearls have sometimes been found still growing and still attached, and they have to be detached. (These are the ones sea-merchants call "pearls-to-detach.") But God knows!

[١]ومن عجايب ما سمعنا من أبواب الرزق أنّ أعربيّا ورد البصرة 2.17.2
في قديم الايّام ومعه حَبّة لؤلؤ تساوي جملة مال [٢]فصار بها إلى عطّار كان يألفه فأظهرها له وسأله عنها وهو لا يعرف مقدارها فأخبرها أنّها لؤلؤة [٣]فقال ما قيمتها قال ماية درهم فاستكثر الأعربيّ ذاك وقال هل أحد يبتاع منّي بما قلتَ فدفع العطّار ماية درهم فابتاع بها ميرة لأهله [٤]وأخذ العطّار الحبّة فقصد بها مدينة السلام فباعه بجملة من المال واتّسع العطّار

في تجارته ٥فذكر العطّار أنّه سأل الأعربيّ عن سبب اللؤلؤة فقال مررتُ بالصمّان - وهي من أرض البحرين بينها وبين الساحل مديدة قريبة - ورأيتُ في الرمل ثعلبا ميّتا على فيه شيء قد أطبق عليه فنزلتُ ووجدتُ شيئا كمثل الطبق يلمع جوفه بياضا ووجدتُ هذه المدحرجة فيه فأخذْتها ٦فعلم أنّ السبب في ذلك خروج الصدفة إلى الساحل تستنشق الريح وذاك من عادة الصدف فمرّ الثعلب فلمّا عاين اللحمة في جوفها وهي فاتحة فاها وثب بسرعته فأدخل فاه في الصدفة وقبض على اللحمة فأطبقَتْ الصدفة على فيه ٧ومن شأنها إذا أطبقتْ على شيْء وأحسّتْ بيد تلمسها لم يفتحْ فاها بحيلة حتّى تُشقّ من آخرها بالحديد ضنّا منها باللؤلؤة وصيانة لها كصيانة المرأة لولدها ٨فلمّا أخذتْ بنفس الثعلب أمعن في العدو يضرب بها الأرض يمينا وشمالا إلى أنْ أخذتْ بنفسه فماتتْ ٩وظفر بها الأعربيّ فأخذ ما فيها وساقه الله إلى العطّار فصارتْ له رزقا

[1]Here's one of the marvels emerging from God's bounty that we've heard about. A long time ago a nomad of the Arab desert traveled to Basra and he had a single pearl with him worth a lot of money. [2]He took it to a perfumer that he knew and showed it to him and asked him about it, since he didn't know what it was worth, and the perfumer told him it was a pearl. [3]So he said, "What's it worth?" "100 dirhams," he said. The nomad thought this exorbitant and said, "Will anyone buy it from me for the amount you said?" So the perfumer gave him 100 dirhams, which the nomad used to buy some supplies for his rela-

tives. [4]The perfumer took the pearl and headed for Baghdad and sold it for a hefty sum, and his business expanded. [5]He mentioned that he'd asked the nomad where the pearl came from, and he said: "I was passing by al-Ṣammān" – in Bahrain, a little distance from the seashore – "and I saw a dead fox on the sand with something clamped down onto its mouth. So I went down and found a dish-like thing, with the inside shining white, and I found this roly-round thing inside it and took it." [6]Then the perfumer realized the reason: an oyster had come out to the shore to take in some air, something they regularly do, and the fox came by and, when it eyed the meat inside it when the oyster's mouth was open, the fox quickly jumped and stuck its mouth inside the oyster and grabbed onto the meat, but the oyster clamped down onto the fox's mouth. [7]It's in an oyster's nature that, when it's clamped onto something and it feels a hand touching it, it won't release its mouth for anything, until one side is split off with an iron tool, saving the pearl from it: it safeguards the pearl like a mother does her baby. [8]When the oyster started suffocating it, the fox went running wild, banging the ground with it right and left, until the oyster had completely suffocated the fox, and it died, and then the oyster died. [9]So the nomad got the oyster and took what was in it, and God brought him to the perfumer, and so the pearl became the nomad's bounty.

8.7 From Bar Bahlul's Syriac Dictionary

See BB 1151-1152 for the text.

ܡܪ̈ܓܢܝܬܐ ܒܢ̈ܝ اللولو الجوهر ܒ̈ܢ المرجان. ܡܪ̈ܓܢܝܬܐ ܒܢ̈ܝ ܘܒܪ ܡܗܘܐ̄
ܗ̄ ܕܐܝܬ ܠܡܫܘܚܬܐ ܡܣܟܐ ܘܠܫܘܪܐ ܒܡܬܬܚܡܢܘܬ ܠܘܩܐ. ܕܢܣܒ
ܥܘܪ̈ܝ ܘܡܫܟܗ ܡܢ ܩܘܠܐ ܕܠܩܘ̈ܫ ܡܠܦܢܐ ܒܡܠܬܐ. ܕܒܠܘ̈ܬܐ

ܕܡܣܬ̈ܟܠ ܒܗܠܝܐ ܒܡܣܡܣܬܗܘܢ ܠܐ ܚܝܘܬܐ ܘܠܐ ܪܓܘܫܬܐ.
ܐܦ ܗܘ ܡܐ ܕܗܘܝܐ ܒܗܘܢ ܐܝܟ ܒܣܪܐ ܡܫܬܡܗ ܣܘܦܬ ܠܝܘܬܐ
ܒܙ ܕܡܐ ܠܬܪܝܗܘܢ. ܘܡܬܦ̈ܬܚܝܢ ܥܠ ܐܦ̈ܝ ܡܝ̈ܐ ܒܡܬܐܬܝ̈ܢܘܬܐ
ܫܐܝܠܬܐ ܘܡܬܩܦ̈ܣܝܢ ܘܡܬܬܚܕ̈ܢ ܒܬܪ ܡܘܟܠܗܝܢ. ܘܡܫܬܒ̈ܩܢ
ܠܬܚܬ ܘܡܬܬܣܝ̈ܡܢ ܥܠ ܐܪܥܐ ܕܝܡܐ ܒܢܩ̈ܦܢܐ ܡܫܩ̈ܬܬܐ.
ܘܡܬܪܒܝܐ ܒܗܘܢ ܘܡܬܩܫܝܐ ܗ̇ܝ ܢܘܛܦܬܐ. ܘܗܘ̇ܐ ܡܢܗ̇ ܗܢܐ
ܠܓܘܫܡܐ ܬܡܝܗܐ اللولو.

ܐܝܬ ܕܝܢ ܐܦ ܠܓܘܫܡ̈ܐ ܐܚܪ̈ܢܐ ܕܫܘܝܢ ܗ̇ܝ ܬܡܝܗܘܬܐ ܡܕܡ
ܒܓܘܢ̈ܝܗܘܢ ܡܫܚ̈ܠܦܐ. ܘܡܚܘܝܢ ܥܠ ܪܒܘܬ ܥܘܬܪܗ ܕܐܠܗܐ.
ܘܡܬܢܣܒܝܢ ܡܢܗܘܢ [1152] ܡܢ ܝܡܐ. ܘܡܢܗܘܢ ܡܢ ܝܒܫܐ.
ܘܡܬܩܪܝܢ ܟܠܗܘܢ ܒܫܡܐ ܓܘܢܝܐ ܕܟܐܦ̈ܐ ܝܩ̈ܝܪܬܐ. ܒܫܡܗ̈ܐ
ܕܝܢ ܝܚܝܕ̈ܝܐ ܐܚܪ̈ܢܝܬܐ ܘܐܚܪ̈ܢܝܬܐ الجوهر الكريم ❖

Pearls (*margånyåṯå*). In one source: "pearls, gems" (*luʔluʔ*); in another: "coral" (*marǧān*). In another source, and Bar Srošway: a pearl is a hard physical object, bright with a doubling of colors, taking its initial constitution from the collection of drops of early rain in oysters, which, when they go up to the surface, then conceive something that is neither animal nor perceptive, even if there's something meat-like in them: it's called a zoophyte, since it's similar to animals and plants. They spread out on the surface of the water with assumed impulses, and then contract and close up after collecting rain-drops; then they're released below and are deposited on the sea-floor, firmly attached. The drop inside them grows and hardens, and from it comes this amazing physical object, pearls.

There are also other physical objects that something of the same amazing quality in their varied colors, and they point out how immense God's riches are. Some are taken from the sea, some from land, and they're all known by the common name of "precious stones," but they have different individual names. Precious gems (*al-ǧawhar al-karīm*).

Bibliography

Abbeloos, Joannes Baptista and Lamy, Thomas Josephus. *Gregorii Barhebraei Chronicon Ecclesiasticum*, vol. 3. Paris and Louvain, 1877.

Adam, Alfred. *Die Psalmen des Thomas und das Perlenlied als Zeugnisse vorchristlicher Gnosis*. Berlin, 1959.

Ahrens, K. *Das Buch der Naturgegenstände*. Kiel, 1892.

Aland, B. "Mani und Bardesanes – Zur Entstehung des manichäischen Systems." In A. Dietrich, ed., *Synkretismus im syrischpersischen Kulturgebit. Bericht über ein Symposion in Reinhausen bei Göttingen in der Zeit vom 4. bis 8. Oktober 1971*. Göttingen, 1975, pp. 122–143.

Allberry, C.R.C. *A Manichaean Psalm-Book, Part II*. Manichaean Manuscripts in the Chester Beatty Collection II. Stuttgart, 1938.

Angelino, Carlo. "Il Canto della Perla: Premessa, traduzione, note." *Synkrisis. Testi e studi di storia e filosofia del linguaggio religiosa* 2 (1983): 7–40.

Annus, Amar. *The Standard Babylonian Epic of Anzu: Introduction, Cuneiform Text, Transliteration, Score, Glossary, Indices and Sign List*. State Archives of Assyria Cuneiform Texts 3. Helsinki, 2001.

Armstrong, A.H. *Plotinus: Enneads 1.1–9*. Loeb Classical Library. Cambridge, Mass., 1989.

Assemani, J.S. *Sancti patris nostri Ephraem Syri Opera omnia quae exstant Graece, Syriace, Latine*. Vol. 3 (Syr & Lat) Rome, 1743.

Barker, James W. *Tatian's Diatessaron – Composition, Redaction, Recension, and Reception*. Oxford Early Christian Studies. Oxford, 2022.

Barney, Stephen A. *Word-hoard: An Introduction to Old English Vocabulary*. 2nd ed. Yale Language Series. New Haven, 1985.

Barthélemy, A. *Dictionnaire Arabe-Français – Dialectes de Syrie : Alep, Damas, Liban, Jérusalem*. Paris, 1935.

Beal, Jane. "The Signifying Power of Pearl." *Quidditas* 33 (2012): 27-58.

Beck, Edmund. "Bardaisan und seine Schule bei Ephräm." *Le Muséon* 91 (1978): 271-333.

———. *Des heiligen Ephraem des Syrers Hymnen de fide*. Corpus Scriptorum Christianorum Orientalium 154 / Scriptores Syri 73. Louvain, 1955.

Bedjan, Paul. *Acta Martyrum et Sanctorum*. 7 vols. Leipzig, 1890-1897.

———. *Histoire de Mar-Jabalaha, de trois autres Patriarches, d'un Prêtre et de deux Laïques, Nestoriens*. Leipzig, 1895.

Betz, Hans Dieter. *Galatians: A Commentary on Paul's Letter to the Churches in Galatia*. Hermeneia. Philadelphia, 1979.

Bevan, A.A. *The Hymn of the Soul*. Texts and Studies 5.3. Cambridge, 1897.

Beyer, Klaus. "Das syrische Perlenied: Ein Erlösungsmythos als Märchengedicht." *Zeitschrift der Deutschen Morgenländischen Gesellschaft* 140 (1990): 234-259.

Bivar, A.D.H. "Gorgān v, pre-Islamic History," *Encyclopædia Iranica* I/2, pp. 96-99, 2012. Available at `https://www.iranicaonline.org/articles/gorgan`.

———. "Kushan Dynasty i. Dynastic History." *Encyclopædia Iranica*, online edition. 2014. Available at `http://www.iranicaonline.org/articles/kushan-dynasty-i-history`.

Böhlig, A. *Kephalaia II (Lieferung 11-12)*. Manichäische Handschriften der Staatlichen Museen Berlin 1. Stuttgart, 1966.

Bonesho, Catherine E. "Language as Power: Aramaic at (and East of) Palmyra." In Kenneth D.S. Lapatin and Rubina Raja, eds., *Palmyra and the East*. Studies in Palmyrene Archaeology and History 6. Turnhout, 2022, pp. 3-22.

Bonnet, M. "Actes de Saint Thomas, apôtre. Le poème de l'âme. Version grecque remaniée par Nicétas de Thessalonique." *Analecta Bollandiana* 20 (1901): 159-164.

Bornkamm, Günther. *Mythos und Legende in den apocryphen Thomas-Akten: Beiträge zur Geschichte der Gnosis und Vorgeschichte des Manichäismus*. Forschungen zur Religion und Literatur des alten und neuen Testaments 49. Göttingen 1933.

Bousset, Wilhelm. "Die Himmelsreise der Seele." *Archiv für Religionswissenschaft* 3 (1900): 136-169, 4 (1901): 229-273.

———. "Manichäisches in den Thomasakten." *Zeitschrift für die neutestamentliche Wissenschaft* 18 (1917-1918): 1-39.

Boyce, Mary. *A Reader in Manichaean Middle Persian and Parthian: Texts with Notes*. Acta Iranica (3rd series: Textes et mémoires) 9. Leiden, 1975.

Brand, Mattias. *Religion and the Everyday Life of Manichaeans in Kellis: Beyond Light and Darkness*. Nag Hammadi and Manichaean Studies 102. Leiden, 2022.

Bresciani, Edda. "Egypt i, Persians in Egypt in the Achaemenid Period." *Encyclopædia Iranica* VIII/3, pp. 247-249, 2011. Available at `http://www.iranicaonline.org/articles/egypt-i`.

Broabribb, D. "La kanto pri la perlo." *Biblia revuo* 4.2 (1968): 23-37.

Brock, Sebastian P. *The History of Holy Mar Maʿin with a Guide to the Persian Martyr Acts*. Persian Martyr Acts in Syriac: Text and Translation 1, Piscataway, 2008.

———. "Later Syriac Poetry," in Daniel King, ed., *The Syriac World*. Routledge, 2019, pp. 327-338.

———. "Poetry and Hymnography (3): Syriac." In Susan Ashbrook Harvey and David G. Hunter, eds., *The Oxford Handbook of Early Christian Studies*. Oxford, 2008, pp. 657-671.

———. *Soḡyâṯâ Mḡabbyâṯâ* ܣܘܓܝܬܐ ܡܓܒܝܬܐ. Holland, 1982.

———. *The Wisdom of St. Isaac of Nineveh*. Texts from Christian Late Antiquity 1. Piscataway, 2006.

———, Aaron M. Butts, George A. Kiraz, and Lucas Van Rompay, eds. *Gorgias Encyclopedic Dictionary of the Syriac Heritage* Piscataway, 2011.

——— and George Kiraz. *Ephrem the Syriac: Select Poems*. Eastern Christian Texts 2. Provo, 2006.

Brockelmann, Carl. *Grundriss der vergleichenden Grammatik der semitischen Sprachen*, vol. 1, *Laut- und Formenlehre*. Berlin, 1908.

———. *Lexicon Syriacum*. 2nd ed. Halle an der Saale, 1928.

Brooks, E.W., I. Guidi, and J.-B. Chabot. *Chronica Minora*, vol. 3. Corpus Scriptorum Christianorum Orientalium / Scriptores Syri 3rd series, 4. Leipzig, 1905.

Buckley, Jorunn J. *The Great Stem of Souls: Reconstructing Mandaean History*. Piscataway, 2005.

———. *The Mandaeans: Ancient Texts and Modern People*. New York, 2002.

Budge, E.A. Wallis. *The Laughable Stories collected by Mâr Gregory John Bar-Hebraeus*. London, 1897.

Burch, Vacher. "A Commentary on the Syriac Hymn of the Soul," *Journal of Theological Studies* 19 (1918): 145-161.

Burkitt, Francis Crawford. *The Hymn of Bardaisan*. London, 1899.

———. Rev. of Preuschen, *Zwei gnostische Hymnen*. *Theologisch Tijdschrift* (1905): 270-282.

———. "Sarbog, Shuruppak," *Journal of Theological Studies* 4 (1902-1903): 125-127.

———. "Toga in the East," *Journal of Theological Studies* 23 (1922): 281-282.

Butts, Aaron Michael. "The Use of *Syāmē* as a Phonological Marker in Syriac," *Hugoye: Journal of Syriac Studies* 18.1 (2015): 95-111.

Camplani, A. "Rivisitando Bardesane: Note sulle fonti siriache del bardesanismo e sulla sua collocazione storico-religiosa." *Cristianesmo nella Storia* 19 (1998): 519-596.

Canney, M.A. "The Life-giving Pearl," *Journal of the Manchester Egyptian and Oriental Society* 15 (1930): 43-62.

Carmi, T. *The Penguin Book of Hebrew Verse*. New York, 1981.

Centore, Giuseppe. "Lo gnosticismo e il canto dell perla," *Studi Storici e Religiosi* 5.2 (1996): 153-176.

Černý, J. *Coptic Etymological Dictionary*. Cambridge, 1976.

Chaumont, M. L. and C. Toumanoff. "Āzād (Iranian Nobility)." *Encyclopædia Iranica Online*, 2011. Available at `https://iranicaonline.org/articles/azad-older-azat`.

Ciancaglini, Claudia A. *Iranian Loanwords in Syriac*, Beiträge zur Iranistik 28. Wiesbaden, 2008.

Ciasca, A. *Tatiani Evangeliorum Harmoniae Arabice*. Rome, 1888.

Clackson, Sarah, Erica Hunter, and Samuel N.C. Lieu. *Texts from the Roman Empire (Texts in Syriac, Greek, Coptic and Latin*. Dictionary of Manichaean Texts 1. In association with Mark Vermes. Turnhout, 1998.

Conley, John, ed. *The Middle English 'Pearl': Critical Essays.* Notre Dame and London, 1970.

Conybeare, Frederick Cornwallis. "The Idea of Sleep in the 'Hymn of the Soul,'" *Journal of Theological Studies* 6 (1905): 609-610.

Corbin, Henry. *En Islam Iranien: Aspects sprirituels et philosophiques*, vol. 2. Paris, 1972.

Crum, W.E. "Coptic Anecdota," *Journal of Theological Studies* 44 (1943): 176-182.

———. *A Coptic Dictionary*. Oxford, 1939.

Culianu, Ioan Petru. "Erzählung und Mythos im 'Lied von der Perle,'" *Kairos* 21 (1979): 60-71.

Davis, Erik. *High Weirdness: Drugs, Esoterica, and Visionary Experience in the Seventies*. London and Cambridge, Mass., 2019.

———. *TechGnosis: Myth, Magic and Mysticism in the Age of Information*. 2nd ed. London, 2004.

Degen, Rainer. *Altaramäische Grammatik der Inschriften des 10.-8. Jh. v. Chr.*. Abhandlungen für die Kunde des Morgenländes 38.3. Wiesbaden, 1969.

del Olmo Lete, Gregorio and Joaquín Sanmartín. *A Dictionary of the Ugaritic Language in the Alphabetic Tradition*. Translated and edited by Wilfred G.E. Watson. Handbook of Oriental Studies, sect. 1, The Near and Middle East 112. Leiden and Boston, 2015.

Donner, Herbert and Wolfgang Röllig. *Kanaanäische und aramäische Inschriften*, vol. 1. 5th ed. Wiesbaden, 2002.

Durkin-Meisterernst, Desmond. *Dictionary of Manichaean Middle Persian and Parthian*. Dictionary of Manichaean Texts 3, Texts from Central Asia and China. Turnhout, 2004.

——— and Enrico Morano. *Mani's Psalms: Middle Persian, Parthian and Sogdian Texts in the Turfan Collection*. Berliner Turfantexte 27. Turnhout, 2010.

Drijvers, H. J. W. *Bardaiṣan of Edessa*. Studia Semitica Neerlandica. Assen, 1965.

———. *The Book of the Laws of Countries: Dialogue on Fate of Bardaiṣan of Edessa*. Semitic Texts with Translations 3. Assen, 1965.

Drower, Ethel S. *The Canonical Prayerbook of the Mandaeans*. Leiden, 1959.

———. *The Haran Gawaita and The Baptism of Hibil-Ziwa: The Mandaic Text Reproduced together with Translation, Notes and Commentary*. Studi e Testi 176. Vatican City, 1953.

———. "Hibil-Ziwa and the Parthian Prince." *Journal of the Royal Asiatic Society* (1954): 152-156.

Duval, Rubens. *Lexicon Syriacum auctore Hassano Bar Bahlule*. 3 vols. Paris, 1901.

Ehlers, B. "Bardesanes von Edessa – ein syrischer Gnostiker." *Zeitschrift für Kirchengeschichte* 19 (1970): 334-351.

Fassberg, Steven E. *A Grammar of the Palestinian Targum Fragments from the Cairo Genizah*. Harvard Semitic Studies 38. Atlanta, 1990.

Ferreira, Johan. *The Hymn of the Pearl: The Syriac and Greek Texts with Introduction, Translations, and Notes*. Early Christian Studies 3. Sydney, 2002.

Fiey, J.M. *Assyrie chrétienne: Contribution à l'étude de l'histoire et de la géographie ecclésiastiques et monastiques du nord de l'Iraq*. 3 vols. Recherches publiées sous la direction de l'Institut de lettres orientales de Beyrouth 22, 23, 42. Beirut. 1965-1968

Fitzmyer, Joseph A. *The Aramaic Inscriptions of Sefire*. Rev. ed. Biblica et orientalia 19/A. Rome, 1995.

Fox, Joshua. *Semitic Noun Patterns*. Harvard Semitic Studies. Winona Lake, Ind., 2003.

Friedrich, Johannes, Wolfgang Röllig, and Maria Giulia Amadasi Guzzo. *Phönizisch-punische Grammatik*. 3rd ed. With the contributions of Werner R. Mayer. Analecta Orientalia 55. Rome, 1999.

Furlani, Giuseppe. "L'Εγχειρίδιον di Giacomo d'Edessa nel testo siriaco," *Rendiconti Della Reale Accademia Nazionale Dei Lincei. Classe Di Scienze Morali, Storiche E Filologiche* 6.5-6 (1928): 222-249.

Gallarta, Israel Muñoz and Lautaro Roig Lanzillotta, eds. *New Trends in the Research on the Apocryphal Acts of Thomas*. Studies on Early Christian Apocrypha 20. Leuven, 2024.

Gardner, Iain. *Kellis Literary Texts*, vol. 1. With contributions by S. Clackson, M. Franzmann, and K.A. Worp. Dakhleh Oasis Project Monograph 4. Oxford, 1996.

———. *Mani's Epistles: The Surviving Parts of the Coptic Codex Berlin P. 15998*. Manichäische Handschriften der Staatlichen Museen zu Berlin 2. Stuttgart: Kohlhammer, 2022.

Garr, W. Randall. *Dialect Geography of Syriac PAlestine 1000-586 B.C.E.*. Winona Lake, 2004.

Gershevitch, Ilya. "A Parthian Title in the Hymn of the Soul," *Journal of the Royal Asiatic Society*, (1954): 124-126 = Gershevitch, *Philologia Iranica*, ed. Nicholas Sims-Williams. Beitrage zur Iranistik 12. Wiesbaden, 1985, pp. 162-164.

Gharib, B. *Sogdian Dictionary: Sogdian-Persian-English*. Tehran, 1995.

Gignoux, Philippe. *Glossaire des Inscriptions Pehlevies et Parthes*. Corpus inscriptionum Iranicarum, supplementary series 1. London, 1972.

———. *Homélies de Narsaï sur la création: édition critique du texte syriaque, introduction et traduction française*. Patrologia Orientalis 34.3-4. Turnhout, 1968.

Gollancz, Israel. *Pearl: An English Poem of the Fourteenth Century*. London, 1891.

Greenfield, J.C. "Early Aramaic Poetry." *Journal of Ancient Near Eastern Studies* 11 (1979): 45-51.

Gzella, Holger. *A Cultural History of Aramaic: From the Beginnings to the Advent of Islam*. Handbuch der Orientalistik I, 111. Leiden, 2015.

Halévy, Joseph. "Cantique syriaque sur saint Thomas." *Revue sémitique d'épigraphie et d'histoire ancienne* 16 (1908): 85-94, 168-175.

Hansman, John. "Characene and Charax." *Encyclopædia Iranica Online*, V/4, pp. 363-365, 2011. Available at `https://iranicaonline.org/articles/characene-and-charax-spasinou-in-pre-islamic-times`.

———. "The Land of Meshan," *Iran. Journal of the British Institute of Persian Studies* 22 (1984): 161-166.

Harnack, Dieter. "ParthischeTitel, vornehmlich in den Inschriften aus Hatra. Ein Beitrag zur Kenntnis des parthischen Staates." In Franz Altheim and Ruth Stiehl, eds. *Geschichte Mittelasiens im Altertum*. Mit Beitragen von Janos Harmatta, Dieter Harnack, Roch Knapowski, Franz F. Schwarz, Zuhair Shunnar, Oswald Szemerényi and Erika Trautmann-Nehring. Berlin 1970, pp. 492-549.

Harris, Rendell and Alphonse Mingana. *The Odes and Psalms of Solomon*. Vol. 1. Manchester, 1916.

Harviainen, Tapani. "Diglossia in Jewish Eastern Aramaic." *Studia Orientalia* 55 (1983): 97-113.

Haspelmath, Martin. "Lexical Borrowing: Concepts and Issues." In Martin Haspelmath Uri Tadmor, eds. *Loanwords in the World's Languages A Comparative Handbook*. Berlin, 2009, pp. 35-54.

Heider, G.C. "Tannin." In Karel Van Der Toorn, Bob Becking, Pieter W. Van Der Horst, eds., *Dictionary of Deities and Demons in the Bible*, 2nd ed. Leiden, 1999, pp. 834-836.

Heinen, Heinz. "Egypt iii. Relations in the Seleucid and Parthian Periods." *Encyclopædia Iranica*, VIII/3, pp. 250-252, 2011. Available at `http://www.iranicaonline.org/articles/egypt-iii`.

Hilgenfeld, Adolf. "Der Königssohn und die Perle: ein morgenländisches Gedicht." *Zeitschrift für wissenschaftliche Theologie* 47 (1904): 229-41.

———. Rev. of Bevan, *The Hymn of the Soul. Berliner philologische Wochenschrift* 18, no. 13 (1898): 389-395.

Hillers, Delbert R. and Eleonora Cussini. *Palmyrene Aramaic Texts*. Publications of the Comprehensive Aramaic Project. Baltimore and London, 1996.

Hillier, Russell M. Review of *A Bloody and Barbarous God: The Metaphysics of Cormac McCarthy* by Petra Mundik. *The Cormac McCarthy Journal* 15 (2017): 96-101.

Hinz, Walther. *Altiranisches Sprachgut in der Nebenüberlieferungen*. With contributions by Peter-Michael Berger, Günther Korbel, and Annegret Nippa. Göttinger Orientforschungen III. Reihe: Iranica 3. Wiesbaden, 1975.

Hoffmann, G. "Zwei Hymnen der Thomasakten." *Zeitschrift für die neutestamentliche Wissenschaft* 4 (1903): 273-309.

Hogrogian, Nonny, illustrator *The Pearl: Hymn of the Robe of Glory – A New Retelling*. Aurora, OR, 1979.

Jeffery, Arthur. *Foreign Vocabulary of the Qur'ān*. Baroda, 1938.

Jonas, Hans *Gnosis und spätantiker Geist*, pt. 1, *Die mythologische Gnosis, mit einer Einleitung zur Geschichte und Methodologie der Forschung*. 3rd ed. Forschungen zur Religion und Literatur des alten und neuen Testaments 51. Göttingen, 1964.

———. "The 'Hymn of the Pearl.'" In *The Gnostic Religion: The Message of the Alien God & the Beginnings of Christianity*. 3rd ed. Boston, 2001, pp. 112-129.

———. "The 'Hymn of the Pearl': Case Study of a Symbol, and the Claims for a Jewish Origin of Gnosticism." In *Philosophical Essays: From Ancient Creed to Technological Man*. Englewood Cliffs, New Jersey: 1974, pp. 277-290.

Joosse, Peter. "An Introduction to the Arabic Diatessaron." *Oriens Christianus* 83 (1999): 72-129.

Kämmerer, Thomas R. and Kai A. Metzler. *Das babylonische Weltschöpfungsepos* Enūma eliš. Alter Orient und Altes Testament 375. Münster, 2012.

Kattan Gribetz, Sarit. "Women as Readers of the Nag Hammadi Codices." *Journal of Early Christian Studies* (2018) 26: 463-494.

Kaufman, Stephen A. *The Akkadian Influences on Aramaic*. Assyriological Studies 19. Chicago, 1975.

———. "Appendix C: Alphabetic Texts." In McGuire Gibson, *Excavations at Nippur: Eleventh Season*. Oriental Institute Communications 22. Chicago and London, 1975, pp. 151-152.

King, Karen L. *What is Gnosticism?* Cambridge, Mass., 2003.

Kiraz, George A. *A Comparative Edition of the Syriac Gospels* 4 vols. Piscataway, 2004.

Klijn, A.F.J. *The Acts of Thomas: Introduction, Text, and Commentary*. Supplements to Novum Testamentum 108. Leiden, 2003.

———. "The So-Called Hymn of the Pearl (Acts of Thomas Ch. 108-113)." *Vigiliae Christianae* 14.3 (1960): 154-164.

Klimkeit, Hans-Joachim. *Gnosis on the Silk Road: Gnostic Parables, Hymns & Prayers from Central Asia*. New York, 1993.

Köbert, Raimund. "Das Perlenlied." *Orientalia* 38.3 (1969): 447-456.

Koenen, Ludwig and Cornelia Römer. *Der Kölner Mani-Kodex. Über das Werden seines Lebem: Kritische Edition*. Abhandlungen der Rheinisch-westfälischen Akademie der Wissenschafter. Sonderreihe Papyrologica Coloniensia 14. Wiesbaden, 1988.

Koltun-Fromm, N. "Re-imagining Tatian: The Damaging Effects of Polemical Rhetoric." *Journal of Early Christian Studies* 16 (2008): 1-30.

Kruse, Heinz. "Das Brautlied der syrischen Thomas-Akten," *Orientalia Christiana Periodica* 50 (1984): 291-330.

———. "The Return of the Prodigal: Fortunes of a Parable on its Way to the Far East." *Orientalia* 47 (1978): 163-214.

Kuehn, Sara. *The Dragon in Medieval East Christian and Islamic Art*. Islamic History and Civilization: Studies and Texts 86. Leiden, 2011.

LaFargue, Michael. *Language and Gnosis: The Opening Scenes of the Acts of Thomas*. Harvard Dissertations in Religion 18. Philadelphia,1985.

de Lagarde, Paul. *Analecta Syriaca*. London, 1858.

Lampe, G.W.H. *A Patristic Greek Lexicon*. Oxford, 1961.

Lanzillotta, Lautaro Roig. "Codex Vallicellanus B 35: An Assessment of the Only Extant Greek Manuscript of *Acta Thomae* including the 'Hymn of the Pearl'." In Israel Muñoz Gallarta and Lautaro Roig Lanzillotta, eds. *New Trends in the Research on the Apocryphal Acts of Thomas*. Studies on Early Christian Apocrypha 20. Leuven, 2024, pp. 43-60.

———. "A Syriac Original for the Acts of Thomas?: The Hypothesis of Syriac Priority Revisited." In Ilaria Ramelli and Judith Perkins, eds. *Early Christian and Jewish Narrative: The Role of Religion in Shaping Narrative Forms*. Tübingen, 2015, pp. 105-133.

Lazard, G. "La métrique de la poésie parthe." In *Papers in Honour of Professor Mary Boyce*. Acta Iranica 25. Leiden, 1985, pp. 371-99.

———. “Prosody iii. Middle Persian.” *Encyclopædia Iranica*, online edition, 2017. Available at http://www.iranicaonline.org/articles/prosody-middle-Persian.

Leriche, P. and F. Grenet. “Bactria.” *Encyclopædia Iranica*, II/4, 2011, pp. 339-344. Available at http://www.iranicaonline.org/articles/bactria.

Lidzbarski, M. *Ginzā, der Schatz, oder das grosse Buch des Mandäer*. Göttingen, 1925.

———. *Mandäische Liturgien*. Berlin, 1920.

Lieber, Laura Suzanne. *Jewish Aramaic Poetry from Late Antiquity: Translations and Commentaries*. Cambridge Genizah Studies 8. Leiden, 2018.

Lieu, Samuel N.C. *Manichaeism in Mesopotamia and the Roman East*. Religions in the Graeco-Roman World 118. Leiden, 1999.

——— and Iain Gardner. *Manichaean Texts from the Roman Empire*. Cambridge, 2004.

Lipsius, R. and M. Bonnet. *Acta Apostolorum Apocrypha*, part 2, vol. 2. Leipzig, 1903.

Löw, Immanuel. “Aramäische Schlangennamen.” In David Günzburg and Isaac Markon, eds., *Festschrift zu Ehren des Dr. A. Harkavy aus Anlass seines am 20. November 1905 vollendeten siebzigsten Lebensjahres*, vol. 1. St. Petersburg, 1908, pp. 27-52.

Lundborg, Patrick. *Psychedelia: An Ancient Culture, A Modern Way of Life*. 2nd ed. Stockholm, 2012.

Lundhaug, Hugo and Lance Jenott. *Monastic Origins of the Nag Hammadi Codices*. Studien und Texte zu Antike und Christentum / Studies and Texts in Antiquity and Christianity 97. Tübingen, 2015.

Luttikhuizen, Gerard P. “The Hymn of Jude Thomas, the Apostle, in the Country of the Indians.” In Jan N. Bremmer, ed., *The Apocryphal Acts of Thomas*. Leuven, 2001.

Macke, K. "Syrische Lieder gnostischen Ursprungs: Eine Studie über die apocryphen syrischen Thomasacten." *Theologische Quartalschrift* (1874): 24-70.

MacKenzie, D.N. "Shapur's Shooting." *Bulletin of the School of Oriental and African Studies* 41 (1978): 499-511.

Mackintosh-Smith, Tim and James E. Montgomery. *Two Arabic Travel Books: Abū Zayd al-Sīrāfī,* Accounts of China and India, *and Ibn Faḍlān,* Mission to the Volga. Library of Arabic Literature. New York and London, 2014.

MacRae, George. "Sleep and Awakening in Gnostic Texts." In Ugo Bianchi, ed., *Le origini dello gnosticismo. Colloquio di Messina 13-18 aprile 1966 / The Origins of Gnosticism. Colloquium of Messina 13-18 april 1966.* Leiden, 1967, pp. 496- 507.

Macuch, Rudolf. *Geschichte der spät- und neusyrischen Literatur*. Berlin: De Gruyter, 1976.

———. *Handbook of Classical and Modern Mandaic*. Berlin, 1965.

Magne, Jean. "Le Chant de la Perle à la lumière des écrits de Nag Hammadi." *Cahiers du cercle Ernest-Renan* 25, no. 100 (1977): 17-28.

Maier, Bernhard. *Gründerzeit der Orientalistik: Theodor Nöldekes Leben und Werk im Spiegel seiner Briefe*. Arbeitsmaterialien zum Orient 29. Würzburg, 2013.

———. *Semitic Studies in Victorian Britain: A Portrait of William Wright and his World through his Letters*. Arbeitsmaterialien zum Orient 26. Würzburg, 2011.

Mairs, Rachel, ed. *The Graeco-Bactrian and Indo-Greek World*. London and New York, 2021.

Marcovich, Miroslav. "The Wedding Hymn of Acta Thomae." *Illinois Classical Studies* 6 (1981), 367-385 = Marcovich, *Studies in Graeco-Roman Religions and Gnosticism*. Studies in Greek and Roman Religion 4. Leiden, 1988, pp. 156-173.

Mariès, Louis and Ch. Mercier, eds. *Eznik de Kołb: De Deo*. Patrologia Orientalis 28. Paris, 1959.

Markschies, Christoph. *Gnosis: An Introduction*. Translated by John Bowden. London, 2003.

Mathews, Jr., Edward G. *The Armenian Commentary on the Book of Genesis attributed to Ephrem the Syrian: An Edition of the Armenian Text with Introduction, English Translation and Commentary*. Ph.D. dissertation. Columbia University, 1996.

——— and Joseph P. Amar. *St. Ephrem the Syrian – Selected Prose Works: Commentary on Genesis, Commentary on Exodus, Homily on our Lord, Letter to Publius*. Edited by Kathleen McVey. The Fathers of the Church 91. Washington, D.C., 1994.

McVey, Kathleen E. *Ephrem the Syrian: Hymns*. Classics of Western Spirituality. New York, 1989.

Mead, G.R.S. *Fragments of Faith Forgotten*. 3rd ed. London, 1931, pp. 392-414.

Ménard, Jacques E. "Le 'Chant de la Perle.'" *Revue des sciences religieuses* 42.4 (1968): 289-325.

Merkelbach, R., *Roman und Mysterium in der Antike*. Munich and Berlin, 1962, pp. 299-325.

Messina, Giuseppe. *Diatessaron Persiano*. Biblica et orientalia 14. Rome, 1951.

Mills, Ian N. "Zacchaeus and the Unripe Figs: A New Argument for the Original Language of Tatian's Diatessaron." *New Testament Studies* 66 (2020): 208-227.

Mokri, Mohammad. "Le symbole de la perle dans le folklore persan et chez les Kurdes fidèles de Vérité (Ahl-e Ḥaqq)." *Journal Asiatique* 248/249 (1960/1961): pp. 463-81.

Moskvina, E.V. (Е.В. Москвина). "Гностический миф о *salvator salvatus* и его элементы в романе Ф.М. Достоевского «Идиот»." *Достоевский и мировая культура. Филологический журнал* 3 (2018): 69-91.

Al-Mubaraki, Majid Fandi. *Diwan Masbuta d Hibil Ziwa: Mandaean Sacred Scroll.* Available at. `http://mandaeannetwork.com/Books/diwans/masbuta-d-hibil-ziwa.pdf`. 2010.

Müller-Kessler, Christa. "The Earliest Evidence for Targum Onqelos from Babylonia and the Question of its Dialect and Origin." *Journal for the Aramaic Bible* 3 (2001): 181-198.

——— and Michael Sokoloff. *The Forty Martyrs of the Sinai Desert, Eulogios the Stone-cutter, and Anastasia.* Corpus of Christian Palestinian Aramaic 3. Groningen, 1996.

Muraoka, Takamitsu. *A Grammar of Qumran Aramaic.* Ancient Near Eastern Studies Supplement 38. Leuven, 2011.

Nöldeke, Theodor. *Beiträge zur semitischen Sprachwissenschaft..* Strassburg: Karl J. Trübner, 1904.

———. *Compendious Syriac Grammar.* Translated by James A. Crichton. With an appendix, edited by Anton Schall and translated by Peter T. Daniels. Winona Lake, Ind., 2001.

———. "Zur orientalischen Geographie." *Zeitschrift der deutschen morgenländischen Gesellschaft* 28 (1874): 93-102.

———. Review of Wright, *Apocryphal Acts. Zeitschrift der deutschen morgenländischen Gesellschaft* 25 (1871): 670-679.

Ogden, Daniel. *The Dragon in the West: From Ancient Myth to Modern Legend.* Oxford, 2021.

———. *Dragons, Serpents, and Slayers in the Classical and Early Christian Worlds: A Sourcebook.* Oxford, 2013.

———. *Drakon: Dragon Myth and Serpent Cult in the Greek and Roman Worlds.* Oxford, 2013.

Oppenheimer, Aharon. *Babylonia Judaica in the Talmudic Period*. In collaboration with Benjamin Isaac and Michael Lecker. Beihefte zum Tübinger Atlas des Vorderen Orients B 47. Wiesbaden, 1983.

Osgood, Charles G. *The Pearl: A Middle English Poem*. Boston, 1906.

Parpola, Simo. "Mesopotamian Precursors of the Hymn of the Pearl." In R. M. Whiting, ed., *Mythology and Mythologies*, Melammu Symposia 2. Helsinki, 2001, pp. 181-93.

Parsons, Richard. *Cebes' Tablet, with Introduction, Notes, Vocabulary, and Grammatical Questions*. Boston, 1887.

Pat-El, Na'ama. *Studies in the Historical Syntax of Aramaic*. Perspectives on Linguistics and Ancient Languages 1. Piscataway, 2012.

Payne Smith, Robert. *Thesaurus Syriacus*. Oxford, 1879-1901.

Pearsall, Derek. *Old English and Middle English Poetry*. Routledge Library Editions: The Medieval World 39. London, 1977.

Pearson, Birger A. *Ancient Gnosticism: Traditions and Literature*. Minneapolis, 2007.

Pedersen, Nils Arne. *Manichaean Homilies*. The Manichaean Coptic Papyri in the Chester Beatty Library. Corpus Fontium Manichaeorum, series Coptica 2. Brepols, 2006.

Penn, Michael, R. Jordan Crouser, and Philip Abbott. "Serto before Serto: Reexamining the Earliest Development of Syriac Script." *Aramaic Studies* 18 (2020): 46-63.

Pereira, A.S. Rodrigues. *Studies in Aramaic Poetry (c.100 B.C.E.-c.600 C.E.): Selected Jewish, Christian and Samaritan Poems*. Studia Semitica Neerlandica 34. Van Gorcum, 1997

Petersen, W.L. *Tatian's Diatessaron. Its Creation, Dissemination, Significance, and History in Scholarship*. Supplements to Vigiliae Christianae 25. Leiden, 1994.

Poirier, Paul-Hubert. *L'hymne de la Perle des Actes de Thomas: Introduction, texte-traduction, commentaire*. Homo Religiosus 8. Louvain-la-Neuve, 1981.

———. "L'Hymne de la Perle et le manichéisme à la lumière du Codex manichéen de Cologne." In Luigi Cirillo, ed., *Codex Manichaicus Coloniensis. Atti del Simposio Internazionale (Rende-Amantea 3-7 settembre 1984)*, with the contribution of Amneris Roselli. Studi e Ricerche 4. Cosenza, 1986, pp. 235-248.

Polotsky, H.J. *Manichäische Homilien*. Manichäische Handschriften der Sammlung A. Chester Beatty 1. Stuttgart, 1934.

——— and A. Böhlig. *Kephalaia 1. Hälfte (Lieferung 1-10)*. Manichäische Handschriften der Staatlichen Museen Berlin 1. Stuttgart, 1940.

Possekel, Ute. "Bardaisan of Edessa, Philosopher or Theologian?" *Zeitschrift für antikes Christentum* 10 (2006), 442-461.

Preston, Todd. *A Handbook of Animals in Old English Texts*. Leeds, 2022.

Preuschen, E. *Zwei gnostische Hymnen*. Giessen, 1904.

Quispel, Gilles. *Makarius, das Thomasevangelium, und das Lied von der Perle*. Leiden, 1967.

———. "Makarius und das Lied von der Perle." In Ugo Bianchi, ed., *Le origini dello gnosticismo: Colloquio di Messina, 13-18 Aprile 1966 = The Origins of Gnosticism: Colloquium of Messina, 13-18 April 1966*. Studies in the History of Religions: Supplements to *Numen* 12. Leiden, 1970, pp. 625-644.

Reiner, Erica and Martha T. Roth, eds. *Chicago Assyrian Dictionary*. 21 vols. Chicago, 1956-2010.

Reitzenstein, R. *Das iranische Erlösungsmysterium. Religionsgeschichtliche Untersuchungen*. Bonn, 1921.

———. "Heilswanderung und Drachenkampf in der alchemistischen Literatur und frühchristlichen Literatur." In Festschrift F.C. Andreas zur Vollendung des siebzigsten Lebensjahres am 14. April 1916. Leipzig, 1916, pp. 33-50.

———. "Zwei hellenistischen Hymnen," *Archiv für Religionswissenschaft* 8 (1904-1905): 167-190.

Richter, Sebastian G. *Psalm Book, Part I, Fasc. 1: Psalmengruppe 1, Die Sonnenhymnen des Herakleides, Die Synaxis-Psalmen.* The Manichaean Coptic Papyri in the Chester Beatty Library. Corpus Fontium Manichaeorum, series Coptica 3. Turnhout, 2021.

———. *Psalm Book, Part II, Fasc. 1: Die Bema-Psalmen.* The Manichaean Coptic Papyri in the Chester Beatty Library. Corpus Fontium Manichaeorum, series Coptica 1. Turnhout, 1996.

———. *Psalm Book, Part II, Fasc. 2: Die Herakleides-Psalmen.* The Manichaean Coptic Papyri in the Chester Beatty Library. Corpus Fontium Manichaeorum, series Coptica 1. Turnhout, 1998.

Robinson, Fred C. and Bruce Mitchell. *A Guide to Old English.* 8th ed. Oxford, 2012.

Robinson, James M., ed. *The Coptic Gnostic Library: A Complete Edition of the Nag Hammadi Codices.* 5 vols. Leiden, 2000.

Rosenthal, Franz. *Ibn Khaldûn, The Muqaddimah: An Introduction to History.* Vol. 1. Bollingen Series 43. New York, 1958.

Russell, James R. "The Epic of the Pearl." *Revue des études arméniennes* 28 (2001-2002): 29-100.

———. "Hymn of the Pearl." In *Encyclopædia Iranica*, vol. XII, fasc. 6, pp. 603-605, 2012. Available at `http://www.iranicaonline.org/articles/hymn-of-the-pearl`.

Ryssel, V. "Poemi siriaci di Giorgio, vescovo degli Arabi." *Atti della Reale Accademia dei Lincei*, ser. 4, *Classe di scienze morali, storiche e filologiche*, 9 (1892): 46–93.

Sachau, Eduard. *Reise in Syrien und Mesopotamien* (Leipzig, F.A. Brockhaus, 1883)

———. *Verzeichnis der syrischen Handschriften*. 2 vols. Die Handschriften-Verzeichnisse der königlichen Bibliothek zu Berlin 23. Berlin, 1889.

Saint-Laurent, Jeanne-Nicole Mellon. *Missionary Stories and the Formation of the Syriac Churches*. Oakland, 2015.

Schulthess, Friedrich. *Kalila und Dimna, Syrisch und Deutsch*, vol. 1. Berlin, 1911.

Schultz, Wolfgang. *Dokumente der Gnosis*. Jena, 1910, pp. 13-23.

Schuol, Monika. *Die Charakene. Ein mesopotamisches Konigreich in hellenistisch-parthischer Zeit*. Oriens et Occidens: Studien zu antiken Kulturkontakten und ihrem Nachleben 1. Stuttgart, 2000.

Seddon, Keith. *Epictetus'* Handbook *and the* Tablet of Cebes*: Guides to Stoic Living*. London and New York, 2005.

Seymour, Michael. *Babylon: Legend, History and the Ancient City*. London and New York, 2014.

Sims-Williams, N. and H. Falk. "Kushan Dynasty ii. Inscriptions of the Kushans." *Encyclopædia Iranica*, online edition, 2014. Available at `http://www.iranicaonline.org/articles/kushan-02-inscriptions`.

Sisam, Kenneth. *Fourteenth Century Verse & Prose*. Oxford, 1921.

Skjærvø, P.O. "Bardesanes." *Encyclopædia Iranica*, III/7-8, pp. 780-785, 1989. Available at `https://iranicaonline.org/articles/bardesanes-syr`.

———, Dj. Khaleghi-Motlagh, M. Omidsalar, and J.R. Russell, "Aždahā." *Encyclopædia Iranica*, III/2, pp. 191-205, 2011. Available at `https://iranicaonline.org/articles/azdaha-dragon-various-kinds`.

Sokoloff, Michael. *Dictionary of Jewish Babylonian Aramaic*. Dictionaries of Talmud, Midrash and Targum 3; Publications of the Comprehensive Aramaic Lexicon Project. Ramat Gan, Baltimore, and London, 2002.

———. *Dictionary of Jewish Palestinian Aramaic*. 2nd ed. Dictionaries of Talmud, Midrash and Targum 2; Publications of the Comprehensive Aramaic Lexicon Project. Ramat Gan, Baltimore, and London, 2002.

Sperber, Alexander. *The Bible in Aramaic*. Leiden, 2004.

Stang, Charles. *Our Divine Double*. Cambridge, Mass., 2016.

Strack, H.L. and Günter Stemberger. *Introduction to the Talmud and Midrash*. Translated and edited by Markus Bockmuehl. Minneapolis, 1996.

Tal, Abraham. "Samaritan Literature." In Alan Crown, ed. *The Samaritans*. Tübingen, 1989, pp. 413-467.

Talon, Philippe. *The Standard Babylonian Creation Myth: Enūma Eliš*. State Archives of Assyria Cuneiform Texts 4. Helsinki, 2005.

Tardieu, Michel. "La diffusion du bouddhisme dans l'empire Kouchan, l'Iran et la Chine, d'après un kephalaion manichéen inédit," *Studia Iranica* 17 (1988): 153-183.

———. *Manichaeism*. Translated by M.B. DeBevoise. Urbana and Chicago. 2008.

Teigen, Håkon Fiane. *The Manichaean Church in Kellis*. Nag Hammadi and Manichaean Studies 100. Leiden, 2021.

Tian, Leilei. "*The Hymn of the Pearl* – Piece for five instruments and electronics, commissioned by Sond'Ar-te Electric Ensemble, Portugal, 2011." Available at `https://www.youtube.com/watch?v=kXrsyiv5OZo`.

Thackston, Wheeler M., Jr. *Shihabuddin Yahya Suhrawardi: The Philosophical Allegories and Mystical Treatises*. Bibliotheca Iranica, Intellectual Traditions Series 2. Costa Mesa, Cal., 1999.

Tropper, Josef. *Die Inschriften von Zincirli*. Abhandlungen zur Literatur Alt-Syrien-Palästinas 6. Münster, 1993.

Tubach, Jürgen. "The Four World Empires in the Hymn of the Pearl." *Journal of Eastern Christian Studies* 56.1-4 (2004): 145-54.

———. "Zur Interpretation des Perlenliedes. Exegetische Prämissen und ihre Schlussfolgerungen." In Dmitrij Bumazhnov and Hans Reinhard Seeliger, eds., *Syrien im 1.-7. Jahrhundert nach Christus: Akten der 1. Tübinger Tagung zum Christlichen Orient (15.-16. Juni 2007)*. Studien und Texte zu Antike und Christentum 62. Tübingen, 2011, pp. 231-258.

———. "Der Weg des Prinzen im Perlenlied." *Orientalia Christiana Periodica* 24 (1993): 87-111.

Van Bladel, Kevin. *From Sasanian Mandaeans to Ṣābians of the Marshes*. Leiden, 2017.

van Tongerloo, Alois. "A Nobleman in Trouble, or the Consequences of Drunkenness." In D. Durkin-Meisterernst, C. Reck, and D. Weber, eds., *Literarische Stoffe und ihre Gestaltung in mitteliranischer Zeit. Kolloquium anlässlich des 70. Geburtstages von Werner Sundermann*. Beiträge zur Iranistik 31. Wiesbaden, 2009, pp. 387-305, with plates 12 and 13.

Vosté, J.-M. and C. Van den Eynde, *Commentaire d'Išoʿdad de Merv sur l'Ancient Testament I. Genèse*. Corpus Scriptorum Christianorum Orientalium 126 / Scriptores Syri 67. Louvain, 1950.

Watson, Wilfred G.E. *Classical Hebrew Poetry: A Guide to its Techniques*. T & T Clark Biblical Languages. London, 2005.

West, M. L. "Akkadian Poetry: Metre and Performance." *Iraq* 49 (1997): 175-87.

———. *Homerus: Odyssea*. Bibliotheca Scriptorum Graecorum et Romanorum Teubneriana. Berlin and Boston, 2017.

White, Monica. "The Rise of the Dragon in Middle Byzantine Hagiography." *Byzantine and Modern Greek Studies* 32 (2008): 149–167.

Widengren, Geo. *The Gnostic Attitude*. Translated by B.A. Pearson. Santa Barbara, Cal., 1973.

———. *Iranisch-semitische Kulturbegegnung in parthischer Zeit*. Köln, 1960, pp. 43–92.

———, ed. *Der Mandäismus*. Wege der Forschung 167. Darmstadt, 1982.

Wikander, Ola. "Job 3,8 – Cosmological Snake Charming and Leviathanic Panic in an Ancient Near Eastern Setting." *Zeitschrift für die alttestamentlichen Wissenschaft* 122 (2010): 265–271.

———. *Unburning Fame: Horses, Dragons, Beings of Smoke, and other Indo-European Motifs in Ugarit and the Hebrew Bible*. Coniectanea Biblica: Old Testament Series 62. Winona Lake, 2017.

Williams, Michael Allen. *Rethinking "Gnosticism": An Argument for Dismantling a Dubious Category*. Princeton, 1996.

Wilson, Emily. *Homer: Odyssey*. New York, 2018.

Witt, Emily. *Health and Safety: A Breakdown*. New York, 2024.

Wolfe, Tom. *The Electric Kool-Aid Acid Test*. New York, 1968.

Wright, William. *The Apocryphal Acts of the Apostles*, vol. 1, *The Syriac Texts*. London, 1871.

———. *Catalogue of Syriac Manuscripts in the British Museum Acquired since the Year 1838*. 3 vols. London, 1870–1872.

Young, Robin Darling, "Notes on Divesting and Vesting in the Hymn of the Pearl." In David E. Aune and Robin Darling Young, eds., *Reading Religions in the Ancient World: Essays presented to Robert McQueen Grant on his 90th Birthday*. Novum Testamentum Supplements 125. Leiden and Boston, 2007, pp. 201-214.

Zingerle, Pius. "Syrische Poesieen, aus zwei Handschriften des Vatican (Cod. Vatican. 63 und 64), enthaltend den Ehe-Ritus der Nestorianer." *Zeitschrift der Deutschen Morgenländischen Gesellschaft* 17 (1863): 730-735.

Index

Typeset in XƎLaTeX by Adam Bremer-McCollum with the following typefaces: Junicode (Roman), Estrangelo Talada and Serto Batnan (Syriac), GFS Porson (Greek), Antinoou (Coptic), Scheherazade (Arabic and Persian), Raanana (Hebrew, JBA, JPA), Noto Sans Samaritan (Samaritan), Mshtakan (Armenian), MPH 2B Damase (Phoenician and Old Aramaic), Noto Sans Nabatean (Nabatean) Noto Sans Palmyrene (Palmyrene), Noto Sans Mandaic (Mandaic), and CPA Genizah ML (CPA). Typesetting completed on February 15, 2025 in Powder Springs, Georgia.

Printed on 70# Sundance Linen paper in Natural. The cover is on 100# Classic Crest in Epic Black, and the dust jacket on 100# Oxford Cover in Wealth.